Street, and J. Smith at Hogarths Head Cheapside Price 1.s

DR JOHNSON'S
LONDON

'When a man is tired of London he is tired of life;
for there is in London all that life can afford.'
Samuel Johnson

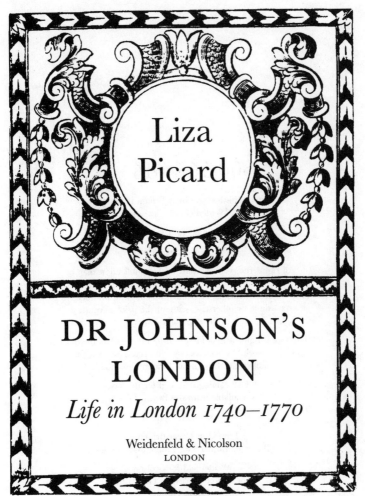

Liza Picard

DR JOHNSON'S LONDON

Life in London 1740–1770

Weidenfeld & Nicolson
LONDON

500 666486

First published in Great Britain in 2000 by
Weidenfeld & Nicolson

© 2000 Liza Picard

Fourth Impression 2000

A CIP catalogue record for this book
is available from the British Library.

ISBN 0 297 84218 8

Printed in Great Britain by
Butler & Tanner Ltd, Frome and London

Weidenfeld & Nicolson
The Orion Publishing Group Ltd
Orion House
5 Upper Saint Martin's Lane
London WC2H 9EA

Contents

Chapter 4   Traffic

Chapter 5   Green Spaces

Chapter 6   The Buildings

PART TWO: THE POOR

Chapter 7   Massie's Analysis

Chapter 8   The Welfare System

Chapter 9   Living Conditions

Chapter 14   Amusements

Chapter 15   Crime and Punishment

PART THREE: THE MIDDLING SORT

Chapter 16   Dentistry, Health and Medical Care

Chapter 17   Childhood, Schooling and Religion

Chapter 18   A Woman's World

Chapter 19   The Middling Rank of Men

Chapter 20   Fashion and Beauty

Chapter 21   Interiors and Gardens

Chapter 22   Parties of Pleasure

Chapter 23   Manners, Speech, Conversation and Customs

PART FOUR: THE RICH

Chapter 24   High Society

Chapter 25   The King

Illustrations

Preface

Welcome gentle reader, to the select company of those who read prefaces, whether before – as I hope – or after – as I usually do – reading the book. This is where I can explain why I wrote the book at all, and how I set about it.

First of all, I should say that I am not a properly trained historian. I am a lawyer by trade, and an inquisitive practical woman by character. I have always enjoyed history, but I have found it difficult, from most history books, to imagine real people going about their daily lives, worrying more about the price of bread than the habits of the nobility. The trend of history writing is increasingly turning towards the man and woman in the street. But even now there is a tendency, it seems to me, to focus on the few rich and the comfortably off, to the exclusion of the majority of people, who were poor. One reason for this is the heritage of buildings and works of art which we still enjoy, and which we identify as typical of the eighteenth century. They have survived because they were built or commissioned or acquired by the rich. The poor were hard put to it to get along at all. They had no money for non-essentials, and no leisure to write diaries or novels. Nothing remains of their lives.

So how could the blank canvas be filled in, between the haves and the have-nots? This book tries to answer that question.

First, I had to choose a period, rather than try to cover the whole century. There were no obvious starting and ending posts, as there had been for my *Restoration London*[1] about the previous century when Samuel Pepys kept his *Diary* for a decade. Samuel Johnson suggested the starting point. In 1740 he had been in London for three years, still struggling to make a living by his pen. There was an idea current in publishing circles, that a new *Dictionary of the English Language* could be a money-spinner. There were several on the market already, but none was satisfactory. Gradually the idea crystallised. Johnson was obviously the man for the job. He drafted a *Plan* for it in 1746.[2] He thought he could finish it in three years, but it was not published until 1755, after many crises. It made his name, although not his fortune; the booksellers got most of the proceeds. In 1770 Johnson was still going strong. He died in London in 1784, at the age of 73. For my purposes, however, his long residence in his much-loved London – nearly fifty years – was too long a period for the kind of detailed account that I wanted to record, so I decided to end the period at 1770, when the east coast of America was still British, the gin-drinking craze was mostly over, and London had taken the shape it would largely retain until the Victorians gave it another mighty shake. The period is arbitrarily chosen, I agree.

Now for the evidence. So far as contemporary witnesses were concerned, perhaps the most impartial were foreign visitors, taking in London as English travellers took in Florence and busily writing up their journals as they went, for publication in their native languages. They had to make their accounts interesting to the readers back home, to ensure that they sold, but they could not afford to diverge too far from the truth for fear of ridicule. They needed to have some individual angle, but still appeal to the general reader. In the period I have chosen, there were several tourists with observant eyes and ready pens. I trusted Monsieur Pierre Jean Grosley most, because he was a lawyer. He was here in 1765, when he was 47 years old. The English translation of his book *A Tour to London* was published in London in 1772. M. Grosley wrote 'I relate things as I have seen them'. His translator explains that he corrected anything that M. Grosley had got wrong. So his book is doubly reliable. He cast a professional eye over the English legal system. He also described going to the theatre, and there is no reason to doubt his account just because it is very funny (see Chapter 22).

A 32-year-old Swedish botanist Per Kalm paused in England on his way to America, in 1748. He saw a different side of London. He took an accurate note of anything growing. He was also intrigued by the habits of Londoners which he could see as he walked about, such as the different methods of not tracking street dirt into the house, and the way coal was delivered. His book was translated into English and published here in 1892.

Then there was Casanova. This is a name that may conjure up all kinds of licentiousness. Indeed I had to go through various hoops before I was allowed to read his memoirs in the Bodleian Library, in case, at my advanced age, they might corrupt me. But all I wanted, and more or less all I found, was what he made of London when he was here in 1763, running an experienced eye over the social and sexual *mores* of Londoners.

Francis Place's autobiography, in his beautiful copper-plate script, can be read in the British Library. He was born in 1771, so his childhood recollections are after our period, but I have used them when the details he recorded are unlikely to have changed.

Since London was such a draw, there was a surge in the production of maps and guidebooks, from the sixpenny pamphlet for the countryman, to the massive *Plan of the Cities of London and Westminster and the Borough of Southwark* published in 24 sheets, together measuring six and a half feet by thirteen, produced by John Rocque in 1747.[3] There were written histories and descriptions covering every parish in London, including a 1754 update 'by careful hands' – anonymous – of John Stow's *Survey of London* first published in 1598, and a *New and Accurate History and Survey of London, Westminster and Southwark* by John Entick published in 1766.

There were publications pleading causes, textbooks imparting information, manuals advising on cooking and home remedies with a bit of DIY thrown in, and periodicals looking to increase their circulation figures. Jonas Hanway is usually thought of, inaccurately, as the first person to use an umbrella in London. He was much more than that – a passionate pleader for young people and a skilful and prolific media man. There was a group of writers on medical matters whose teaching was the received wisdom of the time. They were not necessarily medically qualified. This was an era when any intelligent man would have a go at diagnosis and treatment. Samuel Johnson prided himself on his medical knowledge; so did John Wesley, who wrote a book about it and set up several clinics for people wishing to try the therapeutic effects of electricity. *The Gentleman's Magazine*, which in the best Fleet Street manner boasted of its circulation figures month by month, was my mainstay for the kind of news item that intrigued people then – not necessarily of world-shaking importance, just interesting, such as the amount of money a lucky bridegroom was marrying. It was aimed at a middle-class readership. ('Middle class' had not yet been coined – the correct phrase was 'the middling sort', which perhaps carries less baggage.)

There was a wide spread of newspapers. Here I have to admit defeat in my pursuit of contemporary evidence. In their paper form, eighteenth-century newspapers are now very fragile, and both the British Library and the Bodleian make them available only on film, which is exceedingly difficult to decipher. There are many issues of many newspapers that I have not read. Fortunately, the gaps are sometimes filled by extracts in the works of earlier historians with better sight or more opportunity to see the originals.

And, of course, there were Samuel Johnson and James Boswell. Johnson's brutally bad manners in conversation, which Boswell displayed like a lion-tamer provoking his charge to roar, grew on him as he got older and more famous. Boswell's *Life of Samuel Johnson* is useful for a picture of literary London, as long as Johnson's worst conversational squibs are recognised for what they were, the triumph of bad manners over accuracy. Boswell's own *Journal* is possibly more readable: an accurate self-portrait of an unlikeable young man.

The eighteenth century was a great time for letter writing. Horace Walpole was a prolific and amusing correspondent, describing events in the capital for the benefit of friends in the country, or abroad. The century also produced novels which are for the first time enjoyable in their own right, apart from their value as historical documents. It was no hardship to read my way through Henry Fielding, Laurence Sterne and Tobias Smollett. Their books show poor people as well as rich: something missing so far, from the sources I have referred to.

There is a delightful pamphlet from which I often quote, published anonymously in 1764, called *Low-Life, being a critical account of what is transacted by people of almost all religions, Nations, Circumstances and sizes of Understanding in the 24 hours between Saturday night and Monday morning in a true description of a Sunday as it is usually spent within the Bills of Mortality ... with an address to the ingenious and ingenuous Mr Hogarth*. It describes what people, especially poor people, were doing, in London, hour by hour throughout a summer Sunday. Here is an example:

> As it is now twilight, reputable young fellows, [such] as students in the law ... dependent Nephews and Grandsons who have been unhappily scarred in the wars of Venus are repairing to their several Quack Doctors and Surgeons pupils to get a safe, easy and speedy cure ... about the same time young Women whose unhappy minute has been taken the Advantage of ... are repairing to Persons of their own sex who live about Ludgate Hill and St Martin's Lane and put out handbills

for the cure of all Distempers incident to Women ... Undertakers who
have a body to bury from their own Houses, which they have sold to
be anatomised, are interring coffins full of rubbish and suffer funeral
service to be devoutly performed over it ... Cowkeepers' carts for three
miles round this Metropolis are driving through the streets to fetch the
grains from the respective Brewhouses they deal with. Women who go
out washing for their livelihood and are to be at work by One o'clock
in the morning, thinking of going to bed.

Turning now to modern authorities, my inspiration was Dr M.
Dorothy George, in whose footsteps I have humbly tried to tread.
Her book was first published in 1925 and has long been out of print
in this country. The title she chose was *London Life in the Eighteenth
Century*, which gives no hint that you will look in vain in it for
Chippendale or hooped petticoats or gracious living. The first sentence
of her Preface blows the gaff. She describes her book as 'an attempt
to give a picture of the conditions of life and work of the poorer
classes in London in the eighteenth century'. Not only does she
resoundingly succeed in her attempt, she includes long verbatim
passages from the original sources she used, which I have most
gratefully read and borrowed from.

The many other contemporary records and academic works of
reference I have used can be identified in the Notes. It would
overburden this Preface to list them here. I will, however, refer to
some modest research of my own. The eighteenth century is not, by
some reckonings, all that distant. There are enthusiasts who still
practise the skills of two hundred years ago. I had the good fortune
to meet, in correspondence, Ian Chipperfield, stay-maker, of Great
Yarmouth, whose knowledge and infectious enthusiasm set me on the
path to the leather stays in Norwich Museum which appear in Chapter
20. This encouraged me to make more enquiries. Alum, for example,
is a mysterious substance which constantly crops up in the eighteenth
century but has dropped out of our experience. It was notoriously
used in making bread, but why? The reply to my letter to the Guild
of Master Bakers provided an answer to this nagging question that I
have seen nowhere else (see note 5, Chapter 9). Mercury was on a
par with alum, in my mind: constantly used in the eighteenth century,
this time in medicine, but unknown to me. Dr Melvin Earles took
the time to answer my letter exhaustively and comprehensibly, a rare
combination.

If such riches could be tapped by just one letter, what about the manufacturers and retailers whose businesses began in the eighteenth century and are still prospering? Bearing in mind that the poor lived on bad bread and gin, I approached both the distillers with whose products I am most familiar. Again, my letters produced the most courteous and informative replies, and enabled me to give a wider readership to the story of the first speak-easy (see Chapter 14). Hamleys, Fortnum & Mason, Twinings – they all answered my letters charmingly and helpfully. Messrs Berry Bros & Rudd put me right about eighteenth-century wines and measures, without – regretfully – my ordering from their stock or visiting their splendidly eighteenth-century premises with that vertiginous sloping floor. Perhaps it was level, two hundred years ago.

The late Dennis Severs showed me his mesmeric house in Spitalfields, so brilliantly restored and furnished by him as a family home which the occupants had, it seemed, only just left. I must thank, too, Mr D. E. Wickham, archivist of the Clothworkers' Company, who shares with me an enthusiasm for the less-frequented byways of history. He sent me copies of documents from the company's archives which suddenly made this august body very human; and, superlatively, let me see the catalogue of a rare book sale which included the Mauclerc collection of ephemera dating from the mid-eighteenth century. Mr Mauclerc had been interested in the wild animals being exhibited at the time – see chapter 22. He would have enjoyed the company of my other kind guides. Lastly, at a late stage, I was able to discuss with Mr Tony Grice of Culworth Forge, blacksmith, chimney-system specialist and history enthusiast, the probable situation of climbing boys – see Chapter 12. Neither of us had been convinced by the picture put out by fund-raisers at the time, but without Mr Grice's immense knowledge and practical experience I would have continued to accept it.

The kindness and enthusiasm of other people have produced a better book than I had in me to write. The librarians to whom I have addressed my stumbling queries have been without exception helpful, knowledgeable and brilliantly adept at pretending that they have never before been asked this most interesting question – even when, as in the Public Record Office out at Kew, I got completely lost and had to ask for the Way Out. The staff of the Patent Office Library just off Chancery Lane share my admiration for their wonderful Victorian building. The Guildhall Library in the City has an unparalleled collection of books about London on its open shelves, and more than usually omniscient librarians. The Wellcome Institute for the History of Medicine is as beautiful inside as the new British Library just along Euston Road, and is equally helpful. The National Art Library roosting at the top of the Victoria and Albert Museum, and the London Library in St James's Square, both combine modern technology with Victorian practicality. I read the records of the Marine Society in the National Maritime Museum in Greenwich. The London Metropolitan Archives in Islington enabled me to read the records of the Foundling Hospital, and even handle some of the clothes worn by foundling babies two and a half centuries ago. I also handled eighteenth-century clothes in the Costume and Textile Study centre at Carrow House, Norwich, a department of Norwich City's museum service. Lastly, and superlatively, the Bodleian Library here in Oxford has been a paragon of all that is best. Someone there has the task of summoning books for the most ignorant of telephone enquirers, which she has performed with calm courtesy, inexhaustible knowledge and a most melodious voice. She must be glad I have finished this book.

I have been overwhelmed by the accessibility of eminent academics such as Professor Sir Roy Porter and Dr Goldbloom of the Wellcome Institute, Professor Wrigley of Corpus Christi College Cambridge and Dr Landers of All Souls College Oxford, all of whom took time to answer my struggling questions in a heartwarmingly encouraging way.

I needed all the encouragement I could, and did, get from Benjamin Buchan, the kindest and most congenial editor. My friend Peter Stalker has continued to extricate me from the computer tangles that only I can create. My two neighbours Alison Jones and Catherine Stokes have been equally patient with my ineducable computer illiteracy. My dear doctor son has at times diagnosed my computer troubles at long distance in the best eighteenth-century way, by telephone in the twentieth-century way, and prescribed effectively. He found time to give me guidance on medical matters in Chapter 16. Any errors in it are entirely due to my misinterpreting his authentically medical handwriting, or applying my own misconceptions.

I am fortunate.

Liza Picard
Oxford
March 2000

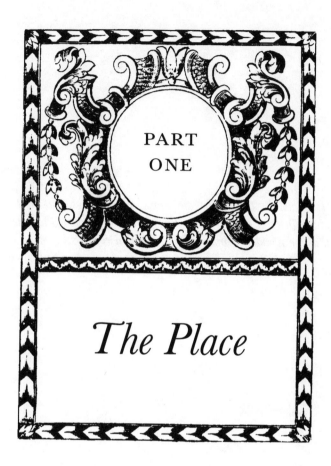

PART
ONE

The Place

'It is not in the showy evolutions of buildings, but in the multiplicity of human habitations which are crowded together, that the wonderful immensity of London consists.'

Samuel Johnson

CHAPTER I

Facts and Figures

The population of England in 1750 has been estimated at 6,140,000.[1] No one knows exactly how many people lived in London. There had never been a census. A Bill 'for registering the number of the people', and also marriages, deaths and births, and even the number of welfare recipients, had been thrown out by the Commons in 1753 because, as Mr Pitt said, it would be too expensive and difficult to administer, and it might even be seen as a prelude to poll tax,[2] which would be unthinkable. Contemporaries such as Malarchy Postlethwaite[3] suggested 1,200,000 at least, a figure adopted by *The Gentleman's Magazine* in its 1766 Supplement. But informed opinion nowadays puts the figure at about 650,000, plus or minus 50,000:[4] over 10 per cent of the population of England.

London had been growing at a fairly steady rate since 1500. By 1650 it had outstripped its European competitors such as Paris and Naples, and by 1750 had overtaken Constantinople,[5] 'Pekin in China' and Cairo.[6] It vastly exceeded other English cities. And as well as housing permanent inhabitants, it was the centre to which perhaps one in six of the total population of England had been drawn at some time in their lives, as tourists, or to 'do the season', or for work in domestic service or apprenticeship.[7]

What was meant by 'London'? The area of one square mile within the walls first built by the Romans, with adjacent areas or 'dependencies' in Southwark and Blackfriars, administered by the Lord Mayor of London? Or all the parishes 'within the Bills of Mortality'? This last description, usually shortened to 'within the Bills', is a reference to the parishes which were bound to make weekly returns, or 'Bills', of the numbers of births and deaths, with the causes of deaths, within their boundaries. This system had begun in 1562, mainly to provide a warning for the well-to-do of the possibility of a plague epidemic, enabling them to leave London in time. The Bills were notoriously inaccurate, but nothing had been evolved to replace them. They covered the 97 parishes within the walls, the 16 dependencies outside the walls, and another thirty or so parishes in Middlesex, Surrey and Westminster – the number of these fluctuated from time to time, as parishes were subdivided or created to keep pace with development.

By 'the City' I mean the city within the walls, and its dependencies: the area administered by the Lord Mayor. By 'London' I mean the built-up area from Chelsea to Deptford, Mayfair to Limehouse, Marylebone to Stepney – in other words, the area shown in John Rocque's *Plan of the Cities of London and Westminster and the Borough of Southwark* published in 1746,[8] and generally corresponding to the area within the Bills. As the *Encyclopedia Britannica* put it, in 1773, 'the form of London including Westminster and Southwark comes pretty near an oblong square, 5 miles in length if measured in a direct line from Hyde Park to the end of Limehouse ... the greatest breadth is two and a half miles'.

Two City tours

The first-time visitor to New York should take a boat round Manhattan Island. Oxford is best seen from the top of an open bus. I suggest we have a quick look at Dr Johnson's London from virtual sedan chairs, in two trips, one into the City and one round the west end.[9] I have taken mid-century, 1750, as a convenient date. I will signal where we are, from time to time, by putting in square brackets [...] a contemporary landmark, so that any tourist map will give you your bearings.

The City

We shall begin at Temple Bar, built by Wren in 1672 at the western boundary of the City, where the Strand becomes Fleet Street [just east of the Law Courts; not the modern structure, but a narrow arch wide enough for one vehicle, with pedestrian passages on either side]. If he had designed it especially to create traffic jams, he could hardly have done better. The habit of impaling traitors' heads on approaches to the City has not quite died out: there are two still on the arch, looking the worse for wear. They have been there since 1746. This part of the City just escaped the Great Fire of 1666.[10] Its medieval timber houses, wildly overdecorated for our pure Georgian taste, overhang the street and lean on each other for support. Dr Johnson lives in a back street tucked away on the left. Ahead of us, up Ludgate Hill, St Paul's Cathedral is already darkening from smoke pollution. Beyond it is Cheapside, a main shopping area. But we shall make a detour north, and find Smithfield – easily done, by the noise and smell of the livestock market. Beside it is St Bartholomew's Hospital, a medieval foundation now in Georgian dress. Then back again past the notorious prison of Newgate [the Old Bailey, or Central Criminal Court, was built almost on its site].

We want to make for the river. The golden fireball on top of the Monument to the Great Fire of 1666 guides us part of the way, then we can home in on the unmistakable smell of Billingsgate, London's principal fish market [demolished and redeveloped now – the smell of old fish lingered for years]. We ignore the boatmen who are shouting for our custom and walk up the muddy steps onto London Bridge. With luck you may hear the lions roaring in the Tower of London. Looking through a gap in the houses on the bridge, you can see the merchant ships and lighters packed together waiting to unload at the Custom House [still there, on the north bank of the river]. Upstream of the bridge the river is covered by small passenger craft, with the occasional royal or plutocratic private barge, like a Rolls-Royce among minis. Near the south bank are two more hospitals, St Thomas's [it has moved since 1750], and a new one founded by a millionaire [Guy's Hospital is still there, just off the Borough High Street]. Then we go to the nearest 'stairs' down to the river again, and take a boat back to the Strand.

Despite the burgeoning prosperity of the west end, it was the City that still represented power. No wonder the monarch had to stop at Temple Bar and symbolically ask the Lord Mayor for permission to enter the City.

The west end

We begin where the muddy road to the hamlet of Tottenham Court heads north, through the fields [Tottenham Court Road tube station]. Looking up it, past the 'pound' or enclosure for stray dogs in the middle of the road, you should see on the left Mr Goodge's brick-drying yards. As we turn west along Oxford Street, the chair-men hurry past the first buildings on the right. They may not be in the same parish as the slums behind us in St Giles's parish, but they have the same reputation as 'the lurking-place of cut-throats'.[11] By the time we get to Rathbone Place we can slow down. This was the first street to be built on the north side of Oxford Street, and it has attracted fashionable residents, who can stroll up to the woods and the windmill at the end of their street. Across Oxford Street from Rathbone Place, Soho[12] Square is lined with elegant houses from the previous century, much favoured still by foreign ambassadors.

As we continue along Oxford Street, look to your right through the gaps between the houses and you'll see open country. Berners Street leads across a patch of waste ground to Green Lane and then through fields, where the Middlesex Hospital stands. About half way along Oxford Street on our right there is a thriving market for fish and meat [Market Place]. A little further along on the left, Swallow Street [replaced by Regent Street] dives straight to Piccadilly. Then Cavendish Square[13] on our right has some sumptuous houses in it, but there are still some vacant sites. It was planned to out-do any other square – quite a few of these squares had such ambitions, when they first came into existence – which meant that buyers were slow to commit themselves. Balancing Cavendish Square, to the south of Oxford Street, Hanover Square was completely built by 1750, of imposing contiguous four-storey houses, complete with church.

Marylebone Lane, originally a winding country track, and Wigmore Row [Street] mark the end of the built-up area north of Oxford Street. Beyond them is farming country. The only sign of city life is Marylebone Gardens, two fields north of Wigmore Row. On the south side of Oxford Street, the houses come to a stop at North Audley Street. After that there are fields on both sides of the road – it has become a road again now, Tiburn[14] Road – as far as the turnpike gate. You won't want to go on further. You can see from the gate the three connected posts where criminals are hanged, and the gallery erected for the greater comfort of spectators [Marble Arch is very near it].

So let us turn south, down Tiburn Lane [Park Lane]. If you look to your left along Upper Brook Street or Upper Grosvenor Street, you should just see Grosvenor Square, the grandest square yet.[15] Hyde Park stretches away to the countryside for miles, on your right. We shall make for the turnpike gate at its south-east corner [Hyde Park corner]. If we headed west, through the hamlet of Knightsbridge, we would get to the village of Kensington, but there is little else to see there except the palace. We will strike south, leaving St George's Hospital [a hotel is now on the site, which from the outside looks much as the pictures of the hospital looked] on our right. We can see another hospital far away in the fields [Chester Street/Grosvenor Place], the Lock Hospital for venereal diseases.

Our chair-men splash through the marshy fields of Pimlico, to Chelsea. Shall we rest in Ranelagh Pleasure Gardens, next door to the Royal Hospital? Or call at the Chelsea Physic Garden? No, we direct the chair-men to Chelsea stairs and take a boat downstream. Vauxhall Spring Gardens [at the south end of Vauxhall Bridge] beckon from the opposite bank, but we land at Westminster stairs, just short of the elegant new Westminster bridge. The ancient buildings of Westminster Hall and the Abbey dominate a maze of medieval streets [Parliament Square].

So to keep clean as well as to avoid pickpockets we take chairs again to St James's Park. The most striking feature of the park is a massive straight 'canal' almost cutting it in half, running from near the Duke of Buckingham's house [not yet a royal residence] to the Horse Guards' parade ground west of Whitehall. Across the park is St James's Palace, where the ruling monarch lives when he is not at his palace at Kensington or in his other kingdom, Hanover in Germany. He allows Londoners to walk through the park, but not to ride in chairs or carriages or on horseback, so we pay off the chair-men and stroll through St James's Park and the Green Park to Piccadilly, where we pick up chairs again.

Going east along Piccadilly, you will see two houses to the left that are very grand indeed – far more in the modern taste than the dilapidated palace of St James – Devonshire House [demolished in the 1920s] and Burlington House [the Royal Academy]. We pass the inns where we could take a coach to the west country, and the Hay Market to the right, and go straight on along Coventry Street and through a narrow alley, emerging into Leicester Fields [Leicester Square]. Here is where the heir to the throne lives: Frederick Prince of Wales, the son of George II, who for some reason cannot stand him. Prince Frederick, sometimes known as 'poor Fred', maintains his princely Court in an unimpressive house on the north side of Leicester Fields, which is not at all a fashionable place to live. His house even has four lock-up shops in its frontage,[16] and a miserable garden. No wonder that Fred spends most of his summer days in the beautiful gardens of Carlton House [now covered by Carlton Terrace], annoying his father.

East of Leicester Fields, through a maze of lanes and alleys, is Covent Garden. By now it has lost its first glamour. Fashionable people have moved away and small traders and brothel-keepers are taking over. But expensive carriages still come through it to drop patrons at the Theatre Royal [Royal Opera House]. Long Acre nearby is where you would come to buy such a carriage. It leads into Drury Lane, which is definitely insalubrious. If you turn left at the top of Drury Lane, you are in one of the poorest and most criminal of London parishes, St Giles. Henry Fielding, author and magistrate, lives very near, in Bow Street, and runs his court from his house. Keep going west and you arrive outside Montague House [site now occupied by the British Museum], with Bloomsbury Square close by, and the open country beyond. A little further and we have finished our tour. We are back at Tottenham Court Lane.

Fashionable London was being built on green-field sites. Londoners still lived within reach of the country. In 1763 two gentlemen walked right round London in seven hours, beginning at Moorfields, to Newington Green, Hackney, Bethnal Green, Poplar, Bow, Limehouse, New Cross, Peckham, Camberwell, Stockwell, Clapham, Battersea, Chelsea, Brompton, Knightsbridge, through Hyde Park, round Tyburn to Paddington, up the road to Islington and along the new City Road to Moorfields again.[7] They were clearly good walkers, but how many tedious days would it take nowadays, to walk right round the metropolitan area?

CHAPTER 2

London and Westminster

The City streets

When the Romans laid out Londinium with their usual efficiency, they built a road north through the gate in the walls which later acquired the name Bishops Gate, a road along the north bank of the river westwards through the gate later called Lud Gate, and another leading to the east, and they built a bridge across the Thames. The pattern they imposed on the city then has remained remarkably unchanged. Successive monarchs tried to limit the size of the city by keeping it within its walls, but all they achieved was the infilling of yards and gardens to produce labyrinthine courts and alleys behind the frontages visible from the main streets. When the City was destroyed by the Great Fire of 1666, the urgency of restoring trade took priority over ideal replanning, and the opportunity to create an elegant metropolis was lost. The streets were rebuilt much as they had been, with a little straightening here and widening there, but still comfortably recognisable to a former resident.

Street cleaning

Street cleaning in the City was still under the jurisdiction of the parochial authorities. Some parishes were poor, crowded and ineffective. Others were rich, thinly populated and powerful. The parish of St Michael Bassishaw contained 142 houses, 'well built and inhabited by merchants of great reputation and fortune',[1] who would see that their frontages were immaculate, in any case. Portsoken ward, which included Whitechapel market, had 1,385 houses and only four scavengers.[2] In theory, the parish scavengers came round every day except

Sundays and holidays, rang their bell to alert residents, and 'stayed a convenient time'[3] for the rubbish to be brought out to their carts. It was an offence to leave rubbish about in front of your own house, and – even worse – in front of someone else's, or in front of a church. 'Throwing any noisome things' – dead cats, for instance – into the highway was just as bad.

Benjamin Franklin found when he was in London in 1742 that when they were dry the streets were never swept, and when they were wet 'there was no crossing but in paths kept clean by poor people with brooms'.[4] The central gutters ('chanels' or 'kennels') are generally made very deep ... and with cross-chanels, render the coachway very disagreeable and unsafe', not helped by 'the too common practice of the lower sort of inhabitants and servants throwing away ashes, rubbish, broken glass ... offals and other offensive things into the streets [which] stop the current of the chanels', making the streets 'much annoyed with mud and ... very dangerous in frosty weather'.[5]

The nature of London street dirt is demonstrated by the value put on it by the market gardeners round about, who bought it by the cartload to spread on their gardens, producing the level of fertility that astonished foreigners.[6] It was a rich, glutinous mixture of animal manure, dead cats and dogs, ashes, straw, and human excrement: see Hogarth's print of *Night*, where a chamber pot is being emptied from an upstairs window on to the hat, and wig, of a passing magistrate.

In frosty weather, walking in the streets was even riskier. 'Everyone must have observed during the late [1756/7] frost, the numberless heaps of horsedung which had been purposely laid in most of the streets of this metropolis and how much after it is dark these embarrass and in some cases endanger those who pass through them on foot.'[7] These regular little piles were an ingenious DIY effort at insulating the lead pipes bringing the domestic water supply. After all, horse dung produced heat in garden hot-beds, why not over the pipes? Unfortunately, it didn't work. The lead pipes still burst 'with an almost incoercible force' and the water froze all over the streets.

Paving and lighting

It was the legal duty of every citizen to pave the street up to the centre line of the street in front of his house, but, predictably, this resulted in even more bumps and holes. As a visiting Frenchman put it,[8] 'it is scarce possible to find a place to set one's foot'. 'A loose stone in a pavement under which water lodges and on being trod upon squirts it up, to the great detriment of white stockings' was known as a 'beau-trap'.[9] If the DIY efforts of the citizens left any stones level, the water companies, the only public utility in the eighteenth century, could be relied on to deal with them. The New River Company alone had 400 miles of wooden pipes under the streets, which were always having to be repaired, and were subject to a twenty-year rolling repair programme when labour could be spared. The water companies were legally obliged to make good their excavations, but somehow it rarely happened.

In 1760 'the ruling part of the City'[10] suddenly realised that if things went on like this they might *lose money* to Westminster or Southwark, which were not quite so filthy. A clean-up campaign was launched. By 1765 the old cobbled paving had become intolerable. 'Every person not bigotted to ancient forms and customs must be convinced of the necessity of a speedy reformation', said the new Commissioners for the Sewers and Pavements of the City, recommending a tax to cover the estimated cost of repaving with 'Scotch stones'. In all, 32,428 yards of paving were to be laid, at 7s 8d per yard, right through the City, from Temple Bar, past St Paul's, along Cheapside and Leadenhall Street to the other side of the City at Aldgate: an astonishing operation.[11] By 1773 granite setts from Aberdeen which, as Dr Johnson noted approvingly, 'hard as it is, they square with very little difficulty'[12] were producing an even surface, and an excruciating screech in conjunction with iron shod wheels.

Instead of sloping down to the central kennel, streets were cambered, with a gutter on each side. Benjamin Franklin found this inefficient, since it halved the force of rainwater that might have scoured away the dirt, dead cats and so on still littering the road. 'It only makes the mud more fluid, so that the wheels of carriages and feet of horses throw and dash it upon the foot pavement which is thereby rendered foul and slippery and sometimes splash it on those who are walking';[13] but then Franklin could always see how to do things better.

The Commissioners brought in contractors to see that the streets were clean and well lit. The Commissioners' officers were to 'behave with all possible good manners towards every inhabitant'. They would need all the goodwill they could muster, because each one had to keep a register of all the streets in his district, noting in it any less-than-perfect paving and gullies and 'frequently to perambulate his district both in the day and the night' to check whether the contractors were fulfilling their contracts, whether the footways were

> daily scraped swept and cleansed ... and whether any pavement is broken or out of repair ... whether any privies communicate with the common sewer [which was not allowed], whether any horse and/or carriage is ridden or driven on the foot pavements, whether signboards were fixed otherwise than in the fronts of the houses and shops to which they belong, ... whether any occupier of a house shall deposit ... any ashes or filth in any part of any street except in some hole or box ... to be provided by the Commissioners...

Broken water pipes had to be mended immediately, by the water company. Wagons were not to 'stand' for longer than an hour, and smaller vehicles for 'longer than is necessary for loading and unloading'; and the Inspector had power to 'seize and remove' an offending cart *with its horses* – there might be as many as eight of them – to a pound. Where there were footways at the side of streets in the City yet another Act, of 1767, for 'pitching, paving, cleaning and enlightening the streets ... within the City' required householders to 'scrape sweep and cleanse the footway' along the front of their houses, before ten o'clock every day except on Sundays.

Lighting had been spasmodic, in the streets of the City. As usual, the inhabitants were under a duty to light the street in front of their houses; and as usual, they didn't. The Commissioners were given powers to enforce the proper lighting of streets, and even to 'direct the placing of private lamps'.[14] Citizens were obliged to hang out, on dark nights, 'one or more lights with sufficient cotton wicks that shall continue to burn from six at night till eleven of the same night, on penalty of one shilling'.[15] Benjamin Franklin spotted a design fault in the lamps used, which produced a feeble glimmer and quickly became sooted up. It was easier to contract with enterprising traders such as William Conanway, who 'furnisheth persons of quality and others with lamps, lanthorns and irons of all sorts, also keeps servants to light them at reasonable rates', or John Clark Lamplighter near St Giles's Church, who also 'furnisheth Gentlemen [but no others, in his case] with all sorts of globular lamps and lights them by the week, or quarter, at the lowest prices'.[16]

Shop signs

The swinging signs that look so quaint in old prints, and which still survive outside village pubs, were declared illegal in 1760. 'How comfortless must be the sensations of an elderly female, stopped in the street on a windy day, under a large old sign loaded with lead and iron in full swing over her head, and perhaps a torrent of rain and dirty water falling ... from a projecting spout', mused Jonas Hanway, the man who popularised umbrellas. No umbrella would help if the sign fell on her.[17] Instead, the signs were fixed flat on the façade of the building, ancestors of today's shop fascias.

Animals

We complain of the pollution caused by petrol-driven engines. Imagine the sheer volume of faeces and urine excreted by the engines of eighteenth-century traffic – that is, horses – let alone the dung of the herds and flocks being driven through the streets to markets and abattoirs. *The Gentleman's Magazine* of May 1761 complained of the 'pernicious practice of driving cattle through the streets of this city'. The Navy's abattoirs on Tower Hill dealt with a huge volume of cattle, sheep and pigs: they all had to get there somehow. Cattle coming up from Kent had to cross the Bridge and walk through the narrow streets of the City, to the market at Smithfield. The direct route to Smithfield from the west country was straight along Oxford Street. And then there were always animals that got away from their drivers. Nowhere was safe.

> A little after two o'clock the people on the Royal Exchange were much alarmed by the appearance of a cow (hard driven from Smithfield) at the fourth Gate, and (though the beast did not run in on 'Change) great confusion ensued; some losing hats and wigs and some their shoes, while others lay on the ground in heaps ... during the alarm, a rumour of an earthquake prevailing, some threw themselves on the ground expecting to be swallowed. The cow in the meantime took [off] down Sweeting's Alley and was knocked down and secured by a carman in Gracechurch Street.[18]

And in 1767, 'while the Court was sitting an over driven ox entered the Guildhall, threw the whole Court into consternation but not liking his company turned about and ran back again without doing any mischief'.[19]

Dogs came and went. There were recurrent scares about people being bitten by mad dogs, which led to orders that all dogs should be killed.

The Watch

The streets were patrolled by the Watch, decrepit old men appointed by each parish and paid a pittance. Londoners could not bring themselves to submit to a properly organised body of law enforcement officers, operating throughout the City. This astonished a French lawyer, Pierre Grosley, accustomed to the high profile of French *gens d'armes*. 'London has neither troops, patrol nor any sort of regular Watch and it is guarded during the nights only by old men chosen from the dregs of the people who have no arms but a lanthorn and a pole; who patrol the streets crying the hour every time the clock strikes; who proclaim good or bad weather in the morning; and who come to awake those who have any journey to perform; and whom it is customary for young rakes to beat.'[20] Grosley missed one other useful function of the Watch. James Boswell managed to put his candle out, in the middle of the night after his fire had gone out. He looked for the tinder-box in the kitchen of his lodgings, but couldn't find it in the dark, so he waited until the Watch came round and got his candle 'relumed' from the old man's lantern.[21] Grosley was not in London during the 1745 rebellion, when the authorities were extremely nervous, the City militia was ordered to patrol the streets and even anti-government talk could land you in trouble.[22]

Night-soil collectors

When good citizens were at home in bed, the night-soil men came out on their rounds. Sewage disposal had not improved much since Samuel Pepys' day when his neighbour's cess-pit overflowed into his cellar and had to be emptied through his house. There were still no sewers in our sense of the term. 'Sewers' were storm-water drains, respectable house-holders had cess-pits, others just threw out of the window.

If they are looked after properly, and regularly emptied, cess-pits should present no problems. The trade card of John Hunt (successor to the late Mr Inigo Brook), Nightman & Rubbish Carter, near the Wagon and Horses in Goswell Street[23] shows two jolly nightmen carrying a tub on their shoulders, being let in by a sleepy servant to the front door of a house. (Houses built in terraces often had no back access.) Their two-horse cart waits outside, with spare barrels. In the distance, the moon shines down on a covered wagon with six horses. Idyllic. But ... John Hunt and his colleagues would charge, and how were the slum dwellers to pay? It took another hundred years and a cholera outbreak to focus the public eye on what it did not wish to see, but which had been under its nose for a long time: 'There are hundreds, I may say thousands, of houses in this metropolis which have no drainage whatsoever, and the greater part of them having filthy stinking overflowing cesspools...'[24]

Street trees

There were elm trees in London streets. 'Nearly all the squares in London were planted round with it. ... So also Moorfields and where the Danish church stands [Austin Friars, in the City]. This and the willow were in short the only trees which were planted along the sides of the streets.' Elm was chosen because 'it gives the best shade, endures the coal smoke very well, stands for a long time green, and keeps its leaves till the autumn',[25] and, I would add for those who have never seen an elm tree in its glory, it is covered with a rufous haze of buds in the spring, and in the autumn its coin-sized leaves turn a lovely pale yellow.

Westminster slums and squares

It may be helpful, here, to remind the reader that Westminster included anything to the west of the City liberties. Ten of the parishes 'within the Bills' were in Westminster. The Strand was in Westminster, Fleet Street was in the City. Both cities were in the county of Middlesex.

In general the problems of Westminster were different from, and lighter than, those of its neighbour. Slums were largely confined to the maze of narrow medieval streets round the Abbey, where Thieving Lane lived up to its name, and open drains carrying excrement still ran down the middle of the streets as late as 1808.[26] The Restoration building boom had produced St James's Square, Leicester Square and Soho Square, the piazzas of Covent Garden and new quadrangles in the Inns of Court.[27] Bloomsbury Square was first built in 1666.

New developments

In their enthusiasm for the fashionable idea of *rus in urbe*, bringing the countryside into the town, the developers of Cavendish Square tried the effect of sheep in the middle of it – 'a few frightened sheep within a wooden paling [with] sooty fleeces and meagre carcases'.[28] A critic suggested painted sheep, but the square was finally embellished by a statue of the Duke of Cumberland 'in the exact modern uniform of the guards, mounted on an antique horse, all richly gilt', sharing his glory with the sheep before they were evacuated. The middle of Hanover Square, according to the same critic, 'had the air of a cow-yard where blackguards [vagrant children] assemble in the winter to play at hussle-cap [?] up to the ancles in dirt'. There must have been uproar one winter day in 1762 when 'a fox was taken up alive in Hanover Square having been pursued for near twenty miles and fairly hunted down'.[29]

The new road

Animals, with the possible exception of foxes, were resented by the nobility and gentry in the new squares. At last a radical decision was taken. A new road – an M25 for animals – must be built through the fields, 'round the suburbs of the city at a proper distance' (Marylebone Road/Euston Road/Pentonville Road follow its route exactly).[30] The wretched animals and their minders could use that outer ring, and leave Oxford Street for the gentry. The new road, opened in 1756, was designed as a drovers' road, 40 feet wide at least,[31] and unpaved, so the flocks and herds plodded through the mud and dust of the ring road just as they had plodded along country roads, except that now a toll had to be paid. The rates evoke the numbers of livestock entering London by this one route alone: 5d per score of oxen, 2½d per score of calves, hogs, sheep or lambs. There was unfortunately no way of compelling the animals to use their new route and leave the nobility and gentry in peace. There were constant complaints that wagoners and drovers ignored this purpose-built road and found their way through the fashionable squares as adroitly as a modern commuter taking a rat-run through a housing estate.

In any case, the new road did nothing for other parts of the city. A letter in *The Gentleman's Magazine* of May 1761 complained of the 'pernicious practice of driving cattle through the streets'. And there were always animals that got away from their drivers, such as the 'large ox' driven by some 'fellows in a furious manner into Southampton Row and endeavouring to force him precipitately through the postern by goading, hoxing and other brutish methods, the generous beast turned ... and at one spring staked himself upon the iron railings next to the Duke of Bedford's wall'. It died.[32]

The Strand

By the eighteenth century, the Strand was completely built up. The territorial magnates' palaces that had lined its south side, with gardens sloping down to the river, had been redeveloped in the previous century, with the massive exception of Northumberland House, a Tudor mansion that adorned the south-west end of the Strand until 1874. The Strand was a shopping mall as famous, and rather newer, than Cheapside in the City. Samuel Johnson called the stretch from Charing Cross to Whitechapel 'the greatest series of shops in the world'.[33] He had a habit of overstating his case; from Charing Cross to St Mary's-le-Strand would have been nearer the mark.

The Grosvenor estate

At the beginning of the eighteenth century, most of the land between Bloomsbury and Westminster Abbey was still open countryside awaiting development. The owners included many old and titled families who had acquired the land by marriage or far-sighted investment. The most famous example was the Grosvenor estate.[34] In the previous century, Hugh Audley, barrister, had thought fit to buy the Manor of Ebury, to the west of London. About 100 acres of it, the northern part, was decent agricultural land. The rest was 500 acres of swamp and marsh, between Westminster and Chelsea. Audley died unmarried in 1662, leaving the Ebury land to the grandson of his sister. The legatee, Alexander Davies, was a scrivener, a kind of lawyer's clerk. He built a few houses at Millbank, served by the horse ferry, but he died of the plague in 1665 before he could complete his development plans. His baby daughter Mary inherited the estate.

By now it must have looked more possible that some day London would stretch out towards the 100-acre site, and Mary was valuable. She was sold in marriage to the heir of Lord Berkeley. She was eight, her prospective husband was ten. But at the crucial moment Lord Berkeley could not raise the necessary £5,000, so she was passed on to Sir Thomas Grosvenor, who duly married her when he was twenty-one and she was thirteen. He died in 1700, leaving her with three sons. Legal complications delayed the development of the northern part of the estate until 1720, when building began on the 100-acre site.[35] The streets were pegged out, 8 acres were reserved for a magnificent square, and the builders moved in. They stayed for nearly 50 years, erecting stately mansions round the Square itself and quite small houses at the edges of the estate. The streets never suffered from the problems that afflicted the City. From the start, they were as well built as modern technology knew how.

Other developments

Lord Grosvenor and his neighbours to the east managed to correlate their street plans, so that for example Upper Brook Street ran east from Tyburn Lane [Park Lane], reappeared after Grosvenor Square as Brook Street, continued out of the Grosvenor estate and across the Conduit estate owned by the City of London, to end up neatly as Little Brook Street at the southern edge of Hanover Square in the Earl of Scarbrough's estate. All this was brought about by com-monsense and mutual interest. There was no overall city plan. It was left to the owner of each estate to develop it as he thought fit.

The result was already clear by 1766. 'This city and liberties are laid out in handsome streets and squares.'[36] But not all the buildings in any square were the same. The ground landlord could enforce a common building line and height, but the size of the sites varied, allowing the nobility and gentry who moved in, a choice of style let alone expense. An obvious example was Berkeley Square. There was a spacious garden in the middle of it, and solid houses on the west side, architecturally friendly but not uniform. Some of the plots on the east and north sides were very small in comparison, and let to such people as tavern-keepers and coffee-house keepers, tucked in among the galaxy of duchesses and earls.[37]

Westminster was kept spruce by no fewer than 80 scavengers appointed by the authorities, who paid out £4,127 annually to subcontractors for contract cleaning.[38]

CHAPTER 3

Water

London Bridge[1]

The wooden bridge that had sufficed the Romans was replaced in 1176 by a stone one, with nineteen 'starlings' or 'sterlings' resting on the riverbed and supporting the bridge piers. This primitive construction lasted nearly 600 years. From time to time the starlings were strengthened by additional stone. A fishpond was built on one,[2] handy for apprentices 'who had the convenience of rope ladders, to let themselves down on the sterlings [to lay] baits and lines to catch eels and other fish'.[3] By 1750 the starlings occupied five-sixths of the riverbed, and the river roared through the gaps like water through the sluices of a dam. The result was that 'shooting the bridge is almost universally dreaded as the risque of life',[4] and the watermen – whose job it was to convey people up and down, and across, the river – complained that their custom was suffering. The arches at the north end were further obstructed by waterwheels to supply water to the nearby district. One had been enough in 1581, but London had grown since then and by 1720 there were four.

Something should be done, but it was far from clear what. Should there be a new bridge, funded by a lottery? Or should the existing one be improved by removing the starlings and enlarging the arches? If the water wheels were demolished, what about the water company's customers? And its shareholders? What about removing the houses and shops on the bridge that for centuries had precariously overhung the river? Would the receipts from tolls outweigh compensation to the house owners and the mounting cost of repairs? According to the most recent survey, the foundations of the bridge were still good, despite the worrying tendency of most of the houses on it 'to decline so much out of the perpendicular',[5] and if the houses were cleared away, it could be made wide enough for four carriageways and a good footway on each side.

Very sensibly, the whole matter was referred to a committee in 1746, which after due consideration referred it to a subcommittee, and there it stayed. Meanwhile the old Tudor houses on the bridge were pulled down. The workmen found 'three pots of money, silver and gold, of the coin of Queen Elizabeth'[6] – at least, they declared three pots. New piazzas were put up instead, in which shopkeepers prospered. Parsimonious ladies drove all the way from St James's, lured by the rumour of bargains on the bridge in pins and needles, gloves and hats and brushes, seeds and prints and wallpaper.

By 1755 things began to move, all too literally. The City decided to demolish all the buildings on the bridge and make the central arch twice as wide by removing one pier. This did not go down well with the inhabitants. A temporary wooden bridge erected over the gap was burned down twice, leaving the City completely cut off from Kent and Europe. The Lord Mayor hurriedly licensed 40 extra boats to ferry passengers and goods across, even *on Sundays*, but their passage was obstructed by beams fallen from the temporary bridge. By April 1758, 500 workmen were employed on the new bridge, every day of the week.[7] Eventually the successor to the medieval bridge emerged, shorn of its buildings and given an elegant Italianate balustrade. It was much admired, although the watermen were still dissatisfied. 'There was so great an eddy at the great arch that craft or vessels passing through were whirled round for a long time before they could get disengaged, and in the utmost danger of being dashed to pieces against the sterlings, overset in the vortex, or staved against each other ... whereby great damage might be sustained as well as lives lost.'[8] Perhaps the improvement was more cosmetic than functional. London Bridge was finally demolished in 1830. Not a bad innings.

Westminster Bridge

The residents of Westminster had been pressing since the previous century for an alternative crossing to avoid the slow detour through the City. Moreover, the Archbishop of Canterbury was anxious to be rid of the ferry that landed horses and vehicles practically on his doorstep, with all the shouting and commotion involved. At last an Act was passed. £389,500 – a huge sum in those days – was raised, mostly by lotteries[9] and the bridge was begun, in 1739,[10] just downstream from Lambeth Palace. Its thirteen arches were built in caissons 'above the high-water mark, and sinking gradually by the weight of the prodigious blocks of stone, the men could work below the level of the water as conveniently as on dry ground'. (If that is not entirely clear, blame William Thornton, whose description it is.)[11] The workmen could work only five hours a day for the first two years, because of the tide, which sometimes rose as much as 22 feet,[12] so it was an achievement to complete it in just under twelve years.

The opening ceremony was quite a party. On 17 November 1750,

> the new bridge at Westminster was opened at twelve o'clock at night with a procession of several gentlemen of that city, the chief artificers of the work, and a crowd of spectators, preceded by trumpets kettle-drums etc. and with guns firing ... [it was] one of the grandest bridges in the world. On Sunday Westminster was all day like a fair with people going to view the bridge and pass over it.[13]

And the excitement did not stop there. 'The surprising echo in the arches brings much company with French horns to entertain themselves under it in summer',[14] which must indeed have startled many a dreaming pedestrian, brooding that 'earth has not anything to show more fair' than the prospect from the bridge (Wordsworth, a little later). Each pier ended in a charming little hooded alcove, like a nightporter's chair, which Boswell found useful for intercourse with a prostitute[15] and thieves adopted as hiding places. The only people less than pleased must have been the watermen who had operated the ferry for so long.

Blackfriars Bridge

In December 1753 the Lord Mayor and his Common Councillors decided that another bridge would be a worthwhile investment.[16] Years passed while a committee was appointed, a site was earmarked at Blackfriars, finance was raised – it was estimated to cost £144,000[17] – and the householders and traders affected were compensated and moved.

Westminster had enjoyed the advantage of a literally green-field site, but the City had to manoeuvre for position. At last, in the summer of 1760, 'the first pile for Blackfriars bridge was drove in the middle of the Thames'. Unfortunately, it was promptly 'broken down

by a west country barge', for which the bargee was fined £5, his
oversight having been accidental not wilful.[18] The bridge was ready
for pedestrians by 1766, for horses by November 1768, and for wheeled
traffic in November 1769.[19] It had mildly exceeded estimated cost, at
£152,840 3s 10d.[20] Boswell was 'agreeably struck with its grandeur
and beauty'.[21] There was an idea that it should be called William Pitt
Bridge, so popular was that politician, but in the end Blackfriars
Bridge it stayed.

Water supply

Most London houses above the poverty line had piped water.[22] It
came through elm pipes laid under the main streets, which needed
frequent repair, especially at the joints. The technique of pipe boring
shown in John Evelyn's *Silva*, published in 1664, is unlikely to have
changed much by 1764. One end of each hollowed-out piece was
pointed and slotted into the next. Elm trees do not grow in straight
lengths like pine trees, so the average length of each pipe would
perhaps not exceed 7 feet or so. A leak was waiting to happen at each
joint, losing about a quarter of the water. Each pipe lasted about
twenty years before needing replacement. Often several companies
laid their pipes along the same stretch of road. No wonder the streets
were uneven.

In 1763 the Duke of Bedford, the ground landlord whose mansion
occupied the north side of Bloomsbury Square, was having the usual
problems with the water company. He wrote fiercely to the New
River Company:

> I am going to new pave the street before this house; and observing that
> the pipes belonging to you are continually breaking and that the
> pavement when taken up to mend the pipes is always laid down in a
> very bad manner, I give you this notice that you may direct that the
> pipes be made good ... [and properly maintained in the future]. I shall
> be sorry to find myself obliged to take any measures that are disagreeable
> to you.[23]

Thomas Lindsay patented 'pipes for conducting water' that were
made of 'fictile' fired pottery in 1766, and his invention was known
to the Home Office,[23] but perhaps there was some technical snag, for
his invention did not take off.

The connection to the household cistern or storage tank, usually made of lead, was by a thin 'quill' or pipe, also of lead. The supply was controlled by a turncock, who did his rounds at three in the morning 'turning the waters on and off for the use of the inhabitants'.[25] It ran only for a few hours, and only two or three days a week. Poor people 'where one cock supplies the whole neighbourhood with water' would 'fill their tubs and pans with a sufficiency to serve them the ensuing seven days',[26] an inconceivably awkward method, especially in cramped spaces. The public conduits of the previous century were largely obsolete by now.

Foreign observers found it surprising that so little water was drunk in London, but had to admit that its taste was 'but indifferent'.[27] Considering the effect of rotting elm and lead, not to mention the miscellaneous refuse, dead dogs and so on that found their way into the supply, a Londoner would not find this surprising at all. Tobias Smollett described London water in *Humphry Clinker* (1771):

> if I would drink water, I must quaff the mawkish contents of an open aqueduct, exposed to all manner of defilement; or swallow that which comes from the river Thames, impregnated with all the filth of London and Westminster − human excrement is the least offensive part of the concrete, which is composed of all the drugs, minerals and poisons used in mechanics and manufacture, enriched with the putrefying carcasses of beasts and men, and mixed with the scourings of all the washtubs, kennels and common sewers within the bills of mortality...[28]

The London Bridge water-wheels

Peter Moritz's water-wheels under London Bridge had been turning since 1581.[29] They were sophisticated pieces of machinery. Each wheel was 20 feet in diameter, and rotated six times a minute at full tide. They were automatically raised or lowered according to the state of the tide.[30] A reasonable pressure was achieved by pumping the water 'to a bason on the top of a high tower of wood which stands on the sterling of the first arch on the north west end of the Bridge. By which means the water is raised to any part of the city.'[31] Not all the Dutchman's hydraulic expertise could counteract the effect of freak tides, when the river had been known to rise as much as 18 feet,[32] or hard winters, such as in 1763, when 'the waterworks at London Bridge are entirely stopped by the severity of the frost, and water in general is now very scarce'.[33]

The New River

Sir Hugh Middleton's New River[34] still flowed, slowly, 38 miles from Amwell in Hertfordshire, to a storage reservoir in Islington. For part of the route, the water flowed along open troughs raised above ground level, leaking at every joint. As a boy, Francis Place used to fish for 'pricklebacks' in the puddles under the joints.[35] The Duke of Bedford paid the New River Company £7 16s a year for the supply to his huge house in Bloomsbury Square.[36] A small house only 14 feet wide, near Leicester Fields, paid a guinea a year.[37] The company owned and maintained, as well as it could, 400 miles of pipes, on a twenty-year rolling repair programme.[38] If an average length of 7 feet is realistic, that means just over 300,000 pipes and joints.

There were other difficulties. In 1754 'a turncock to the New River Company took a carp out of the pipes, in Swallow Street Golden Square, two feet long',[39] and ten years later ' a fine freshwater eel was taken alive out of one of the pipes near the Maypole, East Smithfield. It weighed twelve pounds three ounces.'[40] Perhaps inspired by it, the next year 'a Frenchman was observed to be busy throwing a composition of paste into the New River in order to intoxicate the fish, which the populace resented so much that they threw him headlong into the river'.[41]

Other companies

By the eighteenth century, several other companies were competing with the older concerns. Power was always a problem. The works at Broken Wharf south of St Paul's used wind power at one stage, but had to change to horsepower when the wind down by the river failed. Going upstream – and to cleaner water – the next waterworks was the York Buildings works, beside the water gate near Villiers Street (now flanked by Charing Cross Station, a reminder of how much wider the river was before the Victorians embanked it). The company tried steam power, but could not get it to work properly. Nearby a competitor, the Hartshorn Lane Company, had the novel idea of using a sewer to drive its pumps. Sewers at this time were supposed to be for surface water, not excrement, but still the idea was unattractive and made a good point for the publicity department of the York Buildings Company. Both these companies supplied water as far as the north side of Oxford Street, in the inevitable leaky wooden pipes.

The Chelsea Waterworks Company, incorporated in 1724, was a different kettle of fish altogether. One of its reservoirs is marked on Rocque's map, as a large circular pool with an 'engine', in the middle of the double line of trees on the east side of Hyde Park, convenient for customers in the Grosvenor developments. Rocque does not show how the water got there, but he does show where it began, in an elaborate grid of leats combining water from the Thames and a tributary, the Westbourn. Although no one had yet thought of filtering water, resting in these leats cleared at least some of the sediment. Anyway, the rivers were cleaner here than down in the City. The Company's steam-powered pumping engine was one of the sights of London. It was not powerful enough to supply Lord Harley's estate 'between Great Portland Street and Marylebone Lane', so a reservoir was made just north of Cavendish Square, adding to the amenities of that semi-rural district.

There were some bitter winters in the eighteenth century. The companies' open reservoirs froze, which produced real hardship not only for those who had thought of washing, but also for dyers and others whose livelihood depended on a supply of water. And an unfortunate woman who 'attempted to drown herself in the reservoir at Marylebone ... could not break the ice'.[42] She managed to hang herself instead.

CHAPTER 4

Traffic

Noise

The screech of iron tyres on cobbles and granite sets, crashing and
bumping over the potholes and drains, horses' metal-shod hooves
clattering, wooden axles squeaking, coachmen and carters shouting,
dogs barking, street vendors yelling, children screaming, musicians
playing out of tune ... Hogarth's print *The Enraged Musician* says all
this and more.

Chairs

At least sedan chairs, defined by Dr Johnson as 'a kind of portable
coach', made no noise. 'Chairs are very convenient and pleasant for
use, the bearers going so fast that you have some difficulty in keeping
up with them on foot ... these chairs are allowed to be carried on
the footpaths ... the bearers go so fast and cannot turn aside with
their burden.'[1] The writer, a young Frenchman, was not quick enough
to move out of the way and was knocked over four times, perhaps
because he didn't understand the warning shout of 'By your leave,
sir'. For the user, chairs were certainly convenient. You could get into
one in the privacy of your own home, and be carried into your host's
home through rain and snow and dirt. This was why chair-men
disapproved so violently of the new-fangled umbrellas, alternative
ways of keeping dry in the rain.[2]

Royalty sometimes preferred chairs to their state carriages. Perhaps
the journey was quicker than in a ponderous state coach with six
horses. *The Gentleman's Magazine* of November 1750 reported that the
Prince and Princess of Wales went from their home in Leicester Fields

to St James's Palace to congratulate his father King George II on his birthday, 'in their chairs', followed by a coachful of children, three princes and a princess. Queen Charlotte, George III's wife, sometimes went about London by chair, and on one occasion offended the always touchy rabble by keeping one of the windows shut.[3] She and her royal husband took their chairs to Drury Lane theatre six days after her wedding. They presumably had the usual guard of Yeomen, who had specially designed partisans (which we would inaccurately call pikes) 'of a shorter and less size being more commodious to be used by our aforesaid Guard when they attend the Royal Chair'.[4] The rest of the royal family went in coaches, attended by the Horse Guards. 'The crowd pressed so violently upon Her Majesty's chair that she discovered [showed] some signs of fear, but upon entering the playhouse she presently collected herself and behaved with great gaiety the whole night after.'[5] Poor girl, what an introduction.

Chairs can't have been comfortable for women. The hoop petticoat had to be squeezed in by bending it up on each side, so that the occupant looked like a captive swan. It was easier for men. 'No man of fashion would cross the street to dinner without the effeminate covering and conveyance of an easy Chair.'[6] But he was wise not to think of walking. Casanova found that 'a man in court dress cannot walk the streets of London without being pelted with mud by the mob while the gentlemen look on and laugh',[7] so he took a chair.

Their construction was ingenious. The roof was hinged so that you could walk in from the front without stooping, and sit down. Then the roof was closed, and you shut and perhaps locked the door in the front. In cold weather you might have a foot-warmer ready on the floor. Wits did say that when the fashion for immensely tall coiffures came in, their wearers had to sit on the floor, but I don't think this would have been possible; more probably the crowning glory poked out through the roof.

The chairs that have survived in stately homes are often elaborately decorated. Like 'best' clothes preserved in museums, these beautiful objects were not necessarily in everyday use. The Duke of Bedford owned several, but his household often hired chairs, and always hired the chair-men.[8] A foreign visitor[9] noted more than 300 chairs for hire near St James's Palace. They were all registered and licensed, the licence fee being five shillings a year. Charges were controlled, at two-thirds of hackney coach fares, and depending on distances.[10]

Horses

Horses could be hired from livery stables, and in a crisis were the fastest means of communication. When George II died unexpectedly in 1760, 'the town was exhausted of Hackney horses ... by the great number of expresses that were sent to persons of distinction all over the country, and yesterday great numbers of nobility and gentry arrived in town and more are hourly coming'.[11] If you just wanted a quiet ride, you might consider one of Mr Tredwell's sprung saddles and stirrups, 'whereby the shake and hard motion of a horse is taken away ... and will also greatly ease the horse'.[12] Riding was good for you. 'The pendulous viscera are shaken and gently rubbed against the surfaces of each other.'[13]

Hackney coaches

Hackney[14] coaches had been plying for hire in the streets of London for 200 years. By 1711 there were 800 licences issued in the City alone, at 5s a week. The officially set rates, and distances, were published in almanacs: for instance, the mile and a half from Westminster Hall to Bloomsbury Square, or from Gray's Inn to Sadlers Wells, would cost a shilling. From Westminster Hall to St Paul's, or the Royal Exchange to Drury Lane Playhouse, would cost 18d. A few hackney coachmen were licensed for Sundays, creating 'an intolerable Disturbance to Divine Worship making such a rattling with their Wheels in Churchtime that those who officiate can hardly hear themselves speak',[15] and no doubt making at least some of the congregation wish they could join the happy throng of Londoners off to enjoy themselves, Churchtime or no Churchtime.

Hackney coaches tended to be 'ugly and dirty ... the body of the carriage is very badly balanced so that ... you are most cruelly shaken, the pavement [road surface] being very uneven and the horses ... fast trotters'.[16]

Hired carriages

For out-of-town journeys something better than a hackney coach would be needed – for instance, a 'handsome Landau and four able horses', which could be hired for 20s a day.[17] Or you could use the post system, hiring a change of horses at each post station. 'If', said

Johnson, 'I had no duties, and no reference to futurity, I would spend my life in driving briskly in a post-chaise with a pretty woman.'[18]

Private carriages

James Newton, the parson of Nuneham Courtney in Oxfordshire on which Goldsmith based his *Deserted Village* (1770), regularly came up to London in his own landau to stay with his mother.[19] Her house had no stabling, so he had to find a 'standing' for the landau. He also had to pay the wheeled vehicle tax of £4.[20] He seems from his diary entries to have been modestly proud of his landau. Certainly it enabled him to take his mother and sister and women friends out and about in London. But it was a hardworking conveyance, doing the journey from Oxford in two days, after which it usually needed repair.

The private carriages of the nobility and gentry could be magnificent. 'Most are drawn by [up to six] fine and excellent horses.'[21] Those belonging to noblemen sported a small gilt coronet at each corner. Two or even three footmen 'attired in rich liveries' rode on the back,[22] their main function being to advertise their employer's wealth by being so ostentatiously useless. The panels of the coach could be made of thin metal sheets, enamelled in gold and brilliant colours.[23]

If these were the gold-trimmed Rolls-Royces of the era, the Venetian Ambassador's coach was a stretch limo. When he went to present his credentials at Kensington in 1745, the procession included 'three fine state coaches, the first being the most magnificent ever seen in this country, being *seventeen feet* [my italics: almost the height of a small house] from the ground', and when he came back in 1763 this prodigious vehicle was drawn by a team of eight horses, part of a procession of miscellaneous horsemen, drummers, etc. and twelve other coaches.[24] It seems odd for the representative of a marine empire to indulge in such ostentatious land transport. How on earth did it get here?

Wagons, carts and chaises

But even the most elegant equipage had to crawl if it was stuck behind a wagon, the HGV of the time. These lumbering vehicles, drawn by trains of up to eight horses and some capable of carrying

10 tons,[25] took their time along the streets, never giving way. Their wide wheels, designed to save the road surfaces outside London by rolling smooth the ruts made by narrow wheels, splashed even more mud and filth on to the pedestrians in London streets. Following traffic had no choice but to wait. If you were very unlucky, you might have to wait a long time: for instance, while twenty wagons crawled through the City to the Bank, loaded with booty from the captured French fleet and guarded by marines.[26] On another occasion, the wagons carrying spoils from the war finally got to the Bank, but had to go on to the Tower, 'as the Bank is not immediately prepared to receive it', which must have held up traffic throughout the City.[27] The best thing to do was to get out and walk. 'This happens every day to persons of the first rank', wrote a French lawyer, amazed at English egalitarianism.[28] Then there were the tradesmen's carts, the street vendors' carts and the scavengers' carts, and a variety of one-seater chaises (cf. sports cars), beloved by their owners but of little practical use.[29]

Stage coaches

Stage coaches were sometimes called 'God permits', 'from that affectation of piety frequently to be met with in advertisements of stage coaches where most of the undertakings are promised with "if God permits".'[30] Short runs to villages near London would cost 6d or 1s and may have been pleasant, on a summer morning.[31] The 1740 edition of a *Complete Guide to London* – a sort of desk diary for the well-organised man – gave the timetable for long-distance stage coaches and carriers. For instance, three coaches ran to Oxford from three different inns, in Fleet Street, Holborn and Warwick Crescent, daily in the summer, three times a week in the winter. The coach for Edinburgh ran from the Black Swan in Holborn, three times a week in the summer, twice in the winter. These inns were considerable enterprises. The George and Blue Boar in Holborn, whence the Glasgow coach left, had forty bedrooms, stabling for fifty horses, and seven coach houses.[32] The four horses were changed at each stage, while the passengers got down to stretch their legs and attend to their comforts in the brief respite allowed by the driver.

In 1763 John Wesley went to Bath in the 'one-day machine'.[33] An average day's journey would be 50–60 miles. Samuel Johnson left London one Thursday in October 1772 at 9 p.m. and arrived in

Lichfield the next day at 11 p.m.; yet he could say that 'a stage coach is not the worst bed'.[34] At least steel springs lessened the jolts, from 1754, but those long journeys must have been purgatorial. The driver and his guard sat up in front, keeping their eyes open for highwaymen in case the blunderbuss was needed. Inside, there were seats for four, sometimes six as coach design, and roads, improved. You might be unlucky in your fellow-passengers. Tobias Smollett, always practical, described the 'pestilential vapours' at a Bath assembly which might equally affect a coach traveller.[35] They included 'mingled odours, arising from putrid gums, impostumated lungs, sour flatulencies, rank armpits, sweating feet ...' And then your fellow-passengers might never stop talking. One day in 1776 Samuel Johnson and Boswell went on a 'jaunt' to Oxford by coach, a thirteen-hour journey,[36] with the architect Gwynn, 'a fine lively rattling fellow'. They had animated discussions all the way. Pity the fourth passenger, a gentleman of Merton College, who must have been heartily sick of them all when he got home at last.[37]

In the country the roads were abominable unless they had been 'turn-piked' and were maintained by a private company which charged for its services (like an autostrada now). In London the best that could be hoped for was those unyielding granite setts, and a skilful driver. If the coachman was wicked he would follow a 'one horse chaise ... passing so close to it as to brush the wheel, and by other means terrifying any person that may be in it'. This incitement to road rage was known as 'hunting the squirrel'.[38]

Processions

Add one more contributor to traffic jams: the habit of expressing solidarity by processions of coaches. On 10 September 1744, when invasion by the Scots and the French was threatened, the Lord Mayor of London waited on His Majesty out at Kensington 'in a grand cavalcade of sixty nine coaches', to express the City's support. The next day the merchants of London did the same, in 144 coaches. After careful deliberation, 'the very lawyers ... thought it time to exert their courage and they on 23 November headed by the Lord Chancellor ... and the rest of the judges proceeded from Westminster Hall in a train of two hundred coaches, each in his proper habit [appropriate robes]'.[39] That must have brought traffic to a standstill for a very long time.

The elephant

'On 27 September 1763 Captain Samson had the honour to present
the elephant brought by him from Bengal to His Majesty at the
Queen's House [soon to be renamed Buckingham Palace]. It was
conducted from Rotherhithe that morning at two o'clock and two
blacks and a seaman [who perhaps knew the way] rode on his back.
It is but a young one and is about eight feet high.'[40] Imagine the
effect of an elephant on a late-night drinker.

Accidents

Put all these coaches and carriages and wagons and carts into motion,
like a model railway. Now add fog, which 'wrapps up London entirely
... during the winter, which lasts about eight months'.[41] 'Carts,
coaches and other carriages ran against each other at noon day.
Much mischief was done and some lives were lost.'[42] Hardly newsworthy. What was surprising was the observation of one foreign visitor
that, although the English lower classes were rude and violent, there
were few road traffic accidents, every driver giving way to others,
except for the wagon drivers, who had no room to move over even
if they wanted to. There was an occasion when

> the coachman of a person of rank, driving furiously along Piccadilly,
> threw down a girl with a young child in her arms, and the wheels going
> over her, bruised her in so terrible a manner that there are no hopes
> of her recovery. The child providentially received no damage. There
> was a lady in the carriage ... who called out repeatedly to the coachman
> to stop but he drove on in spite of her orders and of the efforts which
> were made by the spectators to seize him.[43]

Otherwise, drivers were anxious to exert all their skill and patience
to avoid collisions, and 'lend each other a hand [which] prevents this
confusion from degenerating into one of those bloody frays which so
often happen', according to M. Grosley, 'in Paris'.

A horseless carriage?

Someone was already dreaming the impossible dream – or was it
always just a hoax? *The Daily Advertiser* of 20 May 1741 reported that
'the surprising travelling coach which runs without horses will be

shown and rode in till tomorrow night and no longer at Green Street
Grosvenor Square'. This was surely the same one as Samuel Johnson[44]
was told about in 1769 – 'a machine which went without horses: a
man who sat in it turned a handle which worked a spring that drove
it forward. "Then, Sir, (said Johnson) what is gained is, the man has
his choice whether he will move himself alone, or himself and the
machine too".'

River traffic

Billingsgate must have been the smelliest as well as the noisiest place
in the City. Fish had been landed and sold there since the eleventh
century,[45] so that the soil was impregnated with ancient fishy smells.
The sea coal shipped from Newcastle was landed there too, for sale
on the wharf or in the Coal Exchange nearby. In the summer there
could be as many as seven hundred collier ships all waiting to
discharge their cargo, jostling the ships laden with perishable fruit
from Spain and Kent.[46] And with all that, it was the terminus for the
wherries carrying passengers and light cargo down to Gravesend,
where many seagoing ships loaded so as to avoid the delay in London.
Because the wherries had to leave at exactly high tide to get through
London Bridge a bell was rung fifteen minutes before sailing, to get
the passengers out of the pubs. When the Thames was frozen, in the
severe winter of 1763, peace and quiet reigned. 'The watermen with
a wherry on their shoulders and one of their number sitting in the
same with oars began collecting money from charitable people, being
disabled by the frost from carrying on their trade', while 'forty sail of
colliers lie off Gravesend but can proceed no further.'[47]

Passengers waiting for the tide at Billingsgate might have a chance
to see some whales. Eight ships arrived in the river from Greenland,
in July 1753, with 35½ (what happened to the other half whale?) and
ten ships with 20 whales, the next summer.[48] They might like to
muffle their ears; 'fish women ... are somewhat apt to leave decency
and good manners a little on the left side'.[49] Occasionally 'porpusses'
arrived: more than twenty 'came up with the tide almost to London
Bridge and after continuing near an hour playing on the water,
returned in a body.'[50]

Boats

The water-taxis of the time were either 'oars' or 'scullers', the latter
costing half the former. The fixed fares were 4d for oars to cross the
river 'directly', 6d from London Bridge to Westminster, 8d from
Temple stairs to Vauxhall.[51] One can see why the watermen were
against any more bridges. Taking a boatman was rather like choosing
a porter at an Indian airport, in 'a horrible noise by shouts and
upraised hands'.[52] But once you had picked one, he did not think it
within the terms of the contract to help you into his boat: which still
seems to me an extraordinarily difficult feat, if you were encumbered
by stays, long skirts and arthritis. Venetian gondolieri do at least take
your hand, as well as your money.

Thames watermen had a monopoly of river transport, so much so
that the City authorities asked for their help to stop *anyone* rowing on
the Thames on Sundays. The watermen themselves were already
forbidden to, but 'many inconveniences [had] arisen from apprentices
going up the river in cutters [perhaps even drinking and singing] to
the great annoyance of sober families on the banks of the Thames'.[53]
Young people...

State occasions

The river was still used for great occasions. Each new Lord Mayor
of London went to be sworn in at Westminster Hall in his barge,
'attended by the different [livery] companies in their barges'[54] each
one elaborately painted and decorated for the occasion, with sixteen
oarsmen in their uniforms at the back, and flags flying, and a band
playing on the steeply inclined prow. In 1749 the Prince of Wales
bought 'a magnificent new built barge after the Venetian manner and
the watermen dressed in Chinese habits',[55] which must have been
quite a sight. ('Venetian' might not have been right. In its next
appearance in *The Gentleman's Magazine*, it has turned into a 'Chinese
barge'.)[56]

CHAPTER 5

Green Spaces

How did Londoners get away from the traffic?

The countryside

They could walk out of London in any direction, to the open country. Hogarth's print *Evening* shows a family with three small children making their way home, on foot, after a day in the country. As on most happy family expeditions, everyone is tired and grumpy at the end of it, even the dog. But no doubt the fresh country air had done them all good. The Swedish botanist Per Kalm took careful note of the market gardens surrounding London, where asparagus and cauliflowers were raised under glass,[1] and the plots beside the road grew flowers for sale to passers-by. One Sunday in May 1748, during the hay harvest, he walked out towards Hampstead. 'A multitude of people streamed out here from all sides of London to enjoy their Sunday afternoon. In all the ... villages there was a superfluity of beer-shops and inns ... there were also small summerhouses [the translator kindly gives us the Swedish word for them: *lust-hus*] built in the gardens with benches and tables, which are now all full of swarming people.'[2] Some of them no doubt had come in those rattling hackneys that had disturbed the congregation, but Hogarth's family group had clearly walked.

The royal parks: Hyde Park

Then there were the royal parks. The biggest was Hyde Park, opened to the public by James I. There was a melancholy spot at the northeast corner, where soldiers were shot for desertion.[3] It was as well to

keep your eyes open for thieves – Horace Walpole was attacked as
he walked home from Holland House by moonlight.[4] The park was
a favourite place for duels, illegal though they were. John Wilkes quite
blatantly fought a Member of Parliament in the park, one day at
noon. He was slightly wounded and honour was satisfied.[5]

There were deer there, and a railed enclosure where on summer
evenings sometimes as many as 300 carriages full of 'fine ladies and
gentlemen come and drive slowly round in order to see and be seen',[6]
which must have been a lovely sight for onlookers, if dizzying for the
participants. When Charles II and his mistress Lady Castlemaine
drove round the Ring in opposite directions, the dust had been laid
by sprinkler carts. I have seen no reference to eighteenth-century
sprinkler carts but surely they were still there. The Quality did not
appear on Sundays, because the populace invaded the park on their
only day off. The very size of the park made it ideal for mass occasions
such as the army review in June 1763, attended by the royal family
and 'a great number of persons of the first distinction of both sexes,
and near 100,000 others'.[7]

Kensington Gardens

Next to Hyde Park were Kensington Gardens. John Wesley thought
them 'more grand than pleasant',[8] but M. Grosley drew a charming
picture of them. He was sure that Londoners were more scared of
crime than he thought justified. To prove his theory he twice went to
sleep in public. Once was near Chelsea hospital. He woke to find
himself guarded by a posse of Chelsea pensioners who gave him a
fatherly talking-to, one of their number having picked up appropriate
French during his active service. His next experiment was in Kensington Gardens, in 'one of those boxes which are scattered up and
down the grass-plats and move around on pivots'. He woke to find
'a company of handsome young women' all round him, quite silent,
in his little box, waiting for him to wake up – and no theft.[9]

St James's Park

St James's Park was the most colourful of the parks. Charles II had
opened it to pedestrians. Notables could drive along one of its avenues
in their beautiful carriages, but only if they had specific royal authority.
The Duke of Portland could go in and out of the park and across

Horse Guards Parade in his coach, and so could the two Principal
Secretaries of State and the First Lord of the Treasury. They would
need to, to get to work in Downing Street. Lady Sheffield's hearse,
on the other hand, and Lord Sheffield's removal wagons, had only
one-way single-trip passes,[10] and the premier peer of England, the
Duke of Norfolk, got a pass to use his carriage, but only 'during ill
health'.[11]

The thing to do in St James's Park was to walk about and, as usual,
see and be seen. M. Grosley could hardly believe his eyes, on an
April day when the park was 'incessantly covered with fogs, smoke
and rain' – and even then 'filled with walkers'.[12] You could never be
sure who might be there, except on Sundays, when 'welldressed
Gentlewomen and ladies of quality [were] drove out of St James's
Park … by Milliners, Mantua-makers, … Staymakers, Sempstresses
… and butchers' daughters'.[13] In 1751 'His Majesty walked with the
Duke of Cumberland in the mall … which is new gravelled, about
an hour, to the great joy of the spectators'.[14] Mozart's father was very
proud when 'the King and Queen came driving by [in the park] …
they knew and saluted us; the king in particular threw open the
carriage window, put out his head laughing, and greeted us with head
and hands – particularly our master Wolfgang'.[15]

In the winter of 1760, the shallow 'canal' or lake froze, causing
complaints of the 'hundreds of skaiters and spectators shouting and
whooping in time of divine service'.[16] An official reassured the com-
plainants that 'a strong press-gang will attend' and the skaters would
find themselves skating on the frozen lakes of Canada, where we
were fighting the French, instead. In the summer there were more
complaints – by the same spoil-sports? – of 'indecent practices … by
a set of disorderly persons playing and betting at unlawful games,
bathing, [and] running of races *naked etc.* [my italics] particularly on
the Sabbath day'.[17] Casanova[18] approved of the park, for just this
reason.

It was as well to watch your feet.

The grass-plats are covered with cows and deer, where they graze or
chew the cud, some standing, others lying down upon the grass; this
gives the park a lively air … [One senses that M. Grosley was more at
home with pictures by Claude Lorraine than with real cows.] Most of
the cows are driven about noon and evening to the gate [into Whitehall]
and tied in a file to posts

to be milked. The milk was 'served with all the cleanliness peculiar to the English, in little mugs at a penny a mug'.[19] When some of the cows died in the epidemic of cattle plague afflicting Europe in the eighteenth century,[20] the milk bar – surely the first ever? – had to be shut.

As well as cowpats, one might have to avoid elephant turds. The elephant[21] that was given to the King in 1763 seems to have stayed on in the Queen's House, and was taken for walks in St James's Park. M. Grosley made a joke about it, always a difficult thing to do in a foreign language. When the British dislodged the French from Canada in the Seven Years War of 1756–63, French settlers made a rush to acquire British nationality so that they could maintain, or reacquire, their Canadian possessions. Their petitions were, rather surprisingly, granted. 'When an elephant kept in the Queen's stables [it *has* to be the same one] happened one morning to be walking in St James's Park, an Englishman, meeting it, enquired "Where the elephant was going?" "No doubt it is going" said a merry wag, "to the parliament-house, to get itself naturalised".'[22]

Despite its royal walkers, St James's Park always had (and still has) a slightly shady reputation, especially at night. Very early in his reign, George III issued orders that should have solved the problem:

GEORGE R   Our Will and Pleasure is that the following Rules and Directions be observed strictly and obeyed by all Persons concerned, under Pain of our High Displeasure.

That the Centinels placed in St James's Park have Orders given them by their Officers, every Guard, and Directions, from time to time, by our Ranger or his Under-Keepers, not to admit any rude Boys, Beggars or people pretending to sell any sort of Wares, or carrying into or through the said Park, any sort of Bundles or Burden whatsoever, but to stop all such persons and to turn them out at the first Publick Gate or Passage. Not to suffer any persons whatsoever to play at any sort of Games, or Dogs to pass through any of the passages leading into the said Park; and to hinder all persons from walking on the Grass or out of the Public Walks, or on the Mall in wet weather; and not to suffer any Persons to disturb the Deer or Fowl or to walk in the said Park with pattens on.

That no coaches Horses or Persons on horseback be admitted into or to pass through our said Park but with our Livery [permission] . . .

[The rules were to be enforced by as many soldiers] as may be necessary to assist our Ranger ... if they resist, to take them up and carry them immediately before the Civil Magistrate.[23]

Although they seem to cover any eventuality except rude Girls, the Rules did not altogether succeed in their objective. 'Old women and children who have filled their pockets with bread at dinnertime [persisted in] feeding the Ducks in St James's Park.'[24] In 1773 there had to be an official clean-up campaign to 'clear St James's Park of gamesters and other loose and idle persons'. 'Gamblers, beggars, nose-gay women and persons selling things, and at night common prostitutes and soldiers were to be apprehended.' After a hectic four days, 'peace and decorum' reigned[25] – for a time.

The Green Park

This airy space stretched from Hyde Park corner to the gardens of Buckingham House, and from St James's Palace up to Piccadilly. It was the most innocent of all the parks. The banks of the Chelsea Waterworks Company's open reservoir along Piccadilly made a pleasant stroll, and a path led down to the Mall, in front of a row of grand houses such as Spencer House. A print of the time shows deer, and cows being milked, and horse riders. Perhaps it was too rural. It was a favourite escape route for highwaymen and robbers earning a dishonest living in Piccadilly.[26]

The park came in useful for the firework display celebrating peace in 1748,[27] watched by the royal family from the side windows of St James's Palace. *The Gentleman's Magazine* followed every move, from the construction of galleries '800 feet long and sixty feet broad for the conveniency of the nobility and gentry, with covering to screen them from the weather',[28] to the rehearsal attended by twelve thousand people in Vauxhall Gardens of the music for the royal fireworks written by Mr Handel (tickets 2s 6d), to the great evening itself. Privy Councillors got twelve tickets each, peers four, mere commoners two.

The occasion was not an unmixed success. Most of the fireworks had to be abandoned when the elaborate pavilion designed for them caught fire. One of the rockets 'darted straight forward [and] set fire to the clothes of a young lady which would have destroyed her but some persons present having the presence of mind to strip her clothes off immediately to her stays and petticoat'. She was only a little scorched. A painter fell to his death, so did a boy up a tree, and a

man drowned in the pond. The young Swiss who had designed the
fireworks got over-excited and challenged His Majesty's Comptroller
of the Ordinance and Fireworks to a duel. He was arrested, to cool
off, and apologised the next day. All this cost 'only' £14,500.[29]

Other spaces

Westminster Bridge was pleasant on a summer afternoon, when there
would be 'some hundreds of people, mostly women and children,
walking backwards and forwards ... for the benefit of the air, looking
at the boats going up and down the river and sitting on the resting
benches to pick up new acquaintance'.[30] In the City, there was an
enjoyable walk round the walls of the Tower of London, 'much
frequented by the ladies in the summer as ... it is shaded by a lofty
row of trees and [has] a delightful prospect of the shipping',[31] which
in those days was indeed a lovely sight. The gardens of the Drapers'
Company

> are pleasant and commodious being open every day except Sundays
> and rainy days for the recreation of genteel citizens to walk in. The
> ground which they occupy is very near a square. The middle is enclosed
> with iron rails and laid out in grass beds, gravel walks and borders of
> flowers with a statue of Flora in the centre. Without [outside] the rails
> are fine spacious walks ... agreeably shaded with rows of lime trees. At
> the South West corner is a very handsome pavilion for the accom-
> modation of company in hot weather.[32]

'Genteel citizens' could also enjoy the peace and quiet of the Inns of
Court − 'all decent company are permitted to walk in them every
day'.[33] M. Grosley, a lawyer himself, noted the statues in Lincoln's
Inn, and the 'part laid out for culinary purposes' in some of them.[34]
Citizens with no pretensions to gentility could walk in Moorfields,
where elm trees shaded broad gravel walks, the middle one being
called the City Mall.[35] Or if they lived near the older squares such as
Soho Square, Red Lion Square and Leicester Fields, they could see
the 'railings of painted wood [containing] gardens with flowers, trees
and paths',[36] even if they could not walk there.

Tenter grounds

Rocque's map still shows many open spaces labelled 'tenter grounds' –
areas used by textile finishers to dry and stretch fabric after dyeing
it.[37] In the previous century, London had been the main centre of
textile finishing. This trade was drifting out of London to places where
labour was cheaper, and the air and water cleaner, so it is the more
surprising to see tenter grounds just north of Moorfields, for instance,
and on the south bank opposite the Temple, and just south of Guy's
Hospital. Granted, they could not be walked on, but they still
preserved a green space in urban surroundings.

Survivals

'Poor women who live in Courts Yards and Alleys [would] bring their
chairs into the streets, where they sit with their constant gossips and
pass their verdict on people going into or coming out of the fields.'[38]
The tenement houses occupied by the very poor had often been
illegally built in the back gardens of old houses. They made no
provision for pleasure gardens, but just as the ruins of houses and
halls survived in odd corners, so, surely, an occasional old pear tree
still gave shade to the squalid courts and alleys. Trees are amazingly
hardy.

CHAPTER 6

The Buildings

The slums

Observant foreigners such as Kalm and Grosley did not penetrate as
far as the slums. No one did if they could help it. The English
chroniclers of London usually wanted to show it in a favourable light.
It was magistrates and doctors who tried to make the better-off aware
of how the poor lived, and their spotlights fell on some very dark
places indeed.

Ruinous houses in the old parts of London might be good for a
few nights' shelter before they fell down – a frequent event in
the eighteenth century.[1] Samuel Johnson referred to 'falling houses
thunder[ing] on your head',[2] and such disasters were often reported,
for instance 'an old lodging house in ... St Giles fell down ... seven
poor wretches were crushed to death and many more desperately
maimed. There being other houses in the court in the like tottering
condition, the mob assembled ... and pulled them down'.[3] But there
was a living to be made out of such houses. One woman managed
to run twenty of them, which generated money at the rate of 2d a
night for a single person, 3d for a couple: four or five beds in each
room, four floors per house: she must have made a small fortune over
the years.[4] 'In the parish of St Giles's there are great numbers of
houses set apart for the reception of idle persons and vagabonds, who
have their lodgings there for twopence a night. In these beds, several
of which are in the same room, men and women often strangers to
each other lie promiscuously, the price of a double bed being no
more than threepence.'[5]

The well-meant policy of previous centuries, of limiting the growth
of London by prohibiting building except on existing foundations,

had by the eighteenth century produced illegally built warrens tucked away from the sight of the authorities, with no amenities such as street lights, piped water or refuse collection. As temporary structures usually do, they lasted, after a fashion, for years. They were a nightmare for law enforcers. Henry Fielding deplored them. 'Whoever considers the great irregularity of their buildings, the immense number of lanes, alleys, courts and by-places, must think that had they been intended for the very purpose of concealment they could not have been better contrived.'[6] 'The houses are divided from top to bottom, and into many apartments, some having two, others three, others four doors opening into different alleys.'[7]

Obviously criminals profited by these multiple escape routes, but other occupants were there through no fault of their own. A woman too pregnant to work might be lying in a garret, 'open to every wind that blows, or in damp uncomfortable cellars underground'.[8] She would at least have company.

> From three to eight individuals of different ages often sleep in the same bed; there being in general but one room and one bed for each family ... The room occupied is either a deep cellar, almost inaccessible to the light, and admitting of no change of air, or a garret with a low roof and small windows, the passage to which is close, kept dark, and filled not only with bad air but with putrid excremental effluvia from a vault [cess-pit] at the bottom of the staircase.

The window tax was imposed in 1695, and progressively raised, so that even these small windows were often blocked up.

Each room was just big enough to house 'a bed, with space for a person to pass it, and so much as is necessary for a fireplace'.[9] The fire would be the only means of cooking, as well as heating and light, and fuel for it could be harvested from the house itself in the shape of bannisters and panelling, if nothing were available outside. By night 'houses which are left open and are running to ruin [are] filled with beggars some of whom are asleep while others are pulling down the timber to sell for firing'.[10]

Some slum property was cleared to make way for the new bridges. Indeed, slum clearance was one of the reasons justifying Blackfriars Bridge. The district round its north end was described as 'filled with laystalls and bawdy houses, obscure pawnbrokers, gin-shops and alehouses; the haunts of strolling prostitutes, thieves and beggars, who nestling thus in the heart of the City become a nuisance which it is worth all the money the bridge will cost to remove'.[11] This was one of the notorious no-go areas known as 'Alsatias'. Samuel Johnson did not recognise the term, but thieves knew it well,[12] as the districts in Whitefriars and over the river in Southwark to which folk memory still attributed some sort of freedom from arrest dating from medieval sanctuary laws long abrogated. As fast as slum tenants were cleared, they set up house somewhere else. The idea of making decent housing available to those who could not afford it was a long way off.

Many of the very poor slept rough. Brick kilns and glass factories were deserted at night, and with any luck the furnaces were still warm.

Small houses

People hanging on to the fringe of self-sufficiency, such as casual labourers, chair-men, porters and journeymen weavers, lived in furnished lodgings in small houses or tenements as near as possible to where they might hope to find work. Hogarth's print *The Distressed Poet* shows a garret with a fireplace and one lattice window; crowded but not squalid. The kind of space we take as normal, at least separating children from parents at night, and having a room for sitting and watching the television and doing homework, was a luxury only the prosperous enjoyed.[13]

Expectations were low. A parish midwife, Mrs Brownrigg, was married to a house painter. They lived in a court off Fleet Street, where he 'carried on a considerable share of business', and they had a lodger, so they lived in reasonable comfort. They were tried for appalling cruelty to the apprentices sent to her by the parish to do the housework so that she could give her full time to her midwifery. One of the reports of the trial[14] described the girls as 'confined mostly in the cellar, where hogs were kept'.

The grand developments in the west end included small back streets, and sometimes, even, small houses in the squares themselves, for local artisans and tradesmen to service the mansions of the rich.[15]

Housing for the middling sort

According to the architect Isaac Ware, the capital cost of a house for 'the middle rank of people' would be about £600 or £700, depending on the 'ornament' and the size of the plot.[16] The kitchen was below ground level, with a space (or 'area') between it and the door to the coal cellar, which was excavated under the street. Instead of coal being taken through the house, it could be delivered straight into the cellar[17] through a round hole in the pavement covered with an iron plate. Many of these plates can still be seen, although their purpose has long gone. There were plain iron or stone steps at the side of the main entrance, down to the 'area basement', for tradesmen and servants. The lead water-storage tank was installed there, filled by gravity from the mains supply in the road. A house 'fit for a small family' was advertised in the *Daily Advertiser* of 8 December 1743, just off Cavendish Square. 'Water comes into the area and back kitchen twice a week.'

The front door was usually raised a few steps above street level. Over it an iron arch held a lamp in a circle in the middle, and in grander houses there were cone-shaped extinguishers for links (torches) at shoulder level on each side, for the linkmen to douse their torches in when they had delivered their charge to his front door. At floor level, Per Kalm was very taken with 'a fixed iron on which the men scrape the ... dirt off their shoes before they step in'. Did they not have mud in Sweden?[18]

The two rooms on the ground floor were parlours – that is, sitting rooms. Ware placed the dining room and main bedroom on the next floor, two storeys away from the kitchen. On the next, another two bedrooms and a closet. The servants, three or four of them, slept in the garrets, or if necessary 'a bed for one manservant or two maidservants is contrived to let down in the kitchen'.

Ware did not concern himself with drains for the middle classes, beyond saying that 'it is necessary that every house has conveniences for discharging its refuse water and other useless and offensive matters'. If there was no accessible sewer into which 'offensive matters' (excrement) could *lawfully* be discharged, the house had to depend on a 'great cesspool' and night-soil men. Yet only fifteen years later, in 1771, a house was to let in Cecil Street, off the Strand, which had not only an Observatory on the top, but 'two neat water-closets'.[19]

To deal at one sitting, as it were, with lavatories/houses of office/conveniences/*lieux à soupape* (places with valves, from which is presumably derived our 'loos')/houses of easement/water closets/ bogs: Ware recognised that the owner of 'a house of considerable estate in a town where there is the advantage of a common sewer' might well expect some kind of sanitation, so he gives him three 'bog-houses' in sequence. The first is in a courtyard but can be reached from inside, the other two are some way away outside, each taking the discharge from its predecessors. Perhaps he was wise. No one really cracked how to design these things to avoid awful smells, until 1775, when Alexander Cummings, a Bond Street watchmaker, put his ingenious mind to the problem, cut off the rising stinks by a U-bend filled with water, and provided a flush in the pan. His patent was improved in 1778 by Joseph Bramah, a cabinet maker, and since then we have never looked back.[20]

The height of these houses, and details such as downpipes to channel rainwater, and the prohibition of projections, were generally still controlled by the building regulations of 1667 passed after the Great Fire. The windows were elegant sashes with narrow glazing bars. Any that are flush with the wall are pre-1708, when building regulations required them to be set at least four inches into the wall for better fire prevention.[21]

Not surprisingly, Londoners were neurotic about fire risks. Eighteenth-century London building regulations (consolidated in the Building Act of 1774, which finally abolished the 1667 regulations) were largely directed to minimising fire risk, in particular by substantial party walls. When Lady Molesworth's house in Upper Brook Street burned, eight or nine people in it died, 'yet the strong party-walls prevented the fire's doing any damage to the houses adjoining'.[22] Old houses still went up like tinder, taking their neighbours with them, especially in hard frosts when the piped water froze and the 'machines' were helpless.

Samuel Johnson lived at one time in Johnson's Court off Fleet Street, which 'hath but a narrow entrance, but opens into a square court with a free-stone pavement and good houses, well inhabited. Out of this court is another which bears the same name but smaller, with one row of houses with pretty gardens behind them.'[23] Bedford Row was another delightful place to live; 'having a prospect into Gray's Inn garden and the fields ... with a broad coachway to the houses which are large and good with free-stone pavement and palisado pales before the houses inclosing little garden plots adorned with handsome flower pots and flowers therein'.[24]

The Adelphi

The Scottish brothers (Greek: *adelphi*) John, Robert, James and William Adam were a family of genius, who were ahead of their time. In 1768 they designed a multi-purpose development on the site of Durham House, on the north bank of the Thames just up-river from Somerset House. They imported Scottish labour, kept in good heart by bagpipes.[25] Four storeys of warehouses filled the slope between the river and the level of the Strand. On top of the warehouses, and running back towards the Strand, four elegant residential streets were built, their façades decorated with the newly fashionable honeysuckle motifs in stucco, framing a splendid Royal Terrace facing the river. The work took five years. But the houses did not sell and the brothers were saved from bankruptcy only by disposing of them by lottery.

Horace Walpole, that devotee of Gothick, disapproved of the Adelphi. 'Warehouses laced [braid-trimmed] down the seam, like a soldier's trull in a regimental old coat', he said.[26] (The Royal Terrace was demolished in 1936–8. A very few of the original houses, with their honeysuckle motifs, survive.)

The great streets and squares

In March 1763 Earl Granville's house in Arlington Street was sold at auction for £15,000.[27] In 1771 Mr Christie advertised the auction of 'a large and elegant messuage with double coach house and stabling for six horses and convenient offices, on the north side of Portman Square ... four gracious rooms on a floor, an elegant hall, superb stone staircase, and brick ditto [for the servants] the whole fitted up with great taste and elegance ... held for a *term of which ninety years are unexpired*' (my italics).[28]

These last words were significant. If a speculative builder had to recoup his outlay and make a profit, he would not spend much on a building that would revert to the ground landlord in twenty, thirty or even forty years. This was the position in most of London. Ninety-nine-year building leases began to be granted only when the noble landowners first began to develop their green-field sites, in the early 1700s. The market they were aiming at was the top end of the trade: substantial houses which would hold their value for the foreseeable future, more than a century or so. They insisted on higher standards of construction. In return the builder insisted on a longer lease, to give him the option of realising some of his investment before the house reverted to the ground landlord. These long building leases were a peculiarly English invention, connected with the English habit of entailing family property: tying it up so that it stayed in the family and was passed to the eldest son, generation after generation. Unless the machinery of family settlements was done away with, which would have been unheard of, no one person could sell the freehold and get rid of the property altogether. The most he could do was to let it.

Grosvenor Square was developed by such long-term leases. There were 51 houses round the square. Sixteen were occupied by peers. In 1750 its west side alone housed a dowager duchess and a duchess, three earls and a lord. Grosvenor Street and Brook Street could field between them two marquises, four earls, four dukes and five other titles.[29] Yet prices seem surprisingly low, compared to the house in Arlington Street. Perhaps it was sold with contents? Number 26 Grosvenor Square was bought in 1743 for £3,750, with 79 years of its lease to go, and was sold fourteen years later for £6,000. Number 39 was bought in 1730 for £3,400 and sold in 1755 for £4,000 and again, furnished, two years later, for £7,500. The biggest house of all in Grosvenor Square was the centre one on the west side, with a frontage of 70 feet, completed in 1728. Perhaps the builder asked too much. He died before it was sold, and his widow was left with it on her hands until 1739, when she disposed of it by a raffle.[30]

Mansions

Territorial magnates still had huge disposable incomes, when land was profitable and taxation low. They poured some of their money into their ancestral estates in the country, employing the latest architect to design Kedleston, for instance, and on a smaller scale often refronting a Tudor pile in the approved flat Georgian style. But if they were to enjoy the London season every year, to marry off their daughters and strengthen their political alliances, they needed appropriate bases. Surprisingly often, they were content with a house in a row fronting on to a square, cheek by jowl with their neighbours, which must have been a strain for anyone accustomed, in the country, to being monarch of all he surveyed. A few were able to find sites for free-standing mansions with gardens and front courtyards, although the garden would be paltry compared to the rolling acres of their country seats.

Spencer House, the sole survivor,[31] was built for Mr John Spencer (later to become the first Earl Spencer) and his new wife. Building began in 1756, to the design of John Vardy, a disciple of William Kent, imbued with the spirit of Palladio and Inigo Jones. The shell of the house was completed by 1759. At this stage the Spencers decided to switch from Vardy and Palladio to James 'Athenian' Stuart and Greece. The change mainly affected the interior decoration, considered in Chapter 21. Magnificent though Spencer House was, and is, the surprising thing about it is its charm. There are no chilly wastes of stone, as in Kedleston, another Stuart commission. Spencer House contains only one room that could be called great, essential for large, fashionable and influential gatherings. The other state rooms are human in scale, no matter how sumptuously decorated. The site did not allow any forecourt in which guests could dismount or leave their carriages or chairs, away from the interested gaze of the populace, who enjoyed watching the stream of rich carriages arriving at assemblies, and frequently managed to chalk popular slogans such as 'Wilkes and Liberty' on them as they waited in the inevitable traffic jam. But there was room for a small garden separating the terrace of the house from Green Park.

The house Isaac Ware designed for Lord Chesterfield in 1748 was on a site large enough to include a courtyard in front, with elegant arcades to two side pavilions. The exterior of the house was almost insistently plain, making a dramatic contrast to the opulent decoration inside.[32] The Countess of Pomfret found a site in Arlington Street nearby, big enough to provide her remarkably gothic Pomfret Castle with a courtyard and a gothic gatehouse.[33] Lord Featherstonehaugh could drive into his courtyard in Whitehall opposite the Banqueting House, but visitors to another house in Whitehall, Gower House, had to go round to the back.

The biggest private mansion in London was, and had been since the early 1600s, Northumberland House looming over the Strand, its gardens still stretching down to the river. It was a vast Tudor red-brick pile with the Northumberlands' lion proudly standing on its roof, but it had become dilapidated over the centuries and needed a thorough refurbishment in 1749. Mercifully, its exterior was changed only by installing modern sash windows. Its palatial interior could accommodate assemblies of 1,500 people – perhaps the figure was exaggerated, and perhaps they did not all come at once – but its Tudor builders had not provided for modern transport; the courtyard and gateway from the Strand were nowhere near big enough to cope with the chairs and carriages of the guests. (It withstood the encroaching tide of shops and offices until 1874, when it was demolished to make way for Northumberland Avenue.)

Royal palaces

Everyone – foreign visitors and English architects – knew that London needed a proper, modern Royal Palace to house its monarch in appropriate splendour, especially considering the magnificence of some of his mere subjects' residences. Plans had been discussed ever since the Court had had to move into old St James's Palace in a hurry when Whitehall Palace burned down in 1698. Nothing came of them, probably because William III lived out of London as much as possible to relieve his asthma, so he used Kensington Palace as his 'suburban retreat'.[34]

St James's Palace had been built by Henry VII in the 1530s.[35] It was neither impressive to foreign diplomats nor comfortable for the royal family. Successive monarchs tinkered with it, but its Tudor red brick remained obdurately un-modern. It looked over St James's Park, but the house at the end of the mall had far better views down the full length of the park looking east, and over open fields to the west. In the end George III was able to buy that house for £28,000, and move in, in 1762.

Buckingham House had been built in 1705 for £8,000, including an elaborate iron staircase by Tijou. It had thirty acres of garden, more than any other property that could be called inner-city. The King should have been in a good bargaining position, because more than half of the house had been built on land that had originally been the royal mulberry garden, leased to the then Duke of Buckingham, and the lease had run out.[36] £28,000 seems a high price in the circumstances.

Buckingham House became known as the Queen's House when by a bit of legal shuffling George III's queen was given it in return for giving up her right to Somerset House, which had been the queen's dower house since James I's marriage to Anne of Denmark. George III and his queen spent their London days here, George going over to the state apartments in St James's Palace for official business like a civil servant going to his office. They divided the house between them, George taking the ground floor and adding four libraries, a bedroom for himself next to them, and a 'riding house',[37] and Charlotte the first floor. *The Gentleman's Magazine* of May 1762 described 'a bedchamber of thirty four feet by twenty seven feet, within it a large closet that opens into a greenhouse' on the ground floor. A lead cistern on the roof 'holding fifty tons of water driven up by an engine from the Thames supplies all the waterworks in the courts and gardens', which included

> a little square green that has a fountain in the middle and two greenhouses on the sides with a convenient bathing apartment in one of them ... At the end of the green house which joins the best apartment is a little closet for books and under the windows of this closet and greenhouse is a little wilderness full of nightingales and blackbirds.

The only note to add to this idyllic picture is that in those days 'wilderness' meant an arrangement of trees planted in a quincunx pattern, not as in 'howling'.

Queen Charlotte had been well advised to get rid of Somerset House, built by Protector Somerset in 1547. It had had its days of regal splendour. Queen Elizabeth had lain in state there, in 1603. James I's queen, Anne of Denmark, had partied there, and Henrietta Maria, Charles I's wife, had scandalised Londoners by observing the Catholic religion in the chapel there, as she was entitled to do by her marriage treaty. But it had fallen into sad disrepair. The lead roof let in water, and the wooden window frames were rotten. It was patched up from time to time, and was just viable as the setting for a ball given by the Russian Ambassador in 1755 and for a reception for the Venetian Ambassadors in 1763. (What can they, coming from the *Serenissima*, have thought of the shabby draughty rooms?) The Prince of Brunswick was lodged there in 1764, but that was the end.[38] It was demolished in 1775, to the consternation of miscellaneous royal hangers-on who had found lodgings there. The present building was designed by William Chambers to accommodate various learned societies in the north wing facing the Strand, and several government departments in the three other blocks round the courtyard – the first purpose-designed government offices.[39]

PART
TWO

The Poor

'Resolve not to be poor: whatever you have, spend less. Poverty is a great enemy to human happiness; it certainly destroys liberty, and it makes some virtues impracticable and others extremely difficult...'

Samuel Johnson

CHAPTER 7

Massie's Analysis

In 1759 Joseph Massie compiled statistics of average family incomes in England, divided by occupation.[1] His analysis can be imagined as a broadly based pyramid. At the bottom is half the total population of England, with an income of £23 or less per family. There are some London occupations here, such as alesellers, seamen – London was still England's biggest port – paupers and vagrants, but the bulk of these poor people are country dwellers, labourers and husbandmen, fending off starvation in the countryside, not in London.

Working our way up the pyramid and concentrating on London, the first Londoner we meet is a labourer earning £27 10s a year. Then we get to solid citizens such as tradesmen, builders and 'manufacturers', at about £40 a year ('manufacturer' was defined by Samuel Johnson as a 'workman or artificer'). The £50 to £100 band covers clergy, the 'liberal arts', and officers in the Army and Navy. The law, a London-based profession, scores £200 a year, alongside a few successful manufacturers, merchants and tradesmen, but is left behind by some merchants who may be making up to £600 a year. Then finally we approach the summit of the pyramid, rank after rank of 'titled gentry'. They draw their wealth from their estates in the country, and many of them live there all their lives, but increasingly they are drawn to London for some part of the year, and own or rent a house in London. The pyramid culminates in ten families with an annual income of almost £27,000 each.

Massie's figures were estimates, and his occupational categories do not fit London life. Is the practice of medicine to be included in the liberal arts? Where do apprentices fit? But at the very least he jolts us into remembering that the rich, even the affluent or the prosperous, were not the only inhabitants of London. There was a visible chasm between the very rich and the very poor.

The poor are given only a walk-on part, if that, in descriptions of eighteenth-century London.[2] Yet without them one is left with what I came to describe in my mind as 'satin and Chippendale'. So I have drawn arbitrary lines across Massie's table, producing three kinds of Londoner. I shall start with the poor, who left no diaries and wrote no letters and are rarely seen in pictures. Then the focus moves to the middling sort, from small tradesmen to prosperous merchants, including the professions. That leaves the gilded plutocrats and royalty for last.

CHAPTER 8

The Welfare System

What happened to the very poor?

There was a system of welfare, administered by parishes. People were not left to starve in the streets, at least not often. But a constable looked into an empty house in St Bride's one day and found five women. Two had already starved to death, the other three were only just alive. One of them had applied for parish relief, but had been turned away.[1] In another account of the same episode, the men who found this awful scene were an estate agent and his prospective client.[2] When Samuel Johnson estimated those who died of starvation at twenty a week, 'Saunders Welch, the Justice, who ... had the best opportunities of knowing the state of the poor, told me that I underrated the number.'[3]

Settlement

If you hoped to tap parochial charity, you had to satisfy the legal requirements – not always easy to do if you are starving and illiterate. The first essential was to prove 'settlement' – that is, some legal link to the parish on whose funds you were claiming. Everyone, almost, had a settlement. The nearest definition in Samuel Johnson's *Dictionary* is 'to settle: to fix oneself; to establish a residence', although it is tempting to use 'to subside; to sink to the bottom and repose there', for the plight of the destitute. Some parishes in the City of London were very small indeed and might be determined to minimise the cost of poor relief to their more prosperous residents. Parishes sometimes paid indigent bachelors in other parishes a small fee – 40s – to marry some of their poor women, effectively taking them off their books and adding them to the husbands' parishes.

Parish authorities were corrupt as well as stingy. They were notoriously adept at cooking the accounts of the Poor Rate, spending the proceeds on feasts for themselves[4] instead of on deserving claimants. If they could find someone else to bear the cost of maintaining a claimant, they would. Deserting husbands and fathers of bastards were pursued and, if found, made to pay. An 'eminent tradesman' who allowed his mother to exist in a workhouse was traced and ordered to maintain her.[5]

A foundling had its settlement where it was found, and could do little about it if this was in a poor parish. Provident and self-sacrificing women sometimes made for a rich parish when they felt the onset of labour, planning to abandon the baby there and trust it to the mercy of the authorities. But the parish officials knew this all too well, and were not above pushing a woman in labour back over the parish boundary to give birth somewhere else. In 1772 an Act was passed recognising this, and providing that 'mothers who are suddenly taken in labour will no longer be subject to be removed from parish to parish as has frequently been the case but must be relieved immediately and the child provided for, by the parish where they happen to be'. But passing a law is one thing, enforcing it is another.

Children born in wedlock took the settlement of their father up to the age of seven, after that their mother's, if their father had died, unless they established a separate settlement of their own.[6]

Parish babies

A baby in the care of a parish was unlikely to survive for long. Parliament was able to ignore this uncomfortable fact until Jonas Hanway rubbed its nose in it, not by appealing to its humanity, but by methodically collecting figures. St Luke's parish poorhouse[7] received 53 children between 1750 and 1755. By 1755 all of them had died. In thirteen parishes, 2,239 children had been born in or admitted to workhouses between those dates, of whom 1,074 had been discharged normally. That left 1,165 children to be accounted for. By 1755 only 168 of them were still alive.

Finally, Parliament could ignore Hanway no longer. A pair of Acts was passed. The first, in 1762, imposed on parish clerks the duty to keep accurate records of the children in the care of the parish, and it became clear that Hanway had not exaggerated. After a five-year period while these statistics were collated, the parish system of children in care was reorganised from top to bottom. All parish children under six were to be sent out of London to be brought up by paid nurses in the country, who stood to make a further 10s for every baby under nine months who survived in their care. Poor people called this 'the Act for keeping babies alive' and they were right. Figures of infant mortality fell, and the old penny-pinching of parish clerks was no longer the approved official line.

Apprenticeship

Parish children could be bound apprentice at the age of seven, to work for their keep alone and often without any hope of learning any useful trade. The boys were bound until they were 24, the girls until 21 unless they got married earlier. Hanway's 1767 Act provided that no apprenticeship should last more than seven years. St George's parish advertised in 1771 'several poor children of both sexes who are now in the workhouse of this parish are ready to be bound apprentice ... the children may be seen any morning before ten o'clock'.[8] But 'few of those poor children now serve out their time, and many of them are driven by neglect and cruelty into such immorality as too frequently render them the Objects of Public Justice'.[9]

The apprenticeship system had been designed in the Middle Ages, to provide vocational training as part of a carefully regulated system of labour relations, dependent on the guilds for enforcement. The guilds were losing their power by the eighteenth century, and the system no longer functioned efficiently. New skilled trades, such as the manufacture of scientific instruments, were profitable. They could be set up outside the crowded City and outside the jurisdiction of any guild. It would be a rare master who took a parish apprentice into such a trade. The openings for parish children were dead-end jobs, at best, in which the master often took on a child solely for the sake of the £2 or £3 premium that the parish paid him so as to get the child off its books.[10]

The Gentleman's Magazine regularly reported cases of mistresses ill-treating their parish apprentices. The most notorious was the case of Elizabeth Brownrigg, a parish midwife, whose trial ran and ran in 1767. According to *The Gentleman's Magazine* she shut her two girl apprentices up in the cellar, 'where hogs were kept' and made them grind pigments there, for her husband's trade – he was a painter and colourman. It should perhaps be said that the girls were sent to her as domestic drudges, to release her for her midwifery. There was never any question of their learning useful skills from her.

The *Newgate Calendar* had a lurid account of the evidence at her trial. One of the girls, Mary Jones, was an ex-Foundling Hospital child whom Brownrigg 'whipped ... with such wanton cruelty that she was occasionally obliged to desist from mere weariness'. Another, Mary Mitchell, got out of this house of horror (as modern tabloids would undoubtedly have called it), but she was caught by Brownrigg's son, who was just as evil, and dragged back. Meanwhile yet a third girl, Mary Clifford, was apprenticed to Brownrigg by the parish overseers. Mary Clifford's sufferings at the hands of the Brownrigg family are too hideous to recount. At last the efforts of an interfering neighbour freed the girls and achieved the arrest of the Brownriggs. The girls were taken to St Bartholomew's Hospital, where Mary Clifford died. Elizabeth Brownrigg and her daughter were hanged. The crowd prayed for their damnation.

Workhouses

The middling sort, who paid the 'poor's rate', had a feeling that the poor were poor because they spent too much on 'a vast torrent of luxury' such as eating, let alone drinking, so it was all their own fault.[11] Welfare should not be too attractive. Work was the answer. Put them in workhouses and make them work for their living. 'The great cure for Idleness is Labour', as Henry Fielding wrote. Divide the poor into

    1   Such Poor as are unable to work
    2   Such Poor as are able and willing to work
    3   Such Poor as are able but not willing to work.

Those in the first category, who were 'but few', could in his view be left to private charity. Those in the third were so intransigent as to merit criminal sanctions. The second category was, as Fielding conceded, 'of great difficulty', in those days when labour disputes and the withdrawal of labour were beginning to be part of London life. Samuel Johnson[12] thought that

it may be questioned whether there is not some mistake as to the methods of employing the poor, seemingly on a supposition that there is a certain portion of work left undone for want [lack] of persons to do it; but if that is otherwise, and all the materials we have are actually worked up, or all the manufactures we can use or dispose of are already executed, then what is to be given to the poor, who are to be set to work, must be taken from some who now have it.

It had been easier in Queen Elizabeth's day, when the Poor Law was first enacted.

Since 1722 parishes had been empowered to build workhouses, where the poor could be stowed away out of sight, children could be given a minimal education and adults given something to do. Occasionally, they functioned well. A child was old enough, at five or six, to begin work. The going rate in the outside world, for winding silk on to bobbins, was a few shillings a week. The children in the London workhouse undercut even that rate.[13] Was this sweated labour? Or sound financial management that enabled the workhouse to keep its hundred children 'in as good order as any private family'? And why, asked Wesley,[14] 'is not every workhouse in London in the same order? Purely for want either of sense or of honesty and activity in them that superintend it.' Marylebone workhouse ran an excellent hospital that was the exemplar of the great hospitals founded later in the century. The Spitalfields workhouse provided silk to be spun, St George's at Hanover Square employed its inmates on making linen and doing plain sewing, but the products were not really saleable. In general, workhouses were terrible places, they had little effect on poverty and they only exacerbated local work shortages.[15]

> These wretched receptacles of misery ... scenes of filthiness and confusion ... young and old, sick and healthy, are promiscuously crowded into ill-contrived apartments not of sufficient capacity to contain with convenience half the number of miserable beings condemned to such deplorable inhabitation ... speedy death is almost ever, to the aged and infirm, and often to the youthful and robust, the consequence of a removal ... to such mansions of putridity.[16]

Clerkenwell workhouse held 320 inmates. It had been built for 150. How could anyone survive, let alone teach, or learn, in such surroundings?

Contracting out

A year after the Workhouse Act of 1722, Parliament thought of an even better idea. London parishes that found it inconvenient to house their poor in a workhouse could farm them out to contractors, who would for a fee cart them – literally – off to where the cost of living was lower. The contract could be either on a per capita basis, for instance at 3 or 4s a week per head, or simply to take all the paupers that a London parish wanted to get rid of. One such contractor was paid £60, to lodge them 20 miles out of London, far away from any possible contact with friends or family. However many he started with, quite soon only eight were left, mostly diseased and starving children who wouldn't last long. Three parishes sent their poor out to Hoxton, at 4s 3d a head per week. Mile End, then a country district, offered much better terms to five other London parishes, at only 3s a head, less than half the weekly budget for a working man.[17]

'No one would undertake a business so productive of trouble and so obnoxious to [sic] such ignominy, without a prospect of ample repayment. The power of oppression is in [the contractor's] hand.'[18] In plainer words, since no saleable product could be expected from these pitiable humans, the only way to make a profit out of them was to skimp on their food. How many died, and how soon, I do not know; but one good thing was, of course, that their deaths did not inflate the Bills, the returns of the number and causes of deaths in each London parish. These pathetic cartloads travelled by night to their unknown destinations, to save them – and the authorities – from the pitying shamed eyes of their fellow-parishioners.[19]

Outdoor relief

Outdoor relief enabling the recipient to stay in her own home seemed to work just as well, with less cost in human misery. A splendid parish overseer in Leytonstone in 1740 gave Beck Milton some money 'to fetch her stays out of pawn'.[20] Single payments, which were until recently the backbone of the welfare culture, could deal with such sudden crises,[21] and payments could be made for nursing and even medical advice, sometimes at the cost-cutting level of the local wise woman. Weekly payments were at the most 2s, so the claimant's income still needed to be supplemented, usually by begging.

Badges

Anyone receiving parish charity was supposed, by an Act of 1697, to wear a badge with the initial of the parish on the shoulder of their right sleeve. This was most bitterly resented, but it was enforced until its repeal at the end of the century. Hogarth's print of *The First Stage of Cruelty* shows a pauper boy with a round 'SG' for St Giles, one of the poorest parishes in London, on his ragged shirt, and there are two little girls wearing the same badge as they sip their gin in *Gin Lane*.

The Irish

The Irish were an intractable problem. They flocked over to England every summer for casual harvest work in the fields surrounding London. Some of them 'return with the savings of their labour to their own country. These are useful, faithful, good servants to the farmer and as they are of great use to the kingdom deserve protection and encouragement. The others are a set of fellows made desperate by their crimes, and whose stay in Ireland being no longer safe come to London ... most of the robberies and the murders consequent on them have been committed by these outcasts'.[22] In the notorious lodging-houses in St Giles, where rot-gut gin was sold for a penny a quartern (quarter of a pint), the inhabitants were mostly Irish. 'If one considers the destruction of all morality, decency and modesty, the swearing, whoredom and drunkenness which is eternally carrying on in these houses on the one hand, and the excessive poverty and misery of most of the inhabitants on the other, it seems doubtful whether they are most the objects of detestation or compassion.'[23]

Death

It was not long before paupers reached their final status symbol, a pauper's grave. Parish churches gave them little sympathy or attention. There were open 'poors' holes' in the churchyards of St Giles's in the Fields, St Martin's and St James's: 'large holes or pits in which they put many of the bodies of those whose friends are not able to pay for better graves, and then those pits ... once opened are not covered till filled with dead bodies. ... How noisome the stench is that arises from these holes so stowed with dead bodies especially in sultry seasons and after rain, one may appeal to all who approach them.'[24]

CHAPTER 9

Living Conditions

The home

An average poor family lived in one furnished room, paying a weekly rent of perhaps 2s, less for a room in the cellar or under the eaves.[1] The house itself might be old, perhaps the dwelling of a prosperous tradesman who had moved out of the City in the previous century; or it might be new, run up out of nothing in the back alleys, or on what remained of the fields out at Bethnal Green or Spitalfields, where the journeymen weavers lived, or along the river, where sailors and workers in the shipping trades lived. A group of such houses might have a nearby standpipe where water flowed at intervals, but it would certainly have no drainage or refuse collection, nor were the Watch likely to look in.

Food

Serious cooking would be impossible in such rooms. Dr Johnson, and no doubt many others poorer than he was, used the baker's oven to have a pie cooked for his Sunday dinner, the baker not baking bread that day.[2] But there was always a takeaway nearby. There was an alley in Covent Garden called Porridge Island, 'where there are numbers of ordinary cook shops to supply the low working people with Meat at all hours'.[3] The cooks 'cut off ready dressed meat of all sorts and also sell soop'.[4] Meat was the Englishman's mainstay. But for those who could not always afford meat, corner shops everywhere sold bread heavily adulterated with chalk and alum[5] to make it white. During the Gin Craze, a baker giving evidence to a parliamentary commission said that bakers had to cut their loaves into halfpennyworths, 'a practice unknown to the trade till gin was so universally drunk by the poor'.[6]

Bad bread was 'a much more general cause of disease than the public is aware of. Bread is bad either when it is made of bad corn or when it is ill made ... [e.g.] adulterated with alum ... [It causes] general weakness, slow fever, a hectic [fever], the rickets and the king's evil.'[7] (The king's evil was a tubercular infection of the lymph glands of the neck.) Such was one medical opinion of the time, which may well have been right. Smollett, himself a doctor, described London bread in *Humphry Clinker* as a 'deleterious paste mixed up with chalk, alum and bone-ashes, insipid to the taste and destructive to the constitution'.[8]

The adulteration of food was a known scandal, but nothing effective was done to stop it. *The Gentleman's Magazine* reported one case of a baker fined £5 for even possessing alum, but he must have been unlucky.[9] As well as the pollution of bread, sulphuric acid was added to vinegar, confectionery and pickles were coloured with copper salts, chalk came in handy again to thicken watered milk, lead was useful to blacken tea and 'improve' wine; and if all this were not enough to cause severe intestinal distress, the acids in some food could react disastrously with the lead in lead-glazed pottery or pewter vessels.[10] The only advantages that the poor had over the rich were that they were unlikely to suffer from improved wine, and if they did do any cooking, they probably used an old iron pot, which would not poison them, compared to the copper and brass pots in affluent kitchens.

The Gentleman's Magazine gave recipes for soups 'designed for such families as are very necessitous', such as 2lb of beef boiled with 6 quarts of water, which 'will support six for a whole day'.[11] Presumably this was not intended to be cooked by the poor, but distributed to them, like the soup given away by the French charity in Spitalfields, but I doubt if it tasted as good.

Other than bread, the kind of food that the poor could afford is difficult to assess. Corner shops sold small bunches of stale greens, farthings' worths of cheese, and paper twists of tea-flavoured dust. You could buy boiled tripe from a tripe shop, wrapped in a bit of paper – there was an insatiable demand, among takeaway food shops, for old paper. Scraps could be begged at rich men's houses.[13] Fish went off quickly without refrigeration. The mackerel boats came into Billingsgate between three and four o'clock in the morning, and any fish unsold by six began to smell and could be bought for very little.[14]

Little 'dabs' of meat could be bought in the market and 'roasted on packthread strings'[15] dangled in front of the fire, and at noon 'poor people that lodge in low-rented houses go to each other and after paying their awkward compliments borrow saucepans and stewpans for the dressing [cooking] peas beans bacon and mackerel for dinner', while poor French immigrants picked dandelions 'in the adjacent fields to make a salad for their dinner'.[16]

A remarkable computation made in 1750 of 'Expenses in Provisions' for the whole estimated population within the Bills of Mortality gives prices for '1,500 hogs @ 20/- each', but does not give any detailed breakdown. More usefully, for our purposes, it reckons 1d a head per day for bread, the same for milk, cheese and butter (all three together), and for 'sea coals, candle and firewood', and one eighth of a penny per head per day for 'roots and herbs both for food and physic':[17] just over 3d a day per head, excluding meat.

A tract of 1734[18] gave a budget for a labouring man, his wife and four children, in London. They needed 6d a day for meat, 4½d for bread, 1½d for butter and the same for 'roots, salt, sugar etc', ¾d for cheese, ¾d for milk, 4½d for small and strong beer – avoiding the perils of water – 2d for coals, and 2¼d for soap, candles and thread; about 4d per head per day. How realistic this was is hard to tell: for instance, the 'labouring man' and his family had two rooms for the six of them, and only paid 1s 6d a week rent; but they may have been garrets in a slum district. We do not know the age of the children. If the 'labouring man' was in the printing trade, he would certainly have spent more on beer, unless he had met Benjamin Franklin, who was shocked to find his workmates drinking *six pints a day*, at 1½d a pint[19] until he weaned them off it on to tea. Journeymen tailors too expected the odd pint during the day, included in the cost of food and drink for the six working days at 11d a day.[20]

Schooling

Earlier in the century, the Society for the Propagation of the Gospel and the Society for the Propagation of Christian Knowledge had both turned their attention to the young heathens growing up on the streets of London, but by mid-century the impetus had died, without much to show for it.[21] Robert Raikes opened his first Sunday school later in the century (1781). But the streets of London were scattered with charity schools, mostly but not always for boys.[22] In 1766 there were

300 boys at the Merchant Taylors' school, founded in 1561. A hundred of them paid no fee, the rest between 2s 6d and 5s a quarter (about 2–4d a week). The syllabus was the usual – Latin, Greek and Hebrew – but at least the boys learned a modicum of social behaviour.

Christ's Hospital had been founded by Edward VI in 1552 as a co-educational school. In 1675 Samuel Pepys and others persuaded Charles II to extend it to include a Mathematical School where promising boys were taught navigational skills such as mathematics and astronomy. The boys had 'long writing desks sufficient for three hundred boys to sit and write at', and they lived in eight wards of 50, with one ward for the girls. They did well to be there: for instance, 'they have beef about twelve days in the year, by the kindness of several benefactors'.

A quick look at some other schools:

Blackfriars School, 40 boys, reading writing and book-keeping, and 30 girls.

Neale's school in Hatton Garden taught mathematics.

Two schools in St Dunstan's, 50 boys taught navigation, 40 girls 'educated, cloathed and put out to service'.

Bridewell trained 100 apprentices in various trades, 'clothed in blue doublets and breeches and white hats', entitled to £10 after their seven years' term.

Two charity schools founded by Sir John Cass, together 90 boys, 70 girls.

A free school for 20 poor children in Seething Lane.

Southwark, a school for 40 boys and 50 girls, and a cluster of schools including Dorothy Applebee's free English school, and a free grammar school, teaching more than 140 boys and 70 girls.

Bermondsey, two schools, 100 boys and 20 girls.

Covent Garden, two charity schools, 30 boys and 20 girls.

Tothill fields, four schools, together 150 boys and 40 girls.

Burlington Gardens, boarding school for 80 girls.

Hackney, Kingsland Road, 50 boys and 50 girls, 'cloathed yearly and have books provided for them'.

Raine's School Shadwell, 50 boys and 50 girls, of whom every year
one was chosen by lot to receive £100 as a marriage portion.

These must have had some impact on illiteracy, where parents were
prepared to forgo the child's earning capacity. Certainly an ability to
read handbills advertising the next wages demonstration was assumed
by those circulating them, and newspaper reports of the latest crimes
were avidly followed in artisans' taverns. 'I have often seen shoeblacks
and other persons of that class club together to purchase a farthing
paper', wrote de Saussure.[23]

Free further education had been available in earlier times, from
Gresham's Institute, but it had been 'suffered to run greatly to decay'.

Fleet weddings

So much for day-to-day expenses. It is so often the unexpected
occasion that wrecks a careful budget. Weddings, for example, can
be expensive, when you count up the cost of the parson and the
church, let alone all the wedding guests expecting to eat and drink at
the expense of the happy couple. Until 1754, when the law was
changed, all that was needed to make a valid marriage was that the
parties should say that they took each other as man and wife. No
need for an expensive ceremony or a wedding feast. And the best
place to go was the Fleet, the main prison for debtors. There were so
many people imprisoned for non-payment of debts in the early
eighteenth century that, rather than build a new prison, or amend
the law effectively, the authorities allowed the debtors to live near
the prison building in the surrounding district, called the Rules,
or Liberties, of the Fleet.[24] There was a chapel inside the prison,
but a couple could be married anywhere, in any private house,
chapel or 'marriage house' in the Rules, including several public
houses.

Although there was no need for a parson, many brides must have
felt they would like one there, so whoever officiated at the ceremony
might wear a cassock, whether or not he was a clergyman. There
were plenty of clergymen in the Fleet or the Rules, who had been
sent there because they could not pay their debts, such as fees due to
their bishops. They welcomed a modest wedding fee – less than the
proper amount laid down by the Church – and certainly didn't worry
about any possible fine that the Church might impose for undercutting

the official rates: they were already in prison for debt, nothing worse could happen.

Obviously it might be handy to be able to prove a marriage, if anyone queried its validity later, so the celebrant, who could at least write even if he were not ordained, recorded weddings in a book that he called a register, as a matter of convenience. These registers were not formal documents, and could easily be forged, for a small bribe. This could have extraordinary consequences. In about 1784 'a woman came to the [parish poor law] overseers and claimed parish aid as the wife of [a man], in consequence, she said, of a fleet marriage some forty years previously'. The parish took her seriously, and advised the man to pay her a weekly allowance. He refused, and the ensuing legal action in the ecclesiastical court cost him £1,000, which helped to ruin him. He was also excommunicated, which hardly worried him at all.[25]

Who were the people who used this opportunity? Not, as I had assumed, prisoners who could not go and be married in a church like other people. By the 1740s *more than half* of all weddings in London were celebrated in the Rules of the Fleet. Abraham Navarre, a weaver from Spitalfields, married Magdalen Le Grand there in 1748. Peter Sebin of Normandy married Mary Agnes Descamps of Lisle in March 1749. John Barnier, a gardener from Nimes, married a girl from Guernsey in 1751. Maybe they wanted to avoid the elaborate – and expensive – wedding feast that the French community would have expected. There is a thin but steady stream of Chelsea pensioners getting themselves wed, perhaps for the sake of their brides' bright eyes, but more probably for the premium they earned from the brides' parishes, for taking their spouses off the parish poor law books. One Saturday in 1741, 'the churchwardens from a particular parish in the City, in order to remove a burden from their shoulders, [as poor law guardians] gave forty shillings and paid the expenses of a Fleet marriage to a miserable blind youth ... who plays the violin in Moorfields [in Shoreditch], in order to make a settlement of the wife and future family on Shoreditch parish.'[26]

There were soldiers, and, particularly, sailors. Indeed, matrimony seems to have awaited the jolly mariners like a land-based plague, as soon as they got their pay. There was a particular pub in Rotherhithe that was popular with sailors and their girls. Couples would set off for the Fleet ten at a time, and come back married. 'The landlord said it was a common thing when a fleet comes in to have two or three hundred marriages in a week's time among the sailors.'[27] Between these surges in trade, profits were maintained by what we would term 'cold calling'.

> I have often been tempted by the question 'Sir, will you be pleased to walk in and be married?' Along this most lawless space [Fleet Street] was hung up the frequent sign of a male and female hand enjoined with 'Marriages performed within' written beneath. A dirty fellow invited you in. The parson was seen walking before his shop, a squalid profligate fellow clad in a tattered nightgown [dressing gown] with a fiery face and ready to couple you for a dram or a roll of tobacco.[28]

The Fleet was the main place for clandestine weddings. Its principal competitor up to 1742 was a widely advertised one-man business run by the Reverend Dr Keith, who lived in a house vaguely resembling a country church, in Curzon Street, next door to the May Fair Chapel, where he solemnised marriages at a cut rate of a guinea a time.[29] His Bishop caught up with him in 1742 and consigned him to the Fleet, which probably had the untoward effect of *increasing* the reprobate clergyman's income, since he shifted his practice to the Fleet and his curates continued his former practice from his house in Curzon Street as his agents. There was a frantic rush to beat the deadline, 24 March, of the 1754 Act that put an end to such weddings. Forty-five couples had achieved wedlock before eleven o'clock. By the end of the day, 'near a hundred pair had been joined together'.[30] They must have been queuing round the block.

Another parson, the incumbent of the Savoy Chapel, was not so lucky. His output of weddings during two years, 1754 and 1755, topped 1,500, but when he was convicted for offences under the 1754 Act, he had no chance to survive in the Fleet – he was transported.[31]

Divorce

Once married, what were the possibilities of untying the knot? In law, none. Divorce was a rich man's privilege. The best remedy was, as it always had been, to cut and run. The chances of escaping any liability to maintain wife or children would be increased by the prudent use, at the ceremony, of a false name. Spelling in those days was somewhat flexible, and given names can be surprising, but even bearing both those factors in mind, one wonders whether Ann Taylor, who in 1749 married a sailor whose name is recorded as Trueand Loyll, ever saw him again after the consummation of the marriage.[32]

Children

In households that supported themselves by begging and stealing, the rare children who survived infancy – few did, in those circles – could come in useful in unexpected ways. Indeed, it might be necessary to acquire stock from outside sources.

> That by which [gypsies] are said to get the most money is, when young gentlewomen of good families and reputation have happened to be with child before marriage, a round sum is often bestowed among the gypsies, for some one mort [gypsy slang for woman] to take the child; and as that is never heard of more by the true mother and family, so the disgrace is kept concealed from the world and if the child lives it never knows its parents.[33]

If a child did not fall into their laps like that, it could be stolen. 'A gypsy woman was ... charged with decoying children into the fields, stripping them of their clothes etc and frequently selling them to beggars',[34] but there were some occupational risks besides the ponderous processes of the law. 'A woman lately tried for stealing young children was detected in St Giles's [stealing another child]. The mob was so exasperated that she was dragged for a considerable time in the kennel [gutter] and afterwards ducked in a severe manner'.[35]

She was lucky to escape with her life, but things could be arranged amicably. One of the Lord Mayor's periodic clean-up campaigns discovered a beggar woman with a child in her arms, 'which upon her examination appeared to be hired at the rate of eight pence a day of its mother in Petticoat Lane. She was committed to Bridewell and the child returned to its parents',[36] who must have resented this sudden drop in income. An 'autem mort'[37] was a female beggar with several such hired or borrowed children.

Clothes

Poor children probably stole whatever garments they could find, to cover their nakedness. There is a pathetic picture in the *Cries of London*[38] of a child shoeblack carrying a basket of cloths and polishes in one hand and a stool in the other, and wearing a strikingly tattered old coat that would have been far too long for him, in its prime. For a very poor woman, the irreducible minimum would be stays and skirt ('petticoat'). The stays were often made of leather, turned black and shiny with wear and dirt. They could not be washed. They provided a cosy home for livestock.

A working woman, or the wife of a working man, would have a larger, and cleaner, wardrobe, but always based on the stays-and-skirt formula. A writer on the history of the 'labouring classes' in 1797[39] said of the working people in London that they 'seldom buy new clothes ... their wives seldom make up any article of dress', except for children's clothes. A woman's wardrobe would include a 'common stuff' (wool) gown, a linsey-wolsey petticoat, a shift, a 'coarse' (working?) apron and a 'check' apron, stockings and shoes and a 'coloured neck-handkerchief', a cap (not the kind of man's cap favoured by east enders early this century, but a close-fitting white coif), a 'cheap sort of hat' and a cloak – both would last two years – and a pair of stays, which would last six years. The whole lot cost, he reckoned, 37s – under £2.

Stays were not treated as out-of-sight underwear. As we have seen, very poor women wore them with nothing else, on their top half, and the effect was of poverty, not indecency. The window of a respectable pawnbroker and silversmith in the City, who 'lends money on plate, watches, jewels, wearing apparel, household goods and stock in trade', displayed several stays.[40] Their elegant shape appealed to Hogarth, who used them as a border for his *Analysis of Beauty*. Apart from those long-lasting stays, what surprises a modern woman is the lack of duplicates. No possibility of 'one on, one in the wash'. But the list was compiled by a man, who may not have thought to ask. Nor did he know about 'coaxing' stockings or 'vampers', 'to pull down the part soiled into the shoes to give a dirty pair of stockings the appearance of clean ones, or ... instead of darning, to hide the holes about the ancles'.[41] Confusingly, stockings were also known in slang terms as 'drawers'. No knickers were generally worn.

The list for the working man himself was a cast-off coat and second-hand waistcoats and breeches, 'a good foul-weather coat (will last very well two years)', stockings, strong shoes, a coarse linen shirt and a hat '(will last three years)'. Again, no duplicates. Another surprising thing to us, in the age of long-lasting synthetics, is the short life of these garments: two years, for a foul-weather overcoat? The list did not include a wig. This may seem reasonable, nowadays, but wearing a wig was so widespread in the eighteenth century that even the poor workman wore one, probably acquired from the 'dip' in Holborn where wigs ended their days. For 3d you could dip into a box and hope that the wig you got was roughly what you wanted. If it was hopeless, you could have another go for half price.[42]

Credit

There were early versions of friendly societies, called 'box clubs', to which you could contribute perhaps 1d a week, to fund some major purchase (a pair of stays?). By the end of the century, legislation was beginning to regulate these clubs, which was very necessary, the box-keeper finding it only too easy to abscond with the painfully contributed funds. At best, the temptation to divide the contents of the box between the members, or some of them, and have a really good party sometimes proved irresistible.[43]

Another way of buying things that were beyond the normal weekly budget was to go to the tallymen, defined in the previous century as men who 'trust poor persons with 20s worth of goods, or rather with twelve or fourteen shillings worth instead of twenty, to pay them by 6d or 12d a week, wherein if they fail to pay, they hurry them into prison with great charges for arrests and proceedings at law, which many times exceeds the said debt'.[44] Better to stay out of the tallyman's clutches.

Less threatening was the pawnshop. In Hogarth's *Gin Lane* the only prosperous business is the pawnshop, run by S. Gripe. The goods he took were said to be 'laid up in lavender', 'on the shelf', or 'under tribulation', at 'uncle's', or the 'two to one shop', it being two to one that the goods pledged were never redeemed.[45]

Imprisonment for debt

To imprison a man for owing money seems to us illogical – how is he ever to earn enough to pay off his debt, if he's locked up? But this was a commonplace in Dickensian novels, and in Dickens' own life, and it had a long and respectable ancestry. 'So bigotted were our legislators ... that it was not until 1759 that [a statute] first provided a formal means of escape from that savage maxim of the common law that a debtor once taken in execution [arrested for debt] was to be kept *in salva et stricta custodia* [in safe and close custody] until the satisfaction of his debt.'[46]

No one could be arrested on a Sunday, which explains the slang expression 'a Sunday man: one who goes abroad [out of doors] on that day only, for fear of arrest'.[47] But on any other day, the bailiffs might catch up with the unfortunate debtor and offer him the choice between prison or the more comfortable ambiance of the bailiff's home, known as a sponging house.[48] If he could afford it (with what? – if he was being arrested for debt anyway), he would obviously choose the sponging house. This is where the principle behind imprisonment for debt dimly emerges – that a debtor was being wicked and perverse in *refusing* to pay when he had the money to do so. This does not logically apply to cases where the debtor had no money and *could not* pay, but when was law ever logical?

The bailiff was all-powerful. 'It has been common for bailiffs when they have arrested a person for debt to drag him to some public house and order liquors of their own accord for which they oblige him to pay. It has also been customary for them to demand more than their legal fees for the arrest, and to exact a further sum ... under the name of "civility money".'[49] He might, for a fee, be prepared to let the debtor live outside the prison altogether, as long as he gave security for being available when summoned. The bailiff could arrange with the creditors that the debtor could continue his trade, working and earning so that he could pay the creditors off. All these concessions, needless to say, cost the debtor money, in the shape of fees both to the bailiff and the creditors. Sometimes the lawyers joined in too. 'In all cases, the parties were plundered to the greatest extent that could be calculated upon with safety to the bailiff and the attorney.'[50]

Only when there was no more to be made out of him was the debtor transferred to a debtors' prison such as the Fleet or the Marshalsea. In 1759 there were 20,000 debtors in prison, reckoned in an impassioned article in *The Gentleman's Magazine* to be 3 per cent of the population of the United Kingdom. A quarter of them, five thousand people, died there every year, 'overborne with sorrow, consumed by famine or putrified by filth. The misery of gaols is not half their evil, they are filled with ... the rage of want and the malignity of despair.'[51]

The Act for the Relief of Debtors passed in that year enabled a debtor to refuse the hospitality of the sponging house, since he could now use his own bedding and linen in prison, and send out for food. Most valuable of all, if the debt was for less than £100 – a considerable amount in the case of a small trader – he could declare himself

Samuel Johnson by Joseph Nollekens, 1777. Johnson objected to this portrait bust of him because it's not wearing a wig, as any gentleman would. But the wigs he wore never fitted, and were usually singed at the side where he held a candle to help his bad eyesight. He looked much better without.

Below: Leicester Square in 1750. The Prince of Wales lived at the north-east corner of the square from 1743 until he died in 1751. Hogarth lived in the house at the right-hand edge of the picture between 1735 and 1762. Sir Joshua Reynolds lived on the opposite side of the square between 1761 and 1791. Note the flock of sheep and two cows.

(Detail from Leicester Square.) The escort in royal livery shows that the occupants of the sedan chairs are the Prince and Princess of Wales.

Birdcage Walk by John Chapman, about 1750, looking onto St James's Park. No carriages or sedan chairs were allowed inside the park, leaving it free for fashionable pedestrians.

Part of a 1767 caricature by L.P. Boitard of 'the Present Age' which lampooned the extremes of current taste, such as the bizarre vehicle with its high-seated driver, and the mish-mash of architectural styles in the house on the left. The sedan chairs, with their hinged tops, were drawn true to life.

Covent Garden, c. 1750. Inigo Jones designed this elegant square in 1631, for the rich and fashionable. By 1750 they had moved west, and Covent Garden became a noisy produce market by day and a notorious red-light district by night.

Cesspits were emptied during the night, by night soil men. If there was no access from the back they had to come through the house – hence the sleepy servant letting them in by the front door.

Iohn Hunt, *(Successor to the Late Mr. Ino. Brook)* Nightman & Rubbish Carter, *near the Waggon and Horses in* Gofwell-Street, near Mount-Mill, *LONDON.*

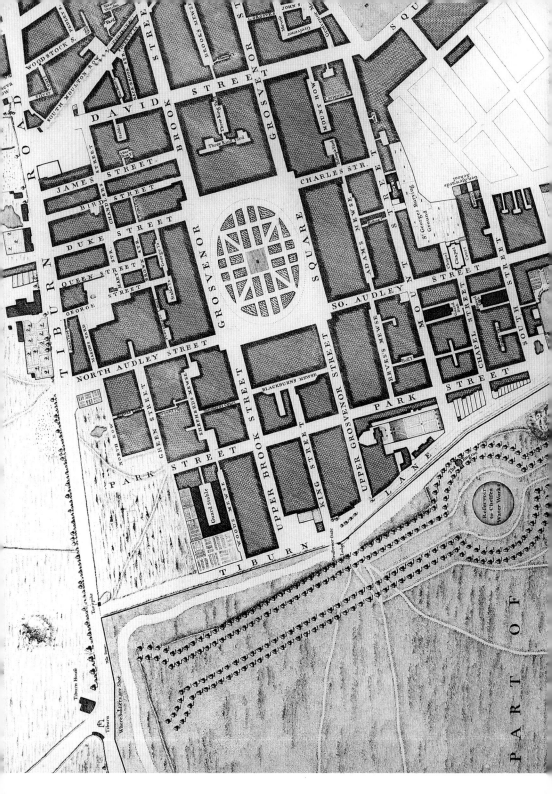

A section of John Roque's 1747 map of London. The triple gallows can just be seen at the junction of Edgware Road and Tyburn Road (Oxford Street). The Grosvenor estate (see page 17) was mostly built between 1720 and 1750. The Berkeley estate to the south was developed slightly later. It is shown blank in this map, except for the corner of Berkeley

Square, which was begun in 1739. Lord Chesterfield (see page 49) was able to find a prime building site just north of Curzon Street. Across Curzon Street lived Dr Keith (see page 70), who made a fortune out of clandestine marriages. The round pond halfway down Tyburn Lane is the Chelsea Waterworks reservoir (see page 25).

Many sailors married in the Fleet district (see page 68). The beaming bridegroom in this 1747 print sits beside his blushing bride, a prostitute whose mother or procuress is listening to the parson's propositions. Another sailor dances, to the music of a peg-legged fiddler. Behind him a cat and dog exemplify married life. The bridegroom is unaware of the bailiffs at the door, about to demand payment for his wife's debts.

A poor woman is given food scraps at the door while the master of the house, in comfortable indoor clothes, leans out of the window to tip the leader of an itinerant band of musicians (Hogarth, 1747).

The Marine Society (see page 81) transformed ragged street urchins into smart lads fit to serve in His Majesty's navy.

The kneeling woman pleads 'For goodness sake, dear your Honour, set him free, he maintains his Father, Mother, Sister and Wife', but the officer in charge of the press-gang (see page 110) replies 'Let them starve and be damned, the King wants Men, haul him on board, you dogs.'

GIN LANE.

Hogarth's *Gin Lane* (1751) helped to end the gin craze (see page 123).

bankrupt and be discharged from his debts. The penalty for fraudu-
lently taking this way out could be death, but as long as a debtor
declared all his assets he could begin life anew, instead of mouldering
in prison indefinitely.

Not surprisingly, the procedure took a little time, because a court
had to examine every application, but if it was granted the debtor
could congratulate himself. At least he could be sure, even if he ran
into debt again, that his clothes, his bedding, and tools to the value
of £10 were sacrosanct. For layabouts who 'choose rather to continue
in prison and spend their substance there' – which if they had any to
spend could make life in prison tolerable, I suppose – their creditors
could compel the disclosure of assets. If a creditor opposed a debtor's
petition, he had to maintain him in prison on an allowance of 3s 6d
a week, which surely would soon become tedious to the most vindictive
creditor.

After 1759 *The Gentleman's Magazine* regularly reported the release of
batches of debtors. 'Upwards of three hundred prisoners from Ludgate,
the two Compters and the Fleet were discharged at Guildhall by the
Lord Mayor' on 24 June 1760.[52] 'Near five hundred prisoners were
discharged from the Kings Bench prison, the New Gaol and Marshalsea on 10 October 1761.'[53] But in the same month a bankrupt
who concealed assets worth £2,100 was condemned to death.[54]

Funerals

Funerals had not yet reached the extravagance of the Victorian era,
but having glanced at the kind of funeral the parish gave a pauper
one can understand that poor people were anxious to avoid that
prospect at almost any cost. The box clubs or friendly societies assured
their members of that – always assuming that there were still funds
in the kitty when the time came. A subscription of 2d a week would
produce a coffin, a rented pall over it, rented cloaks and mourning
wear for three, six pairs of black gloves and two porters. No hearse
was needed – the coffin would be carried through the streets on the
mourners' shoulders.[55] According to a report at the end of the century,
the funeral of a poor person might cost as much as £15, which was
certainly an appalling burden on the property that would otherwise
have gone to the surviving spouse and children.[56] Yet it could be
much less, and still avoid the gruesome poor's pit.[57] Many poor people

'carried their dead children nailed up in small deal boxes into the fields to bury them privately and save the extravagant charge of parish dues'.[58]

CHAPTER 10

Philanthropy

Private enterprise

Decent citizens increasingly felt that something had to be done about the poor. After all, 'the poor are a large as well as useful part of the community ... they have a just claim to the protection of the rich ... If affluence and independence could universally prevail, the benevolent would not experience the inexpressible pleasure of relieving the distressed.'[1] The state did not yet concern itself with welfare. At parish level, the administration of the Poor Law left much to be desired. It was unlikely that an individual would ever again have the money and the inclination to found a charity on his own. So, despite the shadow over joint-stock companies since the South Sea Bubble had burst in 1720, the answer had to be a joint exercise of concerned individuals. By mid-century an Englishman could pride himself on 'the many noble Foundations for the relief of the miserable and the friendless, [and] the large annual supplies from voluntary charities to these Foundations'.[2]

Foundlings

Think of a pregnant girl without resources, employed in a job – almost certainly domestic service – which she will lose if she bears a child. She may well apply to the local wise woman/abortionist. But if she does produce a live baby, what is she to do? She could leave it somewhere where it would be bound to attract attention and, with any luck, care, as Tom Jones's mother left him in kind Squire Allworthy's bed.[3] 'On Thursday night a fine young male child was left at the door of a house ... It was laid in a basket with some new frocks and other cloathing, and the basket tied to the knocker of the door.'[4] Or she could see that it gets to the parish authorities, which will end her problem and, almost certainly, the baby's life. But to do this she has to disclose her identity and admit her 'sin'. She could stifle the child straightaway; or she could just abandon it.

The Foundling Hospital[5]

Captain Thomas Coram began his campaign to provide for abandoned babies in 1722. Looking at his portrait by Hogarth, anyone can see that his greatest asset was one of which he was totally unconscious – his own robust charm, especially to great ladies who had probably never seen someone of such rectitude in their lives. He insisted that they should interest themselves in – of all unlikely objects – babies, and illegitimate babies at that. It took him nearly twenty years, but in 1741 the Hospital for the Maintenance and Education of Exposed and Deserted Children, very soon known as the Foundling Hospital, was ready to take in 30 of the babies whose mothers crowded at the doors. It began in a house in Hatton Garden. It was soon able to open purpose-built premises in the fields north of Gray's Inn.[6]

'All persons who bring children are requested to affix on each child some particular writing or other distinguishing mark or token so that the child may be known hereafter if necessary.'[7] A detailed receipt was given to the mother. 'It is desired that it may be carefully kept, that it may be produced if the child should at any time be claimed', perhaps years later. This meticulous record-keeping was very different from parochial records.

Then the child was given a Christian name and a surname. The first two children admitted were named after Thomas Coram and his wife Eunice. The governors lent their illustrious names, but this occasionally raised the child's hopes unduly in later life, so it was safer to name them Elizabeth Foundling, or even Robin Hood.

There was a running argument going on in the medical profession, breast feeding versus 'artificial' feeding. The Hospital was strongly in favour of breast feeding, which involved it in some desperate recruiting drives. At one time the Bishop of Worcester was approached in case he knew of any possible breast-feeders. As soon as the babies had recovered from the trauma of admission, and the weather was clement, they were dispatched to the country to be breastfed for as long as proper, and generally looked after for their first two to four years – the period varied.

At about three years old, the children came back to the Hospital, and life for them changed abruptly. First of all, they were inoculated against smallpox, which was usually fatal to small children. This policy of early inoculation was farsighted for its time. Then they were eased into Hospital life. Hogarth designed their uniforms, brown serge dresses with stiffened bodices – no stays – for the little girls, and jackets and breeches for the little boys, with cheerful touches of red. Up to the age of six they had almost a recognisable childhood, unlike the wretched parish children. As well as learning to read,[8] they were 'exercised in the open air and employed in such a manner as may contribute to their health and induce a habit of active hardiness ... their diversions [shall] be innocent, active and requiring exercise'. The little boys had bats and balls and tops, and there was even talk of a 'dart or javelin' for them, to 'inure them for a proper sleight in throwing a harpoon in the Greenland [whale] Fishery'.

Vocational training could not begin too soon. From the age of six, the little girls began to take a share in the housework involved in running the Hospital, to make them 'useful servants to such proper persons as may apply for them'. The boys continued their education a little longer, but 'at twelve years the boys be sent to sea or husbandry [agricultural labour] except so many as may be necessary to be employed in the garden ... which is intended ... to supply the house and parts adjacent with vegetables and to have in readiness boys instructed in gardening for such persons as may incline to take them into their service'.

The children's diet was 'plain and simple ... their bread coarse and their drink water'. Fortunately, there was a pure well in the Hospital grounds, and the Hospital made its own bread, avoiding the heavily polluted commercial bread. The governors acted on the best available medical advice in planning the children's meals, and the children no doubt did better than their contemporaries in the outside world. The 'distempered eyes', deformed limbs and 'scorbutic eruptions' noted in the records were symptomatic of rickets and scurvy, and would have been alleviated by a different diet, but the Governors were not to know that.

The weekly religious service became a fashionable event. At the first baptism of newly taken-in children, the 'large collection' included a bank note for £100, a huge sum in those days.[9] When the foundation stone of the Chapel[10] was laid, tickets for the ceremony were issued at 2s 6d each, and the collection raised £590 more.[11]

Nevertheless the Hospital needed funds. In 1756 Parliament agreed to subsidise it, on condition that *all* babies offered must be accepted. This almost overwhelmed the Hospital organisation. In the first four weeks of the 'general reception', 425 babies arrived from all over the country, and had to be taken in, no matter whether they were sick, disabled or dying, as many of them were. In under four years, June 1756 to March 1760, almost 15,000 babies were admitted.[12] Over 10,000 of them died. Yet even then, the survival rate was better than in parish workhouses. And even then, only four babies were lost in the paperwork.

After 1760 the Hospital reverted to being a private charity, but changed its admission policy from rigorously observed anonymity to signed petitions. The usual petitioner was a domestic servant who stood to lose her place, and her livelihood, unless she could find a safe home for her baby. These petitions make sad reading. The shortest I saw read 'seduc'd and reduc'd'. One of the longest came from a Bostonian girl who had unfortunately given birth more than a year after her husband had died. Her brother would take her back to Boston, but only if he never knew of her bastard. Not all the babies were illegitimate. A soldier's wife had nine children to maintain, and couldn't manage. A French woman's husband had gone incurably mad, in Paris, leaving her with their children. The oddest story was of a country parson's daughter who was 'seduced by a man who promised to marry her' – so far, nothing new – but with her mother's help came to London and bore the child. 'After some little time she returned home unsuspected and has since lived a very penitent and virtuous life, her Father knowing nothing of it'. All these petitions were endorsed 'to be received'.

These children must have been very desirable apprentices if they observed even half of the Instructions drummed into them. They were already well trained. They even had immunity to smallpox. The only negative factor is the small scale of the operation, excluding the four years of the general reception. In July 1749, a typical month in a typical year, 20 babies were received out of the 83 who applied.[13]

Perhaps the most salient achievements of the Foundling Hospital were to demonstrate the effectiveness of individual effort, and to give a shining example of record-keeping.

The Marine Society

The Marine Society was the creation of Jonas Hanway as much as the Foundling Hospital had been created by Thomas Coram. Hanway was a merchant, a member of the Russia Company, with evangelical leanings and a passion for righting the wrongs he saw in society, combined with a practical patriotism. When the Seven Years War broke out in 1756, Britain was as usual unprepared. Her Navy had been dangerously run down, and needed bringing up to strength quickly. At the same time, Hanway was all too aware of the gangs of boys infesting London streets and getting into trouble. Put the two problems together. Enlist the boys in the Navy.

On 25 June 1756, twenty-three gentlemen met at the King's Arms tavern in Cornhill, including Jonas Hanway and other City merchants and Hanway's brother, Captain Thomas Hanway. They discussed 'a Plan of the Marine Society [just founded] for contributing towards a supply of two or three thousand mariners for the Navy'.[14] The press-gangs were already scouring the streets of London and other ports. The Society proposed to get 'able-bodied landsmen' from the countryside to enlist, by supplying them with the necessary outfit of clothes etc. A month later, Henry Fielding got in touch with Hanway. The Captain of HMS *St George* had asked him for thirty boys, whom he could supply – he dealt with all too many in his court in Bow Street – but he had no funds to outfit them. Could the Marine Society help? By the end of the year, the Society was regularly collecting boys, washing and outfitting them, giving them a quick burst of education, and sending them off to ships in Portsmouth. Thirty-seven went in January 1757, and 126 the next month.

The project appealed to the merchant community. Funds rolled in. Mr Handel was asked to donate the proceeds of a performance of *Judas Maccabeus*. King George II, who had a reputation for meanness, contributed personally the huge amount of £1,000, the East India Company £200, the Russia Company £100. The boys made a public appearance at a performance of *Acis and Galatea* at Ranelagh, and regularly marched through the City and over Westminster Bridge on their way to Portsmouth, a stirring sight to loosen the pursestrings.

The Society put out press releases stressing that no boy would be accepted unless he came voluntarily and could produce the written consent of his parents or, if he were an apprentice, his master. He had to be fourteen 'unless very stout [strong] and tall at thirteen'. He must be quite sure that he wanted to go to sea, 'which requires a brisk and active genius, and such boys only can be expected to turn out intrepid mariners'. He must be at least 4 feet, 4 inches tall,[15] and 'stout and well made and have no disorders on [him], other than the itch', which the Society reckoned to be able to cure quickly. A criminal record was no bar, but 'Mr Fielding [was] to be asked to warn the Society of any boys known to be pilferers or not to be trusted.' A hundred and fifty boys were to be taught to play the fife, in fourteen days. 'It is presumed that this will be an introduction to their knowledge of several other musical instruments [surely optimistic], being informed that musicians are much wanted on board His Majesty's ships.'

What was in it for the boys? An outfit of decent clothes and bedding that had a market value if they could abscond with it. (After a while, the escorting officer was told to keep the clothes until the boys were actually on board.) An appalling and dangerous life at sea, which the boys never saw till too late, and uproarious spells of leave ashore, which the London boys, at least, must often have seen and envied. And the remote chance that if they survived and if their ship took a prize, they might have more money than they could possibly imagine.

The Marine Society had set out to provide two or three thousand landsmen for the Navy, when the Seven Years War broke out. When the war ended, it had provided 5,452 landsmen and 4,787 boys, all with decent outfits and – unlike some of the miserable wretches caught by the press-gangs – in good health. It foresaw that there would be problems facing the boys on demobilisation after the war. The Society found apprenticeships in sea-related trades for about half the boys it had taken on, the others going to other trades. It issued a public notice: 'There are yet some boys discharged and not provided [for], and great numbers of others already lurking about the streets … in imminent danger of becoming the most profligate kind of fellows, being totally without instruction or protection except that which they receive in the nurseries of Thieves and Murderers.' Such boys were invited to apply to the Society.

By 1769 the Society had set a new course. 'The principal object of the Society shall be to place out boys apprentice to waterborne businesses of every denomination.' Priority was to be given to '(1) boys found wandering or in any particular distress, then to (2) boys whose parishes are unknown [so that they had no settlement] or distant (3) orphans of sailors or soldiers'. They did well to be wards of the Society. Under the Vagrancy Act, they could have been sent straight into the Army or Navy as they stood.

The Female Orphan Asylum

Jonas Hanway and Henry Fielding cornered the market in charity for boys. For girls, several philanthropists seem to have thought of the same idea at the same time: catch them young, before they have had a chance to stray on to the streets, then, if they have, get them back. John Fielding, Henry Fielding's half-brother, published a tract on the subject in 1758, so did another lawyer, Saunders Welch, and Joseph Massie himself.[16]

The Female Orphan Asylum for 'poor deserted girls' between the ages of eight and twelve[17] was founded by John Fielding in 1758.[18] Preference was given to the orphan daughters of servicemen. 'As they are to be constantly employed in the several offices of good house-wifery, in order to qualify them for domestic servants, diseased or infirm children will not be received.' (As with the Foundling Hospital, one wonders what happened to those unfortunates.) By the standards of the time, the girls had not a bad life. The older ones even had a bed each, only the little ones sharing. They got a new outfit every Easter, and clean clothes twice a week.[19] Their food included 'garden stuff' four times a week, and salads. Their days were full, but the timetable allowed five and a half hours for 'meals and play', as well as learning to knit, spin, cook, wash and iron, make shirts and shifts, knit stockings and do housework, and how to 'read a chapter in the Bible, write a legible hand, and cast up a sum in addition'. Few gently-bred girls would know more.

'The objects thus trained are to be bound apprentice for seven years at the age of fifteen, or sooner if qualified, as domestic servants in reputable families, the greatest care being taken ... to enquire of the character of master and mistress.' These girls must have been worth their weight in gold, as unpaid domestic drudges for seven years.

The Magdalen Charity

Prostitutes who wanted to come off the streets could apply to the 'Charity for the Reception of repenting Prostitutes ... called the Magdalen Charity'. The published plan for this enterprise was anonymous, but the copy in the Bodleian Library is marked 'Hanway' in pencil, and indeed in its mixture of practicality and idealism it could hardly have been written by anyone else.

> Of the whole race of Adam there are surely none who stand in greater need of help than these unhappy women. ... There is I believe no city in the world where such gross enormities prevail as in this great metropolis ... [Prostitutes are] the abject slaves of an abandoned procuress, sold body and soul for half a crown ... our streets ... are a disgrace to human nature...

Strong stuff, and apparently on the side of the women. But the next paragraph reverts to the accepted view of them as wicked. The plan was 'to induce women who have lived as prostitutes to forsake their evil course of life'. It would provide, for women under 30 who passed a medical examination and survived one month's probation, 'a retreat for them where they may pass their time in comfort and safety under no other confinement than ... absolutely necessary for their own preservation, and what they shall themselves have voluntarily consented to'. Just as one is looking askance at this threat of custody – but no worse than being dried out for alcoholism nowadays – one is disarmed by the promise 'to treat them with such regard and civility as shall convince them that nothing more is meant than their own happiness ... [and] to dismiss them when it shall appear for their service, and to conduct the charity in such a manner as it shall be considered as a very high favour to be accepted'.

The regime was not too onerous. 'Each person is to lie in a separate bed and have a chest for her cloathes and linen under lock and key to be kept by herself.'[20] They had separate cubicles, and a uniform of 'light grey of a durable but soft and agreeable manufacture', and their own clothes would be cleaned and either 'ticketed and laid by' for them when they left, or sold, the proceeds kept for them. They got two pints of beer a day – 'it is not meant to stint them' – and a reasonable diet.

The snag was that they had to work, which may have been a novel experience to some of them at first. 'It is a fundamental principle of this institution that those who can and will not work shall not eat.' The nature of the work presented difficulties, just as it did in parochial poorhouses. Hanway did not specify what they should do, but imaginatively suggested 'mending silk stockings as in Italy' – that is, invisibly. There would have been a huge market for this, but I have found no other reference to it anywhere. The wages they earned would be saved for them and added to a small present when they left. They could be expelled only for 'absolute non-conformity to the rules of the house'.

The staff included a matron, who was to be 'a single woman of about forty in full health and of good spirits ... she shall not disdain the conversation of the most sensible and polite of these Magdalens'. The physician and surgeon, seemingly a combined office, had to be over 40 and married or a widower, 'with a more humane and polite conduct than perhaps is necessary in any other public hospital'. The Magdalen House Charity sounds pleasantly human. For example, when its sponsors were invited to the annual fund-raising, prayers were scheduled for eleven o'clock 'and dinner will be on the table at three o'clock'.[21]

Foreigners

Immigrants had no parish in which they could claim when they most needed to, before they found their feet, so if they fell on hard times they were entirely dependent on the charity of their friends. The Scots Corporation existed 'for the relief of poor natives of Scotland residing within the cities of London and Westminster and for educating the orphans of Scots parents within the same limits'.[22] 'La Soupe' had been doling out excellent bread and soup to the Huguenots in Spitalfields since at least 1733,[23] and there was a hospital (in the sense of refuge or alms house) for 146 poor French men and women where they were 'supplied with all the necessaries of life'.[24] The Jewish communities looked after their own, although by mid-century the prosperous Sephardic community that had settled in London since the Commonwealth was beginning to find it hard to answer the demands of the poor Ashkenasi immigrants from eastern Europe, fleeing anti-Semitic reaction there.[25]

The old

Scattered through Rocque's map are 'almshouses', where ten or twenty old men or women could live if they fulfilled the founder's criteria. As well as individual charities, there were almshouses funded by, and confined to, members of the ancient guilds and liveries. But again, these can have had a minimal effect on those Londoners who

were too old to work. The workhouse loomed, for them. At least they
were unlikely to last long there.

Impulse giving

If you have some loose change on you, do you feel like giving it
away? You could always give to beggars. But maybe you disapprove
of open begging. Then, give a few trusses to a hospital. St Bart's was
always glad of them. The heavy manual labour of those days often
caused hernias, and the only treatment was a truss, except on board
ship, where the treatment was to hang the sufferer upside down by
the heels until the prolapse was reduced.[26] Or you could go to the
nearest debtors' prison and pay off some debts.

In November 1751, 'two gentlemen went to the several gaols in
London ... and discharged a great number of persons confined for
small debts',[27] and in 1767 'a lady released at the Marshalsea prison
one and twenty debtors and gave each a shilling'.[28] Perhaps it was
her twenty-first birthday. At the other end of life, the Duke of Somerset
ordered 88 'poor wretches' to be released from Whitechapel prison,
their debts paid and 10s given to each one, in March 1746. He died
three years later at the ripe old age of 87.[29] Another 'generous
benefactor' paid off 26 debtors in one prison and went on to another
the next day for several more.[30] What an 'inexpressible pleasure' this
must have given him.

Some prisoners were not so lucky. There was no obligation on the
prison authorities to feed the inmates, so if they had no kind friends
to keep them from starving, they 'could be admitted to the begging-
grate',[31] to push their hands through the grating, at ground level, or
they could let a box down from an upper window on a long string
(called 'angling for farthings'),[32] and hope that a passer-by would be
kind. Samuel Johnson remembered walking through Temple Bar
when its top storey was used as a prison, and 'being struck with
horror by a rueful cry which summoned me "to remember the poor
debtors" '.[33]

If you were a market trader, you could contribute in food or cash
to the Lord Mayor's Christmas collection.[34] It would presumably do
you no harm to be seen doing it by his Lordship. In cold weather
such as the severe winter of 1767–8, contributions for the poor flooded
in, the Lord Mayor had 50 lb of beef boiled every day and distributed

it, with the broth it was boiled in, and the gentlemen at Almack's collected £200 between them as they rested for a moment from gaming for far higher amounts.[35]

CHAPTER II

The Sick Poor

A poor person, especially a child, already weakened by poor diet and the chronic ailments of poverty, who fell ill or was injured in the squalid slums and crowded streets of London had little hope of recovery. What remedies were available to the poor?

Magic and folklore

Folk remedies, and neighbourhood 'wise women', still flourished. Crowder's Well in the City was reputed to be 'salutary in many disorders'. It had been 'made at the charge of Sir Richard Whittington',[1] and was said to be particularly good for eye problems. Occasionally, a remedy found its way into print that must have had its origins in folklore. *The Gentleman's Magazine* of January 1750, for example, recommended the application of a live toad to the kidneys, in a case of retention of urine. Another treatment[2] relied on pure magic, and would need some prior organisation. Two men had been hanged. 'A child of about nine months old was put into the hands of the executioner who nine times with the hands of each of the dead bodies stroked the child over the face. It seems that the child had a wen [cyst] on one of its cheeks and that superstitious notion which has long prevailed, of being touched as before mentioned, is looked on as a cure.'

The old hospitals

Otherwise the only hope lay in the hospitals, St Bartholomew's next to Smithfield livestock market and St Thomas's over the river in Southwark. If they would accept you, you would at least be sure of regular meals and cleaner surroundings, until nature took its course, one way or the other.

Saint Bartholomew's

St Bartholomew's was founded in 1123. It survived the dissolution of the monasteries in the sixteenth century and the Great Fire of 1666. In 1729 its medieval confusion of green spaces and monastic buildings was replaced by James Gibbs's spacious quadrangle (much of which, with the gateway, still survives). There were four storeys in each of the three blocks, the fourth being the entrance gateway. The wards were 22 feet wide, with high ceilings, and about fifteen beds to each ward.[3] Elegant it may still be, but – when it was built there were no lavatories in it.[4] It had an Accident and Emergency department, handy for Smithfield. It charged 2s on admission (1s for the sister, 6d for the beadle or porter and 6d for the nurse) for a 'clean' patient, and 25s 8d for a 'foul' one with venereal disease; not forgetting the cost of two months subsistence at 4d a day, and a deposit of 17s 6d for a burial fee,[5] refundable, of course, if you left alive: a lot for a poor person to find. Fees were not charged to anyone producing a governor's letter of recommendation, but they tended to be wrapped up in red tape.

There were 420 beds in the main building, plus 66 in two outlying hospitals for venereal cases and 'a great number of out-patients'.[6] In the year 1762, Bart's had 'cured and discharged' 6,178 patients and buried only 390, 'remaining under cure 536' – they may have been sharing beds? 'Cure' in those days meant 'care' rather than total recovery. Generally an incurable patient was discharged to die else-where. (The buildings are still there but the hospital's long history as a teaching hospital has ended.)

Saint Thomas's

St Thomas's Hospital for the Sick and Poor was founded in 1173, near St Saviour's church (now Southwark Cathedral) and the south end of London Bridge. By 1749 it stretched back from the street leading to the bridge, in three linked quadrangles holding nineteen wards, 474 beds.[7] Its rules forbade 'suspicious talk' and matrimony.[8] Its statistics for 1762 were much the same as St Bartholomew's – 'cured and discharged 6,399, buried 369, remaining under care 480, with 220 outpatients'.[9] (St Thomas's still flourishes, on a new site to which it moved, beside Westminster Bridge, so that London Bridge station could be built.)

Bedlam

The third ancient hospital was The Hospital of St Mary of Bethlehem, known as Bedlam, specialising in insanity. It had been rebuilt in 1675, and was generally thought to be one of the finest buildings in London, which is not altogether surprising, since its planners had copied the Tuileries in Paris. 'Louis XIV was so incensed ... that he ordered a plan of the palace of our monarch at St James's to be taken, for offices of a Cloacinean nature'[10] – in other words, Louis modelled his palace lavatories on our sovereign's residence.

Bedlam patients were cheered by the figures on the entrance gates, representing raving and melancholy madness, and by a constant stream of visitors who came to gawp. Samuel Johnson went with a party, in 1746, and had 'his attention aroused by a man who was very furious, and who, while beating his straw, supposed it was William Duke of Cumberland, whom he was punishing for his cruelties in Scotland': diverting indeed. In the final plate of Hogarth's *Rake's Progress*, showing Tom Rakewell in Bedlam, two fashionable silk-clad ladies are enjoying *frissons* of horror at the sights to be seen over their fans. M. Grosley went in 1765.

> I happened to enter a hall filled with women who were dressed very neat and clean and drinking tea together. The President of the Assembly ... spoke French [M. Grosley spoke no English] ... and forced me to drink a dish of tea ... This was the gayest and most noisy of all the coteries I have seen in London ... one entire ward contains a row of large cells in each of which was a poor wretch chained down in bed.[11]

The new hospitals

The position began to change, as an urge towards philanthropy coincided with lay interest in medical knowledge. Prosperous men of goodwill wanted to do good to the sick poor. The existing hospitals were patently inadequate to care for the growing population. The same impulse that had driven medieval men to endow monasteries to care for the souls and bodies of the poor impelled eighteenth-century philanthropists to found hospitals to care for their bodies. The concept of funding a project by joint effort had become familiar in business circles, and could be applied to hospital-building, despite the slight reverse to its reputation caused by the collapse of the South Sea bubble in 1720. Cliques of well-heeled gentlemen, often of the same political persuasion, with an appropriate president at their head, gathered together to found hospitals.

It may be that the advance in medical knowledge, itself, was a contributory cause of this wave of new hospitals: yet I doubt it. The new knowledge tended to be theoretical. While the Royal Society astonished itself by almost transfusing blood from one animal to another, blood transfusion as a therapeutic technique was centuries away, and the best thing to do with blood was to 'let' it – take it away. But certainly the new hospitals provided a forum for the dissemination of medical teaching and, to a limited extent, experimentation on living subjects.

The Westminster

Westminster Hospital was founded by four gentlemen including the banker Henry Hoare in 1720,[12] 'the first of its kind in this kingdom',[13] in that it offered care 'for the relief of the sick and needy from all parts', not just London or nearby, and was funded entirely by voluntary contributions. No fees were asked on admission, nor any security for the cost of burial.[14] In 1734 a ward for incurables was opened. In 1747 it had treated only 2,336 patients, compared to the seven thousand and over treated by Bart's, St Thomas's and the London.[15] Rocque shows it as one block, at the end of Petty France, looking over open country. This was to be the policy from then on. Hospitals were sited at the edge of the built-up area, but still accessible. (The Westminster still flourishes, on a nearby site. The original one was too low-lying to be healthy.)

Guy's

Guy's Hospital was founded in 1723, by the munificence of a single man, Thomas Guy, a bookseller in Lombard Street. He had 'amassed a prodigious fortune, not indeed with great honour to himself or good to the community'.[16] This was a guarded reference to the sources of his wealth, which came from buying up seamen's tickets (pay books, which could be assigned) at a discount, illegally importing Bibles from Holland against the monopoly of the Universities, the King's Printer and the Company of Stationers,[17] and getting out of the South Sea Company in 1720 at the top of the market when so many held on too long and lost everything. He had already endowed three wards in St Thomas's. Dr Mead, an eminent physician who was on the staff there, suggested that he should build another whole hospital nearby, with three storeys, twelve wards and 435 beds.[18]

Guy died in 1724, when the building was just finished. He instructed his executors 'to receive and entertain therein four hundred poor persons, or upwards, labouring under any distemper, infirmity or disorders thought capable of relief by physic or surgery'. He had originally meant it to be for 'the indigent and the wretched who should be discharged out of other hospitals as incurable. It is much to be regretted that this intention was not fulfilled'[19] – although it seems that for some years it did function as a hospice for incurables, as its founder first intended. In view of its massive endowment fund, the hospital was able to limit its governors to a manageable 40, unlike the crowds of governors who were the financial mainstay of other hospitals.

The original wards had 30 wooden beds in each, with wooden testers or canopies over them, all infested with bugs when John Howard inspected the hospital in 1788.

Saint George's

St George's Hospital for the Sick and Lame was founded in 1734 by a breakaway group of governors from the Westminster. It was just beyond the turnpike at Hyde Park corner, where the built-up area gave way to scattered houses along Knightsbridge, so that it had 'all the benefit of a clear and pure air',[20] unlike the marshy site of the Westminster. By 1747 its patient through-put was midway between the giants – Bart's, St Thomas's and the London – and Guy's and the Westminster, at about five and a half thousand.[21] Like the rest of the hospitals founded after it, it was funded by voluntary contributions,[22] such as legacies, donations and the fees paid by governors on their election. These gentlemen were a very select body indeed, including dukes and bishops, with the monarch as President.[23] The hospital had three large and three small wards for men, and the same for women. Howard disapproved of its underground kitchens, and found 'a good cold bath [a favourite therapy then] but not used'.

The London

The London Hospital had begun as an 'Infirmary' in 1740, near Moorfields. By 1752 its governors were able to begin building on a green-field site on the eastern edge of London at Whitechapel.[24] It promised 'the admission of poor objects at any hour and without expense',[25] with a particular bias towards sick and wounded seamen, who proliferated in that part of London. Building progressed gradually until 1778, when there were six wards, each a spacious 60 feet by 15 feet, each – a remarkable innovation for those times – with a privy. It was managed by 'the most considerable merchants and gentlemen in London'. For thirty guineas, you could be a governor for life. Five guineas bought a year's worth. The hospital could also count on handsome donations at the annual governors' meeting. In 1768 the collection came to £2,062. (The London still serves the east end of London, in Whitechapel. Astonishingly, its eighteenth-century buildings can still be discerned among its modern development.)

The Middlesex

The Middlesex Hospital was founded with 30 beds in 1745 just off Tottenham Court Road, 'for the relief of the numerous poor of St Giles's and the neighbouring parishes',[26] at that time among the poorest in London. It gave its patients 'medicines, lodging and diet [food] and no security required for their burial. Married women *only* [their italics] are admitted in the last month of their pregnancy. They are to be under the care of the man-midwife, Mr Layard, to be delivered by him and furnished with all necessaries at the charge of the hospital. ... Tuesday is the day of admission but accidents [casualties, not accidental pregnancies] are admitted every day without recommendation' – that is, no governor's letter was needed. In 1755 the hospital moved even further into the country, to 'Marylebone Fields' (where it is now, just north of Oxford Street).

The Lock Hospital

The New Lock[27] Hospital for venereal disease was founded in 1746, in the open country beyond St George's. This was a very necessary institution, but not so attractive as a fund-raiser. Up to March 1752, according to *The Gentleman's Magazine*, it had raised only £3,083 in contributions. Nevertheless 1,495 patients were said to be

> under cure, among them several married women, children and infants, and many naked and starving. Above fifty children had the sad distemper [syphilis] given them from a received opinion among the lower people, both male and female, that if they had commerce [sexual intercourse] with a sound person they will get rid of the disease [and to be sure of anyone being 'sound', the younger the better] ... it requires the most extensive publication in order to prevent such horrid acts of barbarity and cruelty.

From the hospital's rules:

> Many a worthy woman has here to lament the diabolical profligacy of an abandoned husband ... Many a young creature of tender years, yea, even in infancy itself, has to bewail the inhuman violence of a diseased and loathsome ravisher. [As to those who had] brought on themselves the disease by their own sin and folly, that is no reason why they should be left to perish. A life lost to the public, from whatever cause, is still a loss.

But profligacy was not encouraged. 'No person whatever, if once discharged, is ever to be admitted a second time', which was hard on those who were discharged apparently cured, according to the then state of medical knowledge, but who possibly survived until the last stage of syphilis affected them years later.

The smallpox hospitals

Inoculation to prevent the worst ravages of smallpox had been amazingly effective. Samuel Johnson defined it, having dealt carefully with its primary meaning of horticulturally 'inserting the eye of a bud into another stock', as 'the practice of transplanting the smallpox, by infusion of the matter from ripened pustules into the veins of the uninfected, in hopes of procuring a milder sort than what frequently comes by infection', which says it all rather more clearly than The Great Lexicographer often achieved. The custom was to inoculate in one hospital and then move the patient to another to be cared for during the ensuing mild attack. Two hospitals were founded in 1746, and a third 'near Pancras' (*sic*)[28] in 1767.

In a sermon at a governors' meeting in 1752, the Bishop of Worcester said that out of 1,500 inoculated patients only three had died; which is so remarkable as to be incredible, were it not for the source. Perhaps the Bishop had succumbed to the usual fund-raiser's enthusiasm. Such was the euphoria that you might assume smallpox had been practically eradicated, until you consult the Bills of Mortality, which do indeed show a remarkably low figure – just under a thousand – for 1751, but an abrupt rise the next year to 3,500 and thereafter annual totals varying between roughly two and three thousand. These figures were probably more reliable than many in the Bills, because even the Searchers (the old women from whose returns the Bills of Mortality were compiled) must have been sure of their ground, confronted with a death from smallpox.[29]

Insanity

There was further provision for mental illness. Bedlam's robust treatment could not always cure inmates. What was to become of them? After a year in Bedlam, they could be received into St Luke's Hospital nearby, as long as they or their relations could raise 5s a week for their keep: a hefty sum in those days. St Luke's seems to have been financially viable. In 1754, after three years in business, it was able to add twenty new 'cells'.

Maternity hospitals

For the first time, poor women were offered the chance to go into hospital and have their babies under skilled supervision using the latest medical knowledge. By 1752, when Dr Smellie's *Treatise on the Theory and Practice of Midwifery* was published, he had given 280 courses on midwifery to 900 young doctors, plus a few 'female students', and delivered more than a thousand women. He used visual aids in his lectures in the shape of 'machines which I have contrived to resemble and represent women and children', for medical students to practise on. He explained how to use forceps in a difficult labour, but only when they were necessary to save the mother or the child. If a forceps delivery was impossible, he explained how to do a Caesarean section, rather than leaving both mother and baby to die. 'The operation has been performed both in this and the last century, and sometimes with such success that the mother has recovered and the child survived.'

From 1747 a clutch of maternity ('lying-in') hospitals opened,[30] all directly or indirectly inspired by his teaching. In addition, the Middle-sex Hospital opened a maternity ward in 1747. Most lying-in hospitals were for respectably married women, but near Grosvenor Square there was one for unmarried mothers, as long as they had the all-important governor's letter. Once admitted, women could count on 'all necessaries for the last stage of pregnancy and the month of lying in'. They could also count, unfortunately, on a high chance of dying from puerperal fever.[31]

The dispensary movement

In 1741 Dr William Smellie began to train midwives and surgeons to attend pregnant women in their own homes. Not only did he attend his patients free, but he also exacted a fee of 6s from anyone on one of his courses, which went to the patient. The Lying-in Charity for Delivering Poor Women in Their Own Homes, founded in 1757, was the first of many such charities.[32] Children were not normally admitted to hospitals under the age of three or four. In 1769 Dr Armstrong opened a Dispensary for the Relief of the Infant Poor in Soho Square.[33] In its first three years, 'time, medicine and advice have been administered gratis to above 3,300 children of necessitous parents'.[34] A year later, a General Dispensary for the Relief of the [Adult] Poor was opened in Aldersgate Street. An apothecary lived in, and a physician took clinics three times a week, followed by house visits. A governor's letter was necessary. There were nearly 300 governors, including 21 women: an innovation. In its first three years, 3,348 patients were seen, 2,727 were discharged, 96 died and 158 were 'discharged for not attending', an admirably low rate.

Hospital governors

Men became hospital governors because it was the thing to do, in this new climate of private philanthropy. But if it is necessary to impute a cynical motive to them, perhaps they made useful contacts. For instance, one of the richest men in England, Sir James Lowther, was a Vice-President of the London Hospital, and the Duke of Richmond was the President. The actual business of the hospitals was done by an inner core of governors functioning as a house committee. Here is where the contracts for supplying beds and straw and food and drugs were allotted. No wonder there was rarely a shortage of governors. The house committee was also the appointing body to posts in the hospital, which were becoming prestigious, although largely honorary. It did no harm to an eminent physician's practice among the rich, to be known to be on the staff of one or more of the great hospitals for the poor.

The ability to nominate a patient for admission, by a governor's letter, could be useful to a governor whose coachman, say, had an accident. His employer would give him a letter to the hospital of which he was a governor, and know that he would be as well looked after as reasonably possible. When the coachman was better, and discharged, the letter was given back to the governor, so that he would know that he could sponsor another patient. Anyone in need could try to find a governor with a spare patient-space and the necessary goodwill, if he could not raise the cash for the various fees or get to a hospital such as the London or the Westminster, where no fees were exacted.

This must have seemed as miraculous as the National Health Service did 50 years ago. The main snag was that familiar problem - knowing the right people. As a correspondent to *The Gentleman's Magazine* wrote, in 1764, 'few poor people know so much as who are governors; if they do it is troublesome and difficult to procure an order [for admission] if they are not personally known ... besides, how can a sick person either go about to enquire who are governors ... or attend for an order?' This produced a rather pompous reply two months later: the names and addresses of hospital governors were published annually; they lived all over London, there was bound to be one nearby. Which seems to me to leave the original query unanswered. Besides, I doubt if there were all that many hospital governors resident in, say, St Giles's.

Hospital administration

In 1745 a writer in *The Gentleman's Magazine* enthused that 'there never was any age or any nation in which such ample provision was made for the sick, the wounded, the indigent and deserted, by benefactions *purely voluntary* [his italics] as is now to be found in this kingdom'. Admissions to all the London hospitals increased rapidly. In the fifteen years ending in 1749, the total admissions rose from just under 13,000 to over 38,000.[35] Inevitably, this was attributed to the gin-drinking habits of the poor. An alternative reason for the growth may have been that the poor took a while to understand this new system, but when they did, they used it to the full.

Say that a poor sick wretch has managed to get the vital piece of paper, what then? From the same 1764 letter:

> no patient can be received but on a certain day in the week called 'taking-in day', except in cases of accidental or sudden hurts [the A and E department] ... when taking-in day comes the patient, whatever their condition, must wait one, two or perhaps three hours before they are received, and ... they seldom have any medicine administered until the next day. [In St Thomas's] there are so many more candidates than can be received, attending every taking-in day, that many sick after they have given their last sixpence for a petition and waited many hours in the cold are obliged to return without relief.

Back comes the answer: there is no waiting list, if you know the ropes, and anyway 'there are two large fires in the waiting hall'. With the exception of reading matter (I well remember whiling away the time at ante-natal clinics, with Jane's *Fighting Ships* and *The Outdoor Tomato Grower*), the picture is a familiar one.

A letter to the *Daily Advertiser* took a robust line. When it was proposed to cut the waiting lists at St Bartholomew's by appointing another physician, an anonymous writer (almost certainly one of the physicians in post) suggested that, although each physician had a list of outpatients numbering anything between 140 and 200, only half of them attended. Of those that did come, three-quarters only wanted a repeat prescription. Thus there were only 30 new patients at most. They should be asked three or four questions 'which will easily satisfy the judicious enquirer what is the matter with his patient'. He could then write not a 'formal prescription', but a 'sort of shorthand' for the apothecary, who would be able to read the doctor's handwriting and follow his shorthand. The apothecary told the patient what to do with his medicine, and the patient went happily home. 'And so the whole number of patients will be as effectually and beneficially provided for as possibly can be, and this without any such great trouble or overload to the Physician ... This is the method in which the Physicians of this and other hospitals have ever proceeded.'[36]

Medical staff were not too overworked, especially if this masterly way of dealing with waiting lists was functioning properly. St Thomas's in 1760 had a staff of four physicians, three surgeons, an apothecary, a sister and a nurse for each ward, various administrative staff such as a butcher and a brewer, nineteen watchmen, and miscellaneous porters and beadles.[37] Other hospitals might have a man-midwife on the staff, or a lithotomist to operate for kidney and bladder stones.

Hospital beds are rarely patient-friendly, but eighteenth-century ones had disadvantages that we do not have to endure: bedbugs. Wooden bedframes gave them a perfect haven. The wooden bedsteads still in use in the Westminster in 1788 were infested with them. Guy's paid £20 to a 'bugg-killer' in 1735, but only four years later the patients were again 'annoyed in a very grievous manner with Buggs'. In 1765 Samuel Sharp, the first permanent surgeon on the staff, recommended iron bedsteads: 'bugs are frequently a greater evil to the patient than the malady for which he seeks a hospital'.[38]

Itching but relieved to be there, you await the arrival of that expertise which you hope will cure you. The ward round is due, when all patients are expected to be in their beds. Wards were divided between male and female patients. At least one consultant attended every taking-in day, each one on a rota of about three weeks. The patients he admitted would remain his patients, and he would see them on his round, two or three times a week. He could also be summoned in an emergency – although without a telephone and modern transport he was surely unlikely to get there in time unless he lived next door. Physicians would be closely followed by their 'walking pupils', who had paid a premium of £21–26 to be trained, and 'house pupils', who were trusted to take case histories.

Surgeons had walking pupils too, who for an annual premium could go on ward rounds and watch operations. They also had 'dressers', who paid a higher premium of £50 and were allowed to do minor operations, including the frequently prescribed bleeding; and apprentices whose indentures had cost them anything between £100 and £300, and who could watch their masters at work and themselves perform minor operations. House pupils, later called house surgeons, had a contract lasting eighteen months or so, and lived in. House surgeons in the Middlesex Hospital had to 'carry pen, ink and paper to minute down all messages to the physicians [from the surgical consultant] or instructions relating to the patients'. The problems of hospital notes are still with us, unlike – as far as I know – bedbugs.

The lowest form of professional life in a hospital, and probably its mainstay, was the living-in apothecary. He too could take fee-paying apprentices, who in the London Hospital, for instance, 'must be constant in attendance, tender and careful to the patients'. The work of physically looking after the patients was done by nurses and 'watchers', probably women who would otherwise be on the parish poor roll, who did what they could for their charges, and 'when they think a poor patient is nearing his exit ... search their pocket books'.[39]

Having survived the ward round, a patient could look forward to the next meal. Hospital food has never enjoyed a gourmet reputation; but the average patient in an eighteenth-century hospital was only too glad to be fed at all. Anyway, you could always wash it down with a stiff gin; there was bound to be a dram-shop nearby, and there were no rules preventing you from drowning your sorrows in the usual way. Patients who had caught the all-too-prevalent 'Hospital Fever' (the same as 'Jail Fever', nowadays called typhus) must have spent the time in a drunken haze combined with delirium, since Dr Pringle, the leading authority, was a great believer in the curative merits of wine. 'There is nothing compared to wine, whereof the common men had an allowance of half a pint a day of a strong kind ... Wine was the best antiseptic and ... cordial.' Convalescents – if any – should have 'a quart a day of French wine'.[40]

If you were awaiting surgery, you probably needed all the Dutch courage you could get. Lithotomy, the operation that Samuel Pepys had survived a hundred years earlier, was still going strong, but had been speeded up, after William Cheselden cut his operating time to 60 seconds. Like the four-minute mile, we cannot all achieve it, but it does make us quicken our pace. Surgery had not otherwise extended its field for centuries. Cancer of the breast was treated by mastectomy without anaesthetic ... Subcutaneous cysts could be excised. An energetic surgeon recommended, in severe cases of consumption, 'opening the breast ... and cleaning the ulcer ... 'Tis surprising [he said] that this method has not been frequently used.'[41]

Did the hospitals do much good? They provided a training ground for the medical profession that had been lacking in England. The patient was able to rest, at least more comfortably than in his poverty-stricken life outside. His family was able to trust that all that could be done for him was being done. On the other hand, did the patient's health improve, in an environment crowded with suppurating wounds and infectious diseases? Life was short, in those days, for the poor. If they died in hospital, at least they would have company round their deathbed.

CHAPTER 12

Work

'Work: Toil; labour; employment. . . . Work is pleasure when we chuse our task – Dryden': Dr Johnson's *Dictionary*. Possibly; but few poor people have that luxury.

Children

Working life began young. Babes in arms were good theatrical props for beggars. The parish nurses could hire their charges out at 4d a day for each baby.[1] 'Orphans who are in a vagabond state or the illegitimate children of the poorest kind of people are said to be sold ... for twenty or thirty shillings, being a smaller price than the value of a terrier.'[2] Their buyers were chimney sweeps, who contracted to get chimneys clean by the labour of their climbing boys.[3] Girls, too, were sometimes used, being admirably puny. Master chimney sweeps took as many as four children at a time to do the dirty. work, since none of them lasted very long, soot being carcinogenic.

In 1785 Jonas Hanway estimated that there were about 550 climbing children in London. They were sometimes sent up even when the chimney was on fire. Extinguishing burning chimneys was the most profitable part of their master's business.[4] They worked in soot and slept on soot, and had no way of cleaning themselves. Besides cancer, soot caused eye infections. During the summer, when few people thought of getting their chimneys swept, the master sweeps went off to the country and made no provision for their boys, leaving them to scrape a living somehow.

There were various career opportunities open to children on the streets. Girls – and no doubt boys too, for there were plenty of

homosexual brothels in London then – always had an opening in
prostitution. Begging might be more to their taste, or even a little
honest work such as sweeping a crossing through the mud and refuse
on the streets, so that well-dressed pedestrians might have some
chance of keeping their stockings clean. If they could defeat the
competition, they might get themselves a bootblack's pitch.

Children could join the 'Black Guard, a number of dirty tattered
and roguish boys who attended at the horse guards parade in St
James's Park to black the boots and shoes of the soldiers'[5] and
generally got up to mischief everywhere, but this could lead to crime.
The Black Guard 'too commonly live upon pilfering sugar and
tobacco on the Keys [quays] and afterwards become pickpockets and
housebreakers, many of whom, at last, have received their due rewards
and made their exits at the gallows'.[6] Children's light weight was also
useful in walking over the Thames mud at low tide to retrieve goods
thrown overboard, by accident or design, by the crews of merchant
ships moored in the river ('mudlarking').

Street vendors

Some of the street vendors in the *Cries of London*[7] are children, and
some of them are ragged, such as the two children selling 'long and
strong two yards long cotton [stay]laces, all a halfpenny a piece', and
an itinerant shoeblack carrying a small stool for his customers' feet.
Other children look healthy enough, such as the newspaper boy
running along with a bundle of papers under his arm, shouting 'Great
news in the London Evening Post', and a girl selling 'sweet damask
roses' for 'two a penny four a penny'. Per Kalm, a Swedish visitor,
'saw ... men women and girls walk or sit in the streets of London
with baskets full of all kinds of flowers bound in small bunches'.[8] The
man who promises (threatens?) to 'come this afternoon to play you a
merry tune' and the women selling 'sheeps hearts livers or lights' and
'baked ox cheek, fat and brown' are not doing well. The more
prosperous-looking vendors are selling fruit, vegetables and herbs, live
lobsters, eels, shrimps and 'Newcastle salmon', gingerbread and hot
cross buns. The man who offers 'your feet to mend – corns to cut' is
almost elegant.

The woman who sold milk in the streets had found a niche market.
She bought her stock-in-trade from a 'cowkeeper' in the fields round
London. She may have had the help of a parish apprentice or servant

to carry it, in pails on a yoke, to her inner-city trading premises in a cellar, where she prepared it for sale by skimming off the cream, and adding chalk, and water from the pump or the nearest horse trough.[9] She would no doubt check her business records – a collection of tally sticks – before setting off on her round. The debt each customer owed would be chalked up on his doorpost. She made about seven farthings (less than 2d) a quart on milk, not allowing for bad debts and her servant's wages, if any. She supplemented her income once a year, on May Day and the days following, when groups of milkmaids would dance through the streets to the music of a fiddler. They wore on their heads an elaborate panoply of flowers and vessels of tin or silver, no doubt specially polished for the occasion, providing a timpani accompaniment to the fiddler. To emphasise their shining annual cleanliness they had a train of sooty little climbing boys, who shared in the bonanza.[10]

Porters

The milkmaid's pails illustrate the hard physical labour that we rarely see nowadays. Suppose you have bought a load of fish at Billingsgate, or ordered some goods from a shop or a warehouse. You need a porter. It should be easy to find a licensed one, wearing a large pewter badge that by their rules had to be 'visibly worn and never lent', and you should take note of his number.[11] A licensed porter might carry anything from an urgent letter to a load of three hundredweight. No wonder hernias were such a problem.[12] Porters were the taxis and vans and motor-cycle couriers of London, without whom it could not have functioned. The major City companies employed 'Tacklehouse porters' exclusively, who guarded their privileges in a closed-shop trade union. 'Ticket porters' worked from the waterside wharfs, in gangs, or from stands in the City. Their organisation was sufficiently prosperous to offer warehousing facilities as well. 'Uptown porters' could be hired at standing places in the City, to carry packages to markets and warehouses. 'Fellowship porters' had the monopoly of corn, salt and coal, the latter constantly disputed with the coal heavers, who won the fight by persuading the makers of the only possible kind of shovel to supply it only to the coal heavers.

Labour relations

For most trades there were crises of poverty. The medieval system of controlling labour by the livery companies – that is, the employers – was breaking down, although a single justice could still sentence anyone refusing to work for 'reasonable' wages to a spell in a house of correction,[13] during which his family starved or applied for parish relief. The concept of employees combining together to negotiate with their employers was beginning to emerge, with its concomitant of scab labour.[14] The Irish were particularly detested for undercutting agreed rates, which seemed to immigrants from that poverty-stricken island riches beyond the dreams of avarice.[15] But unions, known as 'combinations', were illegal. As early as 1761,

> a number of bills of indictment [prosecutions] were preferred . . . against the rebellious journeymen cabinet-makers, who have lately combined together to raise their wages and lessen their hours of working, etc. The combination among journeymen peruke-makers [when every man wore a peruke, i.e. wig], shoemakers, taylors, cabinet-makers, etc. is a growing evil and wants to be remedied . . .[16]

Whether the cost of living had gone up, and compelled the working man to fight for his subsistence, or whether expectations of a higher standard of living had risen, or perhaps both – labour relations were in an uncomfortable state of ferment. Some workers banded together, broke the law, and extorted some kind of settlement. How lasting or effective those agreements were is debatable. Others looked to the authorities to take pity on them – probably with as much lasting effect.

Silk weavers

Master silk weavers lived in the elegant houses in Spitalfields (just east of Liverpool Street Station), some of which have been lovingly restored. But life for the average weaver was nearer to starvation than elegance. One of the problems of the silk trade was the effect of fashion on those who wove the beautiful fabric. Last year's patterns were sold at much reduced prices.[17] Meanwhile, fashionable Court ladies would pay anything for silk fabric imported, illegally, from France or Italy, no matter whether the King disapproved or whether it was smuggled – indeed, this made it even more desirable.

In May 1762, 8,000 weavers 'paraded' to St James's Palace. They

were dispersed by soldiers and went home, pausing only to break the
Duke of Bedford's windows. But the very next day a crowd of 50,000
'assembled in Spitalfields and marched to Westminster by beat of
drum',[18] which must have been a frightening show of force, even
allowing for journalistic exaggeration. It did achieve two things: the
immediate promise by the silk merchants to cancel all their contracts
for foreign silk fabric and immediately set the journeymen to work,
and an Act prohibiting the import of foreign silks. 'Several thousand
weavers went to St James with colours flying and music playing', to
say thank you.

But in April 1764 they 'waited on His Majesty' once again to
impress on him 'the miserable condition of the silk manufacture from
the clandestine importation of French silks'. A large book of several
thousand French patterns had been seized, which was being 'privately
handed about to the mercers [silk merchants] by French emissaries'.[19]
The unspeakable emissaries had covered the market, from 5s up to
£5 a yard. How could a struggling London weaver hope to compete?

In May 1765 they called on the King again, 8,000 of them (?), and
three years later they went and thanked His Majesty again – they
were nothing if not polite, and it got them a long way – for reducing
the periods of Court mourning, which ruined the fashion trade.[20] But
by 1767 they had finally despaired of achieving a living wage by
peaceful means, and had taken to armed gang violence, breaking into
the workshops of masters whom they suspected of employing scab
labour, and destroying ('cutting') the fabrics on the looms.[21] It took
the hanging at Bethnal Green of two of their leaders to reduce them
to quiescence.[22]

Tailors

The journeymen tailors too were starving. They sat cross-legged on
benches under the window to get the best light, 'crooked hump-
backed lame figures',[23] but in winter, when the demand came for new
fashionable clothes, there was little daylight and they often sewed on
from six in the morning till the small hours, by candlelight. During
the summer, when the gentry deserted London for their country
houses, it was 'cucumber time' for tailors: the Covent Garden vendors
shouted, 'Cucumbers two a penny, tailors twice as many.'[24]

In 1750 their rate of pay was fixed by the Middlesex magistrates at
2s 6d a fourteen-hour day in the summer – if they could get work at

all – and 2s in winter for a shorter day. 'This order was very acceptable to the journeymen',[25] according to *The Gentleman's Magazine*, but it was still too little to live on, even with the 1½d allowed them for breakfast. 'Two journeymen who refused to work for the usual wages were sentenced to six months imprisonment, and one of them to be whipped.'[26] The master tailors brought in 800 scab labour tailors from as far as France, Germany and Holland, and broke the incipient strike.[27] The tailors' only resource was to 'cabbage', a custom that even Dr Johnson knew – 'a cant word among tailors: to steal in cutting clothes', by substituting cheap fabric for what had been given them to make up, and selling the good fabric. There were surely easier ways of making a living.

Coal heavers

The men who unloaded the collier ships had the power to bring the industrial and commercial life of London to a stop, if they withheld their labour. In 1768 *The Gentleman's Magazine* gave full coverage to the coal heavers' wage dispute, and the collier sailors' sympathetic strike. In April 'the business of delivering [unloading] ships in the river is at a stand[still]', but a peaceful settlement was negotiated – it seems amazing how often this happened – and everyone went back to work. A few days later, however, the coal heavers assembled in Stepney Fields and marched through the City to Palace Yard Westminster, where Sir John Fielding met the ring leaders and yet again their 'differences were accommodated'. The men got all the coal wharf masters along the river to sign an undertaking to pay the wage rises they had negotiated, and this time went off to the Lord Mayor with the document, who 'very prudently declined intermeddling with their affairs'.

In May the collier fleet arrived from Newcastle, and any accord between the coal heavers and the collier sailors already in London came violently unstuck. There was 'a terrible fray between the coal heavers and the sailors belonging to the colliers in the river, in which many were killed. The sailors having been long detained in the river by the coal heavers refusing to work had begun to deliver their ships themselves, on which a body of coalheavers fell upon some of the sailors by surprise and killed two or three ... the quarrel became general.' In June there was another 'terrible battle' between the coal heavers and the sailors. The residents of Wapping began 'removing

their goods and chattels for fear of an insurrection this night',
according to an urgent message to the Home Office, requesting a
hundred soldiers immediately, without going through the proper
channels.[28] 'The coal heavers are grown a terror to the whole
neighbourhood of Stepney and Wapping. ... The gaols are full of
these fellows, who would neither work nor let others work, so that
the business on the river has been greatly obstructed', but imprisonment was no deterrent, and by July they were parading the streets
in armed gangs, shouting '£5 for a sailor's head, £20 for a master's'.
Two coal heavers were charged with the murder of a sailor, and
hanged at Tyburn on 11 July.[29] And there this story ended, at least in
The Gentleman's Magazine, and the inhabitants of Stepney and Wapping
could rest easy in their beds.

Seamen

Sailors in the merchant fleet, apart from colliers, were rioting too,
and asking the merchants of London to 'augment their wages' – the
usual phrase. The merchants solemnly replied that this would not be
good for trade. Anyway, an unmarried sailor was paid quite enough,
and married men could rely on 'the benignity of our parochial laws'.[30]
Cold comfort indeed. In 1768 '5,000 – some say 15,000 – sailors
passed through the City to petition Parliament to augment their
wages. When they were in Palace Yard they were addressed by two
gentlemen on the roof of a hackney coach', who reassured them that
their petition would be considered, 'on which they gave three cheers
and dispersed'.[31] Sir John Fielding was able to tell the Lord Mayor
that his firm stand had succeeded, and he 'dares say that they will
never meet again in the same manner'.[32]

    After the battles between the sailors and the coal heavers had
culminated in murder, the sailors quietened down. But a month later,
'a tumultuous body of seamen boarded outward-bound vessels, English
and foreign, and disabled them from proceeding on their voyages by
unbending their sails, striking their yards and topmasts, and compelling
their crews to leave them'.[33] Bamber Gascoyne MP watched them
marching 'in solemn procession ... twelve in a row with each man
his hand clenched in his neighbour's, right and left. They came on
with vast shouts and to the best of my calculation they were then six
thousand in number, very fine fellows, a most formidable body. ...
They were in no way riotous.'[34] This threat to the City's lifeblood,

trade, alarmed the authorities, and urgent messages winged their way round government offices readying troops and alerting the Navy.[35] An armed cutter arrived and once again the tumult subsided. All the sailors wanted was an increase to 37s a month.[36]

London working men had what seems to us a touching faith in their elected Parliament and their father figures, the King and the Lord Mayor. But the authorities were in fact very nervous. There was a rumour that the sailors would call a general strike, and their skill in 'disabling' merchant ships caused horror in commercial circles. Troops and armed naval vessels were ready. But they were stood down by September 1768. Street violence did not break out in earnest until the Gordon riots in 1780.

Sailors in the Royal Navy lived in unimaginable conditions. When they first went on board their ship, they were given a ticket, on which was entered, at the end of the voyage, the pay due to them. It was a vital document, which could be cashed by a publican or assigned to a creditor, or to a wife – hence the keenness of some women to marry sailors? – or stolen, or forged, for which the penalty was death.[37] Even if, avoiding the press-gangs and thieves, a sailor managed to present himself with his ticket at the Navy pay office, he had to wait unconscionably long to get his hard-earned money, and even longer for the share of any prize money to which he was entitled. So when at last he had money in his pockets, no wonder he celebrated. There was nowhere for him to go except an alehouse, and few women to go with him except prostitutes. It must have been obvious when a ship had been paid off, by the number of rioting sailors.[38]

Watermen

Watermen too felt aggrieved. They had a monopoly of river passenger transport, but their rates had not been raised since the last century. In April 1768 they went to the Lord Mayor, who promised to present their petition to Parliament. The same day, the hatters went on strike – in an era when every man wore a hat – and presented their petition too.

Casualties and industrial diseases

It seems astonishing that there was so little violence. When battle was joined between the coal heavers and the collier sailors, all of them robust and strong, there were some casualties, and there was some shooting by soldiers brought in to keep order. This was not reported directly by *The Gentleman's Magazine*, but is to be inferred from a report of inquests on two people who died at a coal heavers' demonstration. They were, as so often happens, innocent bystanders: 'Mary Jeffs who having a basket with oranges to sell was shot dead in removing them, and William Bridgeman who was shot on the top of a haycart as he was looking at the fray at a distance.'[39]

Sympathy for those whose work ruined their health had not produced any practical help. The rich called for remedies; the poor just wanted to get back to work.[40] It was known that goldsmiths and gilders became asthmatic and paralytic because of the mercury in the manufacturing process; they had 'taken too little care to avoid the mercurial exhalation' by turning their faces away from it. Working with antimony or arsenic could cause chronic coughs and bloody urine. Potters shook and trembled from the lead in the glaze. Glassmakers could work only in winter because of the extreme heat of their furnaces, and should stop work at 40. The sulphur used in bleaching textiles caused runny eyes and chest troubles. Plasterers would insist on working without masks and so inhaled plaster dust, blacksmiths 'are usually bleary-eyed', tanners and the makers of cat-gut strings for musical instruments risked oedema and shortness of breath. 'Many uncommon disorders ensue on the excessive use' of tobacco and snuff, so the mouth and nose should be covered when grinding it. Workers in the brewing trade ran the risk of intoxication from inhaling the 'vapours'. Bakers and millers 'are generally troubled with lice' and should use 'liniments containing mercury, killed in spittle'. People who had to stand at work, including courtiers, got varicose veins. Porters were recommended to wear trusses 'by way of precaution'.

'Doubtless there are many things in common use that are taken to be inoffensive because they injure only gradually and insensibly till some chance or other exposes their occult malignity.'[41]

Holidays

The life of a skilled or unskilled man or woman in the middle of the eighteenth century was unenviable. Hours were long, from five in the morning till seven at night from mid-March to mid-September, otherwise dawn to twilight, with one and a half hours off for meals,[42] for a six-day week. Christmas, Easter and Whitsun were the only official holidays, plus the eight 'hanging days' a year when the London journeymen went to watch the executions at Tyburn. No wonder that their only day off on Sunday tended to be more riotous than the middling sort of people approved. And there was one saving grace: 'Saint Monday'. In theory this was a holiday only observed on 25 October, St Crispin's day, and only by the shoemakers, whose patron saint he was, but with a peculiarly English pragmatism St Crispin had adopted all workers, and his day had spread to include every Monday.[43] 'In a moderate calculation above 2,000 artificers, journeymen and labourers absent themselves from their work on Mondays' because they had gone back to the pub for a 'hair of the dog'.[44]

The press-gangs

The practice of forcibly enlisting able-bodied mariners to serve the king in time of war was 'founded upon immemorial custom allowed for ages', it being necessary for the defence of the realm.[45] So said Lord Mansfield, the Chief Justice between 1756 and 1788, but he could not find any better legal justification for it.

The captain of a press-gang was paid £1 a day, and £1 was shared between his men for each recruit they caught. The gang varied from two to twenty men. They made their headquarters, called a 'rondy' or rendezvous, in a convenient alehouse, where in their free time they were 'a roistering, drinking crew ... never averse from a row'. They were armed with cutlasses and clubs, which they used freely. When a porter 'made some resistance they without ceremony knocked out one of his eyes'.[46] They were supposed to take only able-bodied men between 18 and 55 who were not freeholders (house-owners), but their view of 'able-bodied' was flexible. They could rely on a local surgeon to give a cursory health check to their catch, at a shilling a head. This was 'the King's Shilling', no longer given to the recruit himself. Pressed men were 'handcuffed like felons and ... marched through the street ... then put into a boat rowed by six of the pressgang and put into the hold of the tender, an old frigate lying off the Tower'.[47] The cynicism of the gang, or its surgeon, so affected HMS *Bristol*, about to sail for the West Indies in 1754, that out of 68 pressed men, only 18 were capable of sea duties. The rest had to be put ashore.

Sailors learned self-preservation. In the 'hot London press' of 1740, the year when 'Rule Britannia ... Britons never never never shall be slaves' was first sung, the riverside slums and the river itself were scoured by the press-gangs. Twenty-four hours after they had gone with their victims, 16,000 sailors emerged from hiding.[48]

Some trades, such as watermen and harvest workers, were exempt, but they had to prove their status by a written 'protection', produced on demand. A harvest worker had left his in his jacket at the side of the field while he worked – he was taken by the press-gang. It might be worth providing yourself with a forged protection, which was sold in London for £3. Even sailors on ships that had just berthed were pressed before they could get ashore, let alone draw the pay that had accumulated for them during the long voyage. In 1756 'the hottest press [was] begun that ever was known, all protections being disregarded and the hands pressed from the merchantmen to the very mate and master', and able-bodied vagrants throughout the country were to be taken.[49] In 1761 'the river [was] swept of sailors'.[50]

Sometimes the press-gangs went too far. 'A lawless body of sailors' broke into Mr Godfrey's house and dragged him 'through the public streets of London with only one of his slippers on' and shipped him into a waiting tender, where he stayed, fuming, for twelve hours until someone got him released.[51] In 1770 a journeyman barber managed to get himself before John Wilkes, who was sitting as a magistrate in the Guildhall. Wilkes 'adjudged the impressing illegal' and the barber was released.[52] Yet the next month 'a press gang entered the house of Mr Lewis, a plate-glass grinder, and insisted on his going with them which he refused upon which they dragged him into the street and he taking hold of the rails before his own house they beat him on the hands with their bludgeons to force him to let go his hold'. The Navy Board offered compensation, but Mr Lewis was determined to go to law.[53]

'A Press-gang took the coachman of a Colonel in the Guards, from the box [of the coach] in Pall Mall, having been informed that he had been a seaman, and the Colonel was obliged to hire a Hackney coach man to drive his carriage home.'[54] The press-gang even tried to take a bridegroom at his wedding, but there was a general fracas in which the officiating parson took part, and the happy couple 'made [their] escape in the fray'.[55] More than a thousand men were impressed on the river Thames in one night, in December 1770.

The press-gangs could be cunning as well as violent. In 1738 two large birds perched on top of St Paul's Cathedral, attracting crowds of sightseers. Noting this, 'the pressgangs placed a live turkey on the top of the Monument which, in a short time, drawing together a great number of idle people', the press-gangs netted almost enough onlookers to man the entire Navy.[56]

CHAPTER 13

Slaves, Servants
and Domestic Work

Slaves

'No man is by nature the property of another.' So said Samuel
Johnson in 1777.[1] William Pitt the Elder had said the same in 1750.
'The liberty of the subject, Sir, is so deeply rooted in our constitution
that no slavery ... can be admitted ... The black slaves of our
plantations become free as soon as they set foot upon this once happy
island.'[2] Stirring stuff. Yet in 1756 'a negro boy warranted free from
any distemper' was advertised for sale in the *London Advertiser* for £25.[3]
In 1761 'a healthy negro girl aged about fifteen years, speaks English,
works at her needle, washes well, does household work and has had
the smallpox' would have been a good buy.[4] In 1763 'a negro boy
was put up for auction and sold for £32',[5] and in 1768

> a foreign gentleman came to England ... and brought with him a very
> agreeable negro girl ... He was obliged to sell his slave for thirty
> guineas with part of which he purchased a lottery ticket, [he] has since
> drawn a prize of £5,000. He has since re-purchased his slave, made
> her free, and settled on her an annuity for her life.[6]

Not every slave had such luck. In 1771 'at a late sale of a gentleman's
effects ... a negro boy was put up and sold for £32. A shocking
instance in a free country.'[7]

The trouble was that no one really knew the legal position of men
and women who had been enslaved in Africa, taken to the plantations –
so far, so good: they were clearly slaves – and then brought here to

the land of the free. The highest lawyers in the land had opined, in
1729, that they were still slaves.[8] The case of the slave James Somerset
was not heard until 1772. It is sometimes cited as authority for the
proposition that no slavery could exist in England, but Chief Justice
Mansfield did not say that at all. His judgement is limited to whether
a sale of a slave in this country was valid, and he held that it was.
What English law would not countenance was the forcible detention
in this country of a slave, with a view to selling him abroad. 'Whatever
inconveniences [to slave traders] may follow from the decision, ...
the black must be discharged'[9] – but the extent of the decision is
carefully circumscribed. After all, as Boswell said in 1777,[10] the slave
trade was a very important and necessary branch of commercial
interest, so it must be right, and anyway the slaves were treated 'with
great lenity and humanity'[11] and (just like a hunted fox) they probably
enjoyed it, really.

Whatever their legal status, by 1764 there were perhaps 20,000
negro servants in London, mostly young men.[12] Whether they were
slaves or not when they arrived here, they realised fairly soon that
their fellow-servants were being paid as employees, and they asked
for the same terms, and left if they did not get them, sinking into the
anonymity of London whence their masters would find it difficult to
retrieve them. It is pleasant to record that

> among the sundry fashionable routs [assemblies] or clubs that are held
> in town that of the Blacks or negro servants is not the least. On
> Wednesday night last no less than fifty seven of them, men and women,
> supped, drank and entertained themselves with dancing and music ...
> in a public house in Fleet Street till four in the morning. No whites
> were allowed to be present.[13]

Domestic servants

Domestic service was the biggest employment sector in London. Even
parish midwives had their housework done by little domestic drudges
from the parish workhouse, to save themselves for their noble profession. As apprentices, these girls got no wages and could not leave
their mistresses. Living-in full-time servants were not, as they are now,
a luxury of the rich. The philanthropic institutions and charity schools
turned them out by the hundred. A tradesman 'in the middling station
of life', with four children, was assumed in a tract on economics to

employ one maidservant,[14] which was perhaps unrealistic. The house planned for a family in 'the middle rank of people' by Isaac Ware in 1756 assumed, more reasonably, that a family of two or three persons would have three or four servants, whom he consigned to the garrets.[15] A friend of Horace Walpole found it impossible to live 'without pinching economy and pitiful savings' with a staff of under seven, while the Duke of Bedford employed 40 in his London house.[16]

Cleaning and laundry work

There was a clearly defined hierarchy. At the foot of the pile were the charwomen and washerwomen. A charwoman was 'a woman hired accidentally for odd work or single days', according to Dr Johnson's *Dictionary*. He quoted Swift – 'get two or three charwomen to attend you constantly in the kitchen, whom you pay only with the broken meat, a few coals, and all the cinders'.

Washerwomen did very slightly better since their skills were more specific, but I doubt if their lives were easier. They might work at home, rising at four and working till midnight,[17] carrying baskets of linen to and fro on their heads. Or they went out to work. They arrived well before dawn, when according to an affecting poem of the time,[18] the maids were often asleep and they had to wait outside in the bitter weather. Once inside,

> Heaps of fine linen we before us view
> Whereon to lay our strength and patience too
> Cambrics and muslins which our ladies wear,
> Laces and edgings, costly fine and rare,
> Which must be washed with utmost skill and care:
> With holland shirts, ruffles and fringes too,
> Fashions which our forefathers never knew.

Their mistress arrives after some hours 'and in her hand *perhaps* [my italics] a mug of ale', to tell them helpfully not to waste soap. Long after nightfall they finish the work. 'Sixpence or eightpence pays us off at last', for a laborious day of eighteen hours or more, with no guarantee of continuous employment.

If the household wash was done by the domestic staff, the maids were up by one or two o'clock in the morning.[19] A rich household 'washed' once a month or so; the middle rank of people probably once a week, since they had no space to dry more wet washing;

poorer people more often as their clean clothes ran out, or less often as their standards slipped. In 1744 a lady writing from Buckinghamshire wanted a laundrymaid. 'Wee wash once a month, she and the washerwoman wash all the small linen, and next day she and the washerwoman wash the buck.'[20] She was an up-to-date lady, so it is interesting to see that her household used these two different ways of getting clothes and bedlinen clean. Washing the 'small linen', such as shifts and shirts, would be done by hand with hard soap, and water heated in a cauldron on the fire, or in a separately heated copper holding about 20 gallons, in which the linen could also be boiled after it had been washed. The water was ladled out into wooden tubs and basins standing about the kitchen on tables or chairs. It must have been drearily back-breaking work, sloshing hot water about and stooping over the tub to rub the clothes with your bare hands. By 1785,[21] perhaps earlier, a primitive kind of washing machine called a 'dolly' – like a three-legged stool with a long handle, which was rolled around the tub stirring the clothes as it went – was in use.

Soap was a major item in a family budget. In a tract on economics, the family 'in the middling station of life' spent over 6s a week on 'soap and washing both abroad and at home', the same as the cost of bread and butter combined.[22] A household of seven in the £600 income bracket used 8lb of soap a week, at 1½d a pound.[23]

Bucking saved on soap, since it used lye made of wood ash and urine. It is possible that the lady out in Buckinghamshire still burned wood, so her household had plenty of wood ash. Coal ash did not work, for lye, but bucking was still done in the 1660s when wood had already given way to coal, so wood ash or ready-made lye must have been available then, and seems to have continued in use. It would be cheaper than soap, for large household items like sheets. Blue could be added to the final rinse to get a good white in the murky London water. Some pieces had to be stiffened by starch. 'Clear-starchers' were another division of skilled domestics.

Drying was always a problem. Some sort of mangle was on the market – 'to pass the wet pieces between two rollers'.[24] In a London garden design of 1791 there were four sockets for removable posts to hold the washing line,[25] with no hint that this was a new idea. People living in one furnished room draped their washing round the room and put up with the drips.

There is a charming picture of *A servant ironing* by Morland, in 1767. She is seated at a table that is covered with something like a blanket, dreamily using a box iron, a hollow box shaped as present-day irons are, but heated by a separate piece of iron inside: a procedure dangerous both to the linen being ironed and to the ironer, who had to take out the cooled one and insert the hot one at frequent intervals. A living-in laundrymaid was paid £5 or £6 a year.[26]

Housemaids

According to Hannah Glasse's *Servant's Directory*,[27] the first thing a housemaid must do is to 'be up very early in a morning ... lace on your stays and pin your things very tight about you or you can never work well'. After that, the wretched tight-pinned maid is a whirlwind of housework, doing every day all the things we sometimes think of doing occasionally, and a lot more, such as polishing locks (oily rag and a little rottenstone), blowing the dust off pictures and stucco work (bellows), and scouring the stairs (wet sand) – and all this is 'before your mistress rises', when she could set about the bedrooms. 'Always leave a little clean water in your chamber chair pans, it prevents any offensive smell.'

Wood floors should be polished with a long-handled hard brush and herbs. They only needed another sweeping when the herbs had dried, and another polishing, for them to 'look like mahogany, of a fine brown'. If the floor is only to be mopped, 'trundle your mop well, drying the room very neat ... sand and water cleans boards better than anything'. When cleaning windows 'always do it with two persons one on the inside, one without' (that is, outside: did she levitate?). In an idle moment she might clean some pictures (vitriol and borax, then revarnish with nut and linseed oil), or more usefully deal with the bugs in the bed curtains. If bugs are a real problem – and even the King had a Bugg Destroyer[28] – fumigate the rooms with 'a pound of roll brimstone [sulphur] and some Indian pepper' (do bugs not enjoy sneezing?), or take the bedstead to bits and paint it with mercury or arsenic, which should kill the bugs and have a remarkable effect on the other occupants.

The question of bugs was never far from a good housewife's mind. 'About twenty years ago they hardly knew here in England what a wall-louse [bug] was but ... there are now few houses in London in which these least welcome guests have not quartered themselves.'[29] Foreign ships were blamed. As for fleas, 'nothing is so sure a rule as thorough cleanliness'. No wonder 'English women ... are not par-

ticularly pleased if anyone comes in with dirty shoes.'[30] The slang
word for a housemaid was a 'mopsqueezer', or a 'six-pounder', from
the wages she usually got.[31]

Chambermaids

The duties of a chambermaid according to Hannah Glasse sound
more like what we would expect from a lady's maid. She should have
at her fingertips all sorts of stain-removal secrets (ammonia, turpentine,
bread), and the nine separate stages of washing lace, in which 'with
a little practice and care you may come to great perfection'. Tender
feet benefit from a rub with gin. Corns should be cut only 'in the
decline of the moon'. Elder berries and wine make a good hair dye,
or 'combing the hair with a black lead comb will make the hair black
but then it comes off on the linen prodigiously' – still, that would be
the laundrymaid's worry. The Duke of Bedford paid personal maids
£8 a year, and the 'head woman' £20, much more than his housekeeper, who got £12.

Nursery maids

'The child must be kept as dry as possible', which is not, for long,
very dry. According to Hannah Glasse, clearly enlightened in child
care, a baby should wear only very light clothing: that is, a shirt, a
petticoat of fine flannel tying behind, a buckram surcingle 2 inches
wide covered with satin, 'which answers every purpose of stays and
has none of their inconveniences', a robe and two caps. The nursery
maid should be wise in remedies for rickets (snails), teething (hare's
brains) and worms (rhubarb and currants: no mercury in her book).

Boys

The only male servant in Hannah Glasse's *Directory* was a scullion,
who did the kitchen cleaning, such as pewter plates. Pile them up
and pour some strong caustic on to the top one, rub it with tow,
scour with sand twice, rinse twice, then deal with the next in the pile.
'Thus you may clean them at any time with very little trouble.' This
was, of course, before the era of rubber gloves. The inside of tinned
cooking pots must not be scoured with sand. 'If any scraping is
required then use your nails.' He also had to clean the wax from the

candlesticks every morning. The fashionable lady would have a page, often black, to precede her chair, and hand refreshments to her guests. Even a thieving whore had 'genteel lodgings, a spinnet on which she played, and a boy that walked before her chair' in 1758, according to Samuel Johnson.[32] In a large establishment there must have been all kinds of boys hanging about, hoping to get on to the permanent strength.

Footmen

The female staff and miscellaneous scullions no doubt kept Bedford House in Bloomsbury Square immaculate. But it was the male staff who impressed the outside world. From the dizzy heights of the Duke's French cook (£60 p.a.), his butler (£57 10s) and his confectioner (£52 10s), the accounts descend to footmen, between four and eight of them, at £6–8 a year, and two 'ushers' paid the same. The stables were ruled by the head coachman (£12–26), and his assistant (£9–10), with a postilion (£6–11) and two post-chaise drivers (£6–20). The head gardener got £30, and his assistant only £4.

What did they all find to do? The function of the highest-paid men was obvious, but what, in particular, did footmen do? The answer is – to look impressive. They were 'absolutely inutile'.[33] In popular slang they were called fart catchers, 'from their walking behind their master or mistress'.[34] True, they waited at table, and cleaned the silver, but when they were on show, these well-built men in their gorgeous plush liveries trimmed with gold and silver lace and elaborate shoulderknots of gilt cord, white silk stockings and powdered wigs, their very uselessness made clear to the world that expense was no object to their employer. In that capacity, they attended members of the family to the opera and to pleasure gardens, and escorted distinguished guests home, and walked in front of the sedan chairs carrying family members (they were, of course, far above actually carrying the things) and stood two, three or even four deep on the back of the coach. They kept their employers' seats in a theatre box until the employer and his lady decided to appear. They paced in a dignified way through the streets to deliver messages, pausing to drop into a favourite pub on the way. It is a mystery to me why they were not snatched by the press-gangs.

Perquisites and tips

It was assumed by both employer and employee that a servant whose
work brought her or him into contact with the outside world would
make what she or he could out of it, in the shape of 'perquisites' or
'fees'. Jobs would be advertised 'with allowance of perquisites',[35] which
meant that a shop supplying the household had to inflate its prices to
cover the backhander to the housekeeper who placed the contract.
Butlers were entitled to keep and sell the ends of candles, an expensive
commodity in the eighteenth century. Parsimonious employers were
known to buy three-hour candles for a function expected to last three
hours, to thwart their butlers – and unnerve the guest who persisted
in staying. Ladies' maids expected their mistresses' clothes as soon as
the fashion changed. They might not condescend to wear them
themselves, but they could always sell or exchange them. A valet who
was paid £4 a year in 1740 made £50 a year out of tips.

London servants became so intransigent that 'the Quality at the
West end'[36] began to look abroad for their domestic staff. The footmen,
in particular, overreached themselves. The custom of guests having
to give tips or 'vails' to other people's servants burgeoned so out-
rageously that it was cheaper to eat in a tavern than to accept an
invitation to a free meal in a grand house. 'If you take a meal with a
person of rank you must give every one of the five or six footmen a
coin when leaving. They will be ranged in file in the hall and the
least you can give them is a shilling each' – five or six shillings for
one free dinner,[37] and if you did not pay up, your next visit would be
made very uncomfortable, and your plate would be whisked away
from you before you had had a chance to eat. It was difficult to
mount an effective protest. The officers of His Majesty's army stationed
in the King's other realm, Hanover, solved the problem neatly when
their servants demanded a higher level of vails, failing which they
would strike. The gallant officers replied, in effect, 'So be it'. So their
staff had no choice but to withdraw their labour and go home – and
were pressed, at the foot of the gang-plank.[38]

Gradually the custom of giving vails died out. In 1764 four footmen
were charged with riotous behaviour at Ranelagh, where they had
'insulted several of the nobility whom they supposed to have been
instrumental in abolishing the abominable custom of giving vails'.[39]
The riotous behaviour had included 'fighting with drawn swords for
some hours'. These were tough young men. By 1765 a footman's job

was advertised at £17, 'but the vails are small'.[40] By 1767 even Jonas Hanway, who saw gloom and doom everywhere, admitted that vails giving was practically over.

Conditions of service

Samuel Pepys in the previous century had expended considerable energy in chastising his servants, beating them with whatever came to hand. It is hard to imagine the independent servant of the eighteenth century putting up with physical chastisement. A country parson accustomed to London ways casually referred to 'administering the whip' to two manservants, in 1761,[41] but one employer was successfully sued by a servant who recovered £40 from him for an 'excessive' beating.[42]

Another aspect of domestic service that nowadays would be unthinkable was the constriction of their servants' quarters. In Lord Dacre's large house in ultra-fashionable Bruton Street, two footmen shared one of the two beds in a garret, the porter having the other to himself. The three maids shared the other garret; the housekeeper and the butler had rooms in the basement. Bad enough sharing beds, but even domestic servants surely had some personal belongings – a Bible, a dress from home, a warm shawl for the winter. Where did they put them? A maid probably had a box, like the one in the first picture of Hogarth's *A Harlot's Progress*, but imagine having all your worldly goods in one small box.

As usual, Hogarth encoded many messages in that picture. The sweet country girl is being picked up by a notorious brothel-keeper. Many perfectly respectable employers went to the London termini of the wagon services, hoping to find an innocent who had not yet learned London ways – with the result that London servants 'go out of town and return perhaps with the next wagonner, and being made free of the wagon (which is the phrase among those sort of gentry for the last favour) the honest fellow gives them a character' (a reference).[43] The Fielding brothers revived an idea current in the previous century, a central Register Office, but the idea did not take on. Rumours of pimps and brothels hung about it, and of respectable-looking women available nearby to give a false reference, for a fee, and of improbably perfect 'vacancies' to attract innocents who would pay for the chance of applying, only to find it had 'just been filled'. The usual recruitment channel was recommendation by friends, or an advertisement in a newspaper.

In the perfect world, faithful servants would spend their lives working skilfully for their benevolent employers, and leave only when pensioned off. This, notoriously, did not happen. Servants had the reputation of leaving on the slightest pretext. They could always get another job that might suit them better.[44] Few stayed in one post more than three or four years.[45] London swarmed with unemployed servants. Hanway estimated that there were two thousand menservants at any time, looking for well-paid places. He advertised for a cook and got a hundred applications. But the humble maid-of-all-work was always in short supply.

One disadvantage of a country-bred girl was that she might not have had smallpox, and was prone to all other London germs. If a servant fell ill, she was usually looked after in her employer's house. The exception was smallpox, which would cause her rapid removal to a smallpox hospital, and the cancellation of any obligation on the employer.

When a servant was too old to work any longer, there were no formal arrangements for pensions. The workhouse beckoned, unless she had managed during her years of service to put away enough for a small shop, or an alehouse. If she married a fellow-servant, they might be able to retire to the country. But meanwhile life in service had its compensations. If the family was accustomed to spending the summer in its country house, some of the staff, probably recruited locally, could look forward to going home to see their own families, and showing off their London finery and manners, firing their sisters with ambition to follow in their footsteps. Some would be left in the London house, on much reduced 'board wages', but with comparatively little to do, except entertain their friends and enjoy the sights of London. The royal servants left in St James's Palace did particularly well when the family left for Kensington and they could show visitors the Royal Apartments – for a fee.[46]

CHAPTER 14

Amusements

'To amuse: to entertain with tranquillity': Dr Johnson's *Dictionary*. Perhaps amusement is not the right word for what the poor did in their free time. Tranquil it was not.

Gin

Drinking gin reached the scale of a mania. It had begun quite innocently. The Dutch made a good warming spirit to keep out the cold damp air. Adding juniper berries increased its medicinal effect and improved the taste. Visiting French soldiers took a liking to it, and called it *eau de genièvre*, juniper water. The next wave of soldiery was English. They couldn't get their tongues round *genièvre*, so it became geneva, which rapidly became gin. It never had any connection with the Swiss city. Samuel Johnson defined it as 'the spirit drawn by distillation from juniper-berries', but for once he was wrong. They were only used to flavour the spirit, which was made by distilling grain. By 1751 gin was being flavoured with anything handy, such as turpentine.[1]

At first, gin was thought by the nobility and gentry to be a good thing, since it provided an outlet for surplus grain and kept the price up. But it gradually deteriorated in quality and increased in quantity until by 1720 it was being consumed by the poor all over London. Parliament became a little worried, but still managed to shoot an own goal by passing the Mutiny Act of 1720, which absolved shopkeepers who ran stills from the liability of having soldiers billeted on them, barracks being thought un-English at the time. By 1721 the shopkeepers had drawn the obvious conclusion. A committee of London justices reported that 'all chandlers, many tobacconists and such as sell fruit or herbs in stalls or wheelbarrows sell geneva'. Parliament tried to get the genie back into the bottle, by various licensing laws, but the only means of enforcing them was by paid informers, who were so unpopular that they risked being torn limb from limb. That was not the way to stop the poor from dram drinking.

In 1730 the poor drank 6,658,788 gallons of 'official' gin, let alone what they bought from wheelbarrows. By 1736 there were 6,000 or 7,000 dramshops in London, and the Gin Act passed in that year was a dead letter. By 1750 every fourth house in the parish of St Giles sold gin, as did every eighth house in Westminster and every fifteenth house in the City, and the poor were putting away 11,326,070 gallons of the stuff in a year. Henry Fielding, in his *Enquiry into the Causes of the Late Increase of Robbery*, published in 1751, deplored

> the remissness with which [the previous legislation] had been executed ... that poison called gin is the principal sustenance (if so it may be called) of more than 100,000 People in this metropolis ... the intoxicating Draught itself disqualifies them from using any honest means to acquire it, at the same time that it removes all sense of fear and shame and emboldens them to commit every wicked and dangerous Enterprise ... Should the drinking this poison be continued at its present height during the next twenty years there will by that time be very few of the common people left to drink it.

By now it was everywhere. It was made and sold – illegally – in prisons and workhouses and hospitals. Weavers sold it in Spitalfields, and parish nurses gave it to the pauper children in their care to keep them quiet, which it did, permanently. Over 9,000 children died of gin, in 1751. The rich even began to worry about the knock-on effect on themselves. As *The Ladies' Magazine* of July 1750 put it, 'an immoderate use of strong liquors imbecillitates[2] the human body ... the preservation of the industrious labourer depends on his not drinking spirituous liquors: on his preservation, that of the Middling people, and on them the support of the wealthy'. It was in everyone's interests that the poor should be dried out.

In February 1751 Hogarth published his twin prints, *Gin Lane* and *Beer Street*. Beer, 'a common necessity which Britons deem to be part of their birth-right',[3] was shown as a good thing, on which a man could contribute a fair day's work to the community. But gin was different. A nursing mother is too drunk to keep her baby from falling headlong to the cellar marked 'Drunk for a penny, dead drunk for two pence, clean straw for nothing'. Behind her a couple are pawning their cooking pots and working tools; they want gin rather than work or food. In the background a woman tips gin into a baby's mouth, and two little parish girls composedly sip their gin outside Kilman's distillery, unperturbed by the fight going on between cripples, or the drunk in a wheelbarrow being fed yet more gin.[4] A baby weeps as its mother's body is lifted into a coffin. A house is falling down. A man cook dances, waving his spit with a baby impaled on it...

Another Gin Act became law in June 1751. The sale of gin was limited to substantial householders. No more wheelbarrow sales. Gaolers and workhouse masters stood to forfeit £100 if they sold it, which some of them still did, reckoning the game worth the candle. This Act worked. From 11,326,070 gallons consumed in 1750–1 the figure dropped to 7,500,000 in the next year, and to 3,663,568 by 1767–8. The worst of the craze was over.

Before leaving it, here are some synonyms for gin: cock-my-cap, kill-grief, comfort, poverty, meat-and-drink, washing, lodging,[5] bingo (also used to mean brandy), diddle, heart's-ease, a kick in the guts, tape, white wool and strip-me-naked. If you had been hicksius-doxius (drunk) you might well feel womblety cropt (hungover) the day after. And the story of the first speak-easy. Captain Bradstreet made a dangerous living by informing on illegal gin sellers. He noticed that no warrant could issue if the name of the owner of the suspect premises was unknown. He bought a house through a nominee, and retired to it with a bulk supply of gin and food for a siege. Trade signs above shop premises were still usual, and his was a cat, with a slot beside it and a pipe under one of its paws. Discreet publicity produced a steady clientele. For every two pennies posted into the slot, the customer got gin from the pipe. Bradstreet retired a wealthy man, while the going was good.[6]

Animal baiting

So what were the poor to do with their spare energy? The streets were their playground, and could be used for some good games. One was 'bullock hunting', which probably explained the 'cow hard driven from Smithfield' and the 'over-driven ox' in the Guildhall, in Chapter 2. On Smithfield cattle market days, a gang of men and boys would gather round a herd, shouting and whistling and brandishing their formidable drovers' sticks. They would pitch on one animal, which

they would detach from the herd and pursue through the streets until
it was finally exhausted, when the drovers' boy could catch up with
it and take it to the nearest slaughterhouse. The bullock hunters
themselves were agile enough to avoid injury, but bystanders could
be injured or killed.[7]

Then there was bull hanking, or baiting, with dogs. A favourite
site for that was behind the Duke of Bedford's house, in Bloomsbury
fields, and his lordship was not pleased. Two thousand people turned
up to watch one bout, but were dispersed by the law before it began.[8]
On another occasion, a man was gored to death when the bull got
loose.[9] Bears and badgers too could be baited.[10]

Watching cocks fight was enjoyed by rich and poor alike, while
'throwing at cocks' could be enjoyed by the poor anywhere, traditionally on Shrove Tuesday. A cock was tethered to a stake, and 'for
a few pence anyone may throw a short wooden club at him and he
becomes the property of the man who kills him'.[11] There were other
pastimes involving 'that cruel treatment of poor animals which makes
the streets of London more disagreeable to the human mind, than
anything what ever; the very describing of which gives pain'. Hogarth,
whose words those were, depicted all too vividly the cruelty he saw
in the streets, in the first of his series of prints *The Four Stages of Cruelty*.

Boxing

The fields near Marylebone were a favourite place for 'bruising
matches' – that is, bare-knuckle boxing. The law broke up one fight
between an Irish sedan-chair carrier and an Englishman, watched by
'five hundred low and well-known wicked ... Irish chairmen', who
managed to rescue their man from the clutches of the law, leaving
the Englishman to face a criminal charge alone.[12] Sometimes 'Bruising
Peg' took the stage, who was even more fun to watch as she 'beat
her antagonist in a terrible manner'.[13]

Ball games

The populace has other amusements ... such as throwing dead dogs
and cats and mud at passers-by on certain festival days. Another
amusement which is very inconvenient to passers-by is football ... in
cold weather you sometimes see a score of rascals in the streets kicking
at a ball and they will break panes of glass and smash the windows of

coaches and also knock you down without the smallest compunction: on the contrary they will roar with laughter...

The English are very fond of a game they call cricket. For this purpose they go into a large open field and knock a small ball about with a piece of wood. I [a visiting Frenchman] will not attempt to describe this game to you, it is too complicated: but it requires agility and skill and everyone plays it, the common people and also men of rank.[14]

Boys

Francis Place reminisced about the gang warfare that he and other small boys waged in the ruins of some burnt-out houses which made a perfect adventure playground.[15] They had splendid games on Guy Fawkes night, fighting with other gangs and extorting money from passers-by to buy fireworks. The boys were 'all armed with bludgeons', which made November the Fifth rather more violent than any modern trick or treat.

Another traditional ploy took place on Twelfth Night. People used to stop and stare into the windows of pastrycooks, at the gorgeous Twelfth Night cakes on sale. As they stood, boys sneaked up and nailed their clothes to the wooden shopfront. 'The noisy mirth which these pranks occasioned was not confined to the boys who did the mischief but was partaken of by grown persons ... not by any means the lowest of the people but by those who were well dressed.' A really clever 'nailer' would secure a man and a girl together, immobile, like butterflies pinned to a board.

Riots

If there was no football or cricket going on, and no other excuse for creating mayhem, the populace was extraordinarily quick to create a general riot. John Wilkes's various entrances and exits were regularly accompanied by rioting crowds. Out of countless accounts of riots in the newspapers and *The Gentleman's Magazine*, one is unforgettable.[16] In July 1749 three sailors were robbed of 30 guineas, four moidores, a banknote of £20 and two watches, in a brothel in the Strand. They,

obtaining no satisfaction, went out, denouncing vengeance, and [the next night] returned with a great number of armed sailors who entirely demolished the goods, cut the feather beds to pieces, strewed the feathers in the streets, tore the wearing apparel, and turned the women naked into the street; then broke all the windows and considerably damaged a neighbouring house. A guard of soldiers was sent for ... but came too late ... [The next night] the sailors renewed their outrages and committed the same acts of violence on two other houses of ill fame in the Strand, in presence of multitudes of people, who huzza'd them

– and a good time was had by all, except the unfortunate prostitutes. It may be relevant here to say that turning a girl out into the street naked except for her stays was the usual punishment inflicted by sailors on prostitutes who infected them with venereal disease.[17]

The affair had a sobering aftermath. One of the people cheering the sailors on was a young Cornishman, Bosavern Penley. Perhaps he didn't move fast enough, being up from the country, and was 'drawn in by seeing such numbers at work with great Mirth and Jollity in so open and barefaced a manner as if they had thought that the Guards, if they came, would ... at least wink at their escape'.[18] He was arrested, with one other man. Unfortunately for him, however, he had not stood idly by, watching the riot. On him were found 'ten laced [lace-trimmed] caps, four laced handkerchiefs, three pairs of laced ruffles, two laced clouts [cloths] five plain handkerchiefs and a laced apron', presumably belonging to the prostitutes, blowing down the Strand in a haze of feathers. To the indignation of the crowds, he was found guilty of stealing and sentenced to death. Henry Fielding, the magistrate concerned, found it necessary to justify this sentence in the press.[19] 'Since one of the rioters should suffer in order to give a sanction to the law so notoriously violated, the only question was [which of the two criminals it should be].' The other man had committed only a breach of the peace, so it had to be Penley who suffered.

The pillory

Is it better or worse to throw things casually at a man immobilised in a pillory than to inflict death on a tethered cock? If a man was sentenced to the pillory for an offence of which the populace disapproved, such as informing, the authorities deliberately, it seems, chose the site of his punishment to inflate the sentence beyond what they could lawfully impose. Two informers were pilloried in Smithfield on a market day. 'Among a gang of merciless drovers, it was not likely they should escape with their lives.'[20] Blackmailers and sodomites could expect the same treatment.[21]

It was well worth saving any dead dogs and cats and rotten fish you might find; you never knew when they might come in useful.[22] Stones and mud could usually be found on site and, although throwing stones at a helpless man in a pillory was illegal, it gave you a fine feeling of having expressed popular sentiment if you threw one that killed him.

Executions

But undoubtedly the best amusements were executions. Eight times a year, the carts left the gates of Newgate and bumped their way slowly along Holborn and Oxford Street to Tyburn, just outside the turnpike gate,[23] between yelling, cheering, booing, catcalling crowds. A prisoner convicted of coining (making false coins) would be tied to a hurdle or 'sledge' that was pulled along the filthy streets, not that he can have been worrying about hygiene by then.[24] Sometimes the execution was arranged in the place where the crime had been committed, which made a nice change of scene for the crowd.[25] The barbaric sentence of hanging a man, cutting him down still alive, disembowelling him and quartering his corpse was still in place, but I found no record of its actually being carried out.[26]

The fun was not only in watching the prisoners dying, but in assessing their demeanour. They varied from the blasé to the terrified. One man offended the delicate sensitivity of the crowd when he 'behaved with shocking impudence and unconcern and espying a woman whom he knew, in a window in Holborn, used very obscene language to her'.[27] When a gang of thirteen young criminals 'most of them boys, the eldest not above twenty two' were all hanged together, 'some of them were greatly affected, others so hardened that they ridiculed the punishment of death and laughed at their companions for being afraid of it'.[28] Sometimes the mob was cheated by a 'reprieve under the gallows'.[29] Sometimes it attempted a rescue.[30] Sometimes it was more terrifying than the hangman himself. A man who had starved his idiot wife to death was 'apprehensive of being torn in pieces and hastened the executioner to perform his office'.[31]

An average mob was at least half female[32] and before 1751 more than half drunk on gin. Sometimes the hangman was drunk too. In 1738 'the hangman was intoxicated with liquor, and supposing there were three for execution was going to put one of the ropes round the parson's neck as he stood in the cart and was with much difficulty prevented by the gaoler from so doing'.[33] When Lord Kilmarnock, sentenced to death for his part in the 1745 rebellion, came to the scaffold, 'the executioner, who had previously taken something to keep him from fainting, was so affected ... that he burst into tears'.[34] At least one can be fairly sure that children were enabled to get a good view. 'At all ceremonies which attract a crowd ... children ... are seen to meet with tender treatment. All are eager to make room for them and even lift them up ... that they may have an opportunity of seeing.'[35]

Executions were rich fields for pickpockets, and ballad singers distributing the hanged man's last words before he had had a chance to say any, and vendors of oranges and fast food. But such enjoyment could become tiring. A permanent gallery was built, to enable spectators to sit comfortably. Imagine the panic when it 'gave way, when one gentleman's leg was broken and twelve or fourteen other people were horribly bruised'.[36] One can only hope they were well enough to enjoy the sights they had come to see.

Even when all was over and there was no more to do except to fight the carters taking the bodies to Surgeons' Hall – on at least one occasion the mob 'carried away the body in triumph'[37] – the home-going crowd still simmered with violence. A visiting Frenchman's manservant had treated himself to a sight of this extraordinary English custom and was quietly making his way back to his master's lodgings when the mob spotted him and set on him, for the sole reason that he was French. Even the hangman joined in. The manservant was rescued by three French soldiers, deserters. No passing Englishman would have bothered.[38]

Clubs

But it was not all violence. In that era of famous clubs, 'even the lowest class have their clubs'.[39] There was a well-known debating club of small tradesmen and workmen, called the Robin Hood, where members paid 6d for a seat and a pint of beer, and the chance to get up and speak for five minutes only – what an excellent rule – on any subject they chose, including politics and religion.[40] Francis Place's father ran a pub that had two 'club rooms'.[41] On Mondays and Fridays it cost a shilling to stay from eight o'clock in the evening until everyone was drunk, which was usually about one or two in the morning. On Tuesdays and Saturdays there was a lottery club, and on Wednesday evenings and Sunday mornings a 'cutter club' of young men who owned a rowing boat on the river. There were also more boisterous clubs called 'Cock-and-hen' or 'Chair' clubs. At each end of a long table was a chair, one for a young man, the other for a girl. The evening began at eight, and wore on with drinking, smoking, swearing and singing 'flash songs'. 'The boys and girls paired off by degrees till by twelve none remained.' There were also 'illegal concerts' ostensibly to raise money for charity, but in fact to sell the services of prostitutes.[42]

The lottery

Hogarth's *Gin Lane* is an unforgettable image. He did not do the same for the lottery, which was just as much of a disastrous craze.[43] The prizes could be huge. In 1769, for instance, there were two prizes, each of £20,000, in consecutive weeks. But the odds against winning were calculated at 35,000 to one.[44] In a society permeated with gambling, it is not surprising to find the poor betting as if they could spare the money, just like their superiors, but it landed them in the pawnshop and the poorhouse.[45]

The sights of London

So it is a relief to turn to innocent and peaceful pursuits, such as a day out in the country or a Sunday visit to one of the parks, putting to flight the fashionables who paraded there on other days. The wild animals in the menagerie in the Tower cost 6d a head to view, making it out of bounds for a large family, yet it must have been a poor man who unwisely put his hand into a lion's cage to take a calf's head that the lion was eating, and got his hand bitten off.[46] The tombs in Westminster Abbey were a splendid sight, and free if you could withstand the importunate guides. And there were frequent royal and state occasions, with processions of chairs and carriages that could be savoured from the pavement.

City occasions

Then there were always the traditional Londoners' shows, such as St Bartholomew's fair for two weeks at the end of August, and the Lord Mayor's procession in November. 'One hundred considerable graziers, salesmen and inhabitants of Smithfield'[47] wanted to clean up the fair, but it survived, although they did succeed in curtailing it from fourteen days to three.[48] Visiting dignitaries could provide a good show, especially the Venetian ambassadors' comings and goings.[49] But it was the young King of Denmark who won the hearts of the masses, when he came to see King George III in 1768. He left a thousand guineas to be distributed to the royal domestic staff, and with the same munificence, 'observing some poor people assembled under his window in Cleveland Row [he] lifted up the sash and threw a handful of gold among them'.[50]

CHAPTER 15

Crime and Punishment

'Crime: An act contrary to right; an offence; a great fault; an act of wickedness': Dr Johnson's *Dictionary*.

The trouble with that definition is that it equates law with morality. The two are not the same. Some acts are immoral and unlawful, such as murder. Others are only unlawful, such as, in modern England, driving on the right. But in general the law tries to keep in step with morality, and lags only a few decades behind. In the eighteenth century, morality tended to coincide with the interests of the property-owning classes.

Children

Children learned pickpocketing early. There were advantages in training them young, not only because they could go where adults could not, but because until they were seven they could not be found guilty of a crime punishable by death, so the risk of their teacher losing the benefit of his training was less. Between the ages of seven and fourteen, children could be executed only where there was 'strong evidence of malice', but over fourteen they were as liable to the death penalty as anyone else.[1]

Little boys called 'faggers'[2] could be put through house windows. They were useful, too, for hat snatching.

> An old way of robbing was revived in the Poultry [a street in the City] by a boy in a baker's basket [carried on a man's head] who snatched off the hats of several gentlemen before he was detected. The third gentleman he had so served was told where his hat was by a person

from a window who observed the stratagem and could not help laughing
at it.[3]

Not only the hat but the wig went too, and wigs could be expensive.

'A man who kept a public house near Fleet Market had a club of
boys whom he instructed in picking pockets and other iniquitous
practices',[4] such as shoplifting. One boy would attract the shopkeeper's
attention, while the other crawled in below eye level and 'took the
tills and anything else he could meet with'. Or two boys would huddle
together under a projecting shop window at night. Whenever it was
safe to do so, they picked the mortar out of the wall and pulled out
the bricks. One boy went in and took what he could find while the
other stayed put to mask the hole.

Pickpockets

Children really came into their own in pickpocketing. They were the
right height to 'dip' into pockets, or even cut the fabric and take the
whole pocket. If detected, they eeled their way through the crowds
and were rarely caught. Everywhere that crowds gathered, to watch
an execution or a procession, the pickpockets moved in. The
approaches to St James's Park and the other places where people
came to enjoy a quiet walk were good pitches in the daytime, and
by midnight 'the public streets began to swarm with whores and
pickpockets'.[5] Ballad singers collaborated with pickpockets, who moved
through the 'crowd of fools which stood about them all evening'.[6]
'When any of these pickpockets are caught in the act ... they are
dragged to the nearest fountain or well and dipped in the water until
nearly drowned',[7] which was a more satisfactory retribution than
waiting for the criminal law. When children grew too big to slip away
through the crowd, they took to mugging and burglary, or bought a
horse with their savings, and took to the road.

Highwaymen

The romantic hero of eighteenth-century crime is the highwayman.
They frequently made the news, yet perhaps the middle classes
frightened themselves into fits about a danger that was unlikely to
strike. Boswell was 'a little afraid of highwaymen' on his way to
Oxford in 1763, 'but met none', and later 'it was very disagreeable

going from Barnet to London at the time of the evening when robberies are committed', but his journey was uneventful.[8] Horace Walpole's story[9] of his encounter with a highwayman is so vivid, and perhaps so typical, that I quote it although it is rather after our period.

Lady Browne and I were, as usual, going to the Duchess of Montrose at seven o'clock. The evening was very dark. In the close [narrow] lane under her park-pale [fence], and within twenty yards of the gate, a black figure on horseback pushed by between the chaise and the hedge on my side. I suspected it was a highwayman, and so I found did Lady Browne, for she was speaking and dropped [stopped]. To divert her fears, I was just going to say, Is that not the apothecary going to the Duchess? When I heard a voice cry 'Stop!' and the figure came back to the chaise. I had the presence of mind, before I let down the glass, to take out my watch and stuff it within my waistcoat under my arm. He said 'Your purses and watches!' I replied 'I have no watch'. 'Then your purse!' I gave it to him; it had nine guineas. It was so dark that I could not see his hand, but felt him take it. He then asked for Lady Browne's purse, and said 'Don't be frightened; I will not hurt you.' I said 'No; you won't frighten the lady?' He replied 'No I give you my word I will do you no hurt.' Lady Browne gave him her purse, and was going to add her watch, but he said 'I am much obliged to you! I wish you good night!' pulled off his hat, and rode away. 'Well' said I, 'Lady Browne, you will not be afraid of being robbed another time, for you see there is nothing in it.' 'Oh! but I am' said she 'and now I am in terrors lest he should return, for I gave him a purse with only bad [false] money that I carry on purpose.' 'He certainly will not open it directly' said I 'and at worst he can only wait for us on our return; but I will send my servant back for a horse and a blunderbuss', which I did.

The resourceful Lady Browne had elaborated the custom that Casanova was told about:[10] 'We English always carry two purses on our journeys, a small one for the robbers and a large one for ourselves.' It obviously worked for day-to-day activities, but might be awkward after a major trading day at Smithfield, when a successful grazier would be carrying home a substantial amount of cash. The butchers of Smithfield were often suspected of giving accomplices a tip-off on a likely victim.[11]

Robbers

Pleasure parties to Vauxhall and Ranelagh invited the attentions of pickpockets and robbers. One particularly nasty case was reported in 1771, but probably was not unique. 'Between eleven and twelve o'clock at night three gentlemen and two ladies returning from Vauxhall by water were boarded by six men ... about two hundred yards above Westminster Bridge who demanded their money without any hesitation or they would throw them overboard.'[12] The thieves' haul was only £20 and two watches. Just as well that this satisfied them.

Grave robbers

A rather more recherché type of theft centred on graveyards. Although some provision was being made to provide corpses for educational dissection by the surgeons, demand exceeded supply. A widow duly buried her husband, but found that his body had migrated to a surgeon's house. She got a search warrant, but no one found anything untoward until she had a look in the boiler 'which was almost full of boiling water ... she took a stick and stirred it when to her great surprise she saw the head and part of the body of her husband'.[13]

Two men stole a baby's corpse from a burial ground; they were sentenced to a year's imprisonment and a public whipping.[14] Two more little corpses disappeared from their graves in St Giles in the Fields,[15] and a two-year-old 'lately buried at Whitechapel' was taken away by two men who were caught, and fined *a shilling each* and sentenced to six months in Newgate.[16] In the same year, a gang of three men and the gravedigger stole 150 lead coffins from another graveyard,[17] presumably – the bodies in them being past their sell-by date – to sell the lead, which could be easily fenced. 'Blue pigeon flyers', who stole the lead from the roofs of churches and houses,[18] would use the same fences.

Kidnappers

Kidnapping was easy in the crowded London streets.

> There went from her friends on Friday last ... and has not been since heard of, a young woman aged sixteen years, rather short but upright in her person, of a fine fair complexion and smooth face except a mark near her eye from smallpox ... [she] had on a flowered cotton gown,

a black cardinal [jacket], and a black bonnet lined with white. As it appears from many circumstances that she did not intend an elopement it is feared that she may have been decoyed and betrayed by some villain, possibly not without some force.'[19]

Only a month later, 'last night about seven o'clock a gentleman coming down St Martin's Lane ... in company with a lady had the misfortune to separate from her in a crowd: and as she is German by birth ... and understands but little English he has been obliged to describe her in the morning papers of this day in order that she may be restored to her disconsolate husband ... She is about eighteen years of age, fair complexion and black hair.'[20] I don't know the end of either of these sad stories, but there was one that may have had a happy ending. *Miss* Lucy Gough was 'forcibly abducted' and 200 guineas were offered as a reward for returning her. Eleven days later an advertisement appeared in the same newspaper: 'I was taken away by *my husband* [my italics] with whom I am happily reconciled.'[21] We shall never know the truth of it.

Counterfeiters

There was a constant shortage of currency, which created a steady market for counterfeit coin. This was viewed very seriously by the authorities. A few citizens more or less, what did it matter? But competing with government by injecting false money into the economic veins of the state might bring trade to a standstill, so it was classed as treason, and merited death by burning alive. Counterfeit coins could come in useful at times, as Lady Browne knew, for paying highwaymen, and for gaming debts,[22] but there were so many counterfeit halfpence about that shopkeepers refused to accept them, which was particularly hard on the poor, who rarely dealt in the higher denominations.

Cheating sailors

The unfortunate sailors were often cheated. Reports of 'personating seamen with intent to receive their wages' and forging seamen's tickets, and even their wills, regularly appeared in *The Gentleman's Magazine*.

Law enforcement

The lowest ranks of the law-keeping establishment were the Watch, often old and decrepit, armed only with a staff, paid a pittance to patrol far more than they could manage, and fond of meeting their fellow-watchmen in a convenient pub to spend the night tippling.[23] Above them were the parish constables, the lowest rank of voluntary parish officials, who were obliged to serve when their turn came, or buy their way out. They were responsible for apprehending malefactors. They tended to extort 'sufferance money' from brothel-keepers in their 'precincts',[24] and no doubt from other people on the edge of the law, who were prepared to pay for a quiet life. If they caught a malefactor, they took him to one of the round-houses scattered through the district, until he could be charged before a magistrate. These buildings were about the size of a garden summerhouse. At least you could get a drink, if you had any money on you, but they were often verminous and, on a busy night, overcrowded. On one hideous occasion in 1742,

> a parcel of drunken constables took it into their heads to put the laws in execution against disorderly persons, and so took up every woman they met, till they had collected five or six-and-twenty, all of whom they thrust into St Martin's roundhouse, where they kept them all night, with doors and windows closed. The poor creatures, who could not stir or breathe, screamed as long as they had any breath left, begging at least for water: one poor wretch said she was worth at least eighteenpence and would gladly give it for a draught of water – but in vain! So well did they keep them there, that in the morning four were found stifled to death, two died soon after, and a dozen more are in a shocking way ... several of them were beggars, who from having no lodging were necessarily found in the street, and others honest labouring women: one of the dead was a poor washerwoman, big with child who was returning home late from washing.[25]

Another set of constables sent to keep the peace at Ranelagh got so drunk that they fought each other instead.[26]

The next tier of law-enforcers were the Justices of the Peace, usually referred to as justices. In the rest of the country, this was a respected and effective office held by a local gentleman, who could be trusted to know his district and to deal with trouble-makers equitably, even if he did not always apply the niceties of the law. In London the

Two winning lottery-ticket holders in this 1760 print are being paid, but there are losers too. The woman hesitating at the door is so busy counting her money that she doesn't notice she is being robbed.

DISEASES and CASUALTIES.

Abortive and Stilborn	597	Evil	7	Lunatick	72	Broken Limbs	3
Aged	1397	Fever, Malignant Fever, Scarlet Fever, and Spotted Fever, and Purples	2472	Measles	696	Bruised	3
Ague	1	French Pox	46	Miscarriage	2	Burnt	1
Apoplexy and Suddenly	191	Flux	5	Mortification	154	Choaked with Fat	6
Asthma and Tissick	294	Gout	39	Pally	66	Drowned	109
Bedridden	—	Gravel, Stone, and Strangury	8	Pleurisy	17	Excessive Drinking	2
Bleeding	4	Grief	1	Quinsy	21	Executed	14
Bloody Flux	8	Headmoldshot, Horshoehead, and Water in the Head	5	Rash	4	Found dead	4
Bursten and Rupture	5	Jaundies	40	Rheumatism	10	Froze to Death	2
Cancer	8	Imposthume	87	Rickets	14	Killed by Falls and several other Accidents	58
Canker	34	Inflammation	9	Rising of the Lights	1	Killed themselves	30
Chicken Pox	8	Itch	—	Small Pox	1273	Murdered	5
Childbed	185	Leprosy	—	Sores and Ulcers	14	Overlaid	26
Colick, Gripes, and Twisting of the Guts	50	Lethargy	2	Sore Throat	5	Scalded	3
Consumption	3411	Livergrown	6	St Anthony's Fire	4	Smothered	3
Convulsion	4417			Stoppage in the Stomach	13	Starved	4
Cough and Hooping	84			Teeth	644	Suffocated	9
Cough	—			Thrush	91	**Total**	**282**
Diabetes	2			Tympany	2		
Dropsy	682			Vomiting and Looseness	7		
				Worms	6		

CHRISTENED { Males — 7347, Females — 6862, In all — 14209 }

BURIED { Males — 8931, Females — 8645, In all — 17576 }

Whereof have died,

Under Two Years of Age	5971	Twenty and Thirty	1362	Sixty and Seventy	1208	A Hundred and Two	2
Between Two and Five	1795	Thirty and Forty	1589	Seventy and Eighty	961	A Hundred and Three	1
Five and Ten	717	Forty and Fifty	1606	Eighty and Ninety	370	A Hundred and Four	1
Ten and Twenty	556	Fifty and Sixty	1368	Ninety and a Hundred	68	A Hundred and Six	1

A summary for the year 1758 of the Bills of Mortality in the City, giving the causes of death. Smallpox was still a major risk. Children under five accounted for almost half of all deaths. People still died of 'lethargy' and 'grief'.

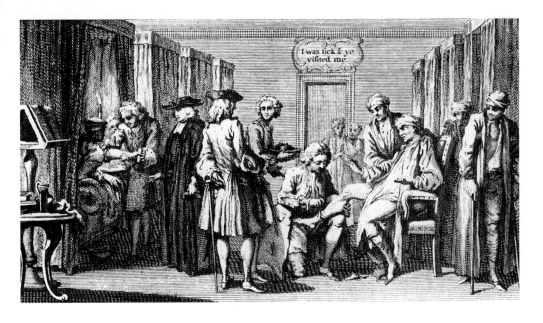

A hospital ward round. On the left a patient extends his arm for blood-letting. The beds have curtains and canopies, which harbour bed-bugs (see page 99).

The panic-stricken exodus from London in April 1750 when an earthquake had been prophesied (see page 270). Traffic jams were frequent, even on normal days.

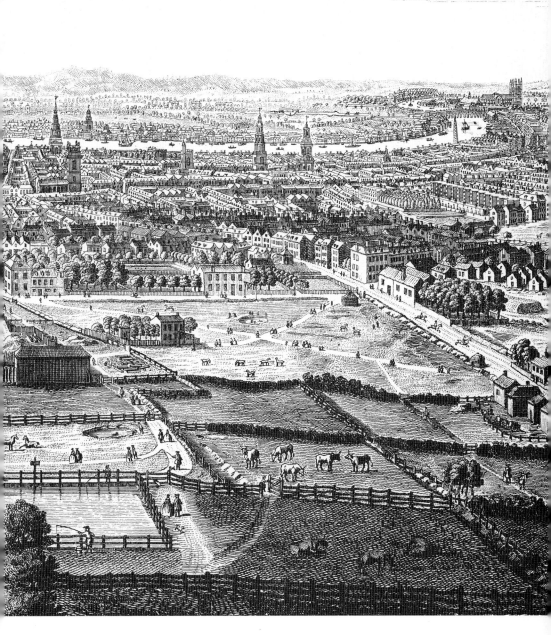

London in 1752, seen from Islington. Westminster Abbey and Westminster Bridge are at the top right corner. The dome marks St Paul's Cathedral. London Bridge is at the left top corner, still lined with houses. The tall white column near it is the Monument. The spires of Wren's churches punctuate the city. In the middle of the picture is the New River reservoir. To the right of it is a yard where tree trunks are being bored for water-pipes (see page 22).

This is the notorious highwayman McLean robbing Lord Eglington, on Hounslow Heath, in 1750. He got away with fifty guineas and his Lordship's luggage. He was caught soon after, and hanged (see page 143).

Tho' such a dismal Sight is here,
Yet not a Briton sheds a Tear.

A judge could order the body of a man executed for murder to be hung in chains. Sometimes the body wore a wig (see page 144).

Hangings were public holidays, attended by huge crowds. The prisoner was taken to the gallows in a cart, with his coffin. Here he is accompanied by John Wesley while the 'establishment' parson travels more comfortably (Hogarth, 1747).

Westminster Hall housed the three principal courts of civil law. This print of 1745 shows two in the far corners and one in the foreground, where the doorkeeper is about to admit counsel (wearing a gown and bands) who seems to be paying a witness. The walls are lined with stalls selling books and fancy goods, regardless of the majesty of the law.

The noise in the streets must have been deafening, considering the ballad singer (note the swaddled baby), the itinerant musician, the knife-grinder, the sow gelder blowing his trumpet, the paviour in the square cap hammering the granite setts … to which would be added the noise of animals and vehicles, not shown in this picture (Hogarth, 1741).

The central figure at this cock fight is Lord Albermarle Bertie, who was blind. Not surprisingly he is being robbed by his neighbour. The shadow over the arena is that of a man who has defaulted on his wager and has been hauled up to the ceiling in a basket (see page 209). He is offering his watch and chain in payment. (Hogarth, 1759.)

justices were seen as 'the scum of the earth, some could hardly write their names',[27] who were so adept at devising occasions for the payment to them of fees for legal procedures that they were known as 'trading justices'.

Justices had two principal functions. They could try those accused of minor crimes, for which they had power to sentence to the pillory, public whipping, a spell in prison or in a house of correction, or a fine, or a combination of the sentences they thought suitable. They also had miscellaneous powers under the Vagrancy Acts and the liquor licensing laws. For more serious crimes they had to consider whether a case had been made out that justified their committing the accused for trial by the assizes held at the Old Bailey.

The administration of law in London began to improve from 1749 when Henry Fielding was appointed chief magistrate of Westminster, with a salary of £550 paid from a secret 'public service' fund[28] (so nervous were the authorities of anything smacking of a central police force), and took up official residence in Bow Street, where his court sat. Henry Fielding died in 1754, but his work was continued by his half-brother John, who had been blind from birth but had the reputation – no doubt carefully fostered by him – of being able to recognise an unbelievable number of thieves merely by their voices.

Bow Street dealt with most felonies. There were other courts in Soho and the Guildhall in Westminster, as well as the Lord Mayor's court in the City. Sir John Fielding set up an office in Bow Street that issued detailed descriptions of stolen property and of wanted persons – the precursor of *The Police Gazette* and also remarkable as the first effort to extend any kind of criminal law enforcement country-wide. He promised 'the immediate despatch of a set of brave Fellows in pursuit who ... are always ready to set out to any part of this town or kingdom on quarter of an hour's notice', the origin of the Flying Squad, although there were only eight of them, mounted on eight trusty steeds.

Trials

Trial procedure would startle a modern lawyer. No wonder that many victims refused to prosecute, since the outcome was so uncertain. The accused might approach them before the trial and offer them money not to go on with the case. This was far more to the point than giving up their time to attend a trial, being required – quite illegally – to pay various fees,[29] and risking mob vengeance if the trial resulted in an execution.[30] No costs were paid to prosecutors or other witnesses for the Crown,[31] who might be kept hanging about for days waiting for the case to come on. When it did, a prudent defendant would be ready with plenty of 'affidavit men' to prove that wherever the crime had been committed, he was somewhere else (*alibi*, Latin for 'elsewhere') at the time. They could be picked up outside the courts, 'ready to swear anything for hire, distinguished by having straws stuck in the heels of their shoes',[32] which was handy. Casanova, who had some experience of legal procedure in Europe, was shocked by 'the facility with which false witnesses may be procured ... I have myself seen the word EVIDENCE written in large characters in a window, as much as to say that false witnesses may be procured within'.[33]

The Gentleman's Magazine constantly reported trials where a high proportion of prisoners were discharged 'for want of prosecution'. For example, 36 were discharged, 60 sentenced in September 1763; and 22 discharged, 31 sentenced in July 1766. Another startling aspect of Old Bailey trials was their speed. In four days in February 1769, the Old Bailey judges tried 40 prisoners, and sentenced three of them to execution, twenty-two to be transported, five to be burned in the hand, and ten to be whipped. They must have been quite glad to discharge another twenty for want of prosecution.[34]

Peine fort et dur

Three features of eighteenth-century court procedure survived from the Middle Ages. Until 1772 *peine fort et dur* still confronted an accused person who refused to plead: that is, to say whether he was innocent or guilty. The point of so doing was to avoid a verdict of guilty, since that would mean that all his property went to the Crown, leaving his family destitute. If he refused to plead, he died a peculiarly painful and lingering death, stretched on the ground naked with weights on his body, fed on stale bread and stagnant water. But since he had not been found guilty, his family received whatever he left, subject no doubt to the various 'fees' extracted by rapacious court and prison officers. In 1770 a prisoner 'at first refused to plead, but being taken down and shown the apparatus for pressing him to death if he refused, he relented'.[35] The last time anyone persisted in refusing to plead was in 1735.

Benefit of clergy

In the Middle Ages, the Church had sole jurisdiction over clerics. They were likely to be the only people who could read, and so if a priest found himself before a lay court, he could claim immunity, proving his status by reading a verse from the Bible. The verse chosen, known as the 'neck verse', came from Psalm 51: 'Have mercy upon me, O God, after thy great goodness: according to the multitude of thy mercies do away mine offences.' The privilege had been extended, illogically but usefully, to anyone who could read, in the fourteenth century, and to women in the seventeenth century.[36] If the claim succeeded, the prisoner did not get off scot-free, but suffered a much milder punishment, such as being burnt on his or her hand. It could only be invoked once; after that a re-offender had to take his chance with the others. Benefit of clergy was not abolished until 1827, but the list of offences for which it could *not* be claimed grew longer, from highway robbery to pickpocketing, until it had little practical importance.

Pregnancy

The man who enabled a woman to 'plead her belly' in capital cases certainly had practical importance, 'every gaol having ... one or two child getters who qualify the ladies for that expedient'.[37] There's a career opportunity for a young man, but, as Filch said in *The Beggar's Opera*, 'one had need to have the Constitution of a horse to go thro' the business. Since the favourite child-getter [in Newgate] was disabled by a mishap I have picked up a little money by helping the ladies to a pregnancy against their being called down to sentence.' The idea was that it would be unlawful to kill a child in its mother's womb, as well as the mother, so if she could satisfy a committee of matrons that she was pregnant, she could delay her death until the baby was born. One prisoner counted on a few more months of life by this means, planning to find a child-getter in Newgate to make good her claim, but the committee of matrons sat on her claim immediately, and dismissed it.[38]

Pardons

In 1748 a special hearing of all the judges considered the case of
William York, aged ten, who had deliberately murdered a five-year-
old girl and hidden her body in a dungheap. The judges declared
that 'he is certainly a proper subject for capital punishment and ought
to suffer [that is, be hanged]; for it would be a very dangerous
consequence to have it thought that children may commit such
atrocious crimes with impunity'. Yet with that inconsequence that is
almost a hallmark of eighteenth-century principles, he did not meet
his so-well-deserved end. After nine years on the equivalent of death
row, he was pardoned on condition that 'he entered the sea-service'.[39]

The more usual course was to refer any case that the judge or the
jury thought suitable for pardon, or where an energetic plea was
made on behalf of the prisoner, to the Home Office, with the judge's
own recommendation. After George III came to the throne in 1760,
he liked to study each case himself. Sometimes the judge was less
than enthusiastic. On a highwayman, 'The judge hoped that, for
example's sake, the terms of mercy would not be too tender.' Yet
Thomas Mayo, another highwayman sentenced to death, was recommended for service in a regiment abroad instead – the 49th Foot,
serving in Jamaica, which must have had a high incidence of deaths
from tropical diseases and was always short of men – 'the prisoner
being a lusty young fellow and it was his first offence'.

The Crown had a nasty habit of granting pardons only just in time.
In the case of another highwayman, 'as His Majesty hopes so to
terrify this unhappy man on the present occasion, that he may not
hereafter be guilty of the like offence, it is the King's intention that
he should not be made acquainted with His Majesty's having extended
his royal mercy towards him till he comes to the place of execution.'
Cally, a slave girl sentenced to death in Calcutta, was pardoned. One
can only hope she was still alive when the good news arrived.

Just occasionally the pardon arrived too late. Edward Woodbridge
had been sentenced to transportation. He got a free pardon, but the
ship had already left for the colonies with him on board. 'The mistake
arose on account of the man's agent not having sent for his pardon
from the office at the proper time. All that can be now done is to
send the pardon after him.' Civil service rules must be observed in
good time. On another occasion, someone muddled the papers and
the prisoner had 'unfortunately suffered' before the pardon arrived.[40]

Peter Donelly was found guilty of assault with intent to ravish (rape) and sentenced to a fine of 13s 4d, three months in Bridewell, and to stand in the pillory. He was let off the pillory, for which, in view of the probable reaction of the mob, he must have been thankful. Mary Prescott was sentenced to transportation for stealing a tea-kettle (probably silver). The judge who sentenced her commented that 'the prisoner had a very bad husband who had driven her into a way of pilfering; but a sister had promised to take care of her'. She was unconditionally pardoned.

The 24 people sentenced to death for riot in July 1767 were all reprieved and sent to the colonies for various terms, thus contributing to the confusion of statistics and showing that the eighteenth-century predilection for savage sentencing was much mitigated in practice. A last example from the fascinating ragbag of Home Office papers. Henry Ludlow, aged eleven years and eight months, a child of the Foundling Hospital, apprentice to John Brice of Islington, watchmaker, had been sentenced to seven years' transportation for stealing a silver spoon. He was sent to sea until he was 21, instead.

Petitions for a pardon did not come cheap. A young man convicted of robbery, for which the sentence was death, managed to get his sentence mitigated to transportation, but it cost his father £300, which ruined him.[41]

If the prisoner was tried and found guilty, and there was no pardon forthcoming, what happened next?

Execution

If he had been condemned to death, he was put into the condemned cell to await his trip to Tyburn. By tradition he tried to look his best on that occasion. On a Sunday afternoon, 'the friends of criminals under sentence of death in Newgate [are] presenting money to the turnkeys to ... take their last farewell and present them with white caps with black ribbons, prayer books, nosegays and oranges that they may make a decent appearance up Holborn' on the way to the gallows.[42] The death cell, which measured 9 feet by 6 feet, sometimes became so crowded with well-wishers that the prisoner had to appeal for a little peace. Fashionable ladies enjoyed the sensation of seeing a man so near to death, especially a handsome highwayman. Three thousand people called on McLean, a highwayman. Walpole remarked that 'I am almost single in not having seen him.' The gaolers must have made a fortune.

Occasionally, the execution took place near the site of the crime. Two rioters found guilty of murder in the weavers' protests were executed at Bethnal Green 'amid an innumerable concourse of spectators', who then went quietly back to work.[43]

Anatomising

The trouble, or one of the troubles, with capital punishment is that it does not deter. On the contrary, the thief may decide that he might as well be hung for a sheep as a lamb, and go further than he had originally intended. You can only die once. In 1752 the authorities thought of a new twist.

> Whereas the horrid crime of murder has of late been more frequently perpetrated than formerly, and particularly in or near the metropolis of this kingdom, contrary to the known humanity and natural genius of the British nation, and whereas it is thereby become necessary that some further terror and peculiar mark of infamy be added to the punishment of death ... be it enacted ... that all persons who shall be found guilty of wilful murder shall be executed according to law, ... [and] that the body of such murderer shall, if such conviction and execution shall be [in London], be immediately conveyed ... to the hall of the Surgeons Company and shall be dissected and anatomised by the said Surgeons...

Hanging in chains

'It shall be in the power of any such judge ... to appoint the body of any such criminal to be hung in chains ...' Monsieur Grosley, arriving from France in 1765, saw no highwaymen on his way to London except 'such as were hanging on gibbets at the roadside: there they dangle, dressed from head to foot, and with wigs upon their heads'.[44] These gruesome spectacles might last for years. The bodies were usually coated in tar to delay natural dissolution. It is understandable that the inhabitants of Smallbury Green petitioned against the body of a murderer being hung in chains on their village green, the site of his crime, and got it transferred to Hounslow Heath.[45]

Imprisonment

Although Samuel Johnson described life in gaol in glowing terms, it was only in contrast to life at sea: 'A ship is worse than a gaol. There is, in a gaol, better company, better conveniency of every kind; and a ship has the added disadvantage of being in danger.'[46] This was definitely one of Johnson's conversational squibs. Life in either was appalling, but a sailor did get some – too much? – of the fresh air lacking in prisons. People in prison died of the 'noisome stench', which in those days was thought to be the source of infection. Reformers were desperately trying to remedy this by installing wind-driven 'ventilators' in prisons and hospitals. It was unpleasant work. One man who caught fever from the foul air infected his family and they all died. The only remedies medically recommended were tobacco and 'a large dram'.[47]

Ventilators perhaps made life more bearable for the inmates, but they did nothing to clean the walls and floors, or help the inmates to clean themselves or their clothes. The eighteenth century has been called the century of typhus,[48] which flourished in those filthy conditions. It was the custom to collect from other prisons any prisoners awaiting trial, and hold them all in Newgate. In 1753 this meant crowding 300 people into two rooms 14 feet by 11 feet, and 7 feet high.

> It appeared afterwards that these places had not been cleaned for some years [a masterly euphemism for 'never'] ... The poisonous quality of the air was still [further] aggravated by the heat and closeness of the court, and by the perspirable matter of a great number of all sorts of people penned up for the most part of the day. The bench [of judges] consisted of six persons of whom four died, together with two or three of the council, one of the under sheriffs, several of the Middlesex jury ... to the number of above forty, without making allowance for those of the lower rank whose death may not have been heard of.[49]

It was not until eleven years later that *The Gentleman's Magazine* proudly reported that 'three cartloads of the most abominable filth' had been taken out of Newgate and it had been cleaned and washed with vinegar. The Old Bailey was scraped down and washed, and herbs were burned before each session,[50] so the judges, let alone those of the lower rank, were more comfortable.

There was a bewildering variety of prisons in London, which had been privatised by the Crown centuries ago. Gaolers and turnkeys made a good living out of them. Some were medieval, some ruinous, some small, some accommodated hundreds. Most, notwithstanding the various Gin Acts, had a tap room where the gaoler sold gin. Life in prison was what you made it. The gaolers had no duty to feed the prisoners. This was to some extent remedied by private charities – Nell Gwynn left some money to feed poor prisoners, for example – but failing that, and any private resources, a prisoner had to rely on 'what arises from the charity of passengers [passers-by] seldom amounting to more than five or six shillings a week, the greatest part of which is given to the beggar at the window for the day'.[51] These were the begging hands pushed out of the grating, or the begging box let down from the window on a piece of string. 'When a Magistrate commits a man to [gaol] for assault he does not know but he commits him there to starve.'

Sometimes official funds supplied bread, but no bedding,[52] sometimes the other way round. Certainly there was no allowance for clothes or washing. The gaoler could make a prisoner's life very uncomfortable indeed, by loading him with iron chains and manacles, unless the prisoner paid his way out of them. And yet these chains seem to have been inexplicably inefficient, in some cases. 'A notorious pickpocket was double-ironed: but less than three hours after his escape [from Bridewell] he sent back his irons in a handkerchief with a letter ... he was much obliged to the keeper for the use of them but now had no further occasion for them.'[53]

The pillory

This could involve anything from death by stoning to release with money. The publisher of number 45 of the *North Briton*, ill-advisedly sentenced to be pilloried during the Wilkes saga, was 'received by the acclamation of a prodigious concourse of people', who passed the hat round for him and raised 200 guineas.[54] Three old men were pilloried for perjury. 'Their tears and grey hairs drew compassion from the people and instead of being pelted money was collected for them.'[55] But mob feeling might veer the other way.

Whipping

'An old notorious gambler who has infested Moorfields for many years corrupting youth by gambling, being tied to a tree near the place where they toss up [a form of gambling] received 66 lashes on his bare back', the first of two instalments of his sentence.[56] More often the whipping was delivered as the prisoner walked, or staggered, a prescribed course, such as the woman who was whipped 'through Fleet Street to Temple Bar for decoying children from their parents and then putting out their eyes in order to beg with them'.[57]

Branding

A first offender who successfully pleaded benefit of clergy was often sentenced to be 'burnt in the hand' with a hot iron, in open court. Sometimes the court would suggest that the iron should not be too hot. A man who discovered his wife in the act of adultery with her lover, and killed him, would be found guilty of manslaughter, but 'the Court commonly orders the sentence of burning on the hand to be inflicted in the slightest manner'.[58]

Transportation

In a wide range of criminal offences, from murder to stealing goods worth more than 40s, the mandatory punishment was death. The judge could recommend any deserving case to the Crown, for the exercise of its prerogative of mercy. Between 1761 and 1765, for example, 567 such cases throughout England were referred to the Crown. In 415 cases the death sentence was commuted to transportation for 14 years. Sixty-one merited transportation for life, 18 for seven years, and two for 21 years.[59] After the Transportation Act of 1718 the judges could impose a sentence of transportation themselves in some cases, instead of recommending it to the monarch.[60] The public conscience was becoming uneasy at the appalling conditions of prisons, which produced no result except death and disease. Building decent prisons would be expensive. Shipping the wretched prisoners abroad to America, where the colonists were crying out for labour, should solve the problem. Out of sight, out of mind. So every April, when the winter was over and the Atlantic was passable, coffles[61] of prisoners would drag their way in chains through the streets of

London from Newgate, where they had been held for up to two months, to Blackfriars, to be loaded into stinking lighters. Of course if you had money you could avoid the coffle and take your own carriage, or a hackney coach, to Blackfriars, where you could agree with the ship's captain that he would for a certain sum make his own cabin available to you for the crossing. But these arrangements could come unstuck as soon as the ship sailed, the captain pocketing the bribe and the optimist finding himself below decks with the rest.

The prisoners were carried in lots of sixty or eighty at a time, chained in the hold, allowed on deck only rarely during the 6–8 week passage. Yet it was in the captain's interest to keep mortality as low as possible. It rarely exceeded 10 per cent. Some captains even outfitted their cargo with clean clothes. That certainly made them sell better. Sales began as soon as the ship docked. Slaves, who might have travelled on the same ship, might fetch up to £44, but of course their service would be for life and any children they had would be included. The average 'transport' was a single unskilled labourer aged between twenty and thirty, and available only for the duration of his sentence, so the contractor who had shipped him out would not realise much more than the £3 per head paid by the government, and perhaps £13 on sale, less expenses. Women, of whom there were always a few, were regarded as poor bargains. Their price would not exceed £10, and they were unlikely to be employed in domestic labour. As Benjamin Franklin said in 1759, 'What good mother would introduce thieves and criminals into the company of her children?'

As soon as the system of transportation was established, a movement in the opposite direction began. Although the penalty for returning was death, the risk was small, if you kept out of the public eye, and placated the Watch with occasional tips. Eighteenth-century record-keeping was chaotic; any prosecution would have to be brought by a private individual, who was unlikely to be motivated unless by some strong personal spite; and how could anyone prove that a man accused of being a 'returner' was the same man as had been sentenced in a different court, by a different judge?

The debates of reformers were cut short when the Colonists rebelled, in 1775. Australia provided a more satisfactory destination, a few years later.

General

The eighteenth century has a reputation for savage sentences. Were the sentences as bloodthirsty as their reputation? They seem so arbitrary to us. The chances of arresting the malefactor were slim, without a police force. If arrested, he might never stand trial. If he did, he stood almost a fifty-fifty chance of acquittal.[62] If he was accused of stealing goods worth over 40s, for which the penalty was death, the jury might well value the goods at just 39s in the face of lists of their value, even including cash of over £2. If he was sentenced to death, he might be pardoned.

It was a problem exercising many minds. But one suggestion was not followed: castration instead of execution, for men. And yet it seemed so appropriate. ' 'Tis an operation not without a suitable degree of pain.'[63]

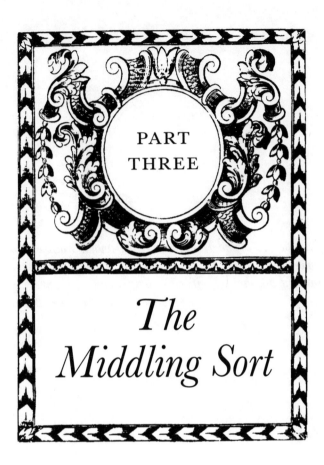

PART
THREE

*The
Middling Sort*

'Middle … a middle station in life, within reach of those conveniences which the lower orders of mankind must necessarily want, and yet without embarrassment of greatness.'

Rogers, quoted in Samuel Johnson, *Dictionary*

CHAPTER 16

Dentistry, Health and Medical Care

Dentistry

'Operators for the teeth' were changing into 'dentists' by the 1760s, leaving behind their mountebank status and writing treatises *On the Disorders of the Teeth and Gums*.[1] Physicians still felt they were a lower form of life than doctors, but Samuel Darkin could advertise himself as 'Surgeon Dentist to his Majesty. Families attended by the year.'[2] Several women combined dentistry with other skills, such as Mme Silvie who made and fitted artificial teeth. 'Those who don't chuse to make their grievances known by asking for the Artificial Teeth-maker may ask for the Gold Snuff-box and Tweezer-case Maker.'[3]

Toothpaste

Dentifrices were marketed with the usual hype. As well as promising a spectacular smile, they often undertook to fasten in loose teeth. Pyorrhoea and scurvy were rampant. Both would loosen teeth,[4] and it would be surprising if toothpaste could firm them up again. Most dentifrices on the market did more harm than good, by destroying the enamel. The leading French dentist Fauchard recommended one's own urine for cleaning one's teeth: always handy. Another cheap way of cleaning the teeth was to bash the end of a wooden skewer, like bashing the ends of rose stems before putting them in water. 'You must clean your teeth with this brush alone, without any powder whatever; and once in a fortnight, not oftener, dip your skewer brush into a few grains of gunpowder ... this will remove every blemish and give your teeth an inconceivable whiteness' (then rinse well, to get the splinters out …).[5] Perhaps the bristle toothbrushes on the market were more comfortable.

Delicate gold-handled toothbrushes, sometimes with replaceable heads, were included in the cases of toilet instruments for the rich. Horace Walpole put his faith in alum. Periodically dissolving a lump in his mouth had, he thought, kept his teeth strong, even at 52, but must have tasted horrid.[6] Toothpicks made of quills were the eight-eenth-century dental floss, except that unlike floss they could be boxed in delicious little jewelled containers. Lord Chesterfield, vainly trying to make his loutish bastard into a polished gentleman, told him:

> A dirty mouth … infallibly causes the decay, as well as the intolerable pain of the teeth, and it is very offensive to his acquaintance for it will most inevitably stink. I insist therefore that you wash your teeth the first thing you do every morning, with a soft sponge and warm water, for four or five minutes, then wash your mouth five or six times … I do insist upon you never using those sticks … or any hard substance whatsoever, which always rubs away the gums and destroys the varnish of the teeth.[7]

Decay

Nearly everyone had carious teeth, even small children.[8] Although sugar was known to cause it, most people, including some dentists,[9] still believed in the tooth worm, which is certainly how an aching tooth feels. A quack excavating a hole proved his skill by putting tiny curls of paper under his nails, which he shed in the patient's mouth. The patient spat out the tiny bloody objects: hey presto, dead tooth worms. The decayed part of the tooth was scraped away with scalpels and files. Any exposed nerve was cauterised with a red-hot wire, before the cavity was filled with lead (imagine the taste), pitch (ditto), beeswax (pointless) or gold (expensive).[10]

Extraction

The fearsome instruments designed to extract teeth usually wrenched them out sideways, once they had been loosened by careful ham-mering. Pulling perpendicularly without damaging the surrounding teeth and gum seems to have been beyond an eighteenth-century dentist, even when he flexed his muscles, put the patient on the floor, and took his – the patient's – head between his – the dentist's – knees.[11]

Transplanting

John Hunter, whose research and skill made dentistry respectable for the first time, endorsed the established practice of transplanting teeth. The chances of success were higher if the tooth came straight from one mouth to the other. It had to be roughly the same size and shape, so several might have to be extracted from the waiting queue of penniless adolescents and tried for size. It was their front teeth they were selling, because only single-rooted front teeth could be transplanted. Once a reasonable match was found, it was pushed into the socket and fixed there by silver wire or silk thread, and with any luck it became attached in its new home. Meanwhile the poor bloody-mouthed donors were slightly richer. Sometimes teeth from cadavers were used, but not surprisingly they didn't take.

False teeth

False teeth could be ordered by post. Mrs Purefoy, living in Buckinghamshire, sent her London 'operator for the teeth' a piece of wood showing where her teeth were, presumably after she had bitten it, and a piece of tape marked with the length of her gums. The teeth she got had to be adjusted only once. They cost her £3 4s.[12] They were probably only a lower set, which stayed in by gravity. An upper denture was made as a curved strip of teeth, not covering the palate, and it tended to slip sideways or down. Teeth 'set in so firm as to eat with them ... not to be taken out at night but may be worn years together, yet they are so fitted that they may be taken out and put in by the person that wears them at pleasure, and are an Ornament to the mouth and greatly help the speech' were an ad-man's dream,[13] unlikely to be true. One way to make them stay in was to connect the upper and lower dentures together by springs at the back of the mouth. The snag was that the springs were so strong that, once your mouth was open, you had to clench your muscles to get it to shut again, which must have looked very curious in company.

The range of material was wide: mother of pearl, silver, enamelled copper, hippopotamus and walrus teeth, elephant ivory, the teeth and bones of oxen, human teeth. Walrus and human teeth discoloured less than the others. Lord Hervey sported lovely agate teeth made for him on his tour to Italy.[14]

Health

'Health: freedom from bodily pain or sickness': Dr Johnson's *Dictionary*.

Expectation of life

The length of the average life was beginning to worry the establishment of the time, which believed that the size of a nation's population was an index of its prosperity in peace and of its ability to trounce other nations in war. Gin drinking by the poor was deplored by the rich because it produced sickly children, or prevented their birth altogether, hence limiting the supply of cannon-fodder. At the other end of the scale, those who read *The Gentleman's Magazine* might be considering life assurance, based on actuarial estimates of life expectancy.

Accurate statistics were lacking. Estimates have been compiled by modern demographers, applying sophisticated modern techniques to imperfect contemporary records, but expectation of life at birth is a notoriously tricky concept. Still, it provides a comparison between the eighteenth century and now. The latest figures available (1995–7) are 74.6 years for men, 79.7 for women. For 1751 the figure for both men and women in England and Wales has been estimated at 36.6 years,[15] but in smoky, crowded, disease-ridden London the figure was probably much lower, perhaps in the mid-twenties.[16]

This does not mean that most people died before their twenty-fifth birthday. It may be helpful to imagine a London woman in a marathon. The race begins at birth. The first stage is strewn with obstacles: between 50 and 60 per cent of London-born children died before their tenth birthday, especially under two, in the period we are looking at. The next difficult stretch comes at adolescence, when crowds of young people come up from the country to look for jobs. They have not acquired the degree of immunity to London germs that to some extent protected London-born survivors of the same age. Many of them fall by the wayside. Once our runner is into her stride, she can look forward to an easier course, with occasional hurdles during child-bearing years and a slight upward slope towards the end. The track behind her, especially the early part, is by now littered with those who were not so lucky. The successful runner can keep going long after 30, even into what we would think of as old age, because she is tough. She has overcome the crises that dealt mortal blows to so many of those who set out with her.

The main source of information was the monthly Bills of Mortality compiled by parish clerks from information provided by the Searchers. They were parish employees, usually old women, who inspected every dead body and diagnosed the cause of death. They seem to have had a form listing the usual causes. They were fond of the general term 'convulsions'. There was a space for 'bitten by a mad dog', although its statistical importance was low. People still died of lethargy and grief. By the eighteenth century, informed opinion agreed that the Bills were hopelessly inaccurate and inadequate, but nothing better was evolved, and one sinister figure was indisputable: the number of christenings in London was always exceeded by the number of burials.[17]

Midwives and accoucheurs

Childbirth has always been a bloody and painful business. Dr Smellie[18] revolutionised obstetric practice, and persuaded midwives to move over and give the new 'man-midwives' or *accoucheurs* space for difficult births, since only they could use forceps. One marked difference between then and now is Dr Smellie's insistence on complete bedrest for four or five days, even after a normal delivery. This could go as far as 'covering the floors and stairs with carpets and cloths, oiling the hinges of the doors, silencing the bells, tying up the knockers, and in noisy streets strewing the pavements with straw'. Anyone who has tried to sleep in a busy ward will relish that thought, even though the bedrest had to be accompanied by 'a constant breathing sweat'. This, with maternal breast feeding, should ward off the fever that all too often followed childbirth, after perhaps four days when all seemed to be going well. If the mother could not feed the baby, a wet-nurse must be found, who should have all the usual ideal qualities of any servant, with the added criterion that 'red haired women are commonly objected to'.

Dr Smellie's ideal doctor 'ought to be endued with a natural sagacity, resolution and prudence, together with that humanity which ... never fails of being agreeable to the distressed patient ... he will assist the poor as well as the rich, behaving always with charity and compassion'. One way of 'being agreeable to the distressed patient' appealed to me. If the mother 'and her assistants' – in other words, her friends gathered round to give her moral support – are 'clamorous' that she should be given medication, first try 'argument and gentle persuasion', but if they still insist, give her 'some innocent Placemus to beguile the time and please her imagination', which demonstrates the good doctor's knowledge of human nature, even if his Latin was a bit shaky.

A new-born baby's first achievement is to breathe for itself. Usually it manages this by letting out a cry, but if not it must be 'moved, shaken, *whipt* [my italics]: the head, temples, and breast rubbed with spirits, garlic, onions or mustard applied to the mouth and nose', and if none of these work, try blowing into the baby's mouth 'so as to expand the lungs' – a very sensible idea.

Infancy

According to Dr Smellie, a new-born baby should be washed in water and dressed. Its clothes should be warm and 'easy' – no more than a cap, a shirt, a waistcoat, a flannel skirt or petticoat tied rather than pinned, and a flannel gown instead of two or more blankets, 'while the head is accommodated with another cap adorned with as much finery as the tire-woman shall think proper to bestow'.

Opinion was divided on the best way to help a teething baby. One method was to pierce the gums with anything handy, such as a sharp-edged coin or a specially sharpened thimble, or a needle. The implement preferred by a dental practitioner was a surgical lancet used 'slightly and carefully',[19] preferably, one infers, by him, for a fee. 'Bleeding at the jugular will also be necessary if the child is strong':[20] how did any of them survive?

Diseases of children

There was a crisis of mortality when the baby was weaned on to solid food, prepared from germ-laden water and milk and polluted bread, in unhygienic kitchens. Infantile diarrhoea was a significant factor in 'Infancy' as a cause of death. Infants' food in some prosperous households tended to be robust. A book on dentition[21] quotes a one-year-old who had been putting away half a 'handsome chicken' daily, with tea and bread and butter, and a baby of seventeen months fed on toast and ale.

Rickets could affect babies between nine and twenty-four months old.[22] According to the writer of the article in the *Encyclopedia Britannica*, they should be treated with a light diet, well-boiled beer, and 'with being carried about in the arms and often shook, swung, and put in motion'. The child should drink four ounces of 'generous French red wine' daily. Another source[23] advised that rickets could be cured by bandaging the deformed limbs and 'a clear warm air'. Rickets is caused by a vitamin deficiency arising from the combination of an inadequate diet and lack of sunlight. Perhaps a 'clear' (outside?) air might have helped. In severe cases, whalebone or tin splints were fitted, and rubbing the affected parts with Oil of Snails should help. Another recipe added earthworms.

That these heroic measures did not always work emerges from Francis Place's autobiography.[24] Looking back to his childhood in the 1770s, he remembered how 'the number of children who had "cheese-cutters", that is with the shin-bone bowed out [with rickets] ... was formerly so great that if an estimate were made now [1824] it would not be believed'. An estimate made in 1773, when living conditions were marginally better than mid-century, reckoned that 'there must be very near 20,000 children in London and Westminster and their suburbs, ill at this moment of the hectic fever attended with tun-bellies, swelled wrists and ankles or crooked limbs'.[25] This was either rickets or kwashiorkor, a disease of malnutrition nowadays seen in Oxfam pictures of pot-bellied starving African children. Rickets rarely kills, but it can cause deformities such as a narrow pelvis which is life-threatening if a girl survives and becomes pregnant.

The infant had next to surmount smallpox, which especially afflicted children between three months and five years old,[26] and accounted for half the deaths in the 5–9-year group. The Searchers were probably fairly reliable on smallpox, from years of seeing its catastrophic symptoms. In 1747 Dr Mead estimated that 'scarce one in a thousand escaped [it]'.[27] One might have expected a steady decrease as the advantages of inoculation became widely known after about 1750, but this does not seem to have happened.

The Gentleman's Magazine regularly carried items on inoculation. In March 1752 the Bishop of Worcester was able to tell the Governors of the Smallpox Hospital that only three out of 1,500 patients inoculated had died. In March 1766, 'their Royal Highnesses the

Prince of Wales and the Bishop of Osnaburg [his younger brother] were inoculated for the smallpox by Pennel Hawkins, Esquire, surgeon extraordinary to His Majesty ... in the presence of the King and Queen, three physicians and another surgeon',[28] and in December 1768 the Princess Royal and her brother Prince William were done: the royal seal of approval. His Majesty's Physicians and Surgeons called Mr Sutton's method 'a great success'. He had inoculated 40,000 people without, *he said*, losing one. 'The art seems to be carried to a very great perfection.'[29] Yet this downward trend was not reflected in the Bills of Mortality. The figures for the period 1746 to 1772 vary between a low (1751) of 998 and a peak (1772) of 3,992, usually running between two and three thousand.

Consumption

Eliza Smith advised treatment with snails boiled in milk, a quarter of a pint to an ounce of snails, or a 'diet drink' of thirteen different ingredients including 'live woodlice bruised' and boiled in small ale.[30] The popularity of snails, particularly in treating chest complaints, can be explained only by the fact that it had always been so. I have not, despite wide research, found any other reason. John Wesley recommended cold baths.[31] According to the Searchers' figures in the Bills, the annual toll from tuberculosis ran at roughly 4,000 to 4,500. Medical opinion of the time suggested that the true figure was only a third of this,[32] and complained that the Searchers' figures would ruin the tourist trade since they gave the impression that consumption was rife in England[33] – which it probably was.

Fevers

A London-born child who had survived into adolescence had acquired a wide spectrum of immunity.[34] But the crowds of young people heading for London from the provinces to see the fabled sights and find jobs had no such immunity, and went down like flies. The Bills of Mortality did not differentiate between the various fevers in terms that a modern physician would recognise. Jail fever (typhus) could, as we have seen, escape from the dock and decimate the respectable people in court, and their families to whom they returned when the trying day was over. Diphtheria, scarlet fever, whooping cough, measles and mumps could be treated only with tender loving care.

There seem to have been epidemics of mumps in 1747 and 1748.[35]

Gout

Gout was 'the English Malady' according to Dr Cheyne. The poor were so fortunate as never to suffer from it; 'only the Rich, the Lazy, the Luxurious and the Inactive'.[36] It was 'the distemper of a gentleman whereas the rheumatism is the distemper of a Hackney coachman', according to that arch snob Lord Chesterfield.[37]

It may have meant a different set of symptoms from those we associate with gout. 'Flying gout' could attack any part of the body. It seems to have been a cover-all word for acute localised pain. It could be avoided by 'that plain diet which is most agreeable to the Purity and Simplicity of uncorrupted Nature', which sounds about as alluring as cold tapioca, but was endorsed by Dr Cadogan forty years later: 'the humours of the gout, in his opinion, are nothing more than the daily accumulation of indigestion'.[38] No one walked any more, 'Coaches are improved with springs, Horses are taught to pace and amble, Chairmen to wriggle and swim along', so that the rich never got a good proper shake-up. Dr Cheyne prescribed a light diet, exercise, and a change of air. Riding in a chaise or chariot counted as exercise – which shows how even the most improved vehicles bumped you about – or 'games [sic] such as hunting, shooting, bowls, billiards, shuttlecock [badminton] and the like or even the flesh-brush' (the kind of massage brush recommended today by beauticians: John Wesley recommended it too),[39] and you should take up a 'hobby-horse'.

The only comfort in all this admirable and familiar advice is Dr Cheyne's idea of teetotalism. To cure himself, he lived on milk and white meats, 'and *only* [my italics] a pint of wine a day'. 'Immoderate venery' should be avoided, although the same authority recommended wine,[40] so it was hard to know what to do for the best. Certainly the agonising pain of a gouty foot would preclude active woman-chasing. The only good thing to be said for gout was that it was thought to protect you from other diseases.

Hernias

Trusses were deeply interesting to an eighteenth-century man who had suffered a hernia, perhaps from excessive physical work such as casual labouring, or even rearranging his statues in his new house. Trusses could be bought by post, and were frequently advertised. 'The widow Hawkins continues to make steel trusses ... for ruptures [hernias] in men women and children.'[41] A country gentleman ordered 'dimmothy' (a kind of stout cotton) trusses for himself six at a time.[42] Dr Percival Potts's *Treatise on Ruptures* came out in 1756, written while he himself was making medical history by letting the compound fracture of his tibia set, instead of having his leg amputated as his medical colleagues advised.[43]

Venereal disease

Gonorrhoea and syphilis had not yet been differentiated. James Boswell managed to catch gonorrhoea several times over, from London prostitutes, no matter how careful he was in his choice of partner and in tying on to his penis a prophylactic sheath. He was philosophical about it, although he resented the surgeon's bill for 5 guineas a time.[44]

Deaths from 'the French Pox' featured regularly in the Bills of Mortality, but in such small numbers that one can deduce that most casualties from this ignoble cause had been transmogrified into martyrs to some more respectable disease, by a present to the Searchers. Treatment for the early stages of syphilis, which seemed innocuous – genital ulcers followed by a general rash and feeling of malaise – might appear to eradicate the disease, but it could lie dormant for as long as twenty years, or resurface after two, with inflammations that destroyed bones and joints and soft tissue such as the nose, and the prospect of paralysis, madness and a hideous death.

There was a theory that a man could get rid of venereal disease by having intercourse with a small child, even a baby, to whom the infection would be transferred, leaving the initiator disease-free. This accounted for some of the baby patients in the Lock hospitals. For a woman, getting pregnant might have the same effect. But 'it is a very idle and wicked Thing ... for women to trust to their delivery in Hopes that by that means alone they may be free of any venereal disease ... an infant born with this Distemper on it is seldom relieved afterwards but makes the case more difficult with regard to themselves'.[45] If for some reason no child or child-getter was available, or the patient could not contemplate anything so horrible, the mercury treatment had to be undergone.

Mercury had been used for many centuries to treat skin lesions in leprosy and scabies. When syphilis first struck, in Italy in the fifteenth century,[46] the Italians naturally turned to mercury[47] to treat the genital ulcers that are its first symptom. The treatment worked, in some cases, and was used up to the last war. But the eighteenth century tended to overdo the dosage. While the disease destroyed the soft tissues of the nose[48] and mouth so that the cheeks fell in and the teeth dropped out, the mercury treatment affected all the glands, particularly the salivary glands, which produced copious black saliva. This was known as 'salivation'. The net result was – unattractive.

Some authorities recognised that the treatment must stop short of that stage.[49] But for others the salivation itself was the goal to aim at: that is, an advanced stage of mercury poisoning. 'When the salivation is thus begun your only business is to encourage your patient cheerfully to go on.'[50] An army doctor who treated soldiers in a camp 'where we had a great number of venereal cases with little accommodation for salivating' published an account in the medical press[51] of a soldier who had been 'put into a salivation for about a fortnight, none of the symptoms disappearing', and concluded that 'a salivation, carried to the greatest height, is still but an uncertain remedy'. Yet five years later he proudly reported complete success with all his patients, except one who managed to go to a 'common woman' during the course, and another who 'frequently contrived to get drunk while he was in the hospital'.[52] One can but sympathise.

Mercury was used for all kinds of ailments as well as venereal disease. The more eighteenth-century medical books I read, the more I am astonished by the liberal recourse to ingredients either known to be potentially fatal or not known to do any good at all. With mercury, the secret seems to have been to take it neat. It was given to children with worms, apparently in the hope of mechanically dislodging the worms in its passage through the gut. Water boiled with mercury was thought to be effective against worms, and was perhaps easier to swallow than the mercury itself. During the panic about bovine distemper, tea-drinkers were advised to boil the water with mercury. Could you pour off the mercury before drinking the tea? John Wesley recommended neat mercury for 'the Iliac Passion' (nervous colic) – 'ounce by ounce, a pound or a pound and a half'.[53] Alternatively, the patient could 'hold a live puppy consistently on the belly', which would be comfortingly warm, at least.[54] For Twisting of the Guts swallow one, two or *three pounds* of quicksilver in water, which again was presumably expected to have a beneficial mechanical effect, but imagine, if you can, the end result.[55] A barium meal is bad enough. The toxicity came from compounds of mercury, such as mercurous chloride, which as calomel crops up everywhere but was not too dangerous, and mercuric chloride, known as corrosive sublimate, which was highly toxic, but good for killing bugs, hence easily available.[56]

Respiratory diseases

The label 'the English malady' has been applied to suicide, flagellation and, as we have seen, gout, but it most accurately, perhaps, describes bronchitis. In the smoky, foggy atmosphere of London, bronchitis and related diseases have always flourished.[57] Pneumonia would usually be fatal. Coughs and colds proliferated.

Insanity

Private madhouses were a profitable line. They were the ideal middle-class way, short of murder, of disposing of unwanted people, especially wives. The approved treatment sounds quite enough to send anyone mad – 'constant but partial discharge of the fluids from the neck and head by perpetual blisters' ... 'all sorts of tolerable irritation', and if none of these worked, 'the concussive force of the cold bath'.[58] But the cases that hit the headlines amounted to imprisonment, not treatment. They became so scandalous that by 1763 legislation to control them was demanded,[59] and there was a House of Commons inquiry at which both of the currently eminent specialists in mental disease gave evidence. Dr Battie said that one husband had 'frankly considered the [mad]house as a kind of bridewell or house of correction'[60] to which he could consign his wife whenever she was troublesome.

Nothing seems to have improved after the inquiry. In 1769 'a gentleman near Whitehall by the assistance of four ruffians forced his lady into a Hackney coach and ordered the coachman to drive her to a private madhouse and there to be confined'.[61] In 1772 a woman was 'decoyed to a madhouse in Bethnal Green', and shut into 'a little apartment the stench of which was intolerable, [she was] chained and handcuffed'. After two days her husband said he was sorry and took her home. She had the courage to try to rescue a fellow-inmate, no more mad than she was. She got a writ of *habeas corpus*, but 'the people at the house refused to send the poor wretch, on which the Justice himself went and insisted on seeing her ... he declared he would not again have done so for £5,000, the place was so intolerably nasty'. She had been there nearly two years.[62]

It was not only women who found themselves immured and helpless. In 1763 a young man was robbed of 'his effects, which were considerable' and shut up in a private madhouse without any means of communicating with the outside world. After thirteen months, 'by getting hold of some Morello cherries and a tooth pick he found means to let his case be known to an acquaintance, who soon procured his liberty',[63] but not, presumably, his effects.

Advice books

Eliza Smith died in 1732, but her *Compleat Housewife or Accomplish'd Gentlewoman's Companion*,[64] principally a cookery book but containing 'above three hundred family receipts of medicines', was still going strong in 1758. 'As to the receipts for Medicines, Salves, Ointments, ... they are generally Family Receipts ... of such Efficacy ... that they have cured when all other Means have failed.' There were no ante-natal clinics in those days, so it is interesting to see Eliza Smith recommending a draught 'to procure easy labour', to be taken twice a day 'six weeks before the time', and another 'to prevent miscarrying'.[65]

The Ladies Dispensatory, or Every Woman Her Own Physician was first published anonymously in 1739. Pregnancy and labour, according to this author, sound rather jolly. The woman should avoid 'every thing that might anyway prove offensive' during pregnancy, but she may 'drink a little wine to comfort her stomach' and 'particular Regard must be had to gratify her desires'. If she gets a bad back – and what pregnant woman doesn't? – 'rest in this case ought to be indulged'. During labour 'wine occasionally diluted with water may be used for common drink for some time before and after delivery. It is customary in the very Hour to administer a Glass of some cordial water [such as gin?] between whiles' and 'when the whole affair is over ... a proper cordial or a glass of hot wine ought instantly to be given her'. I have to admit that this round was not gin, but six spoonfuls of a herbal mixture including 'liquid laudanum', which, after the midwife had put her hand up the poor woman's vagina on several occasions, and gone in for the usual pulling and pushing, her patient must have badly needed.

If labour lasted longer than *four or five days* and none of the midwife's pet methods, such as changes of posture or dilating the vagina with her hand, had worked, an 'able and skilled Operator' – perhaps one of Dr Smellie's graduates – would have to be called in to apply 'the Instrumental Method of Delivery' (i.e. forceps), which midwives did not use. Between three and six days after delivery, the mother might be feverish, 'but this fever is seldom dangerous', said Eliza Smith reassuringly, if inaccurately.

Once the baby is delivered, he should, according to Eliza Smith, be washed in small beer and butter, and ' 'tis a usual thing to give him a little fresh butter and sugar' to clear his breathing and 'purge off excrementitious matter from the Bowels, but he should not have brandy, geneva, aniseed water or any of the like fiery cordials'.[66] Certainly not. Newborn babies being very weak, however, 'a little warm wine should be poured down the throat or squirted up the nostrils'. Yet a modern echo of cot death comes from the same author's pages. The baby 'should lie with his head comfortably raised, that the Phlegm ... may the readier be discharged, and suffocation prevented. The sudden deaths of young children ... are very often owing to a neglect of this Caution.' The anonymous author of *The Ladies Dispensatory* also supported breast feeding. 'Can you think that nature should have furnished women with those two beautiful excrescences for ornament alone?' Surely the author was a man, but not Dr Smellie, for this was not his style at all.

The Ladies Dispensatory also dealt with child care. For a restless or teething child, and if your household was not one where gin was the obvious remedy for everything, try fifteen drops of that invaluable Liquid Laudanum.

The eighteenth century seems to have had a fixation about masturbation.[67] *The Ladies Dispensatory* was exceedingly worried by this 'secret vice'. Women had been known, it said, to refuse advantageous Matches, 'because they are capable of pleasuring themselves ... and keeping up a show of chastity'. This seems a curiously limited view of matrimony. Masturbation ruined the complexion, could cause madness, sterility and frigidity, and, confusingly, gave women at the same time an 'insatiable appetite of venery'. This being so, it is a little surprising to find that the recommended antidote contained a hefty proportion of cantharides, an aphrodisiac.

Household remedies

Old ways die hard, and folk medicine was still relied on in pregnancy and indeed in any other medical context. Often it would be handed on from woman to woman, or written down in the book kept in many households for cookery and useful tips.[68] They included some remarkable ingredients, such as powdered roast mouse (good for incontinence), cow dung fried in butter (for a sore breast), and peacock dung with black snails (consumption). Sometimes the writer relied on magic, although she may not have recognised it when she saw it. But why else insist, in a remedy for rickets, that the blood from the ear of an unfortunate child who has endured blood letting in its ear, 'when the moon is nine days old', should be wiped away with 'a handful of *black* wool from a living sheep's ears', or that to make Calves Pluck water for consumption you should take the lungs of a *red bull calf*, with the usual snails?

Patent medicines

If you could find nothing useful in a book, you could have a look at the newspapers, and the handbills on every street corner. The eighteenth century was the golden age of patent medicines. Daffy's Elixir, 9d a bottle, and 'the original Godfrey's well known cordial for children, 6d'[69] had been going strong since the last century. In 1748 *The Gentleman's Magazine* published a list of over 200 'nostrums' being sold over the counter, including a 'confect for impotency' at 5s a pot, a girdle for the itch at 1s, Dr Belloste's pills for smallpox at 2s 6d a box, and many pills and 'liquors' for the Pox.[70] Between 1751 and 1768, 285 new patents were registered. Of these, 27, nearly 10 per cent, were medicinal.

Most of the specifications in the Patent Office are splendidly evocative. Joseph Fraunches's 'female strengthening pill' contained the best rhubarb, and salt of vipers. It also came in liquid form as an Elixir, for 1s 6d a bottle.[71] George West's Pectoral Elixir began with 4 gallons each of garden snails and millipedes, 'bruised to a perfect paste', as well as dozens of other ingredients. James Collett's Oleum Vitae or Ladies' Nervous and Cordial Drops for Lowness of Spirits were made of distilled river water and the best Madeira wine, which surely made the ladies more cheerful. William Lowther's Medicinal Compound included *pulvis humani cranum* (powdered human skull). It was good for epilepsy, worms, loss of memory and retention of urine, and could be given to month-old babies. A sufferer from gout who had been advised to lessen his alcohol intake could safely rely on Collett's medicine, consisting of 7 gallons of Madeira, 5 gallons of French brandy, various herbs, and 'volatile salt of millipedes': dosage unspecified. Maredant's Drops were good for scurvy, leprosy and evil (the King's Evil: that is, scrofula, a tuberculous infection of the neck glands). They contained mercury sublimate, but the proportion and the dosage are not specified.

Pre-eminently, there were remedies for venereal disease. Walter Leake's Restorative Pills contained calomel, antimony and steel. A Frenchman – could he be assumed to be an expert on the French Pox? – Coy la Blache patented his Royal Military Drops, for venereal diseases, the King's Evil 'and all scrophulous distempers'. They included mercury and that widespread element *acqua pluvialis*. Thomas Jackson promised an immediate cure with his Venereal Lotion, containing sublimate of mercury and 'sal vitrioli' (hydrochloric acid). But the practitioner who cornered the pox market was Dr Rock. His Cathartic Electuary would cure 'the most inveterate degree ... without impairing the constitution'. It had fourteen ingredients, including rhubarb and salt of vipers, and mercury, and cost 6s a bottle – a serious amount in those days.[72] He sold his magic pills and potions in person from a cart in Covent Garden, as well as advertising in the press.[73] His 'original Jesuit Drops for the cure of all stages of the secret disease' – and in the context this was the French Pox, not masturbation – cost 2s or 4s a bottle.[74] (Better take the large size – you never know when you might need it.)

Dr Marten's famous Chymical Drops were the Viagra of the time. After one teaspoonful night and morning, 'men have been made so fit for the marriage bed that their effects that way have been wondered at ... as thousands of people *many of them of the first rank* [my italics] can testify'.[75]

Dr Dominicetti's 'machines'[76] could fumigate each body part – legs, arms, hands, feet, the neck, the head, the penis – giving it the benefit of 'vaporous effluvium' in a steam bath or baking it in dry heat, 'to cure and preserve men women and children'. For once we have feedback on this patent, in a discussion recorded by Boswell in 1769.[77]

Dominicetti being mentioned, [Dr Johnson] would not allow him any merit. 'There is nothing in all this boasted system. No, Sir; medicated baths can be no better than warm water: their only effect can be that of tepid moisture.' One of the company took the other side, maintaining that medicines of various sorts ... are introduced into the human frame by the medium of the pores; and therefore when warm water is impregnated with salutiferous substances it may produce great effects as a bath ... Johnson ... talking for victory [and who was not overfond of baths himself] ... turned to the gentleman: 'Well, Sir, go to Dominicetti, and get thyself fumigated; but be sure that the steam be directed to thy head, for that is the peccant [ailing] part.' This produced a triumphant roar of laughter from the motley assembly...

I must say I don't find it particularly funny, but then I would not have approved of Johnson's manners anyway, and I deplore Boswell's style.

Quack doctors

'Physic [is] a prostituted trade to gull people out of their Wealth and Health ... Women, Farriers, Mountebanks and such like Sham Pretenders ... vend about town their infallible Specifics ... doing what is altogether impossible to be done by any single medicine.'[78] This diatribe came from perhaps a surprising source – an almanac written by a licensed physician and surgeon of, he says, twenty or thirty years' experience. He goes on blandly to recommend his own medicine for rickets, which 'also cures wens and all scrophulous tumours without cutting', which seems a fairly tall order, if not 'altogether impossible'.

Perhaps the quack doctor most known to us is Dr Misaubin, in plate three of Hogarth's *Marriage à la Mode*. Hogarth made the engraving in 1745, by when Misaubin had been dead more than ten years, but his wife, the formidable figure in the picture, advertised that she 'continues to sell his famous anti-venereal pills at her house in St Martin's Lane',[79] and the trade was still going strong years after her death in 1749. The message in Hogarth's picture was that the famous anti-venereal pills had not worked.

Electricity

Electricity, like most things, was known to the Greeks, but its medical potential had not been appreciated until the eighteenth century.[80]

After Stephen Gray, a master at Charterhouse, had electrified a boy (a pupil? – we are not told) in 1730, the idea seems to have occurred to academic circles all over Europe. By 1745 or so, the Leiden accumulator jar made things easier by doing away with the metre-long glass tube used till then.

Electricity could certainly do some amazing things. If you got a regiment of soldiers, or a community of monks, all holding on to an iron chain a mile long, and put an electric charge into one end, they would all fall over like a set of dominoes: *magnifique* (it happened in France), *mais* – where did it get you? More to the point were reports that it could cure paralysis and 'palsey',[81] gout and haemorrhoids,[82] which must have been good news for those who were still treating their piles with leeches. By 1753 it had cured epilepsy and a stroke.[83] John Wesley, who prided himself on his self-taught medical expertise, thought highly of it, and 'ordered several persons to be electrified who were ill of various disorders, some of whom found an immediate, some a gradual cure. From this I ... appointed an hour in every day wherein any that desired it might try the virtue of this surprising medicine.' So many people desired to try its virtue that he had to open three clinics, and by 1756 'hundreds, perhaps thousands, have received unspeakable good' from it.[84] By 1763 the quack doctors were using it, no doubt to dramatic effect,[85] but Wesley held to his view that 'it is a thousand medicines in one, in particular that it is the most efficacious medicine in nervous disorders of every kind which has ever yet been discovered'.[86] The orthodox medical world was soon investing in it. The Middlesex Hospital bought a 'machine' in 1767.

Bloodletting and cupping

The ancient Greek idea of the four humours, which had to be 'balanced' for a healthy life, was being discredited in progressive medical circles, but it still hung about in the lay world. It seems to have been generally accepted that to lose some blood would almost always be a good thing. Some people had it done as a matter of routine, although Samuel Johnson, whose doctorate was in letters, but who was 'a great dabbler in physic, disapproved of periodical bleeding'.[87] Cupping involved upending small heated cups on to the patient's skin, usually on his back. The vacuum formed as they cooled raised blisters which were pricked and carefully kept open so that the serum in them could be periodically drawn off. John Rigg, Cupper, traded at

the hummums [Turkish baths] in the Little Piazza Covent Garden, with a back door from Charles Street, where GENTLEMEN only may be always accommodated (if not full) in the best and neatest manner with Lodging, Sweating, Bathing or Cupping, and with the utmost decorum as has always been kept and preserved for near an hundred years. Likewise Ladies are permitted only to Sweating, Bathing and Cupping, with great Care and proper attendance. NB Gentlemen or Ladies who desire to be cupped at their own houses either in Town or Country shall be waited on. There is likewise a good cold bath.[88]

Qualified practitioners

'As it is now twilight, reputable young fellows, [such] as students in the law ... who have been unhappily scarred in the wars of Venus are repairing to their several Quack Doctors and Surgeons' pupils to get a safe, easy and speedy cure.'[89] The medical hierarchy just recognised the existence of surgeons' pupils, who were trusted to do elementary procedures in hospitals. This is an interesting sidelight on their more profitable private practice. Those patients who had no reason to skulk in the twilight could go to them for other complaints, or the local apothecary. In 1747 *The London Evening Post* carried an advertisement for 'a journeyman apothecary ... capable of ... directing for sick people as may be occasionally required of him'.[90]

Dr Mead, the leader of the medical profession, was reputed to make an income of £12,000 a year. Physicians called on their patients only if the patients were rich enough. Clinics had not yet been invented. Physicians had a reputation for prescribing very small amounts on each visit, so as to necessitate a further call – and a further fee. Once you had called in a physician, you could not avoid his fees by going to a cheaper colleague, or to an apothecary. You were the physician's patient until you no longer needed his professional skill, one way or another.

The scope for major surgery was limited to 'cutting for the stone' (lithotomy: removing stones or gravel from the bladder), which seems, to judge from the number of patent medicines guaranteed to cure it, to have been still as great a worry as in the previous century when Samuel Pepys survived his 'stone-cutting' operation. Miscellaneous sub-cutaneous lumps and bumps could be dealt with. Surgeons would make house visits, 'laying plaisters on sore breasts, broken shins and other maimed parts'[91] Mastectomy for cancer was undertaken. But apart from very rare Caesarean sections, no surgeon would open the chest or abdomen.

There were no anaesthetics. The patient might be given a small dose of opium, 'one of the most noble remedies in the world. But ... medicines sometimes prove poisonous. Those who take a moderate dose of opium are commonly so transported with the pleasing sense it induces that they are, as they oftentimes express themselves, in Heaven ... No happiness in the world can surpass the charms of this agreeable ecstasy.'[92] There was no overt warning against addiction. Possibly alcohol was a safer bet.

Marriage

Marriage could do you good. A certain noble lord 'had by some irregularity brought his health into a very critical state and the physicians recommended marriage to him as the most certain method of ... restoring his constitution'.[93]

Old age

'Old men's diseases are hard to cure but easy to prevent',[94] if the right measures are taken. For instance, the diet should be carefully considered. Ass's milk is more digestible than cow's milk (and possibly less tubercular).

> A cup of chocolate, not too strong, is a good breakfast. Coffee I cannot advise generally, but the exceptions against tea are in a great way groundless. If the old man likes it he need not deny it to himself for breakfast ... Three moderate cups with a little sugar and a good deal of milk ... let him eat with it a thin slice or two of good bread with a little butter. A little wine is necessary to old men ... carrots are to be avoided, potatoes are innocent and parsnips are nourishing ... The passions demand great regard in preserving health ... It is not worth his while to be angry. Quiet is his business, and as he is above the fluttering pleasures of youth let him place himself above its troubles. Of all passions the old man should avoid a foolish passion for women.

... Let him who is gloomy banish the fear of death by warmer foods, and wine.

If he can't sleep, he should take a warm bath and 'a glass more wine'. If he has a stomach upset, try syrup of – as usual – snails. A tincture of sage 'will give old men the spirit and the advantages of youth' (surely not), but 'the company of agreeable friends will be the best medicine'.

CHAPTER 17

Childhood, Schooling and Religion

Toddlers

Family portraits, which now develop the charming habit of including children, show toddlers in floor-length gowns, under which both sexes wore stiffened bodices or stays. Little boys and little girls were dressed the same, and treated the same, until the boys were 'breeched' somewhere between four and seven and went into a man's world. Meanwhile, they were distinguished by the artist by attributes, like medieval saints, such as a masculine drum or a feminine doll.

Children's games

Most children's games had not changed much for centuries. Pat-a-cake pat-a-cake baker's man, the baby clapping game, is surprisingly late, 1698.[1] In 1760 William Hamley saw the market potential of toys for the better-off, and opened a shop called The Noah's Ark, in Holborn, selling rag dolls and tin soldiers, hoops and wooden horses.[2]

Another change was the arrival of books for children. There had been pamphlet-sized books in every chapman's pack, telling folk tales and fairy stories, but in about 1740 Thomas Boreman had the brilliant idea of making child-sized books.[3] He even made a joke of them, calling them *Gigantic Histories* – they were about the size of two bouillon cubes. One recounted 'The Curiosities of the Tower of London', with a recognisable picture of a porcupine (why a porcupine, when the Tower had all those lions?), so that the reader could nag her parents into taking her there. Boreman's idea was taken up by John Newberry, and the children's book trade was born. *Tom Thumb's Pretty Song Book*, 3 inches by 1¼, came out in 1744; *The Circle of the Sciences* began in 1745; *Little Goody Two-Shoes* launched her career in 1765. Meanwhile, the chapbooks were still in business, publishing *The Arabian Nights*, surely an expurgated version, in 1706,[4] *Robinson Crusoe* in 1719, and *Gulliver's Travels*, treated as a book for children, in 1726.

Board games followed books. In 1750 an uninspiring game called Goose had little competition, except Cupid from another publisher. They were both roughly on the Snakes and Ladders principle, except that they wound round like a snail shell. Nine years later, A Journey thro' Europe hit the toyshops.[5] Like the others, it was played on a printed sheet of paper, which tended to be torn in the heat of battle and thrown away after it, so that few survive. On a map of Europe, from Iceland, top left, to Cyprus, bottom right, was a zigzag course, with rewards and penalties according to the throw of the dice. For instance, 'he who rests at 28, Hanover, shall by order of the King of Great Britain who is Elector be conducted to 54 at Gibraltar to visit his countrymen who keep garison [*sic*] there'.

The next year, geographic dunces such as I could play with 'dissected maps', mounted on wood this time, and cut into easy pieces with a saw. The jigsaw had not yet been invented.[6] Fortunate little girls had dolls, and elaborate 'baby-houses' to play with, fully furnished even to the dolls' family silver, and perhaps got a turn on their brothers' rocking horses.

Female education

Francis Place's sisters went to 'a very respectable day school' near the family home, in Arundel Street, where they learned 'various kinds of needlework and the rudiments of the French language'.[7] These were the daughters of an illiterate baker/innkeeper/prison officer, whom his son later described as a 'tradesman in respectable circumstances', definitely within the category of middling rank, albeit on its lower echelons. The teaching of French even to these little girls seems curious. It certainly gave the wrong impression to M. Grosley. 'For some years past, the French language has been taught as universally as the English in all the boarding schools of London [and some of the day schools too], so that French will soon be by choice the language of the people of England as it was by constraint under the Norman conquest.'[8] Little did he know that English people can be taught French for decades, with no effect whatever. Johnson had learned it in his youth, but the wretched French refused to understand him, so he spoke Latin when in France,[9] loudly no doubt.

Some men deplored the education inflicted on middle-class girls. John Wesley warned Methodist parents 'who would send your girls headlong to hell, send them to a fashionable boarding school'[10] such as, perhaps, the one kept by Mrs Masquerier at the *upper* end of Church Lane, Kensington:

> Board, including French, English, Writing, Arithmetic, Geography, Needlework and Dancing for twenty guineas a year, and one guinea entrance. Parents or Guardians may depend on the utmost care taken of the Young Ladies morals and manners, and a particular tenderness shewn to their Persons.
>
> NB The house is genteel and the situation remarkably healthful.
>
> To those who do not chuse to learn all the above branches, a reasonable deduction will be made.
>
> A Shilling Stage to Holborn, Wood Street and the Bank, several times a Day.[11]

The last sentence, in very small print, seems to imply that the hoped-for Young Ladies might be the daughters of City merchants, sent to acquire a marriageable veneer. On the whole, it does not sound a 'hellish' institution.

Captain Coram, always a modernist, thought that

> it is an evil amongst us here in England to think girls having learning given them is not so very material as for boys to have it. I think and say it is more material, for girls when they come to be mothers will have the forming of their children's lives and if their mothers be good or bad the children generally take after them, so giving girls a vertuous [*sic*] education is a vast advantage to their posterity as well as to the public.[12]

Daughters higher up the social ladder were educated at home by governesses and visiting tutors. Little Lady Caroline Russell's 30 writing lessons cost £2 12s 6d, with an extra 6s 8d for 'half a hundred best pens' and a copy book.[13] Her 56 singing lessons cost over £22, she learned French and Italian, the harpsichord and the guitar, and she had three and a half months of dancing lessons. But the governesses charged with the education of the female upper classes 'complain very much of the indocile disposition of their scholars'.[14]

And yet *The Ladies' Diary or Woman's Almanac* for 1760 assumes an alarming level of mathematical ability. Try this one. If three spheres of brass are in contact, and their diameters are 8, 9 and 10 inches respectively, and they support a fourth sphere weighing 12lb, what quantity of weight does each supporting sphere sustain? (I haven't the least idea.) But the 'Ænigmas' were set by women, for women, and the answers (which I did not understand either) were published in the next year's almanac. Another almanac aimed at the feminine market, *The Ladies' Complete Pocket Book*, is more down to earth, in reminding them of useful dates, such as

24 Feb. St Matthias: not one of the twelve.

29 Feb. Hare hunting goes out.

30 March. Palm Sunday so called in memory of our Saviour's Triumphal entry into Jerusalem.

31 March. Bank notes of £10 and £15 each were now first issued 1759.

29 June. St Peter and St Paul were co-operators under our Saviour in the Conversion of the World.

30 June. Buck-hunting comes in.

26 Dec. Stephen the first martyr.
        Fox hunting comes in.

It also gives a most useful précis of the rules of the Stock Exchange, 'for the use of such ladies who may have occasion or are desirous of understanding the price of STOCKS'.

Boyhood

Hogarth, childless himself, must have had a great liking for small boys. There are always some about in his paintings. In *Morning*, one of *The Four Times of the Day* published in 1738, he shows the back view of two, with huge triangular hats, and satchels the same size and shape on their backs, off to school in the wintry dawn. Francis Place, who lived near Fleet Street, went to school at the age of four, to a dame school nearby. When he left three years later, he knew how to read, but that was all. His next school had 120 boys in two large rooms, taught by a master and three 'ushers', two of whom looked after the smaller boys and 'taught them or neglected them as they pleased'. This was the kind of post Dr Johnson refused with horror. Francis and his brother learned reading and writing and 'ciphering'. The hours were from nine to twelve, two to five, with catechism from twelve to one every day, half holidays on Thursdays and Saturdays, and ten days' holiday at Christmas, Easter and Whitsuntide. There was no homework. Unpunctuality and other sins, such as absence without a parental note, were punished 'with a stout cane', up to fourteen strokes on the hand for serious offences. It 'would bruise the hands sorely'.[15] Very sensibly, Francis learned punctuality, and also boxing.

He then progressed to 'a sort of finishing day school where Latin was pretended to be taught as well as bookkeeping and navigation ... to fit boys for the sea'. There were two other schools nearby, one memorable because its boys regularly fought pitched battles with Francis and his schoolmates, another because it taught French, with German and 'to be pushed in mathematics'. 'The manners of my schoolfellows were coarse and vulgar', Francis wrote, many years later when he was recalling his youth, but the picture he drew was of healthy, naughty boys letting off steam, and learning at the same time; attending schools near their homes – no stressful school run – and acquiring reasonably marketable skills.

Francis Place had an acute ear for social class.

> The children of the richer and prouder class immediately above the tradesmen, those who instead of frequenting the public house assembled at Coffee Houses and Taverns, were sent to boarding schools some of which taught little more than the common day schools, but it was a mark of distinction and encouraged pride by inducing the boy to consider himself a gentleman.

The trade card (publicity hand-out) of such a school read:

> Young gentlemen are instructed in the various branches of English and French, including washing, book-keeping, algebra and mathematics, and the use of the globes. Thirty pounds per annum. NB – Young gentlemen wearing light trousers etc. the washing will be 10/- per year extra.
>
> To instruct the youthful mind in moral and religious principles forms an essential part of the rules of this seminary.[16]

Poor young gentlemen, trying to keep their light trousers 'etc.' clean. Francis had much more fun. He added to his pocket money of a penny a week by doing odd jobs, such as cleaning out the street drains and selling the old iron he found – a vivid commentary on the scavengers' standard of work – and chopping wood, for 1½d an hour. With these riches he bought a kite taller than himself, with 'a pair of glass eyes and fine fringed tassels'. The first time he flew it, he accepted an offer for it, of 10s 6d. He and his friends used to play in the ruins of some old wooden houses that had been burned down, but 'contrary to the usual practice the ruins had not been dug out by the Fire Insurance Office and a large quantity of iron and lead remained in them'. A gang of 'black guards' (poor street children) from Drury Lane spotted the potential of the site, as well as Francis and his mates, but after a few fights 'lines of demarcation were drawn' and Francis was able to make so much money from his spoils that he began to follow his father's disastrous footsteps into gambling on games of chance.

When he was about eleven, 'I saw boys not older than myself swim across the Thames at Millbank at about half tide. ... Logs lay on the mud and shingle waiting to be sawn by purchasers. On these logs hundreds of boys used to dress and undress for the purpose of swimming.' He learned to swim himself, nearly drowning in the process. Sometimes he and his friends followed the New River to where its leaky pipes crossed the fields, and fished in the ditches for 'prickle-backs'. With all their limitations, his schooldays were a mixture of learning and the kind of innocent fun that would be hard for an inner-city child to find nowadays.

The Dissenting Academies

The shortcomings of standard education were recognised. The old grammar schools were lethargic. The further education purveyed by the only two universities in England was inappropriate to modern life, and in any case inaccessible to non-Anglicans. The Inns of Court, which had supplied a veneer of culture with a legal bent in the previous century, had relapsed into a long slumber. The only gleam of pedagogical enthusiasm lay in the Dissenting Academies, which taught sciences, modern languages and commercial subjects. There were, however, only two in London. One was the Academy at Newington Green which Daniel Defoe attended and which had a member of the Royal Society on its staff.[17]

Public schools

Westminster School had been 'for many years past ... the place of education of many of the sons of the nobility and gentry'.[18] Young Lord Tavistock went there in 1754, aged ten,[19] at a cost of £25 'board for a year' plus £10 'the room' and an extra £5 for a fire. A year later he had to have extra lessons in writing, at 8 guineas a year. Lord Chesterfield dismissed it as 'the seat of illiberal manners and brutal behaviour'.[20]

St Paul's School and Eton College were not dissimilar. The emphasis was on the classics. A governing class emerged from them who could not only, if they wished, converse with continentals in Latin (although the pronunciation might have presented severe problems),[21] but also swap Latin tags in the House of Commons like the code of a secret society, and who were familiar with the noble sentiments of Romans in public life: which cannot have been all bad. It also explains the slightly odd dress code of statues commemorating eighteenth-century statesmen: togas were worn.

The foreign tour

After years at Eton or Westminster, which 'has little or no effect upon the English',[22] the affluent male's education was rounded off by a foreign tour. As Lord Chesterfield put it,

> few fathers care much for their sons, or, at least, most of them care more for their money: and consequently content themselves with giving them, at the cheapest rate, the common run of education; that is, a school till eighteen; the university till twenty; and a couple of years riding post through the several towns of Europe; impatient till their boobies come home to be married.[23]

In Italy one could be fairly sure of meeting old friends, or at least compatriots, doing the same thing, so there was not too much danger of having to speak a foreign language or mix with the natives. A young man's main task was to acquire a stock of statues and paintings by, or after – sometimes a long way after – old masters, to adorn the ancestral home and show a level of culture that need never be demonstrated again, in view of these mute witnesses. Fortunately, the labour of finding suitable pieces could usually be delegated to the accompanying tutor.

Apprenticeship

Apprenticeship loomed for some. These young men were not the poor drudges that the parish bound out almost before they could think, but lads of fifteen or more, bound for a seven-year term at the end of which they would have got adolescence out of their system, some experience of a trade or profession into their minds, and a network of useful contacts. 'Wanted an Apprentice to a wholesale and retail Grocer in the City ... nothing less than 100 guineas will be taken.'[24] Attorneys and solicitors called their apprentices articled clerks by now, and advertised vacancies for lads of sixteen or less: 'a handsome premium will be expected'.[25] Samuel Whitbread's father paid £300 to apprentice him to a brewer. Twice that amount, equivalent to the annual income of a prosperous gentleman, was required by a banker,[26] and some rich men's sons paid as much as £1,000.[27] 'Walking pupils' of physicians and surgeons paid an annual fee of £20–30, but a formal seven-year apprenticeship to a surgeon cost anything up to £600, and to an apothecary up to £300.[28]

Grosley observed acutely that if the apprentice was diligent he would learn the master's trade, to the prejudice of the master, so some City masters preferred to take the money and allow the apprentice to 'spend his whole time in taking pleasure'. The strictness of the Tudor apprenticeship system was indeed mitigated in practice. An unnamed apprentice who was shot as a mugger was receiving an allowance, presumably from his master, and £10 a year pocket money,[29] quite against the old idea of an apprentice working for his keep only, exchanging his labour for his master's expertise. After all, even in the eighteenth century, why would a young apprentice need money, when he had 'reasonable pleasures such as reading proper books, enjoyment of fine weather, fresh air, and all the beauties of nature'?[30] He should show a 'decent deference' to his master's wife, both in the business and in domestic affairs, and generally behave as a paragon. 'Some necessary matters to be retained in the memory' included the invaluable information that 'cuttle-bones, oranges and lemons, chair-nails, tacks and tenter hooks ... are bought and sold by the thousand', and that a pipe of wine equals 120 gallons.

Religion

It may seem odd to put such an important subject at the tail end of this chapter. But religion was no longer a burning issue. It was part of the mental equipment of anyone born in the eighteenth century, more than it is now perhaps, but it did not occupy the forefront of their minds. Take the date of Easter, which had agitated ecclesiastical circles for centuries. It had been the starting point for many proposals to change the calendar, so that everyone could know in advance when to celebrate what. Quite suddenly, it seemed, Lord Chesterfield, who as Ambassador to France had got bored with trying to live by two different systems, brought in a carefully drafted bill to synchronise the continental/Catholic calendar and the English/Protestant one. It was done without even mentioning Easter, by simply deleting the eleven days 3–13 September 1752 from that year's calendar.[31]

Children were still taught their catechism. Samuel Johnson was scandalised when two little Foundling Hospital children appeared not to know it, but they were probably too taken aback by this fearsome encounter to be able to answer him. Everyone was obliged to attend their parish church on Sunday, but the extent to which this obligation was observed is hard to tell, in the face of the crowds streaming out of London to the countryside on the only day off they had. All official and public posts, including teaching, and entry to the universities in England, were barred to non-Anglicans, but an occasional communion sufficed, and foreign universities including the Scottish ones, and the Dissenting Academies, gave a much better education than Oxford or Cambridge.

The Gentleman's Magazine regularly reported the Quakers' refusal to wear mourning or shut their shops when some member of the royal family died, but the tone of the reports implied a sneaking envy that good merchants did not see any need to give up business for such a remote cause, and respect of the Quakers for their united stand, rather than disapproval. Quakers demonstrated their practical benevolence, even to combatants, by subscribing to buy woollen waistcoats 'for the soldiers to wear under their clothes when obliged to keep the field in winter', waiting to repel the Scottish advance in 1745.[32]

There was a brief moment during 1753 when it looked as if Jews might be able to take British nationality, but the City woke up, after the bill had become law, and objected so loudly that it had to be repealed the next year. The objections were not on religious grounds, but because the City merchants feared they might be out-smarted by Jewish competitors if the disadvantage of alien nationality were removed. M. Grosley was 'surprised by the sweetness as well as the agreeable simplicity' of the singing in a synagogue he attended. It may have been the one in Duke's Place in the City, where the congregation sang so heartily that it competed with the Anglican church nearby.[33]

Grosley found that Roman Catholic services, in theory limited to the private chapels of Roman Catholic ambassadors, were in practice 'winked at by the government', and quoted a saying by Lord Chesterfield to an English Jesuit: 'It is to no purpose for you to aspire to the honour of martyrdom. Fire and faggot are quite out of fashion.'[34] *The Gentleman's Magazine* regularly reported instances of Roman Catholic gentlemen – there might have been others, not so newsworthy – who had seen the error of their ways and publicly recanted and joined the Anglican faith, but the level of religious ardour was on the whole low.

It would be unfair to take Hogarth's print *The Sleeping Congregation* of 1736, reissued in 1762, as a direct representation of church attendance, but it convincingly shows the chasm between the Anglican Church and the people. An indication of the status of the very poor is a letter to *The Gentleman's Magazine* in 1756. 'It were much to be wished that in the churches of this populous city there were some place set aside for the reception of the common people who at present are obliged to stand in the aisles.'[35]

So it is not surprising to find the poor deserting the aisle of the parish church, to hear John Wesley (1703–91). He began his ministry in 1738, with his brother Charles. 'We began preaching inward present salvation as attainable by faith alone.' He saw himself as a member of the Anglican Church, but this was not reciprocated. He was barred from preaching in churches, so he took to preaching in the open air. This proved to be the making of the movement that came to be called Methodism. 'It is field-preaching that does the execution still; for usefulness there is none comparable to it'.[36] Its most marked success was among unskilled labourers, miners and craftsmen in the increasingly industrial midlands and the fishing communities in Cornwall.

In London Wesley extended the hope of salvation to condemned prisoners, whom he would accompany on their terrible Newgate journey to the gallows. He visited the poor and upheld their cause. 'I found some in their cells underground, others in their garrets, but I found not one of them unemployed who was able to crawl about the room. So wickedly, devilishly false is that common objection, they are poor only because they are idle.' Not surprisingly, they flocked to him. 'Great numbers of [poor] people of all nations, circumstances and sizes of understanding [are] going to the bantering booth on Windmill Hill Upper Moorfields to hear their beloved apostle Mr Wesley'.[37] Even Walpole went to hear him in 1766, 'a lean elderly man, fresh-coloured, his hair smoothly combed but with a *soupçon* of curl at the ends. Wondrous clean, but as evidently an actor as Garrick'.[38]

Samuel Johnson, a devout and religious man, attributed the Methodists' success to 'their expressing themselves in a plain and familiar manner, which is the only way to do good to the common people.'[39] Salvation by faith may sound like an easy option, but Wesley expected more of his followers. He expected them to be *methodical* in their inward religious observance, and self-controlled in their outward life, eschewing drunkenness, idleness and laziness. Not all who attended his open-air meetings stayed the course. Those who did were expected to contribute a penny a week towards a fund from which repayable loans could be made to other members of the congregation. Poor people realised that they themselves could help their brethren without hand-outs from charity or the state.

CHAPTER 18

A Woman's World

'Marriage has many pains, but celibacy has no pleasures': Dr Johnson.[1]

Emigration

There have nearly always been surplus women. In some societies, the problem is solved by marrying them. Henry VIII went in for serial marriage, but not every man has his capacity to dispose of unwanted wives. Another expedient is to export them. Out of sight, out of mind. In 1746 'a great number of women have enlisted on board the fleet bound for Cape Breton [now Halifax, Nova Scotia, in Canada], and continue to enter daily. They are given £10 each and their provision during the passage, and when they arrive are to receive further encouragement.'[2] By July of that year, 6,000 had already gone, and another 10,000 were going in the next sailing.[3] If they missed that boat, they could always realise their own capital worth. In 1752, twenty women sold themselves for four years to a captain bound for Philadelphia. 'As women are wanted in our colonies, and we abound with them here, it is thought that none of them will come back.'[4] If they could raise £1,000 – an impossibly large sum in those days – they should try America,

there existing scarcely any employment to which they can now turn themselves, the very few that decency and policy had set aside for their sex being usurped by a flight of commercial hermaphrodites [this does seem unfair, hermaphrodites having the best of both worlds] ... It is incontestable that about £1,000 industriously employed in America on the quantity of land that the Provincial Governor is instructed to give to a settler so qualified will ensure an immediate subsistence and lay the foundation of wealth.[5]

Career women

Commercial hermaphrodites possibly included man midwives, who were taking over childbirth from traditional midwives in some fashionable circles. Women monopolised the rag trade (in the modern sense) and they had a foothold in dentistry and silversmithing. They ran dame schools. They had a market value if they were available as wet-nurses. The new lying-in hospitals were convenient labour exchanges for lactating women needing an income supplement. Women wrote novels, and books of household hints, and advice to the young: each of them a small niche market.

Highway robbery would not seem to offer much of a career opportunity, but it is hard to tell. In 1763 a gentleman and his lady were attacked on the Harrow Road by two highway persons. One of them 'insisted the gentleman should do her a favour under a thick hedge'. The other, observing that 'one good turn deserves another', got the lady to do the same under the other hedge. The usual transfer of valuables had already taken place, but the highwaywoman 'heard the ticking of a watch when under the hedge' and requested its delivery, which the gentleman did 'with some reluctance'.[6]

But did surplus women really 'abound'? A hundred years earlier they had. A quarter of women never married, about the time of Charles II's Restoration. But the figure for the middle of the eighteenth century has been calculated at only 5 per cent.[7]

Marriage

How did so many women find themselves husbands? Domestic servants often married their colleagues, or the tradesmen they had dealt with on household business. Other women might answer a lonely-hearts advertisement, such as the one by 'a gentleman not much on the wrong side of thirty' (39?), who has expectations from a relative aged 60, so he will soon be rich. Meanwhile he can't, just at present, make the normal marriage settlement, but he 'is very desirous to form an alliance with a lady of clear, independent and ample fortune ... who is not an antidote to a man's wishes [as ugly as the back of a bus?] and has sufficient enterprise to quit her situation ...

he is ready at a moment's notice'.[8] A 'marriage register office' – that is, a dating agency – was set up in 1764 to promote 'honest matrimony', but *The Gentleman's Magazine* had its doubts.[9]

The main attraction was money, and somehow women had to give the impression that they had it, as they revolved on public display at Ranelagh and Vauxhall, the theatre and the opera. Their partner in this mating dance might interpret the signals wrongly. In 1761 Elizabeth Raper met a young man whom she rather fancied. Once he was sure she would accept his proposal of marriage, he checked with her mother, and had a nasty shock. 'He seemed vastly surprised that so rich as Father and Mother were reputed to be, they could not give me in [at?] present about [above?] 200 a year. This astonished him greatly' – and when Elizabeth's mother, with a gleam in her eye, added that her daughter could not possibly marry unless he provided a coach, the flustered young man made his excuses and left.[10] The match between the rich alderman's daughter and the dissolute son of a cash-strapped noble, so mercilessly portrayed in Hogarth's *Marriage à la Mode* in 1745,[11] was not unusual.

The Gentleman's Magazine liked to tell its readers of any unusual wedding, such as a 97-year-old marrying a young widow of 67. In most issues it gave the size of the bride's fortune as a matter of course: 'Joseph Burdett to Miss Carolina Burdett of St James's Square, 20,000£,'[12] and 'William Baker Esquire, one of the Sheriffs of London, to Miss Juliana Penn, daughter of – Penn [*sic*] proprietor of Pennsylvania, with £200,000'.[13] A cynical Scottish doctor wrote:[14]

> The Asiatic is careful to improve the breed of his elephants ... The Englishman, eager to have swift horses and victorious cocks, grudges no care and spares no expense to have the males and females matched properly, but ... he will calmly match himself with the most decrepit and diseased of the human species ... considering nothing but the fortune he is, by her alliance, to convey to an offspring [which will be] by diseases rendered unable to use it.

Love did sometimes take a hand in the game. 'We often find the passion called love triumphing over the duty of children to their parents, and on the other hand we sometimes find the passion of pride or avarice triumphing over the duties of parents to their children.'[15] And if a girl could not bear the man her parents had chosen, she had a right of veto, and even a convenient precedent, in *The Complete Letter-Writer*, for conveying the bad news to her admirer:

'I am sorry to say that my disapprobation of your address is insu-
perable.'[16]

The minimum age to contract a valid marriage was twelve for a
girl, fourteen for a boy. Until 1753 there was no legal formality
required, other than a declaration by each party that they took the
other there and then (*de praesenti*) as their spouse,[17] as opposed to a
promise to marry in the future. This was illustrated by a suit for
£10,000 damages for breach of promise of marriage brought against
the Reverend Dr Wilson, a prebendary of Worcester Cathedral.[18] 'It
was proved by several witnesses and letters that the Doctor had
frequently promised to marry her and prevailed on her to promise
him: that they both had declared the same publicly in a solemn
manner: and that he afterwards having denied making such a promise
... this action was brought to justify her reputation.' Her story is
curious, but the court must have believed most of it, because they
awarded the poor jilted plaintiff £7,000, which must have gone a
long way towards repairing her matrimonial chances.

Obviously it would be prudent to have witnesses to declarations of
matrimony *de praesenti*, who could give evidence if the marriage were
ever disputed, but their presence did not affect the validity of the
ceremony.

Lord Hardwicke's Act

Abductions of heiresses by unscrupulous fortune-hunters became so
scandalous, and the validity of Fleet marriages (see above, pp. 68–70)
so questionable, that at last Parliament passed Lord Hardwicke's
Clandestine Marriage Act, in 1753. Thereafter public notice of intention to marry had to be given three times in the parish church of
each party – and this was a time when most people went to their
parish churches, every Sunday, and would listen carefully, as did one
woman who interrupted the service to say that she had been married
to the proposed bridegroom for fourteen years and had seven children
by him.[19]

The marriage ceremony does not seem to have inhibited the
participants unduly. One bridegroom added to the words 'and with
this ring I do thee wed', 'and with this fist I'll break thy head', which
the blushing bride treated as a joke.[20] When asked whether she would
'take this man to be her wedded husband', one woman said, 'No and
I have often told him so.' The parson asked the obvious question –

why was she there? 'Only to tell you, before him, that I would not marry him', and she left the church, and her swain.[21]

Scottish law was, and is, different from English law. Lord Hardwicke's Act did not apply in Scotland, so a romantic couple who decided to elope needed only to cross the border, and exchange vows, to be validly married, even after 1753. Of course, it was as well to have a witness to their mutual bliss, so they stopped at the first settlement over the border, which happened to be the smithy at Gretna Green, for the blacksmith to earn a fee as witness. 'A young lady eloped from her guardian, who being informed that she had taken the road northward immediately pursued her and found her on Finchley Common in a herse [sic] with her lover in the box driving her.'[22]

In 1769 *The Gentleman's Magazine* published a helpful 'Explanation of Matrimony'.[23] 'Matrimony is celebrated in the morning because men are most serious at that time [the pubs not having been open long?] ... When God made the society of marriage he made man superior because he knew equality would breed confusion.' Logically he had another option.

Household duties

Supervising the servants could be exhausting. The Duke of Newcastle had 22 of them in his house in Lincoln's Inn Fields,[24] who must have been falling over each other. Another problem was that they were always coming in and out of rooms, to mend the fire, draw the curtains, bring the tea, or just to say 'You rang, madam?' at an inconvenient moment. Lord Lowther was driven to consummate his seduction of a noble lady in her box at the opera, being the most private place available.[25]

Food shopping

Marketing and cooking would be done by the housekeeper and the cook, in affluent circles. But the lady of the household would still need to have a basic knowledge of their skills, if only to fill in the gaps between their departures and the arrival of their successors. Some cookery books gave clear advice on choosing food.

Eggs: hold the great end to your tongue, if it feels warm, be sure it's new; if cold, it is bad ... Pork: If it be young, the Lean will break in pinching between your fingers, and if you nip the skin with your nails it will make a dent. As for old or new killed, try the Legs, Hands and Springs by putting your fingers under the bone that comes out, for if it is tainted you will find it there by smelling your finger ...[26]

I suppose the danger of a pork joint being unsaleably mangled by these hands-on methods was minimised by not selling tainted meat. Fishmongers had a nasty habit of 'blowing' fish: inflating it through a quill up the vent, which made it look fresher. Poultry and pork could be blown too.[27] Occasionally turtles were landed, from Ascension Island, over 300lb in weight, and 'sold at a very high price'.[28]

Markets

Most food was still sold in markets. There were several scattered about the City, including the rambling buildings of Leadenhall market (which still functions). The weavers' district out at Spitalfields had a thriving market. There was one just north of Oxford Street and another near Bloomsbury Square. The foul Fleet ditch had been covered over and its site used for a market. Housekeepers to the grandees who lived in St James's Square could do their shopping in St James's market nearby, unless they thought it worth their while to make the trip to Covent Garden for fresh vegetables and fruit. Markets were open from six in the morning to eight at night, four days a week – apart from fresh country produce, which could be sold every day except, of course, on Sundays. Housewives did their shopping in the morning, leaving the afternoons to 'retailers and Traders of the City who buy and sell again',[29] including street vendors.

Food shops

The grand developments to the west had a different system. Rocque's 1747 map, in which Grosvenor Square is immediately recognisable by its wide space criss-crossed with paths, shows only one market anywhere near, Shepherd's Market just off Curzon Street. The two weeks of the May Fair held on the market site must have ruled out serious shopping then,[30] and in any case the buildings were cramped.

The pattern of household shopping changed as the west end grew.

Specialist shops grew up, such as the one set up in Piccadilly in 1707 by William Fortnum, a retired royal footman, in partnership with a friend called Mason, who had a stall in St James's market. In 1761 William's grandson Charles entered the service of Queen Charlotte. The perquisites that he was entitled to far exceeded his grandfather's modest line in used candles, profitable though these had been. Charles's perfectly proper title to food, coals, house linen and wine enabled the business to expand.[31]

Thomas Twining had been selling tea and coffee at the sign of the Golden Lion since 1716.[32] There was a Ham Warehouse just off the Strand, selling ham 'calculated for the Nobility at 7½d a pound' and for lesser mortals a penny cheaper. The establishment would deliver free to Royal Navy Commanders in Portsmouth, so presumably would do the same for a good customer in London.[33] You could get turtle soup and 'all sorts of made dishes' to take away or eat in, at the corner of Vere Street,[34] if you were in one of those awkward cook-less gaps.

Street vendors

To some extent it was possible to let your shopping come to you, without leaving the house, but it would not have been quite so fresh. A set of playing cards illustrating the *Cries of London*, published in 1754,[35] shows five vendors of fish, three selling vegetables, a girl selling 'sweet damask roses', three selling fruit and two selling meat, four selling cakes and buns, and a rather cross-looking milk maid waving her tally stick and shouting 'Come quick for I'm a-going'. Asses could be 'drove to any persons house in town or country' if an invalid needed ass's milk.[36]

These street vendors were not shy. Their raucous shouts were pitched to carry into neighbouring streets over the uproar of the traffic. The backgrounds of the playing cards are mostly a standard cityscape, sometimes recognisable as London Bridge or St Paul's. It is hard to imagine the august dwellers in Grosvenor Square putting up with such disturbance to their peace. Nor would the food always be particularly palatable. It was mostly carried on the vendors' heads, horridly open to birds, and projectiles and liquids from upper storeys. Sometimes the vendors could rise to horse-drawn carts. The number of 'higlers and market folk ... wholly engaged to bring veal, pork and smaller things from house to house' as well as to the markets from the country, was estimated at 30,000 'and every one of them have a horse', which didn't help the traffic problem.[37]

Cooking

Reading cookery books of the time, one is struck by the labour-intensive methods, by the emphasis given to preserving food, and by the use of parts of animals and fishes that do not, as far as one knows, see the light of day in our kitchens. As to methods, our '30 minutes at 20°C' was not of course possible. You had to be expert in getting your coal-burning fire to obey you. 'To roast a pig ... spit it and lay it to the fire, taking care that your fire burns well at both ends, or till it does, hang a flat iron in the middle of the grate' to deflect the heat from the heart of the fire.[38] 'Bake all kinds of cake in a good oven according to the size of your cake, and follow the directions of your receipt, for though care has been taken to weigh and measure every article belonging to every kind of cake, yet the management and the oven must be left to the maker's care.'[39]

This writer, Elizabeth Raffald, gives a recipe for a wedding cake that must have needed amazing muscle power. The raw ingredients weighed 18lb plus 32 eggs and half a pint of brandy. 'First work the butter [4lb] with your hand to a cream, then beat in your sugar [2lb] a quarter of an hour ... beat your yolks half an hour at least ...' Eliza Smith outdoes her. A rich seed cake needed beating for two hours, once the butter had been creamed and the 35 eggs had been added. Granted, the kitchen maid would do most of the beating – but someone had to.

Strong nerves, too, were needed. 'To roast a pig. Stick your pig just above the breastbone, run your knife to the heart. *When it is dead* [my italics] ...'[40] 'If the heart is not touched it will be a long time dying.'[41] 'To stew carp. Take a live carp, cut him in the neck and tail and save the blood ...'[42] Tench and eels 'should be dressed alive'.[43] This was known as 'crimping', 'a cruel manner of cutting up fish ... in order to make it eat firm'.[44] Turtles should be killed the night before they are to be cooked, by cutting their throats while they lay on their backs.[45]

Thirty-five eggs are a lot of eggs, but they were smaller than the ones we use. Poultry was smaller. Pigs were not the gross mountains we know, but agile creatures more like wild boar. Massie (see Chapter 7) reckoned that the household of a gentleman with £600 a year, his wife, four children and seven servants – prosperous, in those times – would consume 28lb of pepper in a year. Taking your pepper pot in your hand, imagine 28lb of it. The household's annual consumption of 2,000lb of sugar seems acceptable, after that. The gentry liked their food rich and highly spiced. No wonder doctors advised a light diet.

When the cook and the kitchen maid had an idle moment, they should get on with pickling and preserving and potting and candying for the winter. Shop-bought pickles 'are made to please the eye by the use of pernicious ingredients. It is too common a practice to make use of brass utensils in order to give the pickles a fine green' – that is, verdigris – 'a very powerful poison'.[46] The number of ways of keeping food for weeks or months, without any refrigeration, is impressive. Many sound delicious. Candied orange flowers and conserve of red roses would cheer any winter day; so would damson wine and cherry brandy.[47] Vegetables could be bottled or pickled, and 'your meat will keep good a long time' if you collar it carefully.[48]

What a lot of food we waste. Lambs' testicles, ox palates, sheeps' plucks,[49] cows' udders[50] ... Cods' heads were roasted, pigs' ears and trotters in 'a bottle or two of Rhenish [Rhine] wine' ate well cold, or heated in the jelly 'makes a very pretty dish'. 'Pigeons transmogrified' were wrapped in pastry, 'pigeons in Pimlico' were stuffed and made into patties.[51] A 'calf's head surprise' was 'a handsome top dish at a small expense'[52] and would certainly surprise you if you got a halved eye on your plate. You might also, unfortunately, meet 'a dozen of larks on a skewer'.[53]

Dinner

The ultra-fashionable time for dinner was five o'clock.[54] The more usual time was between three and four,[55] after the Exchange had closed at three and the merchants came home. Elizabeth Raffald, 'unwilling to leave even the weakest capacity in the dark', suggests how to prepare a 'grand table' in the winter, 'January being a month when entertainments are most used'. There were two courses, but utterly unlike our idea of a course. Each could comprise 26 separate dishes, with two more when the two soups were 'removed' and replaced with something else. The essential was not to repeat anything.

Raffald's suggested first course for January includes small dishes of bottled peas, broccoli and salad, but otherwise it is a nightmare of meat and poultry, with Mock Turtle (calf's head again) as a centrepiece.

The next course tempted the guest, if still hungry, with pheasant, hare and collared pig, crayfish and snipe, but offered a change in the shape of elaborate puddings as well, such as 'transparent pudding covered with a silver web' (spun sugar) as a centrepiece, and 'moonshine', 'rocky island' and pistachio cream as outworks.

You might think you had eaten enough, but no: there is still dessert. The remains of the first two Gargantuan courses are cleared away, and the tablecloth is 'drawn'. One can see why at this stage, a hundred years earlier, everyone got up and went to another room, or out to a banqueting house in the garden, while the 'dessert' (also 'desert', from the French *déservir*, 'to clear the table'), was done – that is, the table was cleared. But by now the word had come to mean the 'fruit or sweetmeats with which a feast is concluded'.[56] Elizabeth Raffald points out the obvious – that 'as many dishes as you have in one course, so many baskets or plates your desert must have', such as those candied and preserved fruits that the cook sweated over a hot stove preparing in the summer. 'As ice is very often plentiful at that time [January] it will be easy to make five different ices ...' Astonishing constructions in spun sugar might even be hired, or used again. The Earl of Northumberland's confectioner went so far as to create a 'baby Vauxhall'.[57]

It is fair to say that Eliza Smith, who is not so up-market as Mrs Raffald, gives her prospective guests only five dishes in each course in winter, the second course including A Turkey Roasted *and* A Butter'd Apple Pie Hot. And the anonymous writer of *The Ladies Complete Pocket-Book* for 1760 only goes up to a mere thirteen. 'By complying with these rules the housekeeper will always avoid blame.'

She is the only source I have found who explains how these astonishing meals worked. How did the food arrive on your plate?

> After the lady at the head of the table has made a beginning by helping those near her, the fashion is for everyone to take care of himself by helping himself to what is next [nearest] or sending his plate to the person who sits near what he likes ... if he give any of the company trouble he is in the way of returning it by helping them in his turn.

This is why Lord Chesterfield nagged at his son: 'Do you use yourself to carve adroitly and genteely, without hacking half an hour across a bone; without bespattering the company with the sauce; and without overturning the glasses into your neighbour's pockets?'[58] Eliza Smith gives a list of terms of art for carving, and instructions. 'May I unjoint this bittern for your ladyship, or would you prefer me to thigh you a woodcock?' How did you eat those bottled peas? Fork or knife? The observant M. Grosley has the answer: for small things like peas, 'recourse is had to the knife, which is broad and round at the extremity'.[59] If someone is too shy to enter into the general free-for-all, 'the lady is to ask him without ceremony whether she shall help him to this dish or that'. Presumably she was still there to distribute the dessert, but after the wine is put on the table, 'the women rise and leave the room',[60] and 'the room being furnished with a certain necessary utensil' – there were more often several chamber pots, stored in a cupboard at the end of the sideboard – '[the men] lean upon the table with their elbows, drink about, and settle the affairs of the nation'.[61]

Breakfast

The day began with breakfast, probably no more than a slice or two of bread or muffins and French rolls fetched from the baker.[62] Lord Ferrers, awaiting execution for murder, took 'a half pint bason of tea with a small spoonful of brandy in it [understandable in the circumstances, perhaps, but he seems to have been so cool that this may have been his normal breakfast beverage] and a muffin' every morning, in the Tower of London.[63] Buttered toast was another option observed by a young Swedish visitor, who found English houses so cold that the butter wouldn't spread any other way. 'Most people pour a little cream or sweet milk into the teacup when they are about to drink the tea.'[64]

Luncheon and supper

If dinner was to be hours away, you might have a mid-morning snack or 'luncheon' – 'as much food as one's hand can hold'[65] – bacon on bread, for instance.[66] The original sandwich was a toasted beef one, consumed absent-mindedly by Lord Sandwich while he gambled for 24 hours running.[67] If dinner had been early, you might have a light supper. Eliza Smith suggests a menu of only seven dishes, from stewed carp, broiled pigeons and very small chickens, to 'tarts of all sorts'.

Presumably you took the precaution of having something to eat at home before you set out for 'Mrs L [who] has a party at cards next Wednesday se'ennight of eight tables: she presents her compliments to Mr S and desires the favour of his company' or 'Mr and Mrs C [who sent] their compliments to Mr and Mrs H and desire the favour of their company Wednesday next, to drink tea and spend the evening'.[68]

Wine

Poor M. Grosley could 'never accustom myself to the wine of London'.[69] The red might pretend to be Burgundy or Bordeaux, but the latter was 'enlivened' with spirits, and both might be polluted with boiled turnips and litharge, a compound of lead. The white wine was 'for the most part made in England'. 'I drank no pure unmixed wine except in two houses' − both French. In the eighteenth century the wine trade suffered from the periodic wars against the French, and from Britain's old alliance with the Portuguese, with whom Sir Paul Methuen had concluded a trade treaty in 1703 giving Portuguese wines − mostly red, called 'port' from its place of origin but not fortified as modern port is − customs preference in return for the Portuguese taking English cloth. French wine, which paid a heavy duty, cost 6s a bottle, but 'Methuen wine little inferior to the best burgundy' could be had for a guinea a dozen (1s 9d a bottle), plus 2½d a bottle, refundable on return.[70]

Massie calculated[71] the household expenses, including tax, of a gentleman with £600 a year − well-off for that time. He buys a pipe, 120 gallons, of 'port' (Portuguese red) a year, but 'cannot afford any claret' (French red). This Portuguese red was probably what M. Grosley was wrestling with. He was not alone. Boswell found it 'a very heavy and a very inflammatory dose' the morning after he and Dr Johnson had put away 2 or 3 pints of 'English port' between them.[72] There is even a theory that Handel's death was accelerated by lead poisoning from the vessels used by the Portuguese wine-makers.[73]

Family planning

We left the ladies retiring from the dining room so that the men could get on with drinking. They may have sat down to cards, but they will have certainly gossiped, and the everlasting subjects of women's talk were servants and children.

The enormous families of the Victorians were not a Georgian experience. The average family has been estimated at about 2.5

children per family.[74] Inevitably, one asks how the Georgians maintained this comfortable rate without modern contraceptive methods.
The first steps of the answer are fairly easy. A woman is most fertile
in the years immediately following menarche: at that time, from about
fifteen to perhaps twenty. The usual age of marriage, 26 or so, missed
those years altogether. A woman's fertility was beginning to decline
by the time she married, and it stopped at menopause, say fifteen or
twenty years later. During those years, the prevalence of fevers and
sub-clinical infections must have meant that the fertility, even the
libido, of most couples in London was not what it might have been
elsewhere or in other times.

Then there is some indication that marital intercourse was avoided,
or at least discouraged, during certain seasons in the church calendar,
such as Lent. *The Ladies Diary or Woman's Almanac* for 1750 printed, in
bold Gothic font:

13 Jan	Marriage comes in
11 Feb	Marriage goes out
23 April	Marriage comes in
19 May	Marriage goes out
10 June	Marriage comes in [and apparently stayed in; no other date is given]

If it is right to read this as a hint that not only marriage but marital
intercourse should not 'come in' for thirteen weeks, a quarter of the
year, and if to these times one adds Sundays, Fast days and menstrual
periods, the days when intercourse was permitted, let alone conception
likely, are getting few and far between. Then, maternal breast feeding
was becoming more fashionable among those who could have afforded
wet-nurses, and was normal among the less affluent. Lactation inhibits
ovulation, and in addition there was a convention that sexual intercourse should be delayed until breast feeding ceased, which might be
as long as two years after the baby's birth.

At last the happy husband approaches to claim his matrimonial
rights. Was there any available contraception? There were condoms,
or cundums, 'the dried gut of a sheep worn by men in the act of
coition to prevent venereal infection',[75] but a wife would have been
insulted, surely, if her husband had come to the marital bed wearing
one, and their efficiency as a preventive barrier is dubious in any
case. There was some professional discussion of the rhythm method,
but the mechanism of conception was not yet understood and the

medics got the rhythm wrong.[76] There were various herbal potions said to inhibit lust, which was not altogether the point, or more realistically to make the man or the woman temporarily or permanently sterile. Some of them may indeed have worked. It is easy to dismiss early, or primitive, reliance on herbs as mumbo-jumbo, but we are finding, just sometimes, that we are wrong. And lastly, there was *coitus interruptus*, withdrawing before ejaculation, or as current slang had it, 'to make a coffee-house of a woman's privities, to go in and out and spend nothing'.[77]

CHAPTER 19

The Middling Rank of Men

'Man: (1) a human being (2) not a woman': Dr Johnson's *Dictionary*.

Coffee-houses and clubs

Coffee-houses, taverns, chocolate houses – they all provided a milieu in which to conduct business. They functioned as an eighteenth-century business internet, as well as social centres. Men interested in the same things, whether business, politics or pleasure, tended to converge on the same establishment. Shipping insurers met at Lloyd's, where they would find all the latest shipping news waiting for them. Garraway's often held auctions of prize goods captured in the war, such as 'one box of chocolate, forty six bags of snuff and one elephant's tooth'.[1] Jonathan's was convenient for stockbrokers. Traders to the Baltic met at the Baltic coffee house in Threadneedle Street. These places were not luxurious. Bare wooden floors and Windsor chairs were the norm.[2] Tom King's coffee-house appears in Hogarth's print *Morning* as an open-fronted lean-to shed on the east wall of the church in Covent Garden market, crowded with beaux and rough porters, where a free fight is in progress and wigs are flying.

Once the business of the day was done, you might shift over to another coffee-house where the politics were to your taste, or the gaming was high, or the conversation sparkled. A 'club' meant 'the shot or dividend of a reckoning paid by the company in just proportions: an assembly of good fellows, meeting under certain conditions'.[3] It survives in our expression of 'clubbing together'. The good fellows normally assembled in an accustomed coffee-house, but could take wing like a swarm of bees and settle elsewhere. Various masonic lodges swirled round from one coffee-house to another, whereas the

Jockey Club, founded in 1750, moved out to premises at Hyde Park corner and stayed there.[4] The 'conditions' could include formal proposal and seconding for membership, and a set subscription. M. Grosley, being a French advocate who did not speak English,

> was admitted [presumably as the guest of a member] to a club consisting of clergymen, physicians and lawyers and likewise frequented by lords and other persons of distinction. The members were seated round a large table on which stood bottles of several sorts of wine, tea, coffee, and everything necessary for convivial jocundity. Every member drank what he liked and in what quantity he thought proper ... A newcomer enters the room quietly and takes the first seat he can get ... after having saluted [the company] with a nod.[5]

Perhaps M. Grosley struck a quiet evening. He described the profound silence that fell when discussion paused, 'all persons looking at each other and reflecting on what they have heard', or perhaps wondering how on earth that foreign chap got in.

There can have been few silences at any club when Samuel Johnson was there. He gathered his friends round him in 1748, to take his mind off his *Dictionary*, 'enjoy literary conversation, and amuse his evening hours', and he was a founder member of the Literary Club founded by Joshua Reynolds.[6] Boswell went to a 'club' that Benjamin Franklin belonged to, at St Paul's coffee-house, every other Thursday. 'Wine and punch upon the table, some of us smoke a pipe ... at nine there is a side-board with Welsh rabbits [*sic*] and apple-puffs, porter and beer. Our reckoning is about eighteen pence a head.'

Rich merchants and traders

These were the men making between £400 and £600 a year, according to Massie, merging with the titled gentry at the very top of the tree.

After morning prayers, rich merchants or tradesmen spent their morning on their accounts,

> after which, being dressed in a modest garb without any footman or attendance they go abroad [out] about their business to the Custom-House, the Bank, the Exchange, etc. ... In the evening of every other day the post comes in [which of course they deal with immediately] ...

They frequently meet at the Tavern in the evening, either to transact their business or take a cheerful glass.[7]

This was the English version. So far as that observant Frenchman M. Grosley could see, bankers and merchants rose late – he may not have known about the family prayers – and went straight off to the coffee-house. At eleven o'clock they came home (for luncheon?) or went to meetings, presumably in other coffee-houses. At two o'clock they went to the Exchange for an hour or so until it shut at 3 o'clock. At three or four o'clock they went to 'lounge a little longer at the coffee house and then dine about four ... dinner concluded the day, they give the rest of it to their friends'.[8]

M. Grosley was struck by English commercial methods. Although double-entry bookkeeping was now widely used, the record most relied on by a merchant was a 'debt-book which [he] carries always in his pocket', so he could carry on his business on the hoof, in coffee-houses or the Royal Exchange, which must have been an astonishing sight. It was open between one and three every day, not only to English merchants, but also to foreigners from as far away as Japan and Moscow.[9] Each trade had its own spot, called a 'walk', in the courtyard, some under the arcades and some, including the stockbrokers, in the open space[10] – no wonder they migrated to coffee-houses.

There is an interesting 'estimate of the necessary charge of a family in the Middling Station of life, consisting of a man, his wife, four children and one maidservant, who sets up business on £1,000, a very substantial start in life'.[11] His household expenses work out to £122 10s a year. If he is to provide for his and his wife's clothes – £16 each – and another child every two years, schooling at 10s a quarter, the maid's wages – slightly under the market rate – at £4 10s, 'pocket expenses, master' at 4s a week and 2s a week to the mistress 'to buy fruit, toys, etc.', returning hospitality (£4) and 'Physic for the whole family [which] may exceed six pounds', let alone rent and taxes (£50), he needs an income of at least £350 p.a.: and this budget is wrecked by the very next figure in my notes – the cost of a man's suit, admittedly in velvet with gold braid, but sometimes it's necessary to look rich, if you want to make money – £23.[12]

Sinecures

The great art, then as now, is to be well paid for doing very little.
'£2,000 to £3,000 ready to be given for a genteel <u>place for life</u> (the
law and army excepted), income to be adequate to such advance,
and no objection to a little attendance.'[13] I doubt if this advertiser
had assessed his market correctly. In 1768, for example, a coal meter's
place in the Port of London, checking that each collier's cargo was
accurately weighed for customs duty purposes[14] for 21 years, was sold
for £6,510, and a corn meter's place for £3,300.[15]

It might be realistic to include membership of the House of
Commons here. In 1749 Lord Chesterfield could tell his illegitimate
son Philip, then aged seventeen, that 'you will be of the House of
Commons as soon as you are of age'. The constituency cost his fond
father £2,000. By 1764 his father was able to tell him that there was
an interested buyer for it, but Philip Stanhope seems to have lost his
seat anyway. By 1767, undeterred, his father

> spoke to a borough-jobber and offered five-and-twenty hundred pounds
> for a secure seat in parliament; but he laughed at my offer, and said
> there was no such thing as a borough to be had now, for that the rich
> East and West Indians had secured them all, at the rate of three
> thousand pounds at least; but many at four thousand, and two or three
> that he knew at five thousand.

One borough changed hands for £9,000.[16] MPs were not paid, then,
but the status was a desirable social asset and could open useful doors.

The professions: law

'The law is a crabbed study and requires uncommon diligence to
master it and were it not for the near prospect of a very considerable
reward few would undergo the unpleasant task.' 'Nine out of ten have
little business',[17] which sounds all too familiar. Massie included law
among the top-earning 5 per cent of the population, at £200 a year.
His category presumably included judges, who were comparatively
well paid then. Conditions of practice at the bar must have been
extraordinary, at least as far as the higher civil courts were concerned.
All three courts sat in Westminster Hall. Like some legal institutions,
it had been in use since 1402, but surely this was carrying the
immemorial sanctity of English law too far. Two courts sat at one

The old Horse Guards barracks in Whitehall and its parade ground, with the Banqueting Hall behind, from St James's Park. By Canaletto, 1749.

Canaletto's view of the Thames on Lord Mayor's Day (c. 1746) shows the wide variety of river craft, from grand oared barges to one-man skiffs. The yacht in the middle of the picture, flying the union jack, has just fired a salute.

Captain Coram (see page 78) by Hogarth, 1740. He is holding the seal of the royal charter granted to the Foundling Hospital. The large black hat at his feet was the only payment he would accept from the Company of Hatters, for whom he did a good turn.

The Foundling Hospital. The fashionable world went there to enjoy pictures and hear music such as Handel's *Messiah*. The arcades at each side are still there.

Golden Cross Inn, The Strand by Samuel Scott. The Strand was a principal shopping area; Northumberland House, a survival from Tudor times, was refurbished with elegant eighteenth-century sash windows. The Percy lion on its skyline moved to Syon House when Northumberland House was demolished in 1874. The equestrian statue of Charles I is still there.

Jonathan Tyers with his family in 1740, by Francis Hayman. Tyers was the proprietor of Vauxhall Gardens. He is wearing his own hair, carefully curled, or perhaps a brown wig. His waistcoat is appliqué with silver lace. The three women wear varying degrees of décolletage. The girls' frilled caps sit on top of their heads, their mother's is tied under her chin. Note the small teacups without handles.

Ranelagh Gardens (see page 247) in 1751: the Rotunda, the Chinese House and masqueraders.

Vauxhall Gardens (see page 245) in 1751. The supper boxes were in the two curved arcades and the orchestra played in the octagonal bandstand.

London Bridge from the east, by Samuel Scott. The houses on it were finally demolished in 1757. A barge has just gone through with its mast lowered, but the ship on the right would stay down-river. Note the white-water turbulence as the river rushes through the narrow arches.

King George III gave a fireworks party in 1749 to celebrate the Peace of Utrecht, and Handel wrote the music for it, but it was a fiasco (see page 39). A month later the Duke of Richmond gave the magnificently successful fireworks party shown here, for the Duke of Modena.

Design for silk fabric, Spitalfields, 1741.

Court dress, 1741. The silver embroidery almost covering the fabric must have made the dress exhaustingly heavy to wear.

Satin shoes embroidered with coloured silks, gold and silver thread and gold lace, with fashionable turned-up toes.

A City Shower by Edward Penny, 1764. This self-possessed young maid-servant has just washed her employer's marble-floored entrance hall. She is wearing pattens to keep her feet dry. She twirls the water out of her mop, regardless of passers-by.

end, each in an enclosure 25 feet square, divided from the general public by a partition. The third court sat in another corner. Where the walls were not taken up by these courts, they were lined with small retail shops.

There was no qualifying examination, unless you count the oath 'in denunciation of the pope'. To take the next step up to King's Counsel meant forswearing transubstantiation as well, which does not sound too difficult.[18] Counsel were distinguishable from the idlers waiting to hear the judgements, or the shoppers chatting, only by their gowns and bands.[19] Far from there being silence in court, Counsel had to contend with spectators 'in deep discourse upon some irrelevant subject ... and young ladies actually sewing each other's clothes together amidst titters and suppressed laughter'.[20]

Then, as now, there was a popular perception that Freemasonry pervaded the judiciary. Hogarth's print of *Night*, published in 1738, portrays a drunken magistrate still in his masonic regalia, being supported home by his clerk.[21] The viewers would immediately have recognised him as a notoriously immoral Bow Street magistrate loathed by the poor not only for his savage sentencing, but for his attempt to enforce the 1736 Gin Act. The legal profession was popularly thought to be not above corruption. An 'ambidexter' was a lawyer who took fees from both plaintiff and defendant,[22] presumably before the case came to trial.

By then there were four principal Inns of Court, providing professional training and discipline, and, to some extent, living quarters for barristers and judges, but all was not well. The Inns were in the doldrums as educational establishments. 'Retirement was here intended to promote knowledge ... but these seminaries are no longer possessed of their intended inhabitants. They are become lodging houses to the mean, the vicious, the ridiculous, the abandoned, to *stockbrokers* [my italics], gamesters ... They come ... not unaccompanied. Their Dulcineas attend them with a long procession of fidlers, cats, monkeys, French horns, dogs, pimps and parasites...'[23]

Medicine

Massie does not mention medicine in his list of occupations. 'It is no easy matter to become a physician. Much reading, much thought and pains will really be required', then, as now. No wonder qualified men resented so bitterly such 'bold and confident pretenders to the art of medicine' as quacks.[24] Dr Mead, perhaps the leader of his profession, is said to have made £12,000 a year from his practice – an inconceivable amount in those days, and all free of income tax, which had not yet been invented. He attended only rich patients – and the Foundling Hospital children. Everyone else he prescribed for on the evidence of the visiting apothecary. He rode about London 'in a gilt carriage drawn by six horses and accompanied by two running footmen'.[25] A vivid glimpse of successful physicians as viewed from the gutter: 'in their chariots poring over Books ... to give the Town a sense of their deep Study when perhaps what they are reading may be a ludicrous pamphlet'.[26]

Surgeons qualified by an apprenticeship or pupillage, working their way up the hierarchy until they too could take pupils. Many physicians took a degree abroad, in Leyden, Montpellier or Edinburgh. Medical students could attend courses of lectures in London, given by eminent practitioners. The *London Evening Post* advertised lectures in midwifery and physic, and several other courses including one by the famous William Hunter on 'the Art of Dissecting, during the whole winter season'.[27] A course of 'anatomical lectures, and for learning to dissect and perform chirurgical operations' was advertised in the *Whitehall Evening Post*.[28] These were the final destinations of executed felons, horribly depicted in Hogarth's *The Reward of Cruelty*.[29] But what if the supply of official corpses ran short? The problem could be solved by a little initiative. 'Undertakers who have a body to bury from their own house, which they have sold to be anatomised, are interring coffins full of rubbish and suffer Funeral Service to be devoutly performed over it.'[30]

Teaching

The status of a teacher was very low. Oliver Goldsmith wrote in 1759, 'is any man unfit for any of the professions, he finds his last resource in setting up a school ... Of all professions in Society I do not know a more useful or a more honourable one than a schoolmaster: at the same time that I do not see any more generally despised or ... so ill rewarded. The care of our children, is it below the State?'[31] Massie does not include the profession, unless teachers were part of his 'liberal arts', earning on average £60 a year.

The Church

The only necessary qualification was a university degree in something. The candidate for ordination need never have set his mind to theology, or even philosophy, but increasingly during the century it helped if he had some powerful connections who could ease him into the profitable recesses of the Anglican Church. Massie divided the clergy between 'superior', of whom he estimated there were 2,000 families in the kingdom with an annual income of £100, and 'inferior', of whom there were 9,000 with an income of £50. The 1754 editors of *Stow*, a mine of information on the people of London, do not even mention the clergy. Bishops were certainly superior. Canterbury at the top of the pile was worth £7,000 a year, Durham £6,000 and Winchester £5,000. The Bishop of Oxford could count on only £500,[32] but he could still join his colleagues in the class of 'superior clergy'.

The parlous state of the inferior clergy was reflected in the accounts of the charity usually called the Corporation of the Sons of the Clergy, established after the Civil War to help the widows and children of 'loyal and orthodox clergy as are poore and indigent'.[33] A hundred years later, 'clerical poverty is almost the chief problem of the Church today', a splendidly narrow view ignoring such inconvenient problems as the teeming poor outside the church door. Whether the charity relieved much clerical poverty is doubtful, but it provided schooling 'to educate, cloathe and maintain the sons and daughters of Distressed Clergymen till of age ... to be apprenticed',[34] and its annual procession and service was one of the events of the musical season. The procession of the children to St Paul's Cathedral was led by whifflers,[35] Dr Boyce amplified Purcell's orchestra with more wind and drums, Handel contributed a Te Deum, Prince George (aged nine) and his young brother came to the 1747 rehearsal and gave a princely £50, but the clergy went on being poor.

The Army and Navy

The way in, and up, was money. It was an uncertain investment. Naval officers were increasingly expected to know what they were doing, but still they had to wait until there was a vacancy in the promotion ladder. Conditions at sea were appalling for officers as well as for men, only slightly palliated by the prospect, during wartime, of prize money.

An army officer[36] had little prospect of this. He could buy an ensigncy – the lowest form of commissioned life – for £170–200, in a 'marching regiment', which might be stationed anywhere in England, Ireland or overseas, and then work his way up the ladder, buying each successive step until when he retired he could expect to realise the capital value of his rank on resale, to keep him in his old age. There was another route, where local commanders were authorised to commission officers. The 49th Foot, to which so many convicted criminals were consigned, had been stationed in Jamaica for decades and must have been constantly short of officers – and men – through tropical disease. But these commissions could not be resold. 'Whoever intends to purchase a commission in the army shall first inform himself whether the commission ... may be sold with the King's leave.'[37]

A high proportion of army officers were the sons of clergymen, Huguenot immigrants and, especially, Scots. For them, or for their families, the cost of an ensigncy compared favourably with an apprenticeship premium in a decent trade. But the pay was minimal and the prospects were poor. Massie assessed 'military officers' at £100 a year, but a contemporary[38] worked out the basic living costs of an ensign at £54 15s a year, living very modestly indeed with no leeway for when more affluent young men joined the mess and expected everyone to run up mess bills and gambling debts. The unfortunate ensign, far from having money to throw about, was budgeting to pay a soldier a penny a day to dress his hair and shave him: it all mounted up. If the regiment were ordered abroad, his 'equipage', such as uniforms, shirts and socks, bed and bedding could cost him up to £400. By the time he reached the dizzy height of Lieutenant-Colonel, and was, say, stationed in Ireland, his pay would be just over £229 a year, but his 'necessary expenses' were £100 more. The answer to the obvious question 'How did they manage?' seems to have been an official system of extra allowances for service abroad, supplemented by various unofficial perquisites.

Amusements: gambling

'To game: ... (2) to play wantonly and extravagantly for money': Dr Johnson's *Dictionary*.

> Britons, 'twere greatly to your glory
> Should those who shall transmit your story
> Their notions of your grandeur frame
> Not as you give, but as you game

–lines on the door of a City church where a charity sermon had raised 29s.[39]

The moneyed classes were as addicted to gambling as the poor were addicted to gin, but, of course, they arranged things to suit themselves, unmolested by the law. High society played in members' clubs, such as White's, and Almack's where their established ritual included turning their coats inside-out, for luck, and wearing leather sleeveguards 'such as footmen wear when they clean the knives', and high-crowned hats adorned with flowers.

Charles James Fox lost £140,000 at cards in three years, which he could not afford. In 1770 Horace Walpole wrote: 'The gaming is worthy of the decline of an Empire. The young men lose five, ten, fifteen thousand pounds in an evening. Lord Stavordale, not one-and-twenty, lost eleven thousand last Tuesday, but recovered it by one great hand at hazard. He swore a great oath – "Now, if I had been playing deep, I might have won millions!"' There were even 'lady [card] sharpers, who stake false money and have even the address to change it for Sterling'.[40]

If there were no cards handy, there was bound to be something to bet on. A man fell down apparently dead, outside Brooks's club. The members immediately betted on whether he was really dead. The suggestion that someone should go and see if he could be revived was regarded as in poor taste, since it would affect the bet.[41]

For those without the entrée to White's, there were plenty of other gaming houses. There was one in Golden Square mainly used by foreign domestic servants, who 'met every Thursday night and played very high';[42] one over the river at Cuper's Gardens,[43] a rather *louche* quarter, another 'by the little turnstile in Holbourne',[44] another in the Strand and doubtless hundreds more. These have surfaced only because *The Gentleman's Magazine* reported raids on them. For example

Justice Fielding having received information of a rendezvous of gamesters in the Strand procured a strong party of guards who seized forty five at the tables, which they broke to pieces, and carried the gamesters before the justice, who committed thirty nine of them to the gate-house [lock-up: overnight prison] and admitted the other three to bail. There were three tables broken to pieces ... under each of them were observed two iron rollers and two private springs which those who were in the secret could touch and stop the turning whenever they had any youngsters to deal with and so cheated them of their money'.[45]

Boxing, cricket, cock-fighting – they all provided opportunities for betting.

Boxing

Boxing bouts had been promoted by John Broughton in Marylebone Fields since 1743. They were fought with bare knuckles and very few rules. Contestants could do anything they liked to each other as long as it was above the belt. Broughton offered tuition in boxing at his house in the Haymarket, 'and [so] that persons of quality and distinction may not be debarred from entering into a course of those lectures they will be given the utmost tenderness, for which reason mufflers [boxing gloves] are provided that will effectually secure them from the inconveniency of black eyes, broken jaws and bloody noses'. These muffled gentlemen were unlikely, however, to join in Broughton's Battles Royal, in which a champion took on seven at the same time, single-handed.[46] The fights took place on an unfenced platform, with several rows of seating for gentlemen, separated from the platform by a gap where the plebs stood, their eyes on a level with the boxers' feet. In one famous fight, 'no less was taken than £300 to see these combatants, who fought as long as they could lift their arms'.[47] 'Many thousands have depended upon a match.'[48]

Cricket

Cricket had been played on the Artillery Ground in Finsbury since at least 1744.[49] There were two stumps only, and a scoop-shaped bat, and a 'popping-hole' in front of the wicket, into which it was the batsman's object to plant his bat, having made his runs, before the wicket-keeper could pop the ball in. The ball, which was red, was thrown fast and hard, under-arm, not by that extraordinary windmill action. It was always played for money. In an epic game on the Artillery Ground in 1744 Kent beat All England, 111 to 110. Kent was captained by Lord John Sackville, and included John Rumney his gardener – cricket was remarkable for ignoring class barriers.[50] By

1763, when Middlesex met Surrey at Finsbury, cricketing news was becoming familiar.[51]

Cock-fighting

Hogarth's print *The Cockpit* (1759) had a political message (referring to Pitt's conduct of the war), but as a straight picture of the scene at a cock-fight it could not be bettered. Boswell added a sound track. 'The uproar, and the noise of betting, is prodigious. A great deal of money made a quick circulation from hand to hand.' And 'on the least demur to pay a bet "basket" is vociferated *in terrorem*',[52] according to the rules, by which 'Should any man make a wager and lose, but not pay his dues and make another wager, he shall be put in a basket and hung up to the eaves of the main, where all men shall see him, and there shall remain till the end of the session, when he shall be cut down and banished from the main'.[53] In Hogarth's print the shadow of a man suspended overhead in a basket holding out his watch as an offer, falls on to the ring. There was no segregation of gentry and commoners. Elegantly dressed nobles wearing orders on their satin coats jostled for a view with the rest. This cockpit was built at the end of the seventeenth century, in Birdcage Walk at the edge of St James's Park. There was another just north of Gray's Inn.[54]

The lottery

The state lottery had been running since 1569 (and would continue until 1826, when William Wilberforce achieved its abolition).[55] It generated funds for several worthy causes, such as bridges across the Thames.[56] In 1755, for example, it raised nearly £4 million, nearly four times the amount aimed at.[57] Just as now, there were pitiful stories of lottery-ticket holders. 'Mr Keys, late clerk to Cotton and Co, who had absented himself ever since the 7th of October, the day the £10,000 prize was drawn in the lottery (supposed to be his property) was found in the street raving mad, having been robbed of his pocket-book and ticket.'[58] A permutation that as far as I know does not apply to the modern version was to insure any number for any amount, against coming up blank. The touts who marketed this scheme, which had huge potential for fraud, were called 'Morocco men', from the elegant leather wallets they used.

Tickets were bought in batches by contractors called 'lottery office keepers', and resold at a profit. Sales were advertised in the daily papers. In 1743 half a ticket could be bought for £2 10s and a sixteenth for 6s 6d.[59] There were several lottery offices scattered through London. One that boasted that it was the oldest was 'directly behind the King on horseback' (the equestrian statue of Charles I at the top of Whitehall, often used in the eighteenth century as a landmark).

The draws were public events, with maximum publicity. At the Guildhall, a Bluecoat boy drew the winning numbers from one wheel and another drew the prize numbers from another wheel. Once, one of the wheels stuck, and one of the boys had to strip and get into it to disengage the crucial piece of paper. News of the winning numbers was flown to outlying parts by carrier pigeon, or taken on horseback at a fast gallop. Betting on the lottery was so widespread that no eyebrows were raised when one lady solicited the prayers of her congregation, for 'a new undertaking' – her lottery ticket.[60] James Newton, in London from his Oxfordshire parish, always bought a ticket, and never won, but it amused him to go and see the tickets drawn.[61]

Swimming

That swimming could form part of a gentleman's life, in those days before efficient heating, may be surprising. Yet by 1743 the Peerless Pool (near Old Street: it used to be called the Perilous Pool, before it was refurbished) was 'an elegant pleasure bath' 170 feet long by 100 feet wide, with a smooth gravel bottom, 5 feet deep in the middle, 4 feet at the sides and 3 feet at one end.

> Access was by several flights of steps ... adjoining to which are boxes and arbours for dressing and undressing, some of them open, some enclosed. On the south side is a neat arcade under which is a looking glass over a marble slab, and a small collection of books for the entertainment of the subscribers ... here is also a cold bath [so was the other one heated, or did 'cold bath' here mean a plunge bath?] the largest in England, 40ft by 20ft ... a very large fish pond [for anglers] 320ft long ... The free use of the place is purchased by the easy subscription of one guinea per annum

or two shillings a visit.[62] It is pleasant to think of James Newton, up from his Oxfordshire parish, treating himself to a visit on a hot August day in 1761.[63] There was another 'Swimming bath which is convenient for swimming or for gentlemen to learn to swim in' out at Goodman's fields, near the London Infirmary. 'It is near 43ft in length and *kept warm* [my italics] and fresh every day, and waiters attend daily to teach gentlemen to swim ... there is also a good cold bath.'[64]

Sex

'As we walked along the Strand to-night, arm in arm, a woman of the town accosted us, in the usual enticing manner. "No, no, my girl, (said Johnson) it won't do".'[65] The only unusual thing about this is that she was alone. Grosley found that 'about nightfall [the women of the town] range themselves in a file in the footpaths of all the great streets in companies of five or six, most of them dressed very genteely. The low tavern serves them as a retreat to receive their gallants in; there is always a room set aside for this purpose. Whole rows of them accost passengers in broad daylight...'[66]

Bagnios and brothels

Casanova was impressed by the London sex scene.

I visited the bagnios where a rich man can sup, bathe and sleep with a fashionable courtesan, of which there are many in London. It makes a magnificent debauch and only costs six guineas ... We went to see the well known procuress Mrs Wells and saw the celebrated courtesan Kitty Fisher who was waiting for the Duke of − to take her to a ball ... she had on diamonds worth 5,000 francs ... she had eaten a banknote for 1,000 guineas on a slice of bread and butter that very day ... [so she said][67]

One would need to know which bagnios were perfectly respectable establishments where you could be cupped and take a healthy swim, such as − unless I am fooled by its publicity − the Turk's Head bagnio in Chancery Lane,[68] and which were simply brothels, or as M. Grosley put it, 'warehouses' kept by 'substantial wholesale dealers', where, he noted, the prices were fixed. A well-organised man about town such as M. Grosley solved this problem by consulting a copy of *Harris's List of Covent Garden Ladies or Man of Pleasure's Kalendar*, 'an exact description of the most celebrated Ladies of Pleasure who frequent

Covent Garden and other parts of this Metropolis. Sold in all the booksellers in London: 2/6.'[69]

Keeping a disorderly house was an offence at common law, recognised by statute in 1752. The penalties were not usually onerous: a small fine, a spell in the pillory – where no one would throw anything too dangerous – and a short spell in prison.[70] An exception was Mary Bunce, who was fined £20 and given six months' imprisonment for running a disorderly house near the Hay Market. 'This was the most celebrated person ever appeared, in her way [business], having no less than 22 houses of the same sort within the Bills of Mortality', and a considerable fortune;[71] an early example, perhaps, of franchising.

Boswell, who took a fancy to copulate with a whore on Westminster Bridge, never, surprisingly, went out to the Folly, a barge moored in midstream with, as a young Swiss described it, 'a few small apartments on the second floor, and a restaurant on the first floor. From the top of the building there is an enchanting view of the city and the river.'[72] Could he have missed the notorious fact that the 'small apartments' were run as a brothel?

Brothels proliferated on the north side of the Strand, in the streets behind it, and also in and round Covent Garden. 'Monday night a little after dusk the [parish constables] began to search the houses of ill fame in those districts. The ladies not expecting so early a visit [it was a dark January day] were mostly taken dressing themselves and before eight in the evening the round-houses were full',[73] but the ladies probably talked their way out quite soon. I hope they were warm enough.

There was a 'black bawdy-house',[74] and 'molly houses', homosexual meeting places.[75] In 1764, 'One John Gill was apprehended in a coach in the Strand dressed in women's clothes extremely gay, and being carried before Sir John Fielding was by him committed to Bridewell. He goes by the name of Miss Beasley about Devereux Court' in the Temple, said to be a homosexual haunt.[76]

There have always been brothels and, as long as they do not involve slavery – and the contemporary literature did not complain of that – or annoy the neighbours, one cannot work up much indignation about them. But the Bridewell at Clerkenwell sounds hellish. Since the county allowance was only a pennyworth of bread and some water every 24 hours, the women prisoners had the choice of dying of hunger or prostituting themselves. The prison staff 'consider all the women their seraglio'. In two wards known as the bawdy houses, a male prisoner or visitor could have a woman prisoner, willing or unwilling, the whole night, for a shilling tip to the keeper. 'The place may be considered a great brothel kept under the protection of the law ... [It is] common for the keeper of a bagnio to come to this place, call for a bottle or two of wine [and] look over the girls ... pay their fees and take them home.' If the girl didn't pay off these 'fees', she would be arrested for debt and thrown into gaol, 'where she is left to perish by nastiness, hunger and disease'.[77]

Prostitutes

Boswell too was impressed at how the available talent ran from 'the splendid Madam at fifty guineas a night down to the civil nymph with white thread stockings who tramps along the Strand and will resign her engaging person ... for a pint of wine and a shilling'.[78] The trouble with the 'civil nymph' – and, indeed, the 'splendid madam' – was that she so often had venereal disease, which if asked she would deny. Smollett, another Scotsman and writer, but with a more realistic, medically trained eye, puts this description into the mouth of one of his characters:

I have often seen while I strolled about the streets at midnight, a number of naked wretches reduced to rags and filth, huddled together like swine in the corner of a dark alley; some of whom, but eighteen months before, I had known the favourites of the town, rolling in affluence, and glittering in all the pomp of equipage and dress. And indeed the gradation is easily conceived: the most fashionable woman of the town is as liable to contagion as one in a much humbler sphere: she infects her admirers, her situation is public: she is avoided, neglected, unable to sustain her usual appearance, which however she strives to maintain as long as possible: her credit fails, she is obliged to retrench and become a night-walker, her malady gains ground, she tampers with her constitution and ruins it, her complexion fades, she grows nauseous to everybody, finds herself reduced to a starving condition, is tempted to pick pockets, is detected, committed to Newgate where she remains in a miserable condition, till she is discharged because the plaintiff will not appear to prosecute her. Nobody will afford her lodging, the symptoms of her distemper are grown outragious [sic] she sues [pleads] to be admitted into a hospital where she is cured at the expense of her nose, she is turned out naked into the streets, depends on the addresses of the lowest class, is fain to allay the rage of hunger and cold with gin, degenerates into a brutal insensibility, rots and dies on a dung-hill.[79]

Pornography

Fanny Hill or Memoirs of a Woman of Pleasure by John Cleland was published in 1749. The authorities were scandalised, the more so because the delightful Fanny does not even incur the wages of sin so blackly forecast by Smollett. They ordered that all copies should be destroyed, but somehow the order was never rigorously carried out, and Arthur Wellesley, the future Duke of Wellington, was able to pack nine copies of it when he went out to India.[80] Some of the huge output of prints were fairly rude. The Bishop of London attributed the earthquake in 1750 to the wrath of God: 'Have not all the abomination of the public stews been opened to view by lewd pictures exposed to sale at noonday?'[81] *Aristotle's Masterpiece*, constantly in print since the last century, has been described as the most common sex manual,[82] but you would need a vivid imagination to get any sexual titillation out of it. Unlike modern manuals explaining cars, personal computers etc, it does not assume that you know already how to do what you are looking for in the manual, but all I found was a charming view of matrimony – 'A married state is the most happy condition (where persons are equally yoked) that is to be enjoyed this side Heaven' – and, bound with it, a copy of *The Family Physician* – 'after a long labour wrap the woman in a freshly removed warm sheepskin, fleshy side to her belly'.

CHAPTER 20

Fashion and Beauty

Female underwear

Women's bodies are extraordinarily malleable. The basic structure remains the same, but the fleshy masses hung on it can migrate in the most remarkable way. The bosom, for instance, is either 'in', as it was during most of the eighteenth century, or 'out', as it was in the 1920s. If it was permissible to have a bosom, what shape should it be and how far should it be visible?

Stays

'A kind of stiff waistcoat made of whalebone, worn by women': Dr Johnson's *Dictionary*. The great lexicographer would have done well to get some expert advice here. The garment was not 'made of whalebone', but of two layers of heavy linen often stiffened with paste or glue, into which more stiffening of cane[1] or straw[2] or narrow strips of whalebone were sewn with rows of minute backstitching.[3] The front, or the whole garment, was covered with a decorative fabric matching or contrasting prettily with the dress. So when a pawnbroker displayed stays in his shop window, they were more like jackets, in our terms, than brassières, and it was not so unthinkable to put this advertisement in the newspaper:

> Lost on Monday last, a blue-green lustring gown lined with white stuff and a pair of small stays, white tabby [a kind of plain woven fabric] before [in front] with Russell or calimanco back. Whoever will bring them to ... [address] shall have half a guinea reward and no questions

asked: if offered to sell or pawn pray stop them and you shall have the same reward...[4]

To save all that sewing, the stays could be made of leather, scored vertically on the same lines as the boning of fabric stays, to make them curve round the body. Those that I have seen[5] are forbiddingly rigid, but so would a pair of heavy leather shoes be if they had been stored away for centuries. If they were worn every day and either dressed from time to time with something like shoe cream, or – more realistically – anointed with the sweat and oil on the skin of the wearer, they would be as comfortable and supportive as a well-worn old pair of shoes. Indeed, a pair have been made and worn recently, and did not 'prove to be an impediment to any household duties'.[6]

Stays were worn by all females, from babyhood. A woman was condemned to death for stripping and robbing a four-year-old girl of 'one stay valued 1/- one pair of stockings one linen bib and an Apron'.[7] There were those, usually medics, who deplored them as leading to 'disorders of the viscera and the death of children in breeding [pregnant] women',[8] but the opposite school of thought – staymakers? – insisted that they avoided or cured the deformities which might otherwise leap on unguarded and unstiffened girls at a moment's notice.

Fashionable women who did not expect to exert themselves wore stays that were boned not only vertically but horizontally as well, at the top of the front, so that it lay flat from shoulder to shoulder,[9] and imposed an admirably upright posture, with the shoulders held back away from the corners of the front, which otherwise would have dug in uncomfortably. The sides sloped down to the waist, extending to a point in the front, which could be further stiffened by a rigid busk of wood or whalebone. These busks could be charming vehicles for sentimental messages from swains, especially sailors who spent some of the long hours at sea etching pictures, in scrimshaw, of ships and whales and hearts on to spatula-shaped pieces of whalebone. The point or stomacher went over the skirt, the rest of the waist was cut into tabs, still stiffened, that went under the skirt. The back of the stays was made in two pieces, ending roughly mid-shoulder blade level, with eyelet holes for stay laces at the middle edges. Ribbons might be threaded through holes in the top, at the back and front, to go round the upper arm, leaving the shoulders bare, but they were not needed to keep the stays up, like shoulder straps. The general effect was the fashionable inverted sugar loaf shape,[10] or in modern terms like an ice-cream cone. Because the warmth and pressure of the body might distort the whalebone stiffening, stays were sometimes made reversible. This also reassured those who feared that stays would encourage any existing lack of symmetry in the body. Each side got equal pressure.

As to how much of the bosom was covered, it could vary according to the occasion. Henry Fielding's *Shamela*,[11] intent on conquest, 'put on my prettiest ... cap and pulled down my stays, to shew as much as I could of my bosom', which was quite a lot, since in their normal position they only just covered the nipples. M. Grosley became quite incoherent when describing this 'most striking article of English beauty ... when in dishabille these ribbands generally falling upon the arms, the upper part of the body, disengaged from all vesture, receives ... the overplus of nourishment which the compression of the lower part distributes to it, which results in the ease and beauty of the shape'.[12]

Stays were usually made to measure by a male stay-maker, and could be altered. In 1756,[13]

Miss —'s stays bound round the top and cut lower before	2/-
Her loose slip altered and made to fit the new stays	5/-
Mrs —'s stays let out a lap on each side and bound	5/-

A pair of 'white ticken turning [reversible] slip bone stays' cost £1 8s in 1761.[14]

Hoops

The stays were worn over a knee-length chemise with the same low neckline as the stays, gathered on a ribbon draw-string and lace-edged.[15] Then came a short straight underskirt, confusingly called a 'coat', and then the most famous eighteenth-century device for falsifying the female form – the hooped petticoat. This could be tied round the waist, to give a bell shape curved all round. To give side fullness only, it was made in two parts worn on the hips as 'false hips' (it was the Victorians who thought it nicer to call them panniers).[16] The stiffening was bands of whalebone or cane. In 1742 a mere 10½ feet was wide enough for a country lady ordering from London.[17] But skirts went on increasing in width, so a stronger structure was evolved, on engineering principles. Three metal U-shapes on each side, connected at front and back, were hinged so that they could be folded up like the roof of a sports car. They succeeded in holding the skirt out in a horizontal line, from the wearer's hips, by more than arm's length:[18] an extraordinarily ungainly fashion that reached its apogee in the 1740s, and remained approved wear at court for twenty years or so.

> Suppose the fine lady coming into a room. First enters, wriggling and sideling [sic] and edging by degrees two yards and a half of hoop, for as yet you can see nothing else. Some time after that appears the inhabitant of the garment herself, not with a full face but in profile. Next follows two yards and a half more.[19]

Although the static pose of portraits implies that these huge skirts were anchored to the ground, their behaviour in a high wind or a rapid walk was far from static. They swayed from side to side, or from front to back, in an alarming – or, if the wearer so intended, an enticing – way, disclosing more of the wearer than seems likely from the painted picture. (Knickers had not yet arrived.) They also provided a refreshing breeze round the wearer's legs as she moved.[20] But they presented difficulties. 'We sit in a [sedan] chair hid up to our very eyes like a swan with her head beneath her lifted wings. The whole side of the coach is hardly capacious enough for one of us. ... With our lifted hoops in our hands we expose such a hollow in coming down [stairs] as surprises all below us.'[21] And like most fashions they did not suit the short. 'I have seen many fine ladies of a low stature who when they sail in their hoops about an apartment look like little children in go-carts.'[22]

By 1760 enormous hoops were out, and a mild tulip shape, still with a pointed bodice, made life much easier, except at Court where the expanse of silk hung from extended panniers lingered on.

Dresses

The 'mantua', usually made by a woman, was a skirt and bodice open in the front to show the decorated stays, the sides of the bodice pinned to the stays or tied across with ribbons, the skirt showing a matching or contrasting underskirt. The 'sack back' or 'sack' or 'sacque' dress, often made by a man, was more intricately cut, with a panel starting at the top edge of the stays at the back and falling to the hem in two wide pleats kept in place by invisible tapes.[23] The bodice was fitted, under the pleats, by lacing at the back. It is surprising that dressmaking charges were so low. In 1757 the 'hoop maker' to Lady Caroline Russell charged £1 8s for a blue hoop, yet the next year a 'professional sack maker' charged only a guinea for 'making a black silk sack and petticoat'.[24]

A filmy apron, so clearly useless that it signalled the social status of the wearer, was worn over the skirt, and an equally filmy scarf covered the neckline of the dress.

Night wear was a loose shift perhaps a little longer than the daytime version. A 'night gown' was not a nightie but a slightly less formal mantua, perhaps to instep level instead of floor length, and with less *décolletage*.

Fabrics

Wool had fallen quite out of fashion. Cotton and silk were in. Silks woven in Spitalfields were ravishing. Delicate flowers in clear colours trailed through rococo mazes:[25] incongruously lighthearted, if one remembers the desperation of the poor weavers who made them. The yardage for a dress can be guessed from an order for 16 yards of cotton for a petticoat.[26] 'The Countess of Falmouth fainted away in the drawing room of Leicester House [the Prince of Wales's Court] occasioned by the excessive weight of her clothes.'[27] Gold and silver were woven into fabrics, embroidered on to them, or both. Jewels were scattered over them. A fancy dress ball in Somerset House, given by the Russian Ambassador in 1755 must have been illuminated by the dresses of the guests. On the other hand, one of those famous beauties the Misses Chudleigh came to a ball dressed in nothing much at all.

Accessories

A small muff or 'muffetees' – wristlets – of fur or feathers of swan, parrot or peacock,[28] and a fan completed the ensemble. Fans had shrunk from enormous, to a mere 2 feet by 1744. Caps of varying sizes were worn on the top of the head, before hairstyles took off for the ceiling. They had side pieces, 'lappets', often of exquisite lace, which could be tied under the chin or left loose on the shoulders. The final touch was a miniature dog. By eight o'clock on a Sunday morning 'servants to Ladies of Quality are washing and combing such lap-dogs as are to go to church with their mistresses that morning'.[29]

Shoes

The shoes that have survived in museums are those which were worn only for special occasions, and they tend to give an unbalanced view of eighteenth-century footwear. They were beautiful. They were made of silk, lined with linen or kid, brocaded or embroidered with silk and metallic thread and spangles, and bound at the seams with metallic braid. The heels, fabric-covered, were 4 to 6 centimetres high, waisted like an old-fashioned lavatory pedestal. The toes were pointed, and in the 1740s turned up at the end: see the second plate of Hogarth's *Marriage à la Mode*, where the Countess is wearing just such shoes. They would never see the streets of London except in a chair. All shoes were made 'straight', with no difference between left and right.

More normal shoes could be protected from the mud by wooden clogs or pattens: overshoes raised on metal or wood platforms, which must have been exceedingly difficult to walk in, on snowy or wet pavements. The main figure in Hogarth's print *Morning* has left a trail of prints through the snow, which look as if they were made by an overshoe of some kind with a rough, even spiked, sole. Everyday shoes were of stout leather with slight heels and leather soles, fastened with plain buckles or leather or linen laces.

Stockings could be silk, linen thread or woollen. Scarlet was a popular colour.

Jewellery

Pearls were imported from the Gulf and the Far East. The Chinese were making artificial pearls. Patience, some seed pearls and chemicals including mercury could 'form large pearls out of small ones'[30] at home. It was in the evening that women who could afford to, coruscated in the candlelight.

Pearls were outshone by diamonds. From the 1730s, the diamond mines in Golconda, India, were supplemented by Brazilian diamonds. The technique of cutting diamonds had vastly improved, and a piece could be given extra impact by mounting diamond flowers or insects on springs, as 'tremblers'. Paste, clear or coloured like rubies or emeralds, was so skilfully made that it could deceive the most critical eye, which could sort the authentic from the imitation only by knowing the wealth of the wearer's husband.

Pieces costing thousands of pounds were turned out by designers in Paris and copied in London. At a ball given by the Duke of Bolton, 'it was said there were £270,000s worth of jewels between three ladies'.[31] Lady Temple managed to trump that at a ball a few months later, 'the jewels she wore being estimated at £150,000'.[32] Massive jewelled stomachers, extending across the top of the stays and down the front, were fashionable up to the 1750s, necklaces tending to dislodge them from that time. Yet a diamond pin for the hair could be bought for as little as a guinea.

A lady who wore a cap could pin it with a diamond, or trim the binding on the edge of it with diamonds. If she had given up caps, she could stick her diamond pins into her hair, or drape single diamonds across it on fine chains. Ships in full sail had not yet arrived, but flowers and feathers − black or white or in diamonds − could be perched in the hair.[33]

For day wear, agates, garnets and other semi-precious stones were made into elaborate *parures* of matching necklace, ear-rings that could be lengthened with pendants for evening or worn as simple 'snaps' (for pierced ears, of course), perhaps a cross to hang from the necklace, an aigrette for the hair, a brooch ... Jewelled pins kept sleeves and panniers and bodices in place.[34]

With all this talk of diamonds, a practical problem remains: *how* do you attach a row of diamonds to a cap? Or, for that matter, scatter them on dresses? Even 'the great diamond in His Majesty's [George III's] crown fell out in returning to Westminster Hall [after his coronation] but was immediately found and restored'.[35] The job of a cleaner after one of the state balls must have been well worth having.

Cosmetics

Ceruse was still going strong, even if its wearers were not. It was 'a preparation of white lead, which is of a white colour; whence many other things resembling it ... are called ceruse; as the ceruse of antimony and the like', according to Dr Johnson's *Dictionary*. It produced the desirable matt white complexion. It also produced lead poisoning, in time. Lady Coventry died of it in 1760. There were other more immediate snags. Its artificial white 'is immediately discovered by the eye at a considerable distance and by the nose upon a nearer approach and ... it had the most nauseous taste imaginable'.[36] This was not, of course, mentioned in the advertisements, which covered the same ground that all such advertisements do – erasing wrinkles, clearing the complexion, etc. – but in those days they also had to promise to obliterate the scars of smallpox. Possibly they assumed a greater degree of gullibility in their users than modern cosmetic advertisements: 'The Royal Cosmetic ... making a person look young though really old ... 3/6 a half pint pot'[37] seems remarkably good value, or 'The Persian Handkerchief of Beauty ... any lady or gentleman after using it for some time will look much younger than they really are ... [it can] be used in company ... by a gentle rubbing, one guinea each.'[38] (A quick rub as your hero comes in sight?)

Black eyebrows seem to have been desirable, but I have found no equivalent of mascara, which would tend to run before modern non-irritating fixatives. If your eyebrows grew in the wrong place, you could pluck them out and replace them higher up with paint, or strips of mouse skin.[39] The apothecaries' shops sold dozens of washes and lotions guaranteed to produce a beautiful face, and most cookery books contained a few useful recipes. Eliza Smith gives a recipe for 'lip salve' containing alkanet root, which will have dyed it a pretty red.[40]

The patches that had adorned the Restoration beauties a hundred years earlier were still being worn. In moderation they can be charming, but the old bawd who met the country coach in the first plate of Hogarth's *A Harlot's Progress* is made even more sinister by a great scatter of patches on her face.

Men's clothes

Unlike the tidal waves of women's hoops, men's fashions stayed much the same. Men showed off their legs in silk or cotton stockings, gartered below the knee or folded over the edge of reasonably comfortable breeches with a 'fall flap' instead of a fly.[41] The breeches hardly showed under the coat, which was worn partly or wholly open, despite the heavily emphasised buttons and buttonholes, reaching to knee length. The skirts of the coat made a faint effort to emulate women's gowns in 1745, stiffened and pleated at the side seams so that they stood out from the waist, but they lost enthusiasm for the contest and gradually deflated. Shoulders were narrow and unpadded. A 'smart' coat meant a fitted one, so tight round the shoulders that its wearer could not possibly undertake any physical work. A gentleman's coat was usually of plain silk or fine wool cloth, perhaps embroidered or trimmed with metal braid at the front edges, and lined with silk.[42] In 1745 the materials for a man's suit, including 12 yards of silk velvet (silk fabrics were usually only 21 inches wide), gold braid, buttons and linings came to just over £23.[43] The Duke of Bedford paid 64 guineas 'to embroider a rich suit of crimson velvet with gold' in 1757.[44] This must have been for a Court occasion, perhaps for the presentation of his daughter in 1758. A tailor near Hanover Square advertised a 'half trimmed frock suit, superfine cloth, £4 18/-' and a pair of silk knit or cotton velvet breeches for £1 12s.[45]

Waistcoats

A man's glory was his waistcoat. These could, of course, be used for the utilitarian purpose of keeping the cold out, worn even two at a time.[46] But when Samuel Johnson thought, mistakenly, that he would have to bow to a cheering audience when his play *Irene* was put on by his friend David Garrick, he dressed up in a 'scarlet waistcoat with rich gold lace'.[47] Spitalfields silks made for waistcoats were woven in small all-over designs lending themselves to elaboration at the fronts and pocket flaps, which were often skilfully woven into the fabric. The visible parts of a waistcoat could be bought ready-embroidered, and made up at home or by a tailor.[48] The back would be a plain material, with a buckled strap to adjust the fit.

Jewellery

Men had by now given up wearing much jewellery, but they still sparkled about the feet, with diamond, paste or cut steel shoe buckles, and at the knees, with buckles on their breeches. They could spend as much as they liked on buttons for coat and waistcoat, and fix the brims of their hats up with jewelled loops. Swords and snuffboxes could combine enamel and precious stones, long canes for flourishing while walking in St James's Park could have jewelled or amber knobs and silver ferrules.

Shirts

Shirts were made of linen, of varying weights. In 1752 they cost 'from 4/- to one guinea, ready made, but can be made to any size at very short notice'.[49] They sprouted attached fold-down collars at the neckline, and embroidered or frilled jabots down the front opening, which could be elegantly displayed by the open waistcoat. The billowing sleeves were gathered into wrist bands, with or without ruffles, which were sometimes, unlike the jabot, made detachable.

Underwear

Male drawers were as you would expect.[50] Benjamin Franklin wore long linen ones in the summer, but he may have been unusual in this, as in much else. The norm was knee-length, tied at the waist and knees. (There was still no elastic, of course.)

The nightshirt was a longer looser version of the daytime shirt – surely many men simply took old shirts for night wear? – worn with a night cap to keep the shaven head warm.

Dry cleaning

M. Grosley found London filthy, and regretted that 'it is a rule ... not to use, or suffer foreigners to use, our umbrellas of taffeta or waxed silk: for this reason London swarms with shops of scourers [dry cleaners] busy in scouring, repairing and newfurbishing' clothes ruined by London smog.[51] Specialist shops claimed to deal with gold and silver cloths and satin, so that they looked 'like new for gloss and colour'.[52] If they were too far gone, they could be dyed. Silk takes dyes – and stains – easily, but it must have been a major test of skill to achieve an even result with the masses of fabric involved in one dress, some parts loose, some pleated, some lined.[53]

Women's hairstyles

Women's hair had not quite reached the towering summit of the 1790s beloved by cartoonists, when the hairdresser had to stand on a ladder and a lady in a coach had to sit on the floor, but it was on the way up. Dark hair was the fashionable colour. An evening newspaper advertised: 'the only true chymical liquor for the hair which gradually changes red, grey or hair of any other disagreeable colour ... into the most beautiful Black ... if it does not prove infallible return the liquor [how? if you've just used it and are still red-haired] and the Money shall be repaid.'[54] A home dye could be made from elder berries and wine, or 'combing the hair with a black lead comb will make the hair black, but then it comes off on the linen prodigiously',[55] and, surely, on anyone rash enough to touch it.

The front hair was curled with curling irons or curl papers, and a few 'buckles' (from the French *boucles*, curls) strayed carelessly, after hours of effort, over the shoulders. By 1760 it had become impossible to achieve the fashionable look by one's own hair, so it was supplemented by pads of wool or tow, and slicked into place with pomatum. Caps[56] were out of fashion by 1765, so that the whole head became visible, putting a severe strain on hair and hairdresser.

A writer on hair[57] in 1768 pinpointed the usual problem. 'While it remains in dress [uncombed] it hath rest at the roots, which saves large quantities that would fall off by frequent combing ... [but] perspiration ... may occasion effluvia rather disagreeable.' A hairdresser asked a lady how long it was since her 'head had been opened and repaired; she answered, not above nine weeks: to which he replied that that was as long as a head could well go in the summer ... it began to be a little *hazardé*.'[58]

For Court and other full-dress occasions, the hair would be powdered with starch, usually white but sometimes coloured grey or pastel tints, and – one sees why – scented. The powder stuck to the pomade with which the hair was smeared. Minute hats were perched on top of these edifices, which M. Grosley thought gave the wearers an 'arch and roguish air [and] vivacity which is not natural to them'.[59] He found the English a sad lot.

Wigs and shaving

George III disappointed the peruke-makers, when he acceded in 1760, by 'wearing his own hair' – no wig. Extraordinary. At least his hair was arranged to look like a wig[60] – but *by his wife*, not a perruquier.[61] Side 'buckles', unkindly described in a recent costume drama as looking like sausage rolls gummed to the side of the head, could be created from the natural hair in the same way as Francis Place described some years later when the vogue for wigs was at last fading in the 1780s. Smart young tradesmen in his circle 'had the hair on the sides of their faces rolled upon pieces of window lead about four inches long, they usually had three and sometimes four of these leads one above the other, the lowest receding most'.[62] A simpler and lighter method was the use of curl papers. In Hogarth's *Marriage à la Mode*, plate 4, 'The Countess's Levée', the Countess is having her hair curled by her French hairdresser, attended by a fop in curl papers.

George III reluctantly took to a 'brown George', still not powdered. In 1765 the peruke-makers asked him to order that all male adults must wear wigs, but he balked.[63] Fashion almost did the job for them. A boy was 'hardly in breeches before he came out with a perruque on his head, which was sometimes not much smaller than himself'.[64] In Hogarth's *Noon* there are two very small boys in full fig, hats and wigs and all. It would be easier to spot the men and boys *not* wearing wigs, in a London crowd, than to count the wig-wearers.

There were innumerable kinds, from the small scratch wig worn by artisans and Samuel Johnson – and his didn't even fit properly, and was usually singed on one side from his holding a candle too near it, to help his poor eyesight – to the majestic floods of curled horsehair worn by judges. Wigs could also be made of human hair, at 5s to £5 an ounce, or even, 'for sporting mode, of mallard's tails'.[65] They could be curled all over or straight; short all round or with a queue or pigtail (popular with the army: officers bound theirs with black leather, soldiers with metal wire and black ribbon, sailors smeared theirs with tar), tied at the back with a big black ribbon bow, or at the front by taking the ribbon round and tying it like a modern black tie. Elizabeth Pollard, peruque-maker, advertised five different models, from 10s 6d ('riding brown bob') to £1 11s 6d[66] ('clean short greys'). There were some unwritten rules as to who wore what kind of wig. Physicians would look ridiculous if they wore a bag-wig (the queue stuffed into a bag at the back of the neck, or just the bag worn);[67] they ought to wear 'cauliflowers'.[68] David Garrick played all parts in a small wig with five curls on each side, whether Roman or gloomy Dane.

Wigs were powdered white with wheat starch for formal occasions. If the wearer had no powdering closet where he could sit masked and caped while the powder was blown on to his wig with bellows, a messenger or footman could take the wig to a wig-maker,[69] which sounds so much easier. To 'flux' a wig was 'to put it up in curl and bake it'.[70] Lord Lovat, the old reprobate who had been found guilty of treason for his part in the '45 rebellion, sent his wig to be combed by the barber the day before he was executed.[71] In hot weather, 'fat unwieldy men who are obliged to walk the street are doubling up their wigs to go in their pockets and putting their handkerchiefs between their hats and their foreheads',[72] which is no way to treat a wig, although they can be very hot.[73]

Boswell paid his barber 6d for shaving him and dressing his wig.[74] Some gentlemen took out an annual contract with their barber/peruke-maker. The going rate in 1747 was 40s. 'For this a gentleman must not only be shaved three times [a week] but have seven wigs dressed likewise', wrote a protesting barber.[75] Shaving brushes were available for 'lathering the head and face ... instead of the hand, by which the disagreeable dabbling by the hand of a servant etc. is avoided'.[76]

Men's hats

Men were as firmly attached to their hats as some are now to their baseball caps. In a print showing one of the many riots in a theatre, some gentlemen are advancing on to the stage, cheered on by the stalls. All are wearing large black triangular hats, rather on the back of their heads. The viewpoint is from the back of the theatre, and the rows of hats in the stalls look like a baker's tray full of blackened apple turnovers. Captain Coram once did a kindness to the Hatters Company, and they wanted to express their gratitude. He would take nothing, so they kept him in hats for the rest of his life – always very large ones.[77] The expression 'old hat' should be avoided, as it was one of the countless synonyms for 'a woman's privities'.[78] In moments of relaxation, such as at a coffee-house, there was usually a peg on the wall, or a candle sconce, where this unwieldy object could be deposited. They could be hired from an ingenious hatter who 'furnishes gentlemen with the loan of three good new hats in the year kept in proper repair for 15s and upwards to £1 1s each warranted worth within 3s of the sum agreed for. Hats dyed, drest and cocked in the genteelest manner.'[79]

Personal hygiene

Dr Johnson 'had no passion for clean linen',[80] and showed no enthusiasm for bathing. Many men must have looked grubby if they were shaved only three times a week. Just how clean people were, by modern standards, is hard to tell. The average wash basin was still no bigger than a mixing bowl: possible for hand washing but not much more. We miss Samuel Pepys's description of his rare and perilous ablutions, which he was sure did him no good. In general terms, I think the idea of daily immersion came over with the

Americans during the last war, and once we were allowed to exceed the permitted maximum of 5 inches of bath water, we lay back and enjoyed it, for the first time.

I have not found, among all the advertisements and household recipes I have read, a mention of deodorant, which did exist a hundred years earlier.[81] It may be that some application of that ubiquitous element, alum (on which it was based), was so accepted as not to need mentioning, or it may be that the seventeenth-century habit had died out. But people did smell, strongly, of stale sweat, tobacco, bad teeth, dirty clothes and unclean bodies, until quite recently, when on a hot day in London's Underground all you can smell is deodorant.

Mourning

One of the troubles that beset the Spitalfields weavers was the regularity with which the Court and fashionable circles round it got their black clothes out of the cupboards for yet another spell of Court mourning. Leaves kept dropping off the spreading royal family tree, all over Europe, and their fall had to be marked in black. In 1751 on the death of the Prince of Wales – the heir to the throne, however much his parents disliked him – courtiers had to provide themselves with the right garments fast, but once they were bought they would do again. Ladies had to wear black bombazine and plain muslin, and creep quietly about in black chamois leather shoes. Men went into black cloth without decorative buttons on the sleeves and pockets, plain muslin cravats, black swords, and the same muffled chamois on their feet.[82] 'It is expected that *all persons* [my italics] ... do put themselves into the deepest mourning (long cloaks only excepted)' within seven days. Full mourning lasted for three months; 'second mourning', during which black might fade to grey, another three months. So a whole season of new colourful silks was lost, and 'by a moderate computation no less than 15,000 persons are now unemployed in the silk manufacture of Spitalfields occasioned by the long mourning'.[83]

The subfusc gloom spread to the fan-makers and carriage-makers. 'All lords' were expected to cover their coaches and sedan chairs, and even their livery servants, with black cloth when George II died in 1760. The streets of London must have looked as if a bag of soot had burst. Only a faint gleam enlivened the footmen's black: they could wear their masters' colours in their braided shoulder knots.[84] By the time the Duke of York, the King's brother, died in September 1767, things were not quite so gloomy. Ladies could wear black silk shoes with their black silk gowns, and carry black paper fans. The men could get out their old black coats if they still fitted. 'It is expected that ... all persons do put themselves into decent mourning.' Army officers toned down their crimson effulgence with a band of black crêpe round their arms.[85]

CHAPTER 21

Interiors and Gardens

Rented rooms

A respectable working man in London rented a furnished room, in a poor part of London such as Grub Street, for 2s 6d a week. The furniture in an agreed inventory was adequate for those times:

> a half-tester bedstead, with brown linsey-wolsey furniture [curtains for the bed], a bed [mattress] and bolster ... a small ... table, two old chairs with cane bottoms, a small looking glass six inches by four in a deal frame painted red and black, a red linsey-wolsey window curtain, an old iron stove, poker, shovel, tongs and fender, an iron candlestick ... a tin extinguisher [to put out the candle] a quart bottle of water, a tin pint pot, a vial for vinegar and a stone white teacup for salt. Also two large prints cut in wood and coloured, framed with deal but not glazed, viz (1) Hogarth's *Gate of Calais* (2) *Queen Esther and King Ahasuerus* ...[1]

The tenant in this case was an unmarried clerk earning £50 a year – well up from the bottom of Massie's pyramid. He had two flights of stairs to climb, but when he got there his room was at the front, and sounds comfortable, for those times.

Boswell paid 17s a week (£40 a year) for 'a lodging up two pair of stairs in Downing Street',[2] and thought of moving to cheaper rooms nearby for £22 a year, but his landlord gave him three rooms for the old price, so he stayed where he was. It was certainly a good address, as well as handy for Boswell's habit of picking up whores in St James's Park, but according to Samuel Johnson a good address was not important: 'you might live in a garret at eighteen pence a week ... for spending threepence a week in a coffee-house you may be for hours in very good company'[3] – and use the coffee-house as an accommodation address so that no one need know where you lived. In 1769 Boswell promoted himself to three rooms in Old Bond Street, a large dining room, a bed-chamber and a dressing-room, 'in the very centre of the court end of town', which cost him 1½ guineas (31s 6d) a week.[4]

Cleland's Fanny Hill worked her way up from a bed for one night for a shilling, to sharing 'a private ready-furnished lodging in D– Street near St James's,' where her lover paid half a guinea (10s 6d) a week for two rooms and a closet on the second floor, to another house where she had the whole first floor and a maid. In 1763 Casanova was able to move straight into a furnished house in Pall Mall when his ex-mistress Mrs Cornelys refused to give him house-room. He found it advertised in the *Advertiser*, for 20 guineas per annum, three floors, each having two rooms and a closet.[5] He seems to have found a bargain. M. Grosley lodged with a compatriot near Leicester Fields, who had to pay the ground landlord 38 guineas a year for a three-storey house including a kitchen basement, and in addition one guinea a year for water, two for poor tax and three for window tax,[6] refuse collection and the Watch.[7] The whole house was only 14 feet wide. A house with 30 windows, in a court off Chancery Lane, could be taken in 1738 for only £2 more.[8]

In 1744 the writer of 'An Estimate of the Necessary Charge[s] of a Family in the middling Station of Life, consisting of a Man, his Wife, four Children and one [overworked] maidservant (the Station in Life of a Tradesman who sets up Business on £1,000, a Very Substantial Start in Life)'[9] estimated an appropriate rent at £50.

Interior decorating

Owner-occupied houses for the middling sort of people and above called for decoration in the modern taste. Gentlemen had been making the Grand Tour to Italy for some time now, bringing home foreign souvenirs and tastes. Not many had been to China, except William Chambers, who published his *Designs of Chinese Buildings, Furniture, Dresses, Machines and Utensils* in 1757 after two visits to Canton. Greece was nearer, but almost as unknown, until James Stuart and a companion braved the Turkish administration and toured Athens, drawing-books in hand. Their book *Antiquities of Athens* came out in 1762. Robert Wood's *The Ruins of Palmyra*, with magnificent prints of its third-century Greek architecture, was published in 1758. Meanwhile, excavations in Rome, Herculaneum and Pompeii were producing yet another style, known as 'grotesque' not because it was ugly but because it came from the underground workings or 'grottos' of the excavators.

England seems to have escaped a severe attack of the baroque, but its lighter relation rococo found favour. All this means a bewildering range of choices for the eighteenth-century decorator, and a confusing medley of terms for the reader. Here is a short guide:[10]

> *Classical* and *neo-classical*: as in ancient Rome, pillars (Ionic, Doric, Corinthian) and round-topped arches.
>
> *Palladian* and *neo-Palladian*: as designed by, or after, Palladio (died 1580); ancient Rome domesticated. Statues often stand on the ends of pediments.
>
> *Baroque*: heavy curves, fat ladies and cupids.
>
> *Rococo*: later: lighter, lop-sided curves, thinner ladies, shells and trellis.
>
> *Grotesque*: light and airy, repeated patterns of flowers and fantasies, often using what look like umbrellas.
>
> *Chinoiserie*: unrecognisable to a Chinese; usually incorporating curly-roofed pagodas, bells, dragons, and a trellis pattern running diagonally.
>
> *Gothic*: unrecognisable to a Goth; usually incorporating a pointed arch and plain straight lines.
>
> *Greek*: based on the ancient ruins in Athens and Palmyra; pillars and pediments, friezes of ox skulls linked by garlands. No arches.

These were the days of architect/designers, who liked to design everything from drains to door handles. William Chambers, who was plain and solid when he was not being Chinese, designed furniture that combined comfort with elegance. James 'Athenian' Stuart, on the other hand, designed stools which might have pleased an ancient Greek but lacked comfort. Pattern books proliferated. Hogarth pokes fun at a rich young couple's indiscriminate taste for pediments and pillars, chinoiserie and rococo, classical and modern, in the second plate, 'Early in the Morning', of his *Marriage à la Mode*.

DIY

For simple people, Eliza Smith[11] gave *Directions for painting rooms or pales* (fences), between a remedy for suppression of the urine (Take of snail-shells and bees, of each an equal quantity ...) and Dr Mead's Receipt for the bite of a mad dog. She begins robustly, with the price of materials:

One hundred weight[12] of red lead   18s
One hundred weight of white lead   £1 2s
Linseed oil by the gallon   3s
A small quantity of oil of turpentine is sufficient

The first coat was the red lead priming. The second coat was white lead with an equal quantity in bulk of whiting, plus the oils. Then (surprising: I would have polyfilled the holes first) make a stiff paste of whiting and oils, beating it with a mallet 'till it is stiffer than dough' – there speaks the practical cook – 'to stop all joints in the pales or wood'. The last coat, of white lead, could be coloured. 'There must be bought six chamber-pots of earth and six brushes, *and keep them to what they belong to* [my italics].' Naturally occurring earths such as ochre could make a good range of browns, reds and yellow. Indigo could produce a soft blue. 'Thus will the work be finished to great satisfaction, for it will be more clean and durable than it can be performed by a housepainter, without [unless] you pay considerably more than the common rates.'

DIY was spreading, to the alarm of the trade. 'Several Noblemen and Gentlemen have *by themselves* [my italics] and servants painted whole houses without the assistance or directions of a Painter, which when examined by the best Judges could not be distinguished from the Work of a Professional Painter', for a quarter of the painter's price.[13]

Plaster

The nobleman or gentleman who wanted something more elaborate than plain painted walls might employ English plasterers or Italian *stuccatori* to create garlands and motifs, pilasters and niches, in the antique mode, or a riot of rococo. Traditional plaster made of lime putty and sand, with a little hair, could be built up layer by layer in astonishing detail. There are eyelashes on the sphinxes on the high ceiling in the hall of Sion House, quite invisible from the ground.[14] The result might be spectacular, but it could take a year to dry out, even if the workmen came every day and the weather held up, and at least six months had to be allowed before a plastered room could be inhabited.[15]

Plaster could be coated with coloured whiting before it had quite
dried out, but because of ancient demarcation disputes between
plasterers and painter-stainers, the plasterers could only use basic
earth colours. Trade whiting or 'distemper' incorporated an animal
size made from animal skins or, for top quality, the scraps of kid left
over from glove making. It had a soft, chalky-looking finish, which
was beautiful but not resistant to abrasion. From 1760 the time needed
to create an elaborate scheme could be radically cut by the use of
gypsum for pre-cast motifs.

Paint

Painting the roundels and cofferings on walls and ceilings in bright
colours had to wait until the plaster had dried out enough for oil-
based paint to be applied by the painters. Isaac Ware recommended
three coats of oil paint, which made a strong and flexible coating
without the glitter of modern gloss paint. Paint could be bought
ready-mixed, conveniently contained in pigs' bladders, from about
1730,[16] avoiding the skilled and labour-intensive process of grinding
pigment and mixing on site. The cheapest colours were wood colours,
and shades of cream and stone (4d per pound would cover 10 square
yards),[17] then olive, pea, ' a fine sky blue mixed with Prussian blue',
pinks and yellows (8–12d). The most expensive was 'a fine deep green'
at all of 2s 6d a pound.

The arsenic in green paint was known to be poisonous, and painters
employed on it were paid extra as danger-money.[18] This was unusual:
the normal view of industrial diseases was that you were lucky to
have a job at all. 'All the world knows that cinnabar [red] is the
offspring of mercury, ceruse [white] is made of lead, verdigris [green]
of copper and ultramarine [a strong blue] ... of silver, for the metallic
colours are much more durable than those of the vegetable extraction',
so painters were apt to suffer from 'trembling of the joints, Cachesy
[coughs], Blackness of the Teeth, discoloured complexion, Melancholy
and loss of smelling'.[19]

Wallpaper

By 1756, when Isaac Ware produced his *Complete Body of Architecture*,
wallpaper was taking over from stucco.[20] It had come a long way
since the single sheets tacked on to the walls of Restoration houses.

Flock paper was still much admired, as a cheap imitation of cut velvet. Unfortunately it was still fairly pricey, so a mock flock, mock cut velvet emerged. In a multi-colour printing, the last coat was a dark shade over parts of the motif, so that in some lights it looked as if it were flocked.[21]

Wallpaper was sold in rolls 12 yards long by about 23 inches wide. There was an unprinted selvedge on both edges which had to be trimmed off on one edge. The first piece was pasted, and tacked on to the wall at the top and down one side, through the selvedge. The next piece overlapped that selvedge, hiding the tacks down the side of the first piece, and so on. The top and bottom rows of tacks could be hidden behind wood fillets. The paste was usually flour and water, unless the paper was heavy, such as flock, when a little size might be added. The paper could be put straight on to the plaster if it was in a reasonable condition, or on to lining paper or boards, always 'observing to make ye flowers join', which was impossible on uneven plaster. If the mismatched joins were too bad, the eye could be soothed by cutting out pieces of pattern – a flower, a link of trellis – and pasting them over the worst bits.

The patterns that English Heritage has removed in fragments from London houses of the period 1740–70 include a particularly nasty mock-flock floral in shades of maroon on grey, a delicate striped pattern found in a house in Berkeley Square resembling a warp-printed Spitalfields silk, an all-over design of classical ruins, and an enchanting plain paper in 'green verditer', the colour of the inside of a kiwi fruit, on to which the craftsman has painted thin architraves wreathed in trailing vines, just the tendrils and occasional small bunches of grapes showing. The *trompe l'oeil* effect is heightened by the shadows, carefully angled as if the light really was coming from the window nearby.

Prices could vary from 6s to nearly £7 a roll.[22] Paper stainers could print paper to match textiles, or vice versa. They could provide *papier maché* motifs and swags, and those beautiful hand-painted scenes of (allegedly) Chinese or Indian life, with pagodas and exotic birds, imported from China since 1720.[23] Prints for the fashionable décor of print rooms could be bought by the set. 'Mr Fry at his house in Hatton Garden is perfecting twelve mezzotinto prints ... calculated to be complete and elegant furniture for one room. Subscription two guineas.'[24]

Other wall coverings

Walls could also be covered with silk damask stretched on invisible batten frames so that it gleamed in the candlelight. Tapestries were still used in old-fashioned houses. Panelling ('wainscot') was painted in light shades, and embellished with mouldings and gilding. Libraries were better without too much gilding: 'the constant fires and candles in that room would so soon turn it black, whereas by having it new painted once in four or five years it will always be clean and cheerful'.[25]

Floors

Plain wood floors were acceptable, but it was possible to have pattern on the floors as well as the walls. In 1739 a pattern book[26] was published showing floor designs in marble and stone, which would have needed strong nerves, particularly the vertiginous pattern known in patchwork as tumbling boxes. The paintings of prosperous family groups that now became fashionable often show the participants tightly juxtaposed on a patterned carpet, leaving a wide border of bare boards. If a carpet was beyond your means you could buy a painted floorcloth, the ancestor of linoleum, which could be painted to your own specification or bought ready-made.

The furniture trade

Large contractors dominated the market, purveying everything from beds to bellows, and in whatever taste, or tastes, the customer wanted.[27] There would be some examples to see, in their showrooms, but much of the trade was by commissions from pictures in their catalogues, the actual making being sub-contracted to craftsmen, such as, perhaps, Henry Sidgier, 'carpenter, joiner and undertaker ... Cabinet and Upholsterers Work done and funerals perform'd NB All sorts of boxes and packing cases made'.[28]

Chippendale

In 1754 Thomas Chippendale published *The Gentleman and Cabinet Maker's Director being a large collection of the most elegant and useful designs of household furniture in the gothic, chinese and modern taste including a great variety of bookcases for libraries or private rooms, commodes, library and writing tables, buroes, breakfast tables, dressing and china tables, china cases, hanging shelves, tea-chests, trays, firescreens, chairs, settees, sopha's, beds, presses and cloathes-chests, pier-glass sconces, slab frames, brackets, candle stands, clock-cases, frets and other ornaments ... with proper [appropriate] directions for executing the most difficult pieces.* He also did coffins. He had an immediate success. The second edition, a year later, sold for £3 13s 6d, mostly to cabinet-makers, but the list of subscribers includes five dukes and three earls, including that arbiter of taste Lord Chesterfield. It was 'calculated to improve and refine the present taste and [was] suited to the fancy and circumstances of persons *in all degrees of Life* [my italics]'.

Turning over the book's huge pages, one is reminded of the rumour that Sydney Opera House began life as a doodle on the back of an envelope, never intended for construction. Some of the monstrosities dreamt up by Chippendale would be nightmarish if perpetrated in full. Who needs crockets on a library bookcase, no matter how rich and gothick? Or a Chinese idol and twenty bells, on a 'Chinese case'? Some of the designs Chippendale had already made – 'I have executed this design and it looks much better than in the drawing' – but all could be left to 'a good workman' to construct, using only his drawings, which give a few dimensions. When his own workmen were making up a piece from his drawing, he insisted on their making a scale model before starting on the real thing.[29]

Chippendale is famous for his chairs, and certainly there are many designs for them in his sales catalogue which are not too fantastic. But his ingenuity is confined to the elaborate carving of the backs and legs. The seats – and surely the seat is an essential part of a chair – are flat and unyielding. Ah, you say, but they will have been cushioned. Yes: but only with thin squabs, tufted to stay square,[30] and contributing very little to comfort. No wonder so many of the figures in family group portraits are standing up.

Tables and desks

One thing Chippendale had in his favour was the importation of mahogany, which is beautiful whether carved or plain. Circular mahogany tables on central tripod legs often appear in paintings. If you have used one, you will know its habits: you cannot lean on the edge without upsetting it. The ladies pouring tea in pictures – very often not looking at what they're doing – were far too stiffly corseted to risk such an informal gesture. Mrs Purefoy ordered 'a round neat light mahogany folding table with four legs, two of them to draw out to hold up the ffolds. It must be 4 ft 2 inches wide', for which she paid £2 7s.

Chippendale designed a desk with a lid that could be propped up to make a slope, and even further raised by a ratchet. It looks horridly unstable to me. Mrs Purefoy ordered – not from him – an ingenious extending desk, but 'wee can't open the Draw but do suppose itt opens in the two slits down the legs. I desire you will let me have a [letter] next post how to open and manage it.'[31]

Beds

The beds that have survived in museums, or are described by Chippendale, still had fabric testers and elaborate drapery which could be closed round them. The visible posts at the foot were carved – of course – in a Chippendale piece, but were not usually elaborate. The canopy or superstructure was sometimes domed. (The maker of the plates in the *Director* describes one as 'doomed'. Possibly: it had a Chinese temple and four dragons on it, for a start.) But earlier in the century, Mrs Purefoy ordered a simple bedstead 'with four posts ... brass ferrels and castors to be taken to pieces and put together by any servant, and to draw about the room on wheels',[32] which makes much more sense of the injunctions to servants to take beds to bits when dealing with 'buggs'.

Lighting

The main rooms were lit by candles in chandeliers of glass, metal or wood. Candlesticks stood on stands, asking to be overturned by a passing hooped skirt or a small child. At least Chippendale designed some that provided holders for six candles on the sides of a reasonably solid pedestal, with another candle-holder on the top of it.

Silver[33]

London was still the main producer of, and market for, silver. The new flatting mills produced uniform silver sheet, which meant faster, and cheaper, production from about 1750. Burgeoning middle-class prosperity encouraged silversmiths to produce a piece of silver for every domestic occasion. They can be seen proudly displayed in the paintings of family groups, as the butler or the servant girl pours the tea from a silver pot with all the necessary equipment, all in silver. Babies were given silver spoons for luck. Fortunate little girls were given miniature silver services, not only to play with, but to teach them how to behave in the big world. A place setting was a three-pronged fork, a knife with a round end to the blade, and a spoon.

The era of purpose-made objects began – a baby's pap-boat in silver, with a small saucepan and heater for it; tongs for asparagus or sugar, cow-shaped jugs for cream, a special spoon for fishing beef olives out of the gravy, travelling toilet sets in shagreen cases, and all the pretty, useless trifles sold in 'toy shops', such as an étui like a Swiss army knife but in silver – scissors, knife, fork, corkscrew, tweezers, ear-scoop, bodkin, pencil and writing tablet. Chocolate and coffee pots were vase- or urn-shaped, with matching cream jugs. Candlesticks to take up to bed were low, for safety's sake. By 1766 a tall adjustable candlestick for reading had evolved, with a shade to shield the eyes.

Gardens

'Garden – A piece of ground enclosed and cultivated with extra-ordinary care, planted with herbs, or fruits for food, or laid out for pleasure': Dr Johnson's *Dictionary*.

Small gardens

Private houses, even quite small houses, had gardens. Per Kalm noticed how

> at nearly every house in the town there was either in front towards the street, or inside [behind] the house and building, or in both, a little yard. They had commonly planted in these yards and round about them, partly in the earth and partly in pots and boxes, several of the trees, plants and flowers that can stand the coal-smoke in London. They thus sought to have some of the pleasant enjoyment of a country life in the midst of the hubbub of the town.[34]

Isaac Ware's plan[35] 'for the middle rank of people' considered the question of gardens for them.

> The general custom is ... if there be any little opening behind, to pave

it. Some attempt to make flower-gardens, but this is very idle. Plants require a purer air than animals, and however we breathe in London they cannot live where there is so much smoak and confinement nor will even gravel continue clean [especially where there are cats about]. Instead of borders ... the best method is to lay the whole with a good sound stone pavement and at the farther part build the needful edifice [the lavatory] and something of similar shape and little service opposite to it. An alcove with a seat is a common contrivance in the space between, but it is a strange place to sit in for pleasure.

One can see his point, especially on hot summer days. 'The vulgar think that a piece of ground stuck full of plants is a garden.' So do I.

For a small garden it made sense to use a jobbing gardener or a contractor. 'Gardens made and handsomely kept by the year by Edward Cooper at the corner house leading to the square in Kensington near London.'[36] Lawns, although part of every gardener's dream, were not practical in the back gardens of London houses – which certainly did not stop gardeners from installing them. But M. Grosley noted that they had to be rolled in the evening, and scythed in the morning before the dew dried, once a week in May and June, although once a fortnight would do in other months. He found them 'inconvenient and troublesome to the feet'.[37]

Grander gardens

But there were some gardens behind houses, where you did not have to sit beside the lavatory. The mansions lining Grosvenor Square put their horses and carriages and male staff into quarters at the end of each plot, giving on to a narrow mews. The blank wall of the stable building facing the garden could be elegantly decorated with porticos and pilasters, and the side walls of the garden had fruit or flowering trees and shrubs trained on them. The considerable space between the house and the stables was laid out in beds and gravel paths.[38] The owners of such grand houses employed full-time gardeners. The Duke of Bedford's gardener was paid £30 a year, and had an assistant who got £4.[39] The Foundling Hospital trained garden boys, who had the additional merit of having been inoculated against smallpox.

Garden planning

Garden planning was a serious business. 'Everything trivial or whimsical ought to be avoided', said the *Encyclopedia Britannica*.[40] A retired clergyman, Joseph Spence,[41] designed gardens for his friends. He set out the precepts he worked by, which could be found in any modern article on garden planning. For instance, the owner's intentions and tastes should first be consulted. The boundaries – party walls, in London gardens – and any disagreeable view should be hidden as much as possible, but any pleasant feature or view should be maximised. His own house in Stretton (now Stratton) Street, off Piccadilly, had a glazed door in the middle at the back, giving on to a gravelled terrace, with three steps down to a gravelled path the same width as the garden door, grass plots on either side and narrow flower beds along the walls, where he trained vines. At the bottom of the garden was a paved area with the unavoidable garden shed and a summer house, covered with jasmine and honeysuckle. The only novel – to me – feature was that the width of the garden paths and plots should exactly echo the width of the windows and doors of the house, which did give a pleasant unity to the view from the foot of the garden. This was the object: no longer to look down on a garden from the first floor windows, as in the previous century, but to walk about in it, enjoying the vista from the garden itself. Spence's plan does not show a necessary house. Perhaps the shed served both purposes.

A garden that Spence designed for a neighbour across the street, Lady Falmouth, who wanted her garden to be an outside drawing-room for the London season, had the two corners nearest the house made into a study and a lavatory, each 6 feet square. The rest of the garden, roughly 50 feet square, had a big round table in the middle, with chairs round it, and flowering trees in a quincunx pattern or 'grovette' shading them, with honeysuckle and jasmine trained up their trunks. Again the walls were masked with vines, and a trellis covered with climbers screened the end wall. 'Blew and gold flower pots' held fragrant shrubs and flowers. On a summer evening it must have been a wonderful place for a party.

There would not be too much room for large trees in an average London plot, but you might fancy a Judas tree or a gingko (introduced in 1730 and 1754: it took about ten years for the price of exotic introductions to fall to a reasonable level)[42] or the old-established laburnum or liriodendron (tulip tree), or some 'lelacs'. Possibly shrubs such as camellias and magnolias would be a better idea. For wall-trained fruit you might chose apricots or peaches, of which there were over 40 named varieties.[43] You would need to spray them against aphids, with a wash of 2lb of tobacco stalks to 1lb of wood soot (where, in coal-burning London, would you get that?) and 3 gallons of boiling water: use when cold.[44] Of herbaceous perennials, you could buy sweet peas (1700) and mignonette (1740), if you wanted your garden to be fragrant, with tazetta narcissus and single and double hyacinths in the spring. Eleanor Coade[45] began to produce her fabricated stone at Lambeth in 1769. Her first garden items were vases in which bulbs would be superb. (Her lions, elephants, nymphs and sphinxes arrived after our period.)

Plants in the borders and beds were staggered neatly in height, and disposed so as to show the whole plant: no solid mass of greenery as in a cottage garden. A repeating pattern was normal, grading heights not only front-to-back but also from one tall specimen – say, a delphinium – to the next one, with the intervening plants neatly following a curve downwards, then up again. That is, if the plants co-operated. The border might be edged by box, or the leg bones of horses or oxen 'round curled end stood upwards', which Per Kalm[46] had last seen near Moscow. They may have looked elegant, but it is hard to imagine. (Memo: definitely no dogs admitted.) Another incongruous note was struck by anti-earwig warfare: 'Earwigs may be destroyed by hanging hogs'-hoofs, the bowls of tobacco pipes or *lobster claws* [my italics] on the top of the sticks which support the flowers, and killing the vermin which will lodge in them every morning.'[47]

As always, there were fashions in plants. The great days of intro-ductions from the East Indies were over, but North America was yielding some enviable plant material. The mania for tulips was not repeated, but a passion for auriculas could be an expensive hobby. 'To be sold by subscription, ten plants of a beautiful seedling Auricula called the Countess of Dartmouth at one guinea a plant [at a time when an assistant gardener was paid four pounds a year] raised by Mr William Redmond of the Lower Street Islington.'[48] Auriculas, of which 'an infinite variety'[49] was available, merited special treatment, in a staged 'theatre' of several shelves where each plant in its pot could turn its best side to the viewer, day by day. They are tem-peramental flowers, needing regular watering that meticulously avoids splashing the petals, and protection from inclement weather. Perhaps their theatres should have been wired for electricity. 'If all vegetables that grow in pots … are daily and frequently electrified will they not have a better growth … and their flowers … be more perfect than those not electrified?'[50]

Suppliers

Plants could be bought by mail order. 'To be sold, near 3,000 tulips and about the same ranunculus … enquire of Mr Kingside Nurseryman in Blandford Dorset, who will answer any letter sent to him post-paid.'[51] But there were plenty of suppliers in and near London, such as Mr Powell of Holborn, who could offer recently imported North American trees and shrubs – very fashionable – or Arabella Morris at the sign of the Naked Boy and Three Crowns against the New Church in the Strand – what a relief when houses were numbered, after 1762 – who 'selleth all sorts of Garden Seeds flower seeds and flower roots; fruit trees flowering shrubs evergreens and forest trees. Also shears, rakes, reels, hoes, spades, scythes, budding and pruning knives, watering pots, mats [for shading], sieves and all sorts of materials for gardening.'[52]

If Arabella was out of stock, you could try Thomas Kirkham or William Lucas, also in the Strand. Most bulbs were raised in Holland and imported. 'Flower roots just imported from Holland sold at Garraway's Seed and Net Warehouse, the Rose, near the Globe Tavern, Fleet Street … A large collection of the finest double red white and blue Hyacinths: clear broke and breeding tulips, Turky Ranunculas, Enemonies, Narcissusses, Martagons [lilies] and all other flower roots …'[53]. You could visit Mr Loudon's well-established nursery at Brompton, or call on John Bush, also known as Johann Busch, in Hackney. He supplied rare plants to Princess Augusta, whose plant collection later formed the basis of the Royal Botanic Gardens at Kew.[54] For a special occasion you might think it more economic simply to hire plants for the evening.[55]

Nurserymen, or 'florists', all round London suffered from theft of valuable specimens. 'Thieving florists [were, at night] stealing their neighbours' best roots and flowers which they replant in their own gardens and swear them to be their own.'[56] This was no mere fiddling the prizes at a church fête; it could threaten a man's livelihood. It became so rampant that the theft of a plant or tree worth over 5s was in 1765 made a felony for which the punishment was death.

Health

Lastly, gardening was good for you. When John Warner of Rother-hithe, merchant, died in his eighty-sixth year, his obituary in *The Gentleman's Magazine* attributed his longevity to 'his temperance and daily exercise in his garden', where among many other marvels he had a flourishing vineyard. Dr Hill in his *Old Man's Guide to Health and Longer Life*[57] recommended gardening. 'Nothing affords so happy or so constant exercise' – not, of course, actually digging, but pruning and 'overlooking'. 'The only danger is this, it is too tempting. Let him who falls into it take an invariable resolution never to let his fondness for the garden carry him out too early or keep him there too late.'

CHAPTER 22

Parties of Pleasure

The pleasure gardens

The most famous eighteenth-century places of amusement were Vauxhall and Ranelagh. Before setting out to describe them, a query: how did the English manage to enjoy themselves so much, in an English summer, out of doors? 'They cry "This is a bad summer!" as if we ever had any other', said Horace Walpole in 1768.[1]

Vauxhall

In 1732 Jonathan Tyers, 'the master builder of delight',[2] took over a 12-acre site in the fields across the river, and transformed it. Throughout the summer months, May to August, anyone looking respectable (known whores were barred) could come in for the price of a shilling ticket. Paved paths through trees ran the length of the site, with cross alleys at right angles, and space near the entrance for a music room, 50 supper boxes adorned with paintings by Hogarth and others, Chinese pavilions, and a round bandstand. Vistas were designed to show off a succession of triumphal arches, and some newly built Italian ruins, and a statue of Handel by Roubiliac valued at a thousand guineas.[3] There was a Turkish tent with doric pillars, and a famous 'tin cascade' at the end of one of the avenues, made of strips of tin and complete with miller's house. At nine o'clock each evening, a bell rang, a watchman shouted 'Take care of your pockets' and concealed lighting played on the shimmering strips.

A concert of instrumental music and some pretty terrible songs that were regularly published in *The Gentleman's Magazine* lasted until 10.30.[4] The only snag was a familiar and predictable one, with all those thousands of people. Men were all right: there were plenty of bushes about. But –

> In sweet Vauxhall I love to stray
> But wish it were completely gay;
> In splendid scenes we eat and drink
> In sordid huts evacuate[5]

Before Westminster Bridge was opened in 1750, the only way there was by water. Walpole described taking a barge, 'with a party of French horns attending', and having a noisy picnic in one of the supper booths which went on until three o'clock in the morning – it must have been a fine night for once.[6] M. Grosley, on the contrary, found that the English were 'as grave at Vauxhall and Ranelagh as at the Bank, at church or at a private club'.[7] The opening of Westminster Bridge should have improved the access to the gardens, but when Horace Walpole went to a 'Ridotto al fresco' there in 1769, he set off from Mayfair at eight in the evening and got stuck in a traffic jam for an hour and a half.

> We then alighted: and after scrambling under bellies of horses, through wheels and over posts and rails we reached the gardens, where were already many thousand persons. ... We walked twice round and were rejoiced to come away, though with the same difficulties as at our entrance; for we found three strings of coaches all along the road, who did not move half a foot in half an hour.

Which does not sound much fun. But the great thing was to see who else was there, and to be seen. For only a shilling entrance fee you might see the Prince of Wales, who went often, and most of the nobility and gentry.

Although the brilliant lighting of the place was much admired – 'a thousand lamps so disposed that they all take fire together almost as quick as lightening'[8] – their beams did not reach the far alleys, which 'Mr Tyers has very prudently shut up to prevent indecencies so much complained of last summer',[9] thereby causing some dissatisfied young male customers to tear up the barriers. That must have been the summer when Casanova 'offered [a woman] two guineas if she would come and take a little walk with me in a dark alley'. She took the money, and ran.[10] Young Kalm, observing the goings-on but not wanting to be too rude, thought that 'it is certain that [Vauxhall] may be in a certain way good but then it is certain that it is also in some ways harmful ... Young ladies, also, might not always be improved to the pitch of perfection here.'[11]

If you did not bring your own picnic, you could buy food there, at notoriously high prices. A shilling bought a plate of ham cut so thin you could read through it. A cold chicken cost 2s 6d, a quart of punch 5s.

Ranelagh

Ranelagh was perhaps more select. 'Two nights ago [24 May 1742] Ranelagh Gardens was opened at Chelsea; the Prince [of Wales], Princess, Duke [of Cumberland], much nobility and much mob besides was there.'[12] It was open from April to July, admission 2s 6d, which included tea or coffee and bread and butter. No alcohol was served. Again, its lighting was much admired. The grounds included a canal, with gondolas. Its main feature was a Rotunda or Dome 150 feet in diameter, with a central bandstand, where music was played from seven o'clock until ten. There were two tiers of 52 boxes, each seating eight people, but the main occupation was to walk round and round and round, listening to the music. The floor was made of plaster of Paris, covered with matting to deaden the sound of feet. 'Not a step is perceived and thus the music is heard in every part of the rotundo',[13] which must have pleased young Mozart and his sister when they appeared there in 1764. Dr Johnson 'deemed [it] a place of innocent recreation', and often went there.[14]

To celebrate the end of the war, in 1749, the King was persuaded to order a 'jubilee Masquerade', which pleased Horace Walpole 'more than anything I ever saw'.[15] Everyone came in masks, the amphitheatre was illuminated and decorated with greenery and orange trees 'with small lamps in each orange, and below them the finest auriculas in pots ... there were booths for tea and wine, gaming tables and dancing, and about two thousand persons.'

Other pleasure gardens

It was no wonder, seeing the huge success of Vauxhall and Ranelagh, that pleasure gardens opened all round the west and north of London, on a much smaller scale and often pretending to medicinal value as spas. They usually offered some combination of allegedly healthy mineral water, a place to walk up and down seeing and being seen, and an 'Assembly Room' for concerts. Sadler's Wells, for example, offered water at 6d a glass and a brick-built music room where 3s would buy you a seat in a box and a pint of red wine, while you watched dogs and monkeys performing,[16] and the wine took away the taste of the water, which was so foul that it must have done you good. Physicians fought a losing battle with the unsupervised sloshing back of spa water without the opinion of a qualified practitioner 'who knows the ... properties of the water and how ... it is to be used' – the patients believed the advertisements.'[17]

Shopping

Ladies whiled away the time by 'a turn to Covent Garden or Ludgate Hill [to] tumble over the mercers' rich silks or view some India or China trifle, some prohibited manufacture or foreign lace'.[18] 'Two, three or sometimes more ladies accompanied by their gallants set out to make a tour through the most fashionable shops and to look at all the most fashionable goods, without any intention of laying out one single sixpence'[19] – a retailer's nightmare. And even if they did buy something, they might insist on having it on trial, like Mrs Purefoy who told her son to buy her a silver watch, 'it must bee new fashioned and a good goer, I suppose about five guineas ... Hee would have it on trial for a month or six weeks to be returned if not a good goer.'[20] Furthermore, it was not usual to pay cash, and the long credit expected by customers could bankrupt shopkeepers, who often called in person on a good customer, ostensibly to offer them a special bargain, but in fact to try to extract payment for previous orders.

M. Grosley was enthusiastic about London's shopping opportunities. 'The finest shops are scattered up and down the courts and passages ... The shops in the Strand, Fleet Street, Cheapside etc. are the most striking objects that London can offer to the eye of a stranger.'[21] He was struck by their 'large plate glass windows', often built out in curves. These were not the huge sheets of glass that we know, but panes 12 by 16 inches:[22] still an advance on the old greenish uneven panes, which gave a wavering and unflattering light.

The shops in the City were built on long narrow sites with a back showroom toplit from a skylight. Often they preserved the medieval street layout in their pattern of a narrow entry every four or five shops, giving access to a court behind, lined with more shops and workplaces, or a tavern or inn with all the necessary facilities for travellers and horses.[23] The shops in the new developments to the west were different. There was space in his Grosvenor Square showroom for Josiah Wedgwood to display whole dinner services, on tables laid out as for a meal. 'It will be our interest to amuse and divert and please and astonish, nay, even, to ravish the ladies.'

Promise, large promise, is the soul of an advertisement, as Samuel Johnson said.[24] One thing Wedgwood shared with Chippendale and many other traders was a faith in good copy-writing. Indeed the retail trade embraced publicity whole heartedly. Progressive traders issued illustrated handbills called 'shop cards', which give enchanting vignettes of shops and shoppers.[25] One of the last trade cards Hogarth made was for his sisters Mary and Anne, who seem to have specialised in boys' clothes and school uniforms, such as suits for the 'bluecoat Boys' near their shop in Little Britain. Hogarth, being Hogarth, could not resist making a dull subject into a vivid tableau of shopping for clothes with bored children. 'Mrs Holt's Italian Warehouse ... at the two Olive Posts in the Broad part of the Strand almost opposite to Exeter Exchange' portrays Mercury, no less, about to rush an express order from Florence to London for 'all sorts of Italian silks', as well as fans, Legorne hats, lute and violin strings, 'and in a back warehouse all sorts of Italian wines, Florence cordials, Oyl, Olives, Anchovies, Capers, Vermicelli, Bolognia Sausidges, Parmesan Cheeses, Naple Soap etc.' What a wonderful smell greeted you when you went in for a gut violin E string.

'Warehouse' was the fashionable name for a shop, just as 'centre' is now. The Eider-down Warehouse sold 'bags made with it to keep the feet and legs warm in travelling ... likewise Night gowns quilted', from 6 guineas.[26] There was a 'Chinese paper warehouse' in Newgate Street, and at least two others where the apprentice unrolled with a flourish a roll of sumptuously flowered wallpaper. If the happy couple agreed on it, the shopkeeper could see to its being 'matched and compleatly put up'.

In Francis Noble's 'Large Circulating Library' near Covent Garden, 'Books are lent to read (both English and French) at half a guinea a year or three shillings a quarter. Note, new books bought as soon as published. Ready money for any library or parcel of books, and books exchanged.'

The Tombs and Lions

The tombs in Westminster Abbey were something every visitor had to see. Those of 'illustrious persons' could be seen any time, free. There were at least 48 reckoned to be worth seeing,[27] but you had to pay 6d each – expensive, for a family outing – to inspect the wax effigies of sovereigns, made for their funerals and then deposited in the Abbey.[28] Henry V's, for instance, 'lay on his monument without a head, which has been cut off by some accident', but there were thirteen other miscellaneous monarchs 'made of wax to resemble life, and dressed in their coronation robes. ... It only remains to observe', as the author did, approvingly, 'that the royal family of the house of Hanover are interred in a vault ... without any monumental inscription.'

Per Kalm was duly taken round the 'rareties in London', including the royal tombs in Westminster Abbey, which he thought 'well worth seeing'. But he thought less of the Coronation Chair, 'an old chair ... which was very badly made. Many a poor old woman with only one room has a better ... made chair than this. ... There is scarcely anyone who now sees it who has not the curiosity to sit upon it.'[29] The guides seem to have been more interested in tips from tourists than in looking after the nation's history.

The Tower of London was the next stop on any tourist's itinerary. 'Those who are inclined to see the rarities in the Tower of London generally take a view of the wild beasts before any other curiosity.'[30] Again, 6d a head, but what riches – if you liked the sight of wild animals in cages. The lions were the great draw. Caesar, a large maned lion, could be 'heard at a great distance' when he roared. There was a bear from New York which had been a present to the Duke of York, who passed it on to the King, who sent it to his menagerie. There had been an ostrich, but it died because people would feed it with bits of metal.[31] All the noteworthy animals had names, but I have not been able to trace their origin.[32]

The next sight was the crown jewels. These could be disappointing. 'The spectators are locked into that half of the room assigned to them, where they sit down close to a grate like that of a nunnery, on the other side of which the person who shows the jewels displays them separately by candlelight.'[33] Jewels cut in the recent fashion would sparkle satisfactorily by candlelight, but the old medieval jewels would look very dull.

The Mint was the next port of call. 'The operation that is permitted to be seen being the manner of stamping it.' A team of four men operated a machine turning out finished coins, the most skilful 'twitching out the coin with his middle finger and putting in an unstamped piece with his forefinger and thumb'.[34] No wonder there was a chronic shortage of currency.

Freakshows and monster-mongers

Londoners could not have enough of human freaks and wild beasts. As well as the annual fairs such as Saint Bartholomew's Fair, proprietors bought, sold and exhibited their collections of rarities at inns, which says a lot for the accommodation available there. The newspapers were full of advertisements, and single-sheet flyers littered the streets.[35]

There were human beings, such as 'a young Oronuto savage from Ethiopia' (he features in several different collections: either there were several Oronuto savages, or one was switched between exhibitions; all of them offer him for sale). There was 'a healthy Man who is covered all over his body with solid quills ... there is likewise a Youth, his son, about seven years of age who is covered all over with solid Quills like his father, except his face, the palms of his hands and the Bottoms of his feet'. They could be bought as one lot, for two thousand guineas. A full description was available from the Royal Society, which had also looked at 'the most astonishing instance of Human Nature that ever was yet exhibited to Publick View; being a most surprising wonderful Elephantiasis Man who is covered all over his body with large scales like unto those of a large fish ...' Here we have the reaction of one visitor: 'This wonder I have seen & found to be no more than a true IMPETIGO, 7th July 1758'.[36] 'The Nobility, Gentry and Curious in General' could see 'the white negro girl', an albino described in pulsating prose. She, at least, was not offered for sale. A handbill preserved in the Bodleian Library offered 'human freaks' such as Miss Hawtin, who used her toes as hands, which she lacked, and a man whose arms were only four inches long. 'If required, Ladies and Gentlemen will be waited on at their own homes.'

Wild beasts of every kind proliferated: a noble porcupine, a mantyger from Bengall who very much resembled human nature, a wonderful and surprising Satyr, an amazing Dromedary from the Desarts of Arabia near the ruins of Palmyra, a half-and-half from

Aethiopia found in a cave, and every kind of miscellaneous beast, bird and insect you can think of, with many more. John Cross and Company in Piccadilly offered anything from a wonderful large crocodile to small lap dogs. His hand-out ends 'Gentlemens Menageries and Merchants served with all sorts of curious Birds Animals etc for ready money only ... Wanted, some Small Dutch Pugs, Lap Spaniels and Italian Greyhounds.' Another handbill preserved in the Bodleian Library reads 'Gentlemen and ladies are admitted at one shilling each' to see an ostrich, at Mr Gough's menagerie at 99 Holborn Hill, 'where Birds and Beasts are bought sold and exchanged'.

I doubt if their cages were spacious. London must have echoed with their unhappy cries and roars. My favourite animal would have been the centaur, half man half horse, advertised in *The Gentleman's Magazine* of April 1751. His name was Mr Manpferdit. 'The hours of showing [the place is not stated] are from ten in the morning to four in the afternoon, the rest of the time being necessary to comb and curry himself, stir up his litter, and study English history.' He 'proposes to let himself out to great ladies to take the air on'. They could have had cosy chats about history as they went. Alas he was found to be only an enterprising sailor with the back end of a stuffed horse.

In 1765 'the man who shows wild beasts in Tyburn Road was brought before Justice Girdler ... for receiving the dead bodies from the felons that stole them from Cripplegate churchyard and giving them to the wild beasts ... He was with great difficulty committed to New Prison, the mob having like to have killed him before he got there.'[37]

The British Museum

The museum opened in 1759, funded by a lottery. Mr Manpferdit might have been able to see his relations here, carved in stone. It was meant for 'the general use and benefit of the public', as well as the learned, but in practice it was only persistent scholars who got through the barricades. Tickets had to be applied for in advance, and were issued weeks or months later. The museum was closed on Saturdays, Sundays – which ruled out the working classes – feast days, fast days, Easter and Whitsun and Christmas, and when it was open you got a 30-minute conducted tour in parties of five – no loitering – between nine o'clock and three, or four till eight in summer. Someone must have been proud of the initial trickle of visitors – 60 a year.[38] By 1761 things had improved, in theory at least. Fifteen timed tickets were issued twice or three times a day, and parties could determine their route by a majority vote. If anyone wanted to 'tarry' at a particular exhibit he could be left there 'under the care of a proper officer'.[39] But in 1765 M. Grosley still 'wished that the public could enjoy the Museum more fully and at its ease', and deplored 'the cursory view that visitors are obliged to be satisfied with'.[40]

The Red Indian chiefs

Eight (or three, accounts varied) Cherokee chiefs, 6 feet tall, dressed in only shirts, 'trowsers' and mantles, 'their faces painted a copper colour and their heads adorned with shells, feathers, ear-rings and other trifling ornaments' arrived in 1762[41] to see the King and remind him of his promise to send them teachers. They went to Vauxhall, where '300 eager crowders were made happy by shaking hands with them'.[42] On their second visit there, 10,000 visitors flocked to watch them get riotously drunk.[43] Their views on the manners of the English were not elicited. They finally left London in August 1762,[44] having been presented to the King. A thousand pounds of public funds was applied to their living expenses 'and for presents to them on their departure',[45] but three of them seem to have been left behind, and were found 'living in a deplorable condition' in 1765. A well-wisher 'equipped them in the English fashion', presumably wigs and all.[46]

The next year some Iroquois chiefs arrived, 'with their ladies ... to settle the limits of their hunting grounds'. *The Gentleman's Magazine* gave them less coverage, only noting that 'at an entertainment on account of the opening of a new organ at Watford the Indian chiefs sung several of their warlike songs'.[47]

The theatre

To survey the theatre in the eighteenth century is a task beyond this book. All I hope to do is to give you the flavour of theatre-going.

First as seen by an excited thirteen-year-old:

> The anxious crowd with eager pace
> Hye to the play to get a place.
> First come the gods who all in rows
> Themselves in loftiest seats dispose.

Next wenches draggled to their bums
On foot; in hackney coaches some.
Now all is husht, and now a song
Wide spreads a laugh throughout the throng.
But if pickpockets intervene
We risk a broken leg I wean,
For oft the noisy voices roar
'Toss o'er the rascal, toss him o'er';
Then oranges in clusters fly
And quids half-chewed rough tars supply.
The music next, with pleasing strains
Close to the ear the soul detains...
The music's done, the roarers scoff
And Gods in thunder cry 'Off, Off'.
The curtain falls, the play is done,
And now the magic art comes on.
The pantomime, where cunning hags
On broomsticks ride, instead of nags,
And at the sound of thunderclap
Together vanish through a trap.
Thus shall we go, each man a play'r
We know not how, we know not where.[48]

Well, he was only thirteen. But our next theatre critic was more
sophisticated. Here is M. Grosley's account of an evening at the play –
unfortunately, he does not say which one. He did not speak or
understand English, so he concentrated on what he saw, and being
an advocate his evidence is probably trustworthy:

The English are very fond of bloody tragedies ... in one, the King flies
into the arms of the Queen ... and they continue to clasp each other
in transport, which excites in the audience the strongest emotions,
expressed by a general applause ... the English stage has certain
customs which greatly hurt a Frenchman who is not used to them. The
last scene of every act is constantly interrupted ... by the tinkling of a
little bell which apprises the music[ians] to be ready to play in the
interval between the acts. The [leading] actresses drag long trains after
them, which have four corners like a carpet, the breadth proportioned
to the importance of the character; and they are followed by a little
boy, in the quality of a train-bearer, who is as inseparable from them
as the shadow from the body. This page, who is sprucely dressed ... in

a livery made to suit his stature within two or three inches, keeps his
eye constantly fixed upon the train of the princess; sets it to rights when
it is ever so little ruffled or disordered; and is seen to run after it with
all his might when a violent emotion makes the princess hurry from
one side of the stage to the other: this he does with all the phlegm and
seriousness natural to the English ... Scenes of battery and carnage are
generally preceded by laying a large thick carpet upon the stage to
represent the field of battle, and which is afterwards carried off with all
the dead bodies, to leave the trapdoors at liberty for the ghosts.[49]

Theatre-going was subject to more risks than flying oranges or half-
chewed quids of tobacco. The confined space of a theatre was a
splendid place for rioting. The famous Bottle Hoax of 1749 in the
New Theatre in the Haymarket was all because the promise to
produce a man out of a bottle was not kept. The house was crowded
with 'nobility and gentry of both sexes', who waited noisily until their
patience gave out and someone threw a lighted candle on to the
stage, 'which alarming the greater part of the audience they made
the best of their way out of the theatre, some losing their cloaks and
hats, others their wigs and swords'. The ones who stayed 'entirely
demolished the theatre'.[50]

When the Prince of Brunswick went to Covent Garden theatre in
1762, 'the eagerness of a titled and fashionable mob was such that the
male part fought their way with drawn swords, the females fainted,
and lost shoes, caps and ruffles quite as rapidly as at the other
theatres'.[51] When David Garrick proposed to abolish the tradition
that anyone missing the first three acts of the usual five need pay only
half price, the audience, led by 'a person of the first rank', rioted and
he had to give in.[52] The damage cost £2,000 to repair.[53] Casanova
went to Drury Lane theatre once, when the King and Queen were
there. The play that had been billed had been changed. Garrick
pleaded with the audience, but they were not to be placated despite
the presence of the monarch. 'The King and Queen and all the
fashionables left the theatre and in less than an hour the theatre was
gutted till nothing but the bare walls were left ... in a fortnight the
theatre was refitted.'[54]

In 1749, at a time when English players were starving, the management of the Little Theatre in the Haymarket saw fit to engage a
French company. The audience was outraged and launched into a
chorus of 'The Roast Beef of Old England'. A magistrate who was

sitting in the pit said he would read the Riot Act, after which a mob
had to disperse or face armed soldiers, but this only resulted in further
uproar. By now it was six o'clock, time for the performance to begin,
and the French and Spanish ambassadors 'and other notables' had
rather surprisingly appeared in the stage box. But when the curtain
rose, they saw 'the actors standing between two files of grenadiers
with their bayonets fixed and resting on their firelocks. At this the
whole house rose and unanimously turned to the justice', who said
he couldn't think how it had happened and the grenadiers withdrew.
'Then began the serenade' of cat-calls and noise, so the actors too
withdrew, and 24 dancers appeared.

> But even that was provided for, and they were directly saluted with a
> bushel or two of peas which made their caperings very unsafe. The
> justice stood up on his seat and held out his hand for candles, to be
> able to read the Riot Act proclamation [which he just happened to
> have on him]. Instead he got the hand of a gentleman who persuaded
> him that the course he proposed might result in people being killed.
> He capitulated, the ambassadors left, the curtain fell, and there was a
> Universal Huzza from the whole house.[55]

But even without a riot, things could be noisy. When George III
went to Drury Lane theatre one evening, 'the crowd was so great
that many people were almost suffocated in the subterranean passages
leading to the pit ... several lost the skirts of their gowns etc. but we
do not hear of any deaths ... in the throng and hurry many of them
paid nothing',[56] which was little consolation for having to appear
before your sovereign skirtless. On another evening, Boswell and some
friends 'sallied into the theatre just as the doors opened at four o'clock,
[and] planted ourselves in the middle of the pit with oaken cudgells
in our hands and shrill-sounding cat-calls [whistles] in our pockets.
... at five the house began to be pretty well filled. As is usual on first
nights, some of us called for the music to play "Roast Beef [of Old
England]".' They found the prologue not to their liking, so they hissed
it.[57]

On another occasion, two Highland officers came into Covent
Garden theatre. The 'mob in the upper gallery hissed and roared
"No Scots, No Scots"', and pelted them with apples. There was a
bizarre episode one evening at Drury Lane theatre, at which the King
and Queen were present, when 'one of the honest tars belonging to
a press-gang, who had taken their seats in the upper gallery' made a

rousing speech in favour of a Spanish war, which the house loudly applauded.[58] Those 'honest tars' – the only time I have seen words of praise for a press-gang – were not there to improve their appreciation of the drama, but to pick up cannon fodder. No wonder they were in favour of war.

Oratorios and operas

– or, in popular slang, roaratorios and uproars.[59]

John Wesley no doubt expressed the views of many, when he wrote in his *Journal* in 1764: 'I heard *Judith*[60] an oratorio, performed at the Lock [hospital for venereal diseases. What an odd place to meet this eminent divine, let alone Judith]. Some parts of it were exceedingly fine. But there are two things in all modern pieces of music which I could never reconcile to common sense. One is, singing the same words ten times over, the other, singing different words by different persons at one and the same time.'[61]

Georg Friedrich Händel was born in Halle in 1685. He had been in royal favour since at least 1711, when he performed for Queen Anne. He became a British subject, and anglicised his name, in 1727, the year of the coronation of the second Hanoverian king and his queen, for which he wrote four of the anthems. He produced a stream of varied and delectable music, instrumental, vocal, secular and religious, operas and oratorios, including suitable music for any royal occasion. His *Music for the Royal Fireworks* was commissioned by the King in 1749. It was performed before the fireworks were let off – not, as in outdoor performances nowadays, having to compete with their crashes and bangs.

In the next year Handel began his long association with the Foundling Hospital. He gave a concert in the almost-completed chapel there, ending with the *Hallelujah* chorus from *Messiah*, which brought the packed audience, including the Prince and Princess of Wales, to its feet.[62] In 1750 and 1751 he gave two performances of *Messiah*, each to an audience of about a thousand people crowded into the chapel. Then demand slackened and one annual performance under his supervision was put on each year until his death in 1759, by when his music had earned the Hospital £6,725.[63] Perhaps an even more profitable gift was that Handel put the Foundling Hospital on the fashionable map. It was the done thing to take the carriage out to the Hospital on the edge of London and see the touching young orphans, listen to some good music, enjoy the pictures on show, have a gossip with your friends, and get a glow of virtue from donating to its funds, all without any risk of those horrid riots that so disturbed an evening at the theatre.[64]

John Gay's *The Beggars' Opera* was first staged in 1728. Gay died in 1732, but his irreverent opera was constantly revived. It was even presented before King George III and his new bride seven weeks after their coronation, 'with which Her Majesty appeared to be highly delighted',[65] her husband's reaction not being reported. Originally it was seen, and welcomed by most, as a satire on the corrupt administration of Robert Walpole (1676–1745: he resigned in 1742), but as time went on it earned a place in popular affection simply as an antidote to the high-falutin characters of proper operas and oratorios. McHeath, the hero, was, after all, a highwayman, and one of the heroines was a jailer's daughter. The chorus was a band of petty criminals and whores, and even the music was stolen from other sources. Some people feared that the glamorisation of crime would have a bad effect on the young, but Samuel Johnson took the robust view that no man 'was ever made a rogue by being present at its representation'.[66]

Castrati still sang, in several of Handel's seasons.[67] On a lighter note, 'On the 17th ult. a man taking [catching] his wife with her gallant in a barn, criminally concerned, with assistance qualified him for the opera, and the patient is in great danger of his life.'[68]

Picture exhibitions

Artists had traditionally been dependent on court patronage, and recommendations by satisfied customers. In the increasing prosperity of the middling classes, artists began to use publicity to reach a wider market. In 1740 Francis Hayman was commissioned by Jonathan Tyers to paint a family group,[69] celebrating his rise to fame and fortune as proprietor of Vauxhall. There they all are, staring at the viewer while one daughter cleverly pours tea into a teacup without looking. Tyers was merely following middle-class domestic habits, but he had as well a very public impact on artistic life. The supper boxes at Vauxhall were open to the view of passers-by, who could see the pictures on the back walls. The great advantage of such interesting décor was that a man could pretend to an intense interest in art while ogling the girl sitting in front of it. These pictures became so popular that engravings of them found a ready market.[70] Most of the paintings were by Hayman, but Hogarth's four *Times of Day* were included.

Hogarth had already assessed the potential of a more exclusive market than Vauxhall, such as the prosperous men who became hospital governors. The governors of St Bartholomew's Hospital saw his *Pool of Bethesda* and *The Good Samaritan* every time they went up the stairs to a meeting.[71] He himself, like Handel, became a governor of the Foundling Hospital, donating his magnificent portrait of its founder, Captain Coram. It was given a place of honour in the girls' dining room, to mesmerise all the fashionable visitors.[72] After all, they might be thinking of having a portrait or a family group painted themselves. Another of Hogarth's masterpieces, *The March to Finchley*, arrived in the Foundling Hospital in 1750, by means of another fund-raising ploy: a lottery, in which 2,000 tickets were sold with appropriate publicity. Hogarth probably intended the Hospital to win it all the time, but instead of making an outright gift he managed to draw in another market, that of habitual lottery investors.

By 1760 the Foundling Hospital had developed its fund-raising to include an annual exhibition of pictures by British artists, 'intended as a polite entertaining and rational amusement for the public', and a source of funds for the Hospital. But there was such a 'rage of visiting the exhibition' that the room was crowded with 'menial servants and their acquaintance ... the professors [artists] themselves heard ... their works censured or approved by kitchen-maids and stable-boys'.[73] This would not do. In 1765 a more select audience was guaranteed by the foundation of the Society of Artists of Great Britain, entitled to add Royal to its name three years later. In 1769 Sir Joshua Reynolds became the first president of the Society (now known as the Royal Academy of Arts and housed in Burlington House in Piccadilly. The exterior has suffered from subsequent developers, but much of the interior is pure eighteenth-century Palladian.)

Balls

The King of Denmark gave a masked ball in 1768, in the Opera House in the Haymarket. Spectators were let into the gallery at seven o'clock, the masked dancers began to arrive by nine, and the King of Denmark came to his own party later, dressed in a domino (an all-enveloping and disguising gown) of gold and silver stuff with a black hat and a white feather. The British King and Queen sat in their private box, screened by one-way blinds. The dancing went on until six in the morning, and 'the shameful custom of gaming was totally prohibited ... The value of the jewels which were worn on this occasion were supposed [estimated] to amount to two millions. Many of the best fancied dresses ... were those of eminent citizens or those who had acquired their fortune by trade.' Imagine the thrill of such social slumming.[74]

It took a German *entrepreneuse* to see the commercial potential of the craze for balls, masked or otherwise. Teresa Cornelys arrived from the continent in 1761, and took a lease of the third largest house in Soho Square. It had begun life as the residence of the Earls of Carlisle,[75] but was going downhill, with the rest of Soho, as the nobility moved west. One would have thought that she could have found a corner for Casanova, the father of her child, when he arrived in London, but she no longer wanted to know him.[76] They seem, from his account, to have had a strictly business conversation, in which she told him that she gave 'twelve balls and twelve suppers to the nobility and the same number to the middle classes in the year. I often have as many as six hundred guests at two guineas a head', and she could seat 400 for supper, at one sitting. Her receipts exceeded £24,000 a year, but, she added hastily, her expenses were enormous.

The house, decorated in the Chinese taste,[77] made a wonderful setting for balls and assemblies. Three or four thousand candles illuminated a masked ball she organised in February 1770. Ordinary dominoes were forbidden; elaborate disguises had to be hired or made. All the noble lords and ladies there were listed in *The Gentleman's Magazine* – so much for their disguises, but where would be the fun of not being named in the press? Several ladies were 'uncommonly rich in diamonds'. But who was the cad who turned up as Adam, in flesh-coloured silk with an apron of fig leaves embroidered on it, 'fitting the body with the utmost niceness' (here having, surely, its original meaning of exactitude), which led to 'unavoidable indelicacy'?[78] The very next month the Gentlemen of the Tuesday Night Club at the Star and Garter Tavern in Pall Mall used her rooms for another masked ball for 800 'persons of principal distinction',[79] most of whom probably met again at a masquerade at her place in May, at which 'a most splendid and numerous company of nobility, foreign ministers and persons of eminence were present'.[80]

Teresa Cornelys did not quite monopolise the market. The Club at Arthur's (coffee-house?) took the Opera House for its masked ball in March 1770, when the usual gang of 'principal nobility, foreign ministers and persons of eminence' met yet again.[81] No wonder, said the censorious, that there were more divorces nowadays.

Some magnates such as the Duke of Bedford could run their own balls in their own houses. For a ball in 1759 he – or, rather, his butler – hired 21 dozen cut glasses for a guinea, and borrowed extra plate. He borrowed extra footmen at a guinea each, and hired a band – three violins, one hautbois, one pipe and tabor, two 'bases' (bass viols?) – for 14 guineas, and a French horn player for another 3 guineas.[82]

Any well-brought-up young person would know how to dance the minuet, and the 'country dances' that followed it. A girl could catch up with the latest steps by studying, for example, *The Ladies Complete Pocket Book*, which gave the words of new songs sung at Vauxhall and Ranelagh[83] as well as the steps of 'Admiral Rodney's Delight': 'Cast off one couple and turn your partner foot across top without turning, right and left at top', which sounds more like knitting a sock than eighteenth-century jiving. But if your education had not covered dancing and you wanted to catch up, you could get in touch with Mr Duke, who gave dancing lessons 'for grown gentlemen and ladies ... in so private a manner as to be seen by none but myself if desired, a Minuet or Country Dances with the modern or true method of footing'.[84]

At the other end of the social scale, the Mitre Tavern at Charing Cross advertised a masked ball, tickets 3s, 'habits [dresses] to be had at the above place, and particular care for a warm room to dress in. Coffee and tea gratis.'[85]

CHAPTER 23

Manners, Speech
Conversation and Customs

Etiquette: the hat

When did men first acquire hats? The soft head-coverings of the medieval man presented, no doubt, other problems, but as soon as a hat has a crown and a brim it has to be carefully settled on the head, and as carefully removed when necessary, trying not to disarrange the wig or hair underneath it. When should you take off your hat? And what do you do with it then?

Restoration man was aware that, when he held his hat in his hand, the inside must be towards him, presumably because it might be so dirty as to be offensive. A hundred years later there has been a volte-face. Hats may, indeed must, show their insides, demonstrating how clean they were. Perhaps they were. Perhaps the wig, which went to the barber to be set at regular intervals, had somehow become cleaner than its seventeenth-century predecessor, and so it kept the hat lining clean, but it is hard to imagine anything staying clean very long in that sooty atmosphere and low level of personal hygiene. Perhaps the idea was to demonstrate your fiscal probity by displaying the stamp showing that you had paid the tax on hats.

Did it matter what you did with your hat? The answer has to be, yes. Earl Ferrers, who was hanged for murder, had his hat and the hangman's noose buried with him. In a more general context, manners for the leisured classes were formal.[1] That was why young gentlemen as well as young ladies took lessons from a dancing master: not only to learn to dance, but more importantly to learn how to move. 'Ease gracefulness and dignity compose the air and address of a man of fashion', as Lord Chesterfield wrote to his son; and 'as you will be often under the necessity of dancing a minuet, I would have you dance it very well. Remember that the graceful motion of the arms, the giving your hand, and *the putting on and pulling off your hat* [my italics] genteely are the material parts of a gentleman's dancing.'

The hat was worn indoors and out of doors. One of its three points had to lie above the left eye. So far, so good. Now proceed to the difficult feat of taking it off. No wonder the ordinary man in the street thought all this was ridiculous. 'Raise the right hand to your Hat gracefully. Put your forefinger in as far as the Crown and your thumb under the Brim and then raise it from your head gracefully and easily.'² A few hours of practice in front of a mirror should get you there.

For informal occasions such as an evening at the club, these unwieldy objects could conveniently be hung on pegs on the wall or, failing that, on the wall sconces.

The bow

Complete mastery of The Hat enables you to grapple with the really difficult matter of The Bow. In a place where you will be bowing left, right and centre, say in St James's Park, it is allowed to carry the hat under your left arm. Then, when you need to, you can take it with your right hand, hold it near the body, and get ready to bow.

What kind of bow? The most casual, and the easiest, was the passing bow. There you are, walking through the trees, when you see someone you know. Say the lady, whom for this purpose I will call the salutee, is on your left. Slide the left foot forward (remember what I said about looking where you step in St James's Park) with your leg straight. Look into her eyes. Bend your back, dropping your gaze to the ground (bad luck, you'll have to get your shoes cleaned) as you go. Bend your back knee slightly, over the turned-out toe of the back foot, and turn towards the salutee. This sounds so difficult that practice is essential, otherwise your feet will be tied in ungraceful knots and you will fall flat on your face. As you come up again, another gaze at the salutee. Do not wave your hat about, just keep it in your right hand quite quietly. Perhaps, after all, this do-it-yourself tuition is too difficult and you should engage a dancing master.

Because we have only just started. Before you enter a room quickly run through the moves for a Bow Forwards. To the count of three, slide leading foot forward, hat off of course, bending the back at the same time, then rise on the 'scraping foot' and in you go. Now for the post-graduate stuff, the Bow to Side. (1) Short step sideways on to right foot, removing hat with the usual grace. (2) Bow the back, not at a right angle but to 'appear rounded'. Caricatures of courtiers of the time catch this perfectly. They all look like woodlice. (3) Move left leg back to the fifth position, your right heel touching your left big toe, feet at right-angles. The directions stop there – find your own way out.

But as you go, bow. Bow sideways when entering a room, greeting someone, beginning and ending a dance, and taking leave. 'If the person taking leave was intending to make his exit to the right he repeated the bow always on the right foot, slowly edging away from the company.'[3] If by some awful chance you encounter royalty, bow, of course, as deeply as you can, or feel like. Then when you are dismissed, walk backwards, bowing, of course, as you go.[4]

Stand easy

While waiting about for another chance to bow, think what you are doing. Your head must be erect, but not stiff. Your feet must be turned out, 'that makes you stand firm, easy and graceful'. Your arms can be tricky. Only servants let them hang down on each side in a tasteless way. But do not put your hands in your pockets,[5] except among close male friends. This is what waistcoats are for. The right hand is inserted into the waistcoat, which remains unbuttoned for this purpose; the left hand goes on to the left hip (do not pretend to be Napoleon: he is the wrong century); the hat may well be tucked under the left arm; the left foot is slightly advanced, with the foot, of course, turned out. Perfectly simple. Walking too is straightforward. Just remember to keep your legs turned out from the hip.

The curtsy or sink

Ladies, with all those stays and stomachers, are allowed to be less supple than men. Again there are various degrees of 'reverences', but the body stays upright throughout. The passing reverence just needs some neat footwork, unseen under the skirt, and a graceful 'sink', hands joined at the waist. The most reverential sink involves sliding one foot forwards, transferring your weight to it, then a small sideways step, transferring your weight to that foot. Slide the first foot to join the other foot, heels touching, toes turned out, bend the knees outwards over the toes, flashing your eyes at the salutee/floor/salutee as in male bows, and that's it.

The language of fans

On no account handle them in a bourgeois fashion. They should normally be held closed, between the thumb and first finger of the right hand. Change hands if you must. Compared to the expertise of the Spaniards there was hardly any language of fans, only the following:

> Fan closed, tip to lips: *hush, we are overheard.*[6]
> Ditto, tip to right cheek: *yes.*
> Ditto, tip to left cheek: *no.*
> Ditto, tip to nose: *you are not to be trusted.*
> Ditto, tip to forehead: *you're out of your mind.*
> Chin on tip: *your flattery annoys me.*
> Cover left ear with closed fan: *keep our secret.*
> Gaze at closed fan raised in front: *make yourself clear.*
> Tip of closed fan to heart (or stays): *you have my love.*
> Yawn behind closed fan: *go away, you bore me.*
> Open fan, hiding eyes: *I love you.*
> Ditto over the head: *I must avoid you.*
> Lower open fan till pointing to the ground: *I despise you.*
> Extended in right hand with palm upwards: *you are welcome.*
> Open fan making brushing-away movement: *I do not love you.*

That seems to cover most things, except 'When will you send the carriage for Gretna Green?' But the snag, as with all phrase books, was the risk of your partner having a different edition, or none at all, and this desperate semaphore getting you nowhere.

Children

As to be expected, they should spend their time bowing and sinking, and standing up until they are told they may sit down. The reality was, as often with children, different. M. Grosley was shocked by the irreverence of 'children of the noblest families' who spent their time throwing bits of apple into the enormous periwig of the Lord High

Steward during Lord Byron's trial for murder in Westminster Hall.[7]

Table manners

No better guide than Lord Chesterfield, writing to his seventeen-year-old son, whom he had dispatched to Europe for polishing after Westminster School, 'the seat of illiberal manners and brutal behaviour', which clearly had not taught him well. 'If at table you throw down your knife, plate, bread etc. and hack the wing of a chicken for half an hour without being able to cut it off, and your sleeve all the time in another dish, I must rise from the table...'

Foreigners' views

Casanova was taken aback in St James's Park, by the sight of the 'hinder parts of persons relieving nature in the bushes'. Surely they could turn round to face the path and hide their bottoms? 'Not at all ... for then they might be recognised whereas in exposing their posteriors they run no such risk ... You may have noticed that when an Englishman wants to ease his sluices in the street he doesn't turn up an alley or turn to the wall.' 'Yes I've noticed them turning towards the middle of the street where they are seen by everybody who is driving in a carriage.' 'The people in the carriage needn't look.'[8] (This curious habit was, I think, still going on in 1810.[9] The street outside public houses was 'extremely unpleasant in summer. Delicacy forbids my adding more on the subject. Would that equal decency in the keepers would *turn their customers backwards* [the writer's italics].')

Nevertheless that observant Frenchman M. Grosley was, on the whole, favourably impressed by English manners.[10] The lower classes, the porters, sailors, chair-men and day-labourers, were 'as insolent a rabble as can be met with', and xenophobic with it. What a contrast to 'the politeness, the civility and the officiousness [helpfulness] of people of good breeding whom we meet in the streets, as well as the obliging readiness of the citizens and shopkeepers'. Violent hand-shaking in which 'the whole soul enters the arm ... supplies the embraces and salutes of the French.' A lawyer himself, Grosley went to see the English legal system in action in the courts and both Houses of Parliament. He must have asked someone a question in French, expecting him to understand it after all those French lessons. He was taken aback by the reaction of the person he spoke to, which was to

Ludgate Hill, 1749. Prostitutes advertised by raising the side of their skirts. The two on the left are well dressed but a third one, further to the right, has not prospered. The street lighting throws a patchy light.

In 1749 a gang of aggrieved sailors broke up two brothels in the Strand (see page 127). The two cloudy patches are feathers from the beds the sailors have thrown out of the windows, with most of the other furniture. The neighbours are delighted –'a good riddance' – but the fat man on the left with medicine bottles in his pocket laments 'Villains, I shall lose all my patients' and the prostitute in the centre says 'Now I must pike [go] to Goodman's Fields' to ply her trade.

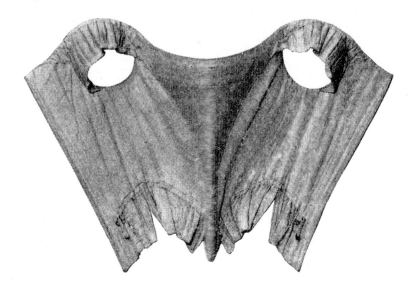

The front of these stays, c. 1770, is in the middle of the picture. The straight edges would be laced up the back, almost to shoulder level.

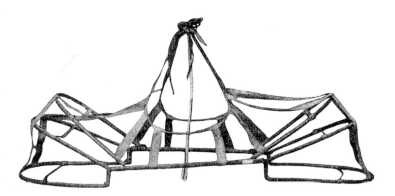

In the extreme of fashion a framework tied round the waist held the skirt out sideways. The U-shaped half-hoops could fold upwards if necessary (see page 217). c. 1750.

A lady's maid is having her hair elaborately dressed in the kitchen while the old washer-woman works.

A barber, his razors in his back pocket, carrying newly-dressed wigs, 1771.

THE CITY TONSOR.

The two upper levels of this pawnbroker's shop window display second-hand clothes, including stays.

Apprentices display patterned wallpapers, rolls of which are stored in fixtures at the back of the shop.

This shop frontage dates from the 1760s and still survives, in London's Haymarket.

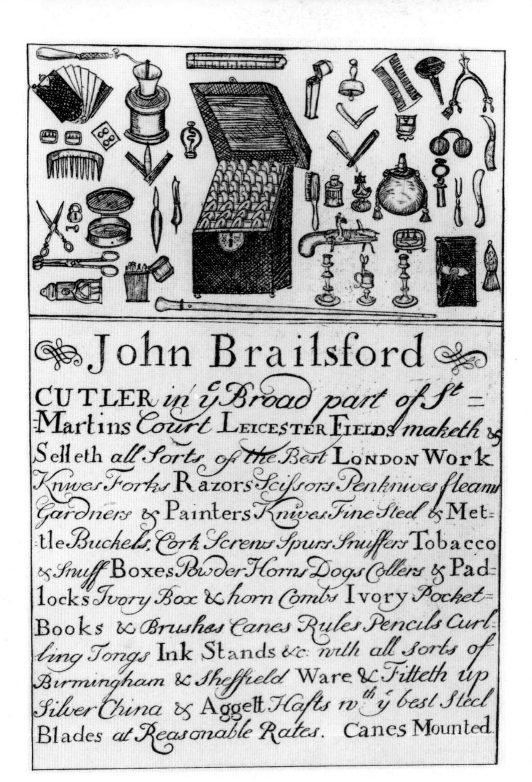

John Brailsford

CUTLER in y Broad part of St Martins Court LEICESTER FIELDS maketh & Selleth all Sorts of the Best LONDON Work Knives Forks Razors Scissors Penknives fleams Gardners & Painters Knives Fine Steel & Mettle Buckels, Cork Screws Spurs Snuffers Tobacco & Snuff Boxes Powder Horns Dogs Collers & Padlocks Ivory Box & horn Combs Ivory Pocket Books & Brushes Canes Rules Pencils Curling Tongs Ink Stands &c: with all Sorts of Birmingham & Sheffield Ware & Fitteth up Silver China & Aggett Hafts wth y best Steel Blades at Reasonable Rates. Canes Mounted

Much of the stock listed on this trade card can be identified in the picture. Small metal-ware manufacture was just beginning to move to Birmingham and Sheffield.

David Garrick and Hannah Pritchard in *The Suspicious Husband* by Francis Hayman, c. 1747. The weight of her skirt must have made it difficult for this actress to move fast. Garrick retained his Staffordshire accent after years on the London stage.

A theatre riot in 1762, when the management of the Covent Garden Theatre threatened to raise seat prices (see page 255). Note the stage lighting, and the boxes overlooking the stage. The two male actors are in 'Eastern' dress appropriate to the play, Arne's *Artaxerxes*; not so the female lead.

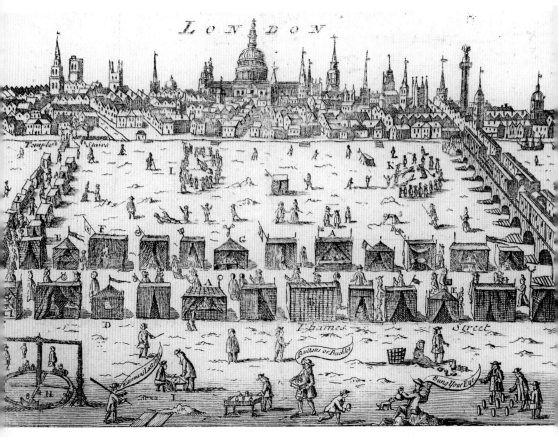

When the Thames froze, as in the winter of 1739–40, it was traditional to hold a Frost Fair. Printing presses on the ice turned out these souvenirs. Near London Bridge people are watching bear-baiting. More people are waiting for a slice of the ox being roasted nearby. Stalls sold jewellery and other fairings.

When English currency was often debased, and foreign currency had to be weighed and valued, a handy pair of scales was essential (see page 294).

disappear as fast as possible. But he soon realised that 'those who did not understand me were eager to look for someone who did', which he thought most kind, especially considering that really the Englishman loved his horses more than his fellow human beings.

Spoken English

It may be easier to speak to a horse than to a fellow human being. M. Grosley wanted to see the Apothecaries' Garden – that is, the Physic Garden, in Chelsea – but he never managed it because he could get no one to understand his pronunciation of Apothecary. 'The English language as generally spoken seems to consist entirely of monosyllables ... the first syllable is pronounced with emphasis, and the rest, being half suppressed, dies away within the teeth.' He was surprised by its idiosyncracies: for instance, that 'surgeon' was pronounced surgeon but written chirurgeon.

There was no way, such as broadcasting, of imposing a uniform 'received' speech. Perhaps the most widely admired speaker was David Garrick, but he apparently[11] spoke with the accent of his native Staffordshire. The examples of this solecism merely confuse. Garrick was said to be guilty of pronouncing gird, birth and firm as gurd, burth and furm. Well yes. He should have used a short 'u' as in 'but', but I don't see how. The same with heard, earth and interred. 'His example was followed by many of his imitators on the stage, who would do well to correct this impropriety', but they seem to have lost the battle. Boswell, not the most sensitive of men, thought it wise to try to get rid of the worst of his Scottish accent, resulting in the compliment from Samuel Johnson that his 'pronunciation is not offensive'.[12] Many vowels seem to have changed their values. Gold was pronounced goold, and Rome Room. Ea before two or more consonants should be pronounced as in realm, which leaves earth, learn, pearl and search due for a change. Au should be pronounced as in hat, which produces hanting, laffing and a drafft.

Several writers set out different rules for the only permitted pro- nunciation. The anonymous author of *The Complete Letter-Writer* – published in Edinburgh in 1768, but purporting to deal with the English language – began with a list of words in which letters were not pronounced, 'but must be wrote', such as the i in devil and venison, the o in carrion and Nicholas, the c in victuals and perfect, the h in herb, humour and host, the l in Bristol ('wrote' in old maps as Bristow) and the n in kiln. The terminal g was dropped in according, dancing, playing, singing and fighting.

Samuel Johnson found 'our speech copious without order, and energetick without rules'. In particular, vowels 'are so capriciously pronounced and so differently modified by accident or affectation'.[13] He launched a characteristic side-swipe at 'most of the writers of English grammar' and their long lists of words pronounced otherwise than how they were spelt. He distinguished between the 'cursory and colloquial', which they used, and the 'solemn', which he was all too prone to use himself. He dismissed the efforts of reformers to tidy up the language. 'Some ingenious men have endeavoured to deserve well of their country by writing honor and labor for honour and labour ... as they have done no good, they have done little harm ... because few have followed them' (except, now, the North American continent and most spell checks in computers). He then set out detailed rules which he modestly suggested might be useful, but 'in English ... much must be learned by example and authority', so he left the field wide open.

English as spoken 'among the better sort in London' was, however, beginning to emerge as the proper way to speak,[14] as long as it avoided the worst of Cockney, such as Potticary for Apothecary (poor M. Grosley) and v for w as in wittles (victuals).

As I read my way through contemporary writers, a few words caught my eye:

> *bingo*: brandy or other spirit
> *birthday suit*: particularly rich clothes worn at a royal birthday
> *bitch*: the worst possible epithet for a woman, worse than whore
> *bread*: employment
> *bucket, to kick the*: to die
> *chatter broth* or *scandal broth*: tea
> *chum*: a friend, or an obliging fellow prisoner who gives up space
> *crack*: a prostitute
> *dosser*: a basket holding two bushels, i.e. large
> *fireship*: prostitute with venereal disease
> *frost face*: pitted with smallpox
> *godfathers*: jurymen
> *homely*: plain
> *honey month*: the first month after marriage
> *looking glass*: a chamber pot

louse ladder: a dropped stitch in a stocking
mama: already in use 1749
mob: coined by the upper classes from *mobile vulgus*, the fickle crowd
niffy-naffy fellow: a trifler
old hat: a woman's private parts
pencil: a little brush
perambulator: a measuring wheel
Quaver tub: Quakers' meeting house
rhino: cash
smart money: disability pension to soldier or sailor
toilette: dressing table

Conversation

What did they find to talk about? The weather, of course. It had
been doing some curious things. The first shocks of an earthquake
were felt throughout London on 8 February 1750: 'the chairs shook
and the pewter fell from the shelves to the ground',[15] which must
have made a resounding clang but did no harm. But the second shock
was worse. 'The water of the River was so agitated that the fish were
seen to leap some distance from its surface.'[16] Even Walpole took it
more seriously.

> In the night between Wednesday and Thursday last (exactly a month
> since the first shock) the earth had a shivering fit between one and two:
> but so slight that, if no more had followed, I don't believe it would
> have been noticed. I had been awake, and had scarce dozed again –
> on a sudden I felt my bolster lift up my head; I thought somebody was
> getting from under my bed, but soon found it was a strong earthquake,
> that lasted near half a minute, with a violent vibration and great
> roaring. I rang my bell; my servant came in, frightened out of his
> senses: in an instant we heard all the windows in the neighbourhood
> flung up. I got up and found people running into the streets, but saw
> no mischief done: there has been some; two old houses flung down,
> several chimneys and much china-ware.

Then panic set in. If the Lord had seen fit to send earthquakes at
such a punctual monthly interval, he would certainly send another
next month, especially considering that he had already sent plagues
of cattle distemper and locusts. (Perhaps not quite a plague, but
'numbers of locusts ... were found in St James's park and places

adjacent ... They sometimes eat each other', but not apparently much else. 'We do not hear that the locusts have done any damage'.[17] Those people who could, left London. The streets were gridlocked with carriages, and 'the fields about the metropolis were crowded with people all of whom passed the night in fearful suspense'.[18] John Wesley hoped that general repentance would avert a further mark of divine displeasure.[19] The Bishop of London did not help the traffic situation by preaching a death-and-damnation sermon linking the locusts and the cattle pest with the earthquakes and the plagues of Egypt. It was immediately printed and widely sold – the emergent power of the media. But 8 April passed without more signs of divine disapproval, and people came back to their London houses sheepishly saying that the weather had been so lovely that they had not been able to resist a short holiday.

Londoners were jumpy about earthquakes for years afterwards, the more so after the terrible earthquake that destroyed Lisbon in 1755. A brawl between two Irishmen on the Royal Exchange in 1763 'gave rise to a report that an earthquake was felt by which some gentlemen were frightened and others had their pockets picked'.[20]

The winter of 1739–40 was bitterly cold, the average temperature never rising above freezing throughout December to February.[21] The Thames, shallower and slower before the Victorians embanked it, froze over. Watermen and others who got their living from the river were starving, and the price of coal rose beyond the reach of the poor. At least it was possible to hold a Frost Fair, with booths and even, following a long tradition, a printing press to run off souvenirs. In 1746, while Englishmen waited with bated breath for news of the Scottish invasion, the wretched soldiers on guard out at Finchley shivered in another unusually cold winter. A subscription list was opened at the Guildhall, to buy them shirts and stockings and woolly caps and gloves and 'spatterdashes' – woollen gaiters.[22] There were ten wet summers in a row, between 1751 and 1760.[23]

In 1760 a terrible hurricane rolled up the lead roof of the Admiralty like a scroll,[24] did extensive damage to the close-packed shipping on the Thames and even covered the Mall in St James's Park with broken branches.[25]

The winter of 1762–3 was again bitterly cold. A man was found frozen to death, in Fleet ditch, standing bolt upright, and another 'with skaits on was found frozen to death upon some floating ice over against the Isle of Dogs'.[26] In the bitter January of 1771 'a waterman crossing the Thames had his boat jammed in between the ice and could not get on shore, and no waterman dare venture to his assistance. He was almost speechless last night and it is thought he cannot survive long'.[27]

But good stories emerged from the river even in normal weather. 'On Friday last a woman took a boat at Somerset stairs, and when the waterman had rowed into the river he attempted to be rude with her, which she resisting, the boat overset and they both drowned.'[28]

If it wasn't the weather, it was the French. They were suspected of planning an invasion to assist Charles Stuart in his attempt to topple the Hanoverian dynasty, and rumours went round London like wildfire, of flat-bottomed invasion barges massing off Dunkirk and landings expected 'every hour'.[29]

Then there was the complicated matter of the new calendar. The British had lived according to their own calendar perfectly peacefully for many years, but suddenly they were expected to join the rest of Europe and synchronise their dates by cutting eleven days out of their life (see note 31, Chapter 17). This involved the equally confused question of the Millennium. There was much correspondence, and doubtless much conversation, about the meaning of Millennium in the New Testament. Should it be taken literally or figuratively? The rule about leap years, too, was changed. Far-seeing scholars worked out that, although an extra day every four years was nearly enough to correspond with the solar year, it needed a minor adjustment every 400 years. Thus, the year 2000 would not be a leap year. (They seem to have got this wrong: 2000 is indeed a leap year.)

There were always Court scandals and appalling crimes, to deplore. But serious science was debated too. Where did swallows go in the winter? Did they conglobulate under water? Was there life on the moon?[30] *The Gentleman's Magazine* could always be relied on for 'cuts' (engravings) of plants and animals in the news, such as elephants, and résumés of medical discoveries.

Customs: weddings

As we have seen, it was not only the poor who chose to get married in the Fleet, with a minimum of ceremony. But in any case, a proper church wedding with its public declaration of worshipping the bride's body was thought by some to impose too great a strain on female sensitivity, so private ceremonies by special licence were popular among genteel brides.[31] Fanny Burney wrote in her diary: 'of all things in the world I don't suppose anything can be so dreadful as a public wedding – my stars, I should never be able to support it'.[32] 'Honey moon' meant merely the first month after marriage.[33] No doubt any bride wished to look her best, and dressed accordingly, but there was no general rule of bridal white. A tragedy was reported in *The Gentleman's Magazine* of November 1763.

> A young lady who died a few days since was at her own request buried in all her wedding garments, consisting of a white negligee [a kind of dress, not a dressing gown] and petticoats ... her wedding shift was her winding sheet, with a fine point lace tucker, handkerchief, ruffles and apron, also a fine point lace lappet head [cap] and a handkerchief tied closely over it, with diamond ear-rings in her ears and rings on her fingers, a very fine necklace, white silk stockings, silver-spangled shoes and stone [jewelled] buckles.

In view of the activities of grave-robbers this charming picture was surely unwise.

Funerals

> Robert Green coffin maker and undertaker ... sells and lets all manner of furniture for funerals, on reasonable terms, viz. velvet palls, hangings for rooms, large silver'd candlesticks and sconces, tapers and wax lights, Heraldry, feathers and velvets, fine cloth cloaks and middling ditto, rich silk scarves, alamode and sarsnet hatbands, Italian crape by the piece or hatband, black and white favours, cloth black or grey baize and flannel ditto, burying crapes of all sorts, fine quilting and quilted mattrices, the best lac'd, plain and Shammy gloves, kidd and lamb ditto, etc. NB All sorts of plates and handles for coffins in brass, lead or tin likewise nails of all sorts, coffins and shrouds of all sizes ready made.[34]

Which seems to cover everything. One would have to work out what could be hired and returned, and what unreturnable items had to be bought. Some families surely had mourning equipment and clothes that could be borrowed by other family members. There is a recipe for 'extracting grease or stains from mourning' (boiled fig leaves),[35] which indicates repeated wear. If not, an average funeral for the middling sort cost about £100,[36] which if Massie's figures are anywhere near accurate was an appalling drain on the resources of the bereaved. The undertaker assessed what the market would bear, offering 'to furnish out the Funeral Solemnity with as much pomp and feigned sorrow as the Heirs and Successors chose to purchase'.[37]

The high cost of hiring the fragile black ostrich feathers might perhaps be dispensed with, but since funerals increasingly took place in the evening, the 'large silvered candlesticks' would be needed, and certainly the coffin would be covered by a pall – a heavy black cloth that hung almost to the ground. The edges of it were held by the pallbearers, who were friends or family members. The coffin was carried on the backs of the undertaker's men. (The general effect looks unfortunately comic in pictures.[38] The coffin moved along like a caterpillar on several pairs of black legs.) Mourners in deep black followed the coffin, others could join the procession in ordinary clothes. Foot processions were still usual. Because of the fear that grave-robbers might dig up and sell the body after interment, 'improved coffins' were marketed,[39] 'the fastenings of these improved receptacles being on such a principle as to render it impracticable for the grave robbers to open them. This security must afford great consolation at an era when it is a well-authenticated fact that nearly one thousand bodies are annually appropriated for the purpose of dissection.'

Funerals could have unexpected results.

At the interment of Mr Cambden, a sugar refiner, in St James's Church Shadwell, minute guns were fired from on board the 'Happy Return', Captain Ross, as a tribute to his memory. The guns however not being properly examined, one of them was fired with two balls one of which went through a house and in it cut the sacking and tick of a bed on which lay an exciseman very ill; it did not hurt him otherwise than by frightening him much to find himself buried in loose feathers on the floor. The other ball went through three chambers in another house without doing any further damage than much frightening the neighbourhood.[40]

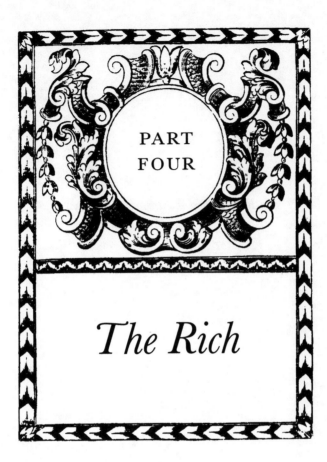

PART
FOUR

The Rich

'Rich beyond the dreams of avarice'
Samuel Johnson

CHAPTER 24

High Society

Money

The people at the top of Massie's pyramid were some of them very rich indeed.

> The whole subject of conversation at present is the death and will of Lord Bath. He has left above twelve hundred thousand pounds in land and money; four hundred thousand pounds in cash, stocks and mortgages; his own estate in land was improved to fifteen thousand pounds a year [and other property of £800,000] and all this he has left to his brother General Pulteney ... though he never loved him.[1]

The Duke of Northumberland managed on only £25,000 a year.[2] 'In a few days a marriage will be consummated [*sic*: surely *The Gentleman's Magazine* meant celebrated?] between Edward Lascelles Esquire ... and Miss Danes ... a beautiful lady with £100,000 fortune.'[3] Lord Chesterfield married money too, but chose a bride past the age of fertility – hence, perhaps, his belated interest in the illegitimate son he had fathered on a respectable French lady.

John Spencer inherited vast landholdings all over England. By the time he became of age in 1755, £240,000 in cash was waiting for him, with an annual income of £30,000 and at least five grand houses, including Althorp in Northamptonshire and two in the Grosvenor development.[4] With that kind of money he could, and did, choose whom to marry without worrying about a dowry. And there was no inheritance tax, no income tax, only 5s in the pound on income from land and multitudinous taxes on status symbols such as footmen and carriages, which could be borne without strain. In 1761 that indefatigable pamphleteer Joseph Massie issued a counter-blast to politicians who were arguing that taxes were too high. In his *Calculations of the Present Taxes yearly paid by a family of each Rank, Degree or Class* he showed that a nobleman with £20,000 income from land was paying £6,378 10s, of which £4,000 was land tax: an effective rate of 6s 5d in the pound of his total income.

Houses

The most splendid example of conspicuous consumption in London was Spencer House. The cost of construction and decoration alone was £35,000, with another £14,000 for the site and unknown amounts spent on the furnishings and *objets d'art*, but John Spencer and his new bride, who had excellent taste, created an interior that delights without overwhelming. It is true that the gold used in the palm room was 23.5 carat, the fireplaces were carrara marble, the walls were exquisitely painted or covered in silk damask: yet the house emerged from the workmen as a monument not to grandeur, but to marital happiness. The biggest room was only 40 feet long, enough for a modest party for 600–700 where everyone could move about and talk to each other with pleasure, instead of being squashed together as notoriously happened at many fashionable parties.[5]

I am not so sure about Lord Chesterfield's house. He specified two grand rooms, one a drawing room and one his library. Tastes have certainly changed since his day, but to my eye his drawing room,[6] which was a riot of gilt curlicues, looked as if a troupe of monkeys – French ones, of course, Lord Chesterfield being francophile – had run riot with pots of gold paint. I concede that the gilding was real gold leaf, and as elegant as it could be, but unlike Spencer House it looks overwhelming and – dare one say it? – vulgar. The most splendid feature of the house was the marble staircase, which Lord Chesterfield picked up in 1747 at the demolition sale of another plutocratic house, Lord Chandos's Cannons, out near Stanmore. His library was comfortably panelled and had direct access to that rarity, a water closet, which inevitably calls to mind his advice to his son:

> I knew a gentleman [himself?] who was so good a manager of his time, that he would not even lose that small portion of it which the calls of nature obliged him to spend in the necessary-house; but gradually went through all the Latin poets, in those moments. He bought, for example, a common edition of Horace, of which he tore off gradually a couple

of pages, carried them with him to that necessary place, read them
first, then sent them down as a sacrifice to Cloacina [Roman goddess
of excrement]; and I recommend you to follow his example. It is better
than doing only what you cannot help doing at these moments; and it
will make any book which you shall read in that manner very present
in your mind.[7]

Pomfret Castle in Arlington Street could not be called vulgar, merely
mad. The Countess of Pomfret liked the Gothick taste, and her own
way. The result, inside as well as outside, was a medieval dream, with
plaster traceries soaring above the stairs as in the nave of a good
cathedral, and fan vaulting in the drawing room glittering with gilt.[8]

The Duke and Duchess of Northumberland had no excuse to knock
down Northumberland House in the Strand and put up something
more to the modern taste. After all, they had Sion House out in the
country. But they did transform its interior into a modern Georgian
mansion by new doors and ceilings and sash windows, and added a
wing to accommodate a picture gallery two storeys high and 160 feet
long, and a ball room 103 feet long lit by four huge crystal chandeliers,
each with 25 candles, which 'light up the room even more brilliantly
than necessary'.[9] Thus refurbished, the place could accommodate a
party of 1,500 'persons of distinction' – were there really so many in
London?

Many houses in squares and terraces could vie with these mansions
in the splendour of their interiors. The Duke of Norfolk lived in St
James's Square. He lent his house to the Prince of Wales and his wife,
who gave birth to the future George III in a room at the back in
1738. When the prince was three years old, the family moved to
Leicester House, the Duke got his house back, bought the house next
door and combined them into a splendid dwelling.[10] His music room
was done in gold and white and mirrors, reflecting the pond in the
middle of the square, and his dressing room was hung with silk hand-
painted with Chinese scenes. The perfection of detail was exemplified
by a basket of porcelain flowers, incorporating a lamp to burn
appropriately scented perfume.[11]

Personal possessions

Lady Temple could grace a mere Lord Mayor's procession wearing
£150,000 worth of jewellery.[12] The Duchess of Northumberland's

jewels at a royal court in 1765 cost about the same.[13] Lady Carteret's mother got a headache from the weight of her diamonds.[14] Mrs Monkton came to a masquerade given by Mrs Cornelys dressed as 'an Indian sultan in a robe of cloth of gold ... the seams embroidered with precious stones and a magnificent cluster of diamonds on her head'.[15] *The Gentleman's Magazine* reporter seems to have been mesmerised by diamonds. At a ball given in the Opera House in 1768, where spectators were admitted to the gallery and he maybe got a free view, he reckoned that 'the value of the jewels which were worn on this occasion was supposed [estimated] to amount to two millions'.[16]

The clothes of ladies and gentlemen of fashion and wealth gave splendid opportunities for showing off, by sewing diamonds on to already fabulous stuffs. And no matter what the law said – or the Prince of Wales, who let it be known that he would be seriously displeased with anyone who attended his Court in French silk – smuggled fabrics for which hefty premiums had to be paid to the handlers were so much smarter than the home-grown article.[17] According to M. Grosley, the preferred route was via the Isle of Man, until 1765 when the Crown bought the island for £70,000 and the smugglers had to leave.[18]

Pictures and statues could enhance the décor of the new mansion. Lord Chesterfield gave *carte blanche* to agents on the continent to track down old masters for his new house, and was surprisingly good-natured when one of them turned out to be a fake. Massive pieces of silver enabled the assemblies of 'persons of distinction' to be properly fed. At the end of the evening chairs like jewel boxes, carriages with gilt and enamel panels and coronets, and matched pairs of horses would transport these favoured humans back to their homes, while the mob looked on. For processions on the Thames, the noble barge would be brought out, rowed by minions wearing colourful livery and silver badges, with musicians and flags, and gilt oars flashing in the sunlight.

Pastimes

What did they find to do? They gave parties. After the mortifying part-failure of the royal fireworks in April 1749, the Duke of Richmond put on a much better show for the Duke of Modena the next month, in the Privy garden at Whitehall and on the Thames, loosing off

'5,000 sky-rockets and 5,000 water-rockets',[19] and nothing went wrong.

They gambled. Their ancestral estates were almost certainly entailed, which meant that the current holders could not sell them to raise money because the land was tied up in legal parcels to hand on to the next heir, on the same terms. This was probably the saving of many estates, which otherwise would have joined the gambler's other assets on the gaming table. M. Grosley found it extraordinary that

> their losses leave no traces on their countenances ... a minister of state [Lord Sandwich] passed twenty four hours at a public gaming table so absorbed in play that during the whole time he had no subsistence but a bit of beef between two slices of toasted bread ... this new dish grew highly in vogue. It is called by the name of the minister who invented it.[20]

Women were as fond of gambling as men. 'At great assemblies play is the only thing that unites both sexes.'[21]

They flirted and bedded. In 1770 Lord Grosvenor finally sued the Duke of Cumberland for damages of £100,000, for seducing his wife.[22] In 1768 the two had been the talk of the town, seen everywhere together by everyone and in bed together by the servants. According to the evidence of the Countess D'Onhoff (this case has everything: that really was the lady's name; she had preceded Lady Grosvenor in the Duke's affections), the pair first had sexual intercourse in her house in Cavendish Square, the Duke having told the servants that he was visiting his 'sister'. He forgot the scar on his face, which made him immediately recognisable. The story reached the level of farce when Lord Grosvenor got restive and banished his lady to his country seat at Eaton, 180 miles from London. She had no choice but to go, but she kept her lover informed of her movements, which were remarkably slow, by letters written invisibly in lemon juice. Unknown to her, the servants knew how to read invisible writing, and kept their master informed, stage by stage. When she finally, after four overnight assignations at coaching inns – *four* nights for a journey of 180 miles in plutocratic transport? – got to Eaton, her swain put up at an inn nearby and they continued their affair in the fields. How undignified and uncomfortable. It was December by now. At last D'Onhoff wrote an anonymous letter to the cuckolded husband, who set off from London for Eaton, and managed to miss the vile seducer, who left Eaton for London just in time.

By 15 December 1769 the story had broken in the press. In January

1770 George III opened Parliament. Lord Grosvenor was there, with other lords such as the Duke of Grafton, who had just divorced his wife for adultery. When the King said, 'it is with much concern that I find myself obliged to open this session by acquainting you that distemper among the horned cattle has lately broken out', Lord Grosvenor and the Duke of Grafton turned to each other and bowed.[23]

The jury in the court action, who had enjoyed every word of the evidence, found Lord Grosvenor's claim for damages justified in principle, but awarded him only £10,000 and his costs, which amounted to £13,000. The Grosvenor/Cumberland affair was a goldmine for the legal profession. The next stage was a suit by Lord Grosvenor for divorce, which his wife contested, bringing evidence from whores bribed and suborned from all over London to show the character of her husband. The case was settled in 1771, out of court, which must have been a disappointment to the press and the lawyers.

Lady Grosvenor bore a son to the Duke of Cumberland, but the baby did not survive. In normal circumstances, most noble ladies preferred to leave their country seats and have their children in their London houses, where a fashionable midwife, male or female, could be booked in good time. The kind of money at stake is shown by a report in *The Gentleman's Magazine* of a case in which 'an eminent man midwife' was sued for not arriving in time to attend the plaintiff's wife. He had to pay £1,000 and costs.[24]

They networked. In effect, the great Whig families governed the country, and parcelled out political offices to their friends and families. It was as well to keep in touch, by giving balls and assemblies and even routs at which rising stars could be greeted and potential sons-in-law marked.

Good works

It is fair to say that the nobility often involved themselves in altruistic good works. The Duke of Richmond was the President of the London Hospital. The Duchess of Somerset was one of the original signatories of the petition to the King launched by Captain Coram, which resulted in the Foundling Hospital. He eventually netted seven duchesses, eight countesses and five baronesses.[25]

Crimes

Lord Ferrers, in whose veins the blood of the Plantagenets (diluted) was said to run, 'was a man of an unhappy disposition. Though of clear intellect, and acknowledged abilities when sober, yet an early attachment to drinking greatly impaired his faculties.'[26] He had been judicially separated from his wife, and the financial arrangements were in the hands of an old and trusted servant, Johnson. All went well for a while, but by 1760 the Earl had convinced himself that Johnson was cheating him, and cold-bloodedly planned to murder him. He sent the menservants away, and told his mistress and their four children to go to her father's house. He summoned Johnson, told him to kneel down, and shot him. The wound was not immediately fatal. There was time to summon a surgeon, who, frightened for his own life, assured the Earl that Johnson was in no danger. So the Earl went off to get drunk, and Johnson was bundled into a chair and taken to his own house, where he died.

A posse went out to the Earl's house, tracked him from room to room, and managed to shut him up in a nearby public house to await events – which followed remarkably quickly. Johnson died on a Saturday morning, and a coroner's court was convened on the following Monday. The jury found that the deceased had died by wilful murder, so the Earl was moved from the pub to Leicester Gaol. 'After remaining [there] about a fortnight he was conveyed to London in his own landau. He behaved with the utmost composure during the journey [92 miles by modern roads: he is unlikely to have done the journey in one day, at that time] and being taken before the house of peers ... he was committed to the Tower.'

His trial took place three months later, before the House of Lords, in Westminster Hall. There was only one possible verdict, once it had become clear, from the Earl's able cross-examination of witnesses, that he was not mad. The sentence was that he should be hanged, like any common criminal. 'This unhappy nobleman petitioned to be beheaded within the Tower: but as the crime was so atrocious the king refused to mitigate the sentence.' On 5 May a mourning coach was got ready, but he was allowed to go to Tyburn in his own landau. Among the many occasions for horse-drawn processions in the London of the eighteenth century, this must have been one of the most macabre. It was headed by five of the Earl's coaches, presumably empty. Then came his landau, occupied by the Earl in his wedding clothes, 'a white suit, richly embroidered with silver', the Sheriff of London and the chaplain of the Tower, and guarded by a party of footguards and warders of the Tower. The mourning coach with six horses came in useful after all for some of his Lordship's friends.[27] Then came the Lord High Steward in his state coach drawn by six horses, and twelve judges, and the Masters in Chancery, each undoubtedly in his separate coach with at least four horses.[28] The procession to Tyburn through the crowds took nearly three hours. The Earl wanted to stop for a drink, as most prisoners were allowed to do, but the sheriff advised against it because 'it would only draw a greater crowd about him', so he agreed. Why had no one thought of bringing a flask? He also wanted to say goodbye to his mistress, but this too was refused. At the very last moment there was an undignified argument between the hangman's assistant, to whom the Earl had given 5 guineas, mistaking him for his boss, and the hangman himself, who wanted the money. Finally, they managed to get down to business. The Earl had brought a white cap with him. It must have been the soft turban-like headgear that men wore when they took their wigs off. This was pulled down over his face, the noose was put round his neck, the raised part of the scaffold on which he was standing was lowered, and he was hanged. A little boy also died, trampled to death by a horse in the crowd, and a girl somehow managed to strangle herself in the strings of her bonnet.[29] The Earl's corpse stayed where it was for over an hour. Then it was put in a coffin lined with white satin and taken in a hearse with six horses to Surgeons' Hall, 'where an incision was made from the neck to the bottom of the breast'. But it was not subjected to the indignities of extensive dissection for the instruction of medical students and the curious, horrifically depicted by Hogarth in *The Reward of Cruelty* nine years earlier. 'After the body had remained some time at surgeon's hall for public inspection it was delivered to his friends for interment', with his hat and the hangman's noose in the coffin. He was buried in St Pancras church. Later his coffin was moved to Leicestershire. Two weeks after the execution his brother Washington took his seat in the House of Lords as a peer.[30]

The trial of Lord Byron in 1765 had a happier outcome. The story began at one of those clubs where gentlemen whiled away their time. This one met in the 'Star and Garter' in St James's Street, renowned for the best claret in London. Three solid hours of drinking it led the fifth Lord Byron to disagree with his friend and neighbour in the country, Mr Chaworth, about the relative values, in terms of game, of their respective estates. They retired to a back room on the first floor, obligingly made available by the management. There someone lit a tallow candle, they drew their swords and set about resolving the argument. Mr Chaworth was killed.[31]

Lord Byron was, like Earl Ferrers, tried by his peers in Westminster Hall, but this time we have M. Grosley's description of the proceedings.[32] He must for once have found someone to translate for him. Weeks before, workmen had begun to put up galleries in the ancient hall, which otherwise could not possibly accommodate all who needed to be there. There were 'two great boxes for the royal family and foreign ministers, ... all covered with crimson cloth'. Four thousand tickets had been issued to the general public, which were changing hands at 6 guineas each by the time the trial began, at 7 a.m. on 16 April, at which unaccustomed hour 'it would be hard to conceive a more brilliant meeting ... all the chief ladies of quality in the three kingdoms [were there] ... none had neglected her attire or forgot her jewels'. Only a few ladies were dressed in the French taste, and 'resembled unfurnished houses' – they had clearly mistaken the occasion. 'All the rest, decked in the finest manner with brocades, diamonds and lace, had no other headdress but a riband tied to their hair over which they wore a flat hat adorned with a variety of ornaments.' It must have taken them hours to get into all that. 'These hats ... filled Westminster Hall.' The function of their wearers, at a trial for murder, is unclear, even more so that of the choristers of St Paul's, who were there too, misbehaving, and the 'children of the noblest families' whom we met before, throwing bits of apple into the Lord High Steward's enormous periwig.

Enter the peers, 250 of them, walking two by two, in their long, red ermine-trimmed robes and '*hats* [my italics] of all shapes and sizes', which two by two they took off to salute the throne with the appropriate bow, disclosing an equal variety of hairstyles and wigs. The defendant was 'dressed in deep mourning'. After all, his friend was dead. The hearing ended eleven hours after it had begun. By some means which is not clear to me, the verdict absolved him of murder but found him guilty of manslaughter. He claimed the privilege of peerage, was not even burned in the hand, paid his fees, got into his coach and went home. 'Five days after the trial I saw him amongst the other peers at the House of Lords.' It must have been a curious experience for M. Grosley.

CHAPTER 25

The King

The king for part of the period covered by this book was the second Hanoverian monarch, George II (1683–1760), who reigned for 33 years from 1727 and died on the lavatory of heart failure. His son Frederick, Prince of Wales, had died nine years earlier, so the crown skipped a generation and came to rest with George III (1738–1820), who reigned for 60 years. After 1811 his powers were exercised by his son, another George, because he was thought to be mad, but the Regency is after our time.

How did Londoners perceive George II in the last twenty years of his reign, and George III as a young man?

George II

During most of the eighteenth century Europe was in a confused state of warfare.[1] Back in 1708, Marlborough and others had won the battle of Oudenarde. Young Prince George was in the thick of it, hacking and thrusting, sweating and swearing like any trooper,[2] and thoroughly enjoying himself. Thirty-five years later, as a man of 61, he had a second chance to show the courage that so endeared him to his British subjects, at the battle of Dettingen. This time he was in command of the allied army, and accompanied by his favourite son, William, Duke of Cumberland. He took an active personal part in the battle. The fact that his horse bolted for the rear at one stage was not his fault, and he stopped it quite quickly, got off and fought on foot, rallying his infantry by shouting, 'Now for the honour of England! Fire and behave brave and the French will run!' – and those French who survived, did.

This personal courage was to the taste of the English. What rankled was the undeniable fact that their brave king was also the ruler of Hanover, and regularly went off there, preferring the life of a small German court to the squabbles and backbiting of his English courtiers. The division of spoils and liabilities between the Hanoverians and the British was far from clear even to statesmen, but the man in the street harboured a grudging feeling that the foreigners were getting the best of it. Britain was against the whole idea of a standing army, so when land forces were needed quickly mercenary troops from Hesse as well as Hanover were hired, and paid from the British treasury. The British had only themselves to blame, but that has never placated a deeply felt popular prejudice.

George II spoke English loudly, fluently and with an execrable accent. 'Boetry and bainting' bored him.[3] The magnificent royal library that had somehow accumulated he donated to the British Museum in 1757.[4] He was notorious for his bad manners and his parsimony. He had married Caroline of Anspach (1683–1737) in 1705. They were reasonably happy together, considering his appalling manners to her even in public, and her far superior intellect. When she was dying, she told her heart-broken husband that he should remarry. Between sobs, he replied, 'Non – j'aurai des maîtresses.' 'Ah mon dieu, cela n'empêche pas', she sighed, after many years of putting up with George's mistresses.

Their first child, Frederick, was born seventeen months after their marriage. In modern terms, his parents failed to bond with him. His grandfather, George I, ordered that the boy should be educated in Hanover, so he hardly saw his parents between the ages of seven and twenty-one. The bitter dislike they shared for him as Prince of Wales is notorious and inexplicable. In practical terms, it meant that when he did come to live in London the Prince ran an alternative Court in opposition to his father's, until his unlamented death in 1751. This made it all the more important for careerist courtiers to be seen to attend royal functions. Their absence would be interpreted as a sign that they had gone over to the opposition. So, year after year and birth after birth, the royal Court was thronged with gorgeously dressed nobility come to offer their felicitations to their sovereign on such auspicious occasions. When he was in London, the King lived out at Kensington or even further out at Hampton Court during the summer, returning to St James's Palace only for the winter months. So slow-moving processions of carriages would queue up in St James's or trek out to Kensington. This made a lovely sight for the mob, who scrawled graffiti on the carriages while they waited.

George II's second son, William, Duke of Cumberland, to whom he had given command of the Army, was wildly cheered for having crushed the Stuart rebellion at Culloden. Londoners felt that he had lifted the awful threat of invasion by not only the Scots – bad enough – but their allies the French, who were hated. But the repressive measures Cumberland ordered against the beaten Scots repelled even the exultant English, and earned him the nickname of Butcher Cumberland. Nor did they appreciate his efforts to inculcate strict order and discipline into English troops to rival the orderliness he was accustomed to in his Hanoverian troops. His attention to detail focused on all aspects of military life, including the length of military horses' tails and the height of foot soldiers. In 1752 he noticed that the massed ranks of foot soldiers were a bit ragged, and ordered that any man under 5 feet 8 inches should be discharged, which depleted three regiments of footguards of a quarter of their strength, but they did look tidier.[5]

George II had five daughters. Anne, the Princess Royal, was bored to distraction by her father's army reminiscences, so in 1734 she accepted the proposal of marriage to William of Orange (or vice versa) with relief. The next, Amelia or Emily, lived in Cavendish Square from 1761 until she died in 1786 at the age of 76. She was an excellent rider and equine doctor, devoting her energies to horses, being rude to people and making mischief.[6] Princess Caroline nursed an unrequited passion for that most unlikely of swains Lord Hervey. Princess Mary was the third embittered spinster. Princess Louise was married off to the King of Denmark. When she reached the Danish Court, she realised that her husband's marital prowess was unlikely to match her enthusiasm, so she took the Court physician to her bed, where, unfortunately, they were discovered and she was removed to prison. She died in 1751.

George III

The accession of George III was welcomed by the mob with delirious enthusiasm. Had he not, unlike his Hanoverian predecessors, been born in London? Did he not speak English? Two prints[7] of the time span the years 1760–70. In the first, *The Reception in 1760*, the windows are crowded with onlookers, and children and men and women, some with babies in their arms, are running along beside the royal coach, shouting 'Long live King George III' and 'Honour and glory to our British King' as well as 'He's a sweet pretty man' and 'Huzza!' The matching print is called *The Reception in 1770*. The same king, the same carriage, but no people. The driver, sitting comfortably on his box instead of standing as he did ten years ago, observes that 'We are no longer plagued with the acclamations of the people'. Two courtiers are bowing with just the proper round-shouldered subserviency, and a man who has already replaced his hat observes, 'Not a creature at any of the windows.' By now the sweet pretty man had yielded his place in popular hearts to that most unlikeable man Wilkes, who managed to make his name synonymous with Liberty, always a rabble-rousing word.

Yet George III was a likeable man. One of his first acts on accession was to publish a proclamation 'to discourage and suppress all vice'. He had to start somewhere. His own domestic life was boringly uxorious. In his own words, 'I do not pretend to any superior abilities, but will give place to no one in meaning to preserve the freedom, happiness and glory of my dominions, and all their inhabitants, and to fulfil the duty to my God and my neighbour in the most extended sense.'[8] He must have found the antics of his uncle, the Duke of Cumberland, and Lady Grosvenor deeply uncongenial.

He had fifteen children, his son George leading the way in 1762 and another Amelia bringing up the rear in 1782. In 1765 *The Gentleman's Magazine* reported that 'gold and silver medals were issued in commemoration of his Royal Highness Prince Frederick's election to the bishopric of Osnaburgh'. This may be at first sight surprising. It was only a case of Buggins's turn in the Holy Roman Empire. Osnaburgh was a small bishopric state next door to Hanover, which was part Catholic and part Protestant, so the right to nominate its ruler was exercised alternately by the Catholic Church and the ruler of Hanover, who was also at the time ruling Britain. In 1761 it happened to be Hanover's turn. The bishop did not have to do anything episcopal, which was just as well because he was a babe in arms.

HRH the Prince of Wales has summarised his ancestor's personality:[9]

> As a young man George III was not particularly attractive and could almost be described as priggish. However as he mellowed and gained

experience his warmth and friendly interest in people – particularly
evident at Windsor and Kew where he used to go walking and visiting
alone, talking to his tenants and behaving as a natural and thoroughly
civilised country gentleman – won him immense popularity. ... Few
have laboured harder at being a good King.

The royal standard of living

It is difficult to assess the amount of money that the King could spend
on his own amusements, so tangled up was it with parliamentary
grants and long-standing debts. But however the royal coffers are
measured, they certainly qualify for the top echelon of Massie's
analysis. When George III went to dinner with the Lord Mayor of
London in November 1761, the City bought a whole new set of silver
and the evening cost £6,898 5s 4d, including six 'necessary women'
and a dish of ducks' tongues,[10] but who knows whether the King
enjoyed himself? Could he have laid his hand on as much cash as
the Lord Mayor? Or John Spencer? Possibly not. There is a picture
of his queen in 1764, sitting at her dressing table, which is draped in
lace. The knick-knacks on the table are gold. The lace cost over a
thousand pounds,[11] but it was already two years old.

The royal family never did build themselves a magnificent palace,
despite the advice of every prominent architect and town planner,
contenting themselves with making over Buckingham House, which
was rapidly overcrowded by progeny. The Queen gave the King a
surprise birthday party in 1763, before all those children arrived. She
contrived 'a most magnificent temple and bridge finely illuminated
with about 4,000 glass lamps ... in the garden' of her newly acquired
Buckingham House,[12] but the royal pair were not known for throwing
wild parties other than the obligatory Court functions. They liked
going about London in chairs. The King enjoyed Ranelagh. They
took no interest in horses, and deplored gambling.

When they came in to St James's Palace from the country, the
King and Queen used 'a very plain equipage escorted by a few light
horse ... coachmen and carmen never stop at his approach and they
take a pride in not bowing to him. ... His palace, which has no guard
except at the gate, is open to every Englishman.'[13] Indeed this was
taken too literally by some. In 1762 'a young gentleman scarce twenty,
dressed in a shabby suit of clothes, bag wig, white silk stockings,
silver-laced hat, brass-hilt sword and a large oaken stick [they were

fashionable, but surely that was asking for trouble?] attempted to get into the drawing room at St James's.' He was evicted.[14] Three years later a better-dressed party tried the same thing. 'Seven female Quakers, very neatly dressed, being desirous of seeing their Majesties come to court, were admitted into the royal apartments.'[15] In 1770

a woman meanly dressed found her way up the back stairs to the Queen's private apartments and entered the room where Her Majesty was sitting with the Duchess of Ancaster ... the woman took a survey of the room with great composure ... at length the Duchess had the presence of mind to ring the bell which brought up the page in waiting who with difficulty turned the intruder down stairs.[16]

The mob and the King

When the mob took to the streets, it was not the King they raged against, but his ministers and their policies. In 1749 'near 1,400 sailors went to St James's to solicit for their prize money. They all escorted his Majesty to the House of Peers and back again.'[17] During the Spitalfields troubles, thousands of silk weavers presented their petitions to the King, before they tried Westminster.[18] The King supported their cause and prohibited the import of foreign silks. 'Several thousand weavers went to St James's, with streamers [of silk] flying, music playing, and drums beating', not to impose their will, but 'to thank his Majesty'.[19] When the sailors asked for a rise and the merchants told them they were being paid quite enough and they could always rely on parish relief, it was to St James's that they marched, 'colours flying and drums beating [to] present a petition to his Majesty praying relief'.[20]

The King and Samuel Johnson

Samuel Johnson defined a pension, in his *Dictionary*, as 'an allowance made to any one without an equivalent. In England it is generally understood to mean pay given to a state hireling for treason to his country', and a pensioner as '(2) a slave of state hired by a stipend to obey his master'. Perhaps he was jealous, and worried by his finances. He certainly worked hard for his 'equivalent'. But as Boswell wrote, 'the accession of George III ... opened a new and brighter prospect to men of literary merit who had been honoured with no mark of royal favour in the preceding reign. ... Johnson having been represented to him as a very learned and good man, his Majesty was pleased to grant him a pension of three hundred pounds a year'.[21]

The pension came out of the Secret Service fund, which the King used for minor benevolences. No one was supposed to know of it, but of course everyone in the literary world of London soon did.[22] Johnson was so pleased that he was speechless – a unique occasion – and was eventually driven to use French, which he famously couldn't speak. He was *pénétré* with his Majesty's goodness, but had cold feet about the definitions in his *Dictionary* and asked his friend Joshua Reynolds if it would be proper to accept. Reassured, he was able to fire off an orotund thank-you letter. Unfortunately, the actual payments took a while to come through, but they transformed Johnson's life.

Now comes the oddest part of the story.[23] The royal librarian had allowed Johnson to use the King's library as often as he liked, which was brave of him because Johnson was notoriously destructive of other people's books. The King said he would like to meet him, so the next time Johnson came and settled down with a good book by the fire the librarian went and got the King, and they had a cosy chat about libraries in Oxford and Cambridge – the Bodleian won on size – and Johnson's current work, a subject any writer can talk about with ease. The King went on to various current academic disputes and recent publications, and even suggested that Johnson should write a 'literary biography' of England, which would have suited Johnson down to the ground, but nothing more came of it. 'During the whole of this interview Johnson talked to his Majesty with profound respect, but still in his firm manly manner, with a sonorous voice, and never in that subdued tone which is commonly used at the levee and in the drawing-room.' It is a vivid picture of both men, and probably mostly true.

Cost of Living, Currency and Prices

To compare the cost of living then and now is difficult. The consumer durables and convenience foods on which we rely were unknown in the eighteenth century, and have no counterparts. House ownership was rare. Crippling mortgages were not a part of the middling way of life; nor were exorbitant costs of commuting to work. Priorities and aspirations were different.

In theory (and carefully placed under the foundation stone of Blackfriars Bridge) there were gold coins of 5 guineas, 2 guineas, one guinea and ½ guinea, and silver coins of a crown, ½ crown, a shilling, sixpence, and two and three penny pieces. There were copper halfpence and farthings.[1] But in practice there was a constant shortage of currency. In 1762 the arrival of a batch of farthings from the Mint made news. 'Most of our crown and half crown pieces have ... been melted down or conveyed abroad. Many of our old shillings and most of our old sixpences are greatly defective in weight.'[2] 'People who have numbers of workmen to pay frequently give 10s in £100 to supply themselves with silver coin.'[3]

To some extent the gaps were filled by trade tokens issued by retailers,[4] and by foreign coins. This must have been extraordinarily confusing, when you had to sort out gold – eleven different kinds of ducats, Venetian sequins and Peruvian pieces of eight – and silver from all over Europe,[5] let alone check the assayed value of foreign gold coins and work out their current value against the official value of the guinea, which varied between 21s and 21s 6d. A Portuguese 'John' piece worth 36s, for instance, was easily mistaken for a two-guinea piece.[6] Other Johns were worth anything between 4s 6d and £3 12s, and there were moidores worth 27s and French pistoles worth 18s.[7] Guineas were often 'clipped' or filed for the market value of their gold.[8] Scales or balances were part of everyday life, to enable both parties to any cash transaction to check the weight of the coins concerned, against the current valuation of bullion.

The market must have been flooded with foreign coins after 1742 and 1762, when British ships captured the Spanish galleons bringing to Spain the year's accumulated treasure from its American possessions. Their value was distributed *in specie* among the crews. The Navy pay office made this as difficult as possible. Litigation dragged on for years. There was a 'monstrous disproportion in the appointment of prize-money in favour of officers' – and complaint was treated as mutiny.[9] The *Covadonga* galleon captured in 1742 was carrying 1,313,843 pieces of eight,[10] with other silver. Anson, as leader of the expedition, was entitled to three-eighths of her cargo, but even sailors and ships' boys eventually got their share. The cargo of the *Hermione*, much of it in coins, 'is said to be worth to the captors £1,600,000'.[11] The seamen got £485 each,[12] the captains of the two victorious ships £64,000 each.[13]

Bank notes for £10 and £15 were issued in 1759. There were notes for £100 and even £1,000. (That was the famous sandwich filling eaten by the prostitute Kitty Fisher. I doubt if there were many in circulation.)

A list of prices and pay may give some indication of how far money could go. I have collected them all from the contemporary documents I read, but I shall not give the individual references because that would be even more tiresome for the reader than the usual endnotes. I have tried to maintain some balance between the mass of poor people and the few middling and rich, but prices paid by the poor tended not to be written up as the Duke of Bedford's household accounts were. I have tried to eliminate obviously aberrant prices, and many could be challenged in detail, one way or another. They changed during the period, and probably from place to place in London, and season to season. Yet it seemed to me that as you scan through them you gather a flavour of eighteenth-century life that almost makes the rest of this book unnecessary.

½d	half a loaf, during the gin craze
1d	enough gin to get drunk on; a day's allowance of coal, candles and firewood for a tradesman's family
1½d	a pound of soap; hourly rate for a boy chopping firewood
2d	enough gin to get dead drunk on

3d   supper of bread, cheese and beer for a journeyman tailor; cost of blood-letting for a poor person; postage of one-page letter going 80 miles (paid by recipient)

3½d   a quart of milk, when 'extremely dear'

4d   a quart of beer; boat across the river

4d–6d a pound of cheese

5d   a pound of hair powder

6d   meat, drink and bread for a journeyman tailor's dinner; paid to a barber to shave a man and dress his wig, or to a sweep for one chimney; a boat from London Bridge to Westminster

6¼d   dinner for a government clerk – cold meat, bread and a pint of porter

8d   Samuel Johnson's dinner; cost of an evening at a coffee-house; turnpike toll for a coach and four horses (six horses, 10d)

8d–10d a pound of butter

9d   cost of an almanac

10d–1s 1 lb of fat bacon (half a pound would do a working man for dinner); a dozen best china or seville oranges

1s   dinner in steakhouse – beef, bread and beer, plus tip; entry to Vauxhall; entry to Ranelagh (but could be as much as £2 2s on masquerade nights); a dish of beef or thin-cut ham at Vauxhall; 1 lb of perfumed soap; a phial of Dr Ward's drops; the first mile in a Hackney chair (after that, 1s 6d); postage of one-page letter from London to New York; 1 lb of Parmesan cheese

1s 6d   1 lb of soles

1s 5¾d–1s 9½d cost of keeping a pauper for a week

1s 6d   cost of hackney coach for first hour (then 1s per hour); rate of window tax per window of house with 12+ windows, 1762

1s 6d–2s 6d cost of drycleaning a coat

2s   twelve yards of gold braid; a pair of washable kid gloves; a curling iron; weekly rent of a furnished room for a tradesman

2s 2d   daily pay award for journeyman tailors

2s 6d   a whole pig; a tooth extraction; dinner sent in from a tavern; a chicken at Vauxhall; half-pint of Dr Daffy's elixir for obstruction or a bottle of Dr Martin's Chymical Drops; a ticket to hear the rehearsal of the music for the royal fireworks at Vauxhall

2s 10d 1 lb of candles

3s 2d   a pair of men's yarn stockings

3s 3d   a barrel of Colchester oysters

4s 6d   a petticoat for a working woman

5s   a pound of Fry's drinking chocolate (plain); a workman's second-hand coat; a pot of patent confect for impotency

4s 9d–6s   1 lb of coffee

5s   cost of lead dental filling (gold cost, 7s 6d); a bottle of claret at Vauxhall; a box at Drury Lane Theatre, 1763

5s 2d   a pint of lavender water

5s 7d   a pair of women's worsted stockings

6s   a pair of stays for a working woman; 1 lb of opium; Dr Rock's Antivenereal Electuary

6s 6d   a gown for a working woman

7s   a dozen rabbits in the market; a pair of strong shoes

7s 6d–16s   1 lb of tea. It varied widely depending on quality

7s 6d   1 lb of Fry's drinking chocolate (vanilla)

8s   a bottle of champagne at Vauxhall

8s 6d   a cane-seated chair

8s 8d   a yard of flowered damask (15½ yards for one dress)

9s   a dozen chickens in the market; weekly wage of an unskilled labourer; a piece (14½ yards) of Indian sprigged muslin

10s   cost of Dr Johnson's *Dictionary*, 1756

10s 6d   cost of dental scaling; a bottle of Dr Prossily's Water for the pox; ticket to hear *Messiah* (Handel on the organ) at the Foundling Hospital; ticket in pit or box of Theatre Royal Covent Garden, 1763

10s 6d–£1 15s   cost of various wigs

13s 10d   a yard of mechlin lace

16s   a pair of men's lace ruffles

17s 4d   pair of men's silk stockings

18–22s   weekly wage of journeymen tradesmen in 1777

18s   wig for a clerk in a public office; a brass barometer

18s 6d   a yard of rich brocaded satin (12¾ yards for one dress)

£1–36s   advertised price of carpet per square yard

£1 1s   a fine beaver hat; journeyman silversmith's weekly pay; annual subscription to the Peerless Pool (or 2s per visit); a ticket to the grand jubilee at Ranelagh; a ticket to a grand gala at Mrs Cornelys'; a special auricula plant; twelve French lessons; a dozen bottles of 'Methuen' wine

£1 2s   stud fee

£1 9s   season ticket to Vauxhall, 1742

£1 10s   a pair of velvet breeches

£1 10s 6d   cost of Boswell's three rooms in Old Bond Street; cost of sack dress

£1 12s   a pair of stout silk-knit breeches

£1 12s 10½d   cost of outfitting a 5-year-old Foundling Hospital boy

£1 15s   monthly pay of East India Company seaman, 1762

£1 18s 6d   tips to six servants by a guest over five days

£2   an annual shaving and wig-dressing contract

£2 2s   a load of hay; a ticket for a ball at Mrs Cornelys'; a month's dancing lessons

£2 7s   a round mahogany folding table

£2 10s   annual pay of a ship's boy

£4 4s   cost of dental care under annual contract

£4 10s   a suit of clothes for a clerk in a public office

£5   a silver hilted sword

£5 5s   a silver watch; a transplant of a live tooth

£5 18s   a chimney glass and a pair of sconces

£6   cost of a night out including supper, a bath and a fashionable courtesan; a 'full dressed' suit

£6–£8   the annual wage of a housemaid

£7 7s   four places and a bedroom to watch George III's coronation procession, 1760

£8   a man's suit; the annual wage of a footman

£10   daily pay of the Duke of Cumberland as head of the army

£10–12   annual cost of maintaining and educating a clergy orphan

£10 10s   monthly rent of a pretty house in Chelsea; fee to dentist for transplanting natural tooth

£12–£26   the annual wage of a coachman

£13 7s 6d   a crimson velvet easy-chair and two matching stools

£14 14s   cost of musicians for a ball

£15   annual cost of liveries for three menservants

£22   lodgings in Westminster (Boswell) or a whole furnished house in Pall Mall (Casanova)

£25   annual cost of boarding at Westminster School (plus £15 for room and fire)

£32   cost of a negro boy, 1771

£40   annual cost of a two-wheeled chaise and horse in London; Boswell's lodgings in Downing Street

£42   price of a lottery ticket a few days before the drawing, 1758

£73 10s–£105   full set of false teeth with gold springs

£77 16s   a coach, 1748

£200   Boswell's annual allowance from his father, to live in London

£300   annual rent of a house in Grosvenor Square, 1751

£350   estimated annual cost of living for a prosperous tradesman's family

£485   seaman's share of prize money from capture of *Hermione*

£3,000   annual salary of the First Commissioner to the Admiralty

£3,780   cost of lace on Queen's state bed

£4,000   annual salary of the First Lord of the Treasury

£10,000   lottery prize, December 1768

£10,356   rent of Covent Garden market, 1759

£20,000   lottery prize, November 1769

£64,000   captain's share of prize money from capture of *Hermione*

Notes

'Notes are often necessary, but they are necessary evils': Samuel Johnson,
Plays of William Shakespeare, London, 1765.

Preface (pp. xv–xxi)

1 Liza Picard, *Restoration London*, London, 1997.
2 Allen Rettick, *The Making of Johnson's Dictionary*, Cambridge, 1990.
3 Unfortunately there is no practicable means of reducing this map to book size.

Chapter 1: Facts and Figures (pp. 3–8)

1 E. A. Wrigley, 'A simple model of London's importance in changing English
society and economy 1650–1750', *Past and Present*, July 1967, no. 37.
2 *Parliamentary History of England*, vol. XIV, 1747–53, London, 1813.
3 Malarchy Postlethwaite, *Universal Dictionary of Trade and Commerce*, London, 1766.
4 E. A. Wrigley and R. S. Schofield, *The Population History of England 1541–1871*,
Cambridge, 1981; W. A. Speck, *Stability and Strife in England 1714–60*, London,
1977; A. L. Beier and Roger Finlay (eds), *The Making of the Metropolis*, London,
1986; a private, and kind, letter from Professor Wrigley.
5 Beier and Finlay, op. cit.
6 John Entick, *A New and Accurate History and Survey of London, Westminster and
Southwark*, London, 1766.
7 George Rudé, *Hanoverian London*, London, 1971.
8 Reproduced, with notes by Ralph Hyde, as *The A to Z of Georgian London*, London,
1981.
9 In familiarising myself with the layout of Dr Johnson's London, I have used John
Rocque's map. I have also drawn on near-contemporary general descriptions of
London, such as Entick, op. cit. William Thornton's *New, Complete and Universal
History, Description and Survey of the Cities of London and Westminster*, London, 1784,
and Thomas Pennant's *Tour of London and Oxford*, London, 1806. For the exact
state of London in 1750 I have relied on Hugh Phillips's meticulously detailed
volumes, *Mid-Georgian London*, London, 1964, and *The Thames about 1750*, London,
1951. To place eighteenth-century buildings in their current context, Edward
Jones and Christopher Woodward's *A Guide to the Architecture of London*, London,

1983, is invaluable. I have cross-checked details in Ben Weinreb and Christopher Hibbert (eds), *The London Encyclopaedia*, London, 1983. More particular references to other sources are given in later chapters.

10 For more about the Fire of London and the subsequent rebuilding, see the author's *Restoration London*, London, 1997.

11 Phillips, *London*, op. cit., quoting Pennant, op. cit. Pennant was reminiscing about his childhood.

12 *Soho!* was a hunting cry that somehow lingered on when this part of London was built in the preceding century. It has no relation to Soho in New York, where the emphasis is on the second syllable and the derivation is from *So*uth of *Ho*uston Street.

13 Cavendish Square is shown by Rocque as blank, but according to Hugh Phillips, *London*, op. cit., houses in it were occupied from 1725. Princess Amelia, one of George III's sisters, lived there from 1761.

14 Rocque's spelling. The river Tyburn seems to have been culverted by then. The road we have been looking at was known as Oxford Street from about 1725, but some people went on using the old names, 'the Tyburn Road' or 'the Oxford Road', until at least 1750.

15 Phillips, *London*, op. cit.

16 Ibid.

17 *London Chronicle*, 1 October 1763.

Chapter 2: London and Westminster (pp. 9–18)

1 John Entick, *A New and Accurate History and Survey of London, Westminster and Southwark*, London, 1766.

2 Ibid.

3 *The Gentleman's Magazine*, October 1753.

4 W. I. Franklin, *Memoirs of Benjamin Franklin*, London, 1833.

5 Report of Commissioners summarised in Entick, op. cit.

6 Per Kalm, a young Swedish botanist who came to London in 1748, was intrigued. 'It is said that [the market gardeners] commonly manure [the fields] every autumn ... with the dung and dirt which is collected in London in the streets and is laid outside the town in large heaps from which they carry it to their meadows.' Kalm, *Account of his Visit to England on His Way to America in 1748*, translated by Joseph Lucas, London, 1892.

7 *The Gentleman's Magazine*, January 1757.

8 P. J. Grosley, *A Tour to London*, translated by Thomas Nugent, London, 1772. M. Grosley was in London in 1765.

9 Francis Grose, *A Classical Dictionary of the Vulgar Tongue*, London, 1785.

10 Entick, op. cit.

11 Ibid.

12 Samuel Johnson, *Letters*, Oxford University Press edition 1952.

13 Franklin, op. cit.

14 Entick, op. cit.

15 William Thornton, *A New, Complete and Universal History, Description and Survey of the Cities of London and Westminster*, London, 1784.

16 Ambrose Heal, *London Tradesmen's Cards of the Eighteenth Century*, London, 1925.

17 John Pugh, *Remarkable Occurrences in the Life of Jonas Hanway*, London, 1787.

18 *The Gentleman's Magazine*, May 1761. The Stock Exchange has always been apt to panic.

19 *The Gentleman's Magazine*, June 1767.

20 Grosley, op. cit.

21 F. A. Pottle (ed.), *Boswell's London Journal 1762–1763*, London, 1951.

22 Ibid.

23 Heal, op. cit.

24 Minutes of Evidence to the Royal Commission on Metropolitan Sanitation 1847, quoted in Stephen Inwood, *A History of London*, London, 1998.

25 Kalm, op. cit. The plane trees that the Victorians favoured are coming to the end of their lives, unlamented by me, although they have their supporters. Their squamous bark may have helped them to withstand air pollution, but their brown leathery leaves fall early and shoot late, and do not even make good compost. They are succumbing to old age, and to the salt that conscientious local authorities spread on their streets in the winter. Elm trees have been subject to disease for generations, but the outbreak in the 1960s destroyed most of them. The only London survivors I know are, or were, in a square in Hackney.

26 Hugh Phillips, *Mid-Georgian London*, London, 1964.

27 Edward Jones and Christopher Woodward, *A Guide to the Architecture of London*, London, 1983: an invaluable guide to the growth of building development in London.

28 Anon., *Critical Observations on the Buildings and Improvements of London*, London, 1771.

29 *The Gentleman's Magazine*, December 1762.

30 Thornton, op. cit.

31 Ibid.

32 *The Gentleman's Magazine*, May 1754.

33 James Boswell, *The Life of Samuel Johnson*, London, 1791.

34 Michael Reed, *The Georgian Triumph*, London, 1983.

35 The Grosvenor story is summarised in Phillips, *Mid-Georgian London*, op. cit. The 500 acres were eventually drained and built over by Thomas Cubitt in the next century, as Pimlico and Belgravia.

36 Entick, op. cit.

37 Phillips, *London*, op. cit.

38 Entick, op. cit.

Chapter 3: Water (pp. 19–25)

1 Except where otherwise noted, I have taken the information about London Bridge from Hugh Phillips's other book, *The Thames about 1750*, London, 1951.

2 *The Gentleman's Magazine*, August 1753.

3 Anon., *Low-Life*, London, 1764.

4 *The Gentleman's Magazine*, Supplement, 1753.

5 *The Gentleman's Magazine*, August 1753. Some can be seen doing just this, in the background to Hogarth's *Marriage à la Mode*, printed in 1745.

6 *The Gentleman's Magazine*, February 1757.

7 *The Gentleman's Magazine*, April 1758.

8 *The Gentleman's Magazine*, July 1767.

9 John Entick, *A New and Accurate History and Survey of London, Westminster and Southwark*, London, 1766.

10 Thomas Pennant, *A Tour of London and Oxford*, London, 1806.

11 William Thornton, *New, Complete and Universal History, Description and Survey of the Cities of London and Westminster*, London, 1784.

12 Pennant, op. cit.

13 *The Gentleman's Magazine*, November 1750.

14 A. S. Turberville (ed.), *Johnson's England*, Oxford, 1933, quoting from *The Gentleman's Magazine* of 1750, month unstated. An irresistible echo of the late Gerard Hoffnung's recommendation to 'try the echo in the reading room of the British Museum' when the British Library was housed there.

15 F. A. Pottle (ed.), *Boswell's London Journal 1762–1763*, London, 1951.

16 Thornton, op. cit.

17 *The Gentleman's Magazine*, July 1759.

18 *The Gentleman's Magazine*, June 1760.

19 The dates are given in the relevant *Gentleman's Magazine*.

20 Pennant, op. cit.

21 F. Brady and F. A. Pottle (eds), *Boswell in Search of a Wife 1766–1769*, London, 1956.

22 Much of the information in this section is taken from Hugh Phillips, *The Thames about 1750*, op. cit.

23 Gladys Scott Thomson, *The Russells in Bloomsbury Square 1669–1771*, London, 1940.

24 Joseph Reddington (ed.), *Home Office Papers 1766–69*, London, 1878.

25 *Low-Life*, op. cit.

26 Ibid.

27 P. J. Grosley, *A Tour to London*, translated by Thomas Nugent, London, 1772.

28 Tobias Smollett, *The Expedition of Humphry Clinker*, London, 1771.

29 In 1767 the then proprietors petitioned for leave to use a fifth arch. Peter Moritz's 1582 grant would expire in 2082. Two more arches were granted to his grandson and another to the petitioners in 1761. Being public-minded, they wanted another arch 'not only to supply the common exigencies of their tenants but also the extraordinary demands for water' if there should be a fire. This difficult matter was referred to four different surveyors, who gave four different answers. The Thames watermen's complaint was only a revised version of a centuries-old grievance. (*The Gentleman's Magazine*, July 1767). Unfortunately, this riveting story was not followed up in subsequent issues, but I can say that the water-wheels stayed until 1822, and the Thames Water Authority is still liable under the 1582 grant. Rosemary Weinstein, 'New urban demands in early modern London', *Medical History*, Supplement no. 11, 1991.

30 Phillips, op. cit.

31 Entick, op. cit.

32 Pennant, op. cit.: in describing the building of Westminster Bridge he gave the figure as 22 feet. Discrepancies in figures can happen in even the most carefully researched works.

33 *London Chronicle*, 4 January 1763.

34 Weinstein, op. cit. The new river began to flow in 1609.

35 Francis Place, *Autobiography*, BL Add MS 35142.

36 Scott Thomson, op. cit.

37 Grosley, op. cit.

38 Translator's note, Per Kalm, *Account of his Visit to England on his Way to America in 1748*, translated by Joseph Lucas, London, 1892.

39 *The Gentleman's Magazine*, April 1754.

40 *London Evening Post*, 7 April 1764.

41 *The Gentleman's Magazine*, June 1765.

42 *London Evening Post*, 1 January 1747.

Chapter 4: Traffic (pp. 26–34)

1 De Saussure, *A Foreign View of England in the Reign of George I and George II*, translated by Van Muyden, London, 1902. De Saussure was in London in 1725–36.

2 Betsy Rogers, *Cloak of Charity: Studies in Eighteenth Century Philanthropy*, London, 1949. The philanthropist in this case was Jonas Hanway, who habitually used an umbrella.

3 P. J. Grosley, *A Tour to London*, translated by Thomas Nugent, London, 1772. Grosley was in London in 1765.

4 Joseph Reddington (ed.), *Home Office Papers 1760–65*, London, 1878.

5 *The Gentleman's Magazine*, September 1761.

6 Anon., *An Estimate of the Manners and Principles of the Times*, London, 1757.

7 Lowell Blair (ed. and trans.), *Casanova's Memoirs*, London, 1958.

8 Gladys Scott Thomson, *The Russells in Bloomsbury Square 1669–1771*, London, 1940.

9 De Saussure, op. cit.

10 If this worried you, you could sit in your chair counting the carriers' steps. There are 5,280 feet in a mile. 'If the step or pace of a man in walking be five feet, 1,056 such paces will be an exact mile', according to a contemporary almanac, the 'step or pace' being of course what I would call two steps, one with each foot. Possibly easier to trust the chair-man and, if his charge was exorbitant, pay him, take his number and complain to the hackney Chair and Carriage Authority.

11 *London Chronicle*, 25 October 1760.

12 Patent no. 816 of 1764. Mr Tredwell was the Henry Ford of eighteenth-century transport, constantly inventing improvements to modes of road transport.

13 *The Gentleman's Magazine*, August 1763.

14 Dr Johnson defined 'hackney' as '(1) a pacing horse (2) a hired horse, hired horses

being usually taught to pace ... (3) a hireling; a prostitute (4) anything let out for hire (5) much used; common.' I can find no link between this and the London Borough of Hackney.

15 John Stow, *Survey of London*, London, 1598, corrected by John Strype, 1720, 1754 edition.

16 De Saussure, op. cit.

17 *The Daily Advertiser*, 20 May 1741.

18 James Boswell, *The Life of Samuel Johnson*, London, 1816.

19 Gavin Hannah (ed.), *The Deserted Village: the Diary of an Oxfordshire Rector, James Newton*, Stroud, 1992.

20 *The Gentleman's Magazine*, January 1747.

21 It is remarkable that when the present Queen goes in her coach to open Parliament, with all possible state, she uses only four horses. I do not know when the magnificent six-horse-power traction unit was given up.

22 De Saussure, op. cit.

23 Patent no. 732 of 1758.

24 *London Chronicle*, June 1763.

25 *London Evening Post*, 7 April 1764.

26 *The Gentleman's Magazine*, May 1747.

27 Reddington, op. cit., 12 August 1762.

28 Grosley, op. cit.

29 A print by L. P. Boitard published in 1767, *The Present Age*, satirising the customs of the day, includes a ludicrously high vehicle, the driver perched on a seat far above his two horses' heads, with two big back wheels and two smaller wheels, and no chassis whatever.

30 Francis Grose, *A Classical Dictionary of the Vulgar Tongue*, London, 1785.

31 Besant, *London in the Eighteenth Century*, London, 1902.

32 A. S. Turberville (ed.), *Johnson's England*, Oxford, 1933.

33 John Wesley, *Journal*, London, 1827.

34 Boswell, *Life*, op. cit.

35 Tobias Smollett, *The Expedition of Humphry Clinker*, London, 1771.

36 Hay and Rogers, *Eighteenth-Century English Society*, Oxford, 1997.

37 Boswell, op. cit.

38 Grose, op. cit.

39 John Entick, *A New and Accurate History and Survey of London, Westminster and Southwark*, London, 1766. Maybe 'accuracy' was here sacrificed to a good round number.

40 *The Gentleman's Magazine*, September 1763.

41 Grosley, op. cit.

42 *The Gentleman's Magazine*, December 1772.

43 *The Gentleman's Magazine*, November 1771.

44 Boswell, op. cit.

45 Stephen Inwood, *A History of London*, London, 1998. The market was closed in 1982, making way for development by a financial house. As Mr Inwood says, 'the smell of fish was gradually replaced by the smell of money', but it was astonishing to drive past the site while the ground was being prepared for building, and inhale the smell of fish – probably medieval cod, for a start.

46 Phillips, *The Thames About 1750*, London, 1951.
47 *The Gentleman's Magazine*, January 1763.
48 *The Gentleman's Magazine*, July 1753 and July 1754.
49 Grose, op. cit.
50 *The Gentleman's Magazine*, July 1747.
51 A detailed list of land and river fares was given in, for example, H. Overton's *Map of London*, London, 1756.
52 Per Kalm, *Account of his Visit to England on his Way to America in 1748*, translated by Joseph Lucas, London, 1892.
53 *The Gentleman's Magazine*, July 1762.
54 *The Gentleman's Magazine*, October 1766.
55 *The Gentleman's Magazine*, May 1749.
56 *The Gentleman's Magazine*, August 1749.

Chapter 5: Green Spaces (pp. 35–41)

1 Literally, in the case of asparagus. Broken bottles were planted round them so that each spear had its own mini-cloche.
2 Per Kalm, *Account of his Visit to England on his Way to America in 1748*, translated by Joseph Lucas, London, 1892.
3 *The Gentleman's Magazine* of February 1752 reported the death of one optimist who had deserted no less than ten times, each time re-enlisting in another regiment, and no doubt pocketing whatever payment was made to recruits. There must have been easier ways of making money.
4 Paget Toynbee (ed.), *Letters of Horace Walpole*, Oxford, 1903.
5 *Owen's Weekly Chronicle*, 19 February 1763.
6 De Saussure, *A Foreign View of England in the Reign of George I and George II*, translated by Van Muyden, London, 1902.
7 *The Gentleman's Magazine*, June 1763.
8 John Wesley, *Journal*, London, 1827.
9 P. J. Grosley, *A Tour to London*, translated by Thomas Nugent, London, 1772. Grosley was in London in 1765.
10 Joseph Reddington (ed.), *Home Office Papers 1760–65*, London, 1878.
11 Ibid.
12 Grosley, op. cit.
13 Anon., *Low-Life*, London, 1764.
14 *The Gentleman's Magazine*, November 1751.
15 E. Holmes, *Life of Mozart*, quoted by M. Dorothy George, 'London and the life of the town', in A. S. Turberville (ed.), *Johnson's England*, Oxford, 1933.
16 *Gazetteer*, 12 January 1760.
17 *Gazetteer*, 21 June 1766.
18 Lowell Blair (ed. and trans.), *Casanova's Memoirs*, London, 1958.
19 Grosley, op. cit.
20 Cattle plague used to be known as rinderpest. *The Gentleman's Magazine* charted its progress, as 'the distemper of horned cattle'. It was highly contagious.

Eventually all movement of cattle was prohibited, infected animals were burned and their hides were buried. Even then unscrupulous hide dealers dug them up. Cattle plague was eradicated from Europe by 1930, so it cannot be linked with BSE; but the anxiety it caused certainly parallels BSE. This information was kindly supplied by the Royal College of Veterinary Surgeons.

21 It was this very elephant that the Company of Cutlers, whose crest was an elephant, borrowed for the Lord Mayor's Show in 1763, according to the *London Chronicle*, 29 October 1763. Poor elephant, it must have resigned itself to London ways by then.

22 Grosley, op. cit.

23 Public Record Office: SP 375/4. Pattens were normal wear in wet weather: a kind of overshoe on a high metal ring that lifted the wearer out of the mud, but would certainly have chewed up grass and gravel alarmingly.

24 *Low-Life*, op. cit.

25 Reddington, op. cit.

26 Hugh Phillips, *Mid-Georgian London*, London, 1965.

27 This marked the end of the War of Austrian Succession by the Treaty of Aix la Chapelle, by which, in general, everyone went back to where they had started: see note 1, Chapter 25.

28 *The Gentleman's Magazine*, November 1748.

29 *The Gentleman's Magazine*, April and May 1749.

30 *Low-Life*, op. cit.

31 John Entick, *A New and Accurate History and Survey of London, Westminster and Southwark*, London, 1766.

32 Ibid. There is a brief history and description of this garden in the previous century in the author's *Restoration London*, London, 1997. It is possible to imagine that the site had been a garden for perhaps 600 years, by 1760.

33 William Thornton, *A New, Complete and Universal History, Description and Survey of the Cities of London and Westminster*, London, 1784. Thornton often lifted bits from Entick, op. cit. The essential 'gentility' of eighteenth-century visitors contrasts markedly with the jolly crowds of office workers who enjoy lying on the Inn grass in the summer, baring as much skin as possible.

34 Grosley, op. cit.

35 Thornton, op. cit. Samuel Johnson defined 'mall' as 'a walk where they formerly played with malls and balls'. This seems a long shot from current American usage.

36 De Saussure, op. cit.

37 It was fixed to wooden frames by hooks, to keep it taut: hence, 'on tenterhooks'.

38 *Low-Life*, op. cit.

Chapter 6: The Buildings (pp. 42–51)

1 A falling house, bricks flying into the street, is one of the emblems of ruin in Hogarth's *Gin Lane*, 1751.

2 Samuel Johnson, *London*, London, 1738.

3 *The Gentleman's Magazine*, July 1758.

4 M. Dorothy George, *London Life in the Eighteenth Century*, London, 1925.

5 Henry Fielding, *An Inquiry into the Causes of the Late Increase of Robbers*, London, 1751.

6 Ibid.

7 Jonas Hanway, *Citizen's Monitor*, London, 1780, quoted in George, op. cit.

8 W. Maitland, *The History and Survey of London*, London, 1756.

9 Dr Willan, *Diseases in London*, London, 1801. Doctors were the first to publicise the appalling living conditions of the poor, which they saw for themselves when they visited patients' homes, as part of the Dispensary movement at the end of the century, or at second hand when they saw patients in hospitals.

10 Anon., *Low-Life*, London, 1764.

11 Quoted in George, op. cit.

12 F. Grose, *A Classical Dictionary of the Vulgar Tongue*, London, 1785.

13 I live in a very small house in a terrace about a hundred years old, said to have been built for the workers at Oxford University Press nearby. I was amused to hear a guide instructing a group of foreign tourists outside my house that the lack of space in the houses explained why men spent so much time in the pubs. Yet he may have been right. My house was probably occupied by a family of six or more, when new.

14 *The Gentleman's Magazine*, August 1767. It is fair to say that in another report in *The Newgate Calendar* there is only one, temporary pig.

15 This applied particularly to Berkeley Square, the north and east sides of which included some very small houses: Hugh Phillips, *Mid-Georgian London*, London, 1964. A tradesman occupier may well have let out rooms, legally or illegally, to those below him in the pecking order, in these fashionable districts.

16 Isaac Ware, *Complete Body of Architecture*, London, 1756, a fascinating view of the reality of the life of the middling sort.

17 Per Kalm was most impressed by this. Perhaps he had not noticed how coal was delivered in Sweden, or perhaps the Swedes used wood, which cannot easily be tipped down a narrow hole. Kalm, *Account of his Visit to England on his Way to America in 1748*, translated by Joseph Lucas, London, 1892.

18 My house has one, but it is a humble little iron bar in a small niche beside the door. My builder thought it was perhaps a very small dog kennel.

19 *Public Advertiser*, 18 January 1771.

20 Lawrence Wright, *Clean and Decent*, London, 1960.

21 C. C. Knowles and P. H. Pitt (eds), *The History of Building Regulations in London*, London, 1972.

22 John Entick, *A New and Accurate History and Survey of London, Westminster and Southwark*, London, 1766.

23 John Stow, *Survey of London*, London 1598, corrected by John Strype 1720, 1754 edition.

24 Ibid.

25 Ben Weinreb and Christopher Hibbert, *The London Encyclopaedia*, London, 1983.

26 Quoted by Sacheverell Sitwell in *British Architects and Craftsmen*, London, 1945.

27 *The Gentleman's Magazine*, March 1763.

28 *Public Advertiser*, 19 January 1771.

29 Phillips, op. cit.

30 M. H. Port, *West End Palaces: The Aristocratic Town House in London 1730–1830*, London, 1955.

31 Joseph Friedman, *Spencer House: Chronicle of a Great London Mansion*, London, 1993. The house is now occupied by the J. Rothschild group of companies, which has funded the unimaginable achievement of restoring the state rooms and the fabric of the building to their former glory while installing necessary modern facilities. It is regularly open to the public, on Sundays at the moment of writing.

32 C. S. Sykes, *Private Palaces*, London, 1985.

33 Phillips, op. cit.

34 H. M. Colvin (ed.), *The History of the King's Works*, vol. V, London, 1976.

35 Jones and Woodward, *A Guide to the Architecture of London*, London, 1983.

36 Colvin, op. cit.

37 Ibid.

38 Ibid.

39 I worked there for many years. Its thick stone walls meant that it was deliciously cool in the summer, but took a while to heat up in the winter once the central heating was switched on. There were fireplaces in every room, but messengers no longer brought coal for them.

Chapter 7: Massie's Analysis (pp. 55–56)

1 I have taken Massie's figures from Douglas Hay and Nicholas Rogers, *Eighteenth-Century English Society*, Oxford, 1997.

2 Exceptions are M. Dorothy George, *London Life in the Eighteenth Century*, London, 1925, and Dorothy Marshall, *The English Poor in the Eighteenth Century*, London, 1926. Sir John Summerson's *Georgian London*, London, revised edition 1988, is a brilliant account of his subject from the viewpoint of an architectural historian, to which considerations of the life of the poor would be irrelevant.

Chapter 8: The Welfare System (pp. 57–63)

1 *The Gentleman's Magazine*, November 1763.

2 James Pellar Malcolm, *Anecdotes of London*, London, 1810.

3 James Boswell, *The Life of Samuel Johnson*, London, 1791.

4 Dorothy Marshall, *The English Poor in the Eighteenth Century*, London, 1926.

5 *The Gentleman's Magazine*, September 1765.

6 Let us suppose that Mary married Tom Brown, whom she met while he was staying with friends in her father's parish of St Giles, in London. He came from Newcastle and his settlement was there. She acquired that settlement by marriage, even though she had never been to Newcastle. They had two children. When Tom Brown died, the children were eight and six. After Tom's death, her father

died and left her some money, and Mary was able to buy a house in St Giles
and became a ratepayer there in her own right, thus acquiring a settlement in
St Giles. The older child took its mother's settlement there. But the younger one
was not yet seven, so it still had its father's settlement in Newcastle, where it had
never been nor wanted to go. Mary Brown marries again. Her new husband,
Bill White, is from Portsmouth, and his settlement is there, and from then on so
is hers, although she has never been there. They sell Mary's house, spend the
proceeds and move to lodgings near her mother. Bill is not a ratepayer in St
Giles, so I would expect his Portsmouth settlement to apply again. Bill and Mary
have two more children, before he falls ill and dies. With four young children
and no money she claims benefit in St Giles, where she and the children are
living. One of her children risks being moved unwillingly to Newcastle, and if
she is treated as settled in Portsmouth, she will go into a workhouse there, away
from her mother and totally unable ever to get to Newcastle. The fact that this
reads like an exam question doesn't mean that it, or something like it, didn't
happen all the time, every parish Poor Law overseer trying to pass the buck to
another, whatever the law might say. It helps to explain why there was a huge
mass of litigation between parishes, about settlements. Maybe Mary would do
well to stay away from the Social Security office (i.e. the parish overseers) and
try to make a go of it by herself, keeping all four children safely with her.

7 'Poorhouse' and 'workhouse' seem to have been used interchangeably, although
their functions were different, a poorhouse providing shelter while a workhouse
provided – in theory – work.

8 *Public Advertiser*, 17 January 1771.

9 William Bailey, *The Utility of Workhouses*, London, 1758, quoted in Marshall, op.
cit.

10 Hugh Cunningham, 'Employment and unemployment of children in England
1680–1851', *Past and Present*, no. 126, February 1990.

11 Henry Fielding, *An Inquiry into the Cause of the Late Increase of Robbers*, London, 1751.
John Wesley passionately denied this.

12 Boswell, op. cit.

13 Peter Linebaugh, *The London Hanged*, London, 1991.

14 John Wesley, *Journal*, London, 1827. Wesley was writing about London in 1739–
73.

15 F. M. Eden, *The State of the Poor: A History of the Labouring Classes in England*,
London, 1797.

16 John Scott, *Observations on the Present State of the Parochial and Vagrant Poor*, London,
1773, quoted in Marshall, op. cit.

17 'The case of the journeymen tailors', 1745, quoted in Linebaugh, op. cit.

18 Scott, op. cit.

19 Ibid.

20 Marshall, op. cit.

21 In my ten years as a part-time Chairman of Social Security Appeals Tribunals I
was never asked to redeem stays. We had no power to commit fraudulent
claimants to prison, but I well remember an old lady who thought I had, and
implored me not to send her down. 'Ain't none of my family never gone to none
of them places', she said, and she didn't want to break the family tradition.

22 Saunders Welch, a London magistrate, in 1753, quoted in M. Dorothy George, *London Life in the Eighteenth Century*, London, 1925.

23 Henry Fielding, another London magistrate, in 1751, also quoted in George, op. cit. It is remarkable to see a magistrate pitying the Irish, usually treated as irredeemable.

24 George, op. cit., quoting a tract of 1721, but the practice persisted throughout the century.

Chapter 9: Living Conditions (pp. 64–76)

1 M. Dorothy George, *London Life in the Eighteenth Century*, London, 1925, on which I have drawn largely, for this section.

2 James Boswell, *The Life of Samuel Johnson*, 1791.

3 Richard Ingrams (ed.), *Dr Johnson (by Mrs Thrale)*, London, 1984.

4 Francis Grose, *A Classical Dictionary of the Vulgar Tongue*, London, 1785.

5 Alum is a compound of alumina, potash and sulphuric acid. It is a strong astringent. This affects the flour during fermentation, making it possible to use wheat that had 'sprouted' in a wet season. Without alum the bread from such flour would have been more like rye bread nowadays – that is, dark and solid. The use of alum declined with the import of foreign wheat in bad seasons, and improved milling methods, but additives to bread were used for centuries. Agene was disallowed in 1950; it was alleged to make dogs go mad. Diox was disallowed in the 1960s, and benzoil peroxide and potassium bromate were disallowed in the 1980s. I owe all this information to Mr I. V. Barrett, who kindly and fully answered my letter to the Guild of Master Bakers. He quoted from Owen Simmons, *The Book of Bread*, published in about 1900. In 1757 *The London Chronicle* (vol. II, July–December 1757) reviewed a recent publication, *Poison Detected, a Treatise on Bread*, by a physician, who listed the 'noxious ingredients in the present composition of bread in London ... to increase its weight and deceive the buyer by its fraudulent fineness, Lime, Chalk, Alum etc. ... It is averred by very credible authority that sacks of old ground bones are not infrequently used by some of the bakers.'

6 James Pellar Malcolm, *Anecdotes of London*, London, 1810.

7 *The Gentleman's Magazine*, May 1765.

8 Tobias Smollett, *The Expedition of Humphry Clinker*, London, 1771.

9 *The Gentleman's Magazine*, July 1759.

10 Thea Molleson and Margaret Cox, *The Spitalfields Project*, York, 1993.

11 *The Gentleman's Magazine*, January 1758. It did not suggest where, how or in what the poor could cook this delicious dish.

12 Dorothy Davis, *A History of Shopping*, London, 1966.

13 Anon., *Low-Life*, London, 1764.

14 Ibid.

15 Ibid.

16 Ibid. French people still pick roadside herbs in country places.

17 *The Ladies' Magazine*, 10 March 1750.

18 Jacob Vanderlint, *Money Answers All Things*, London, 1734. He was campaigning for an increase in wages for the poor.

19 W. I. Franklin (ed.), *Memoirs of Benjamin Franklin*, London, 1833.

20 'The case of the journeymen tailors', 1745, quoted in Peter Linebaugh, *The London Hanged*, London, 1991.

21 M. G. Jones, *The Charity School Movement*, Cambridge, 1938.

22 John Entick, *A New and Accurate History and Survey of London, Westminster and Southwark*, London, 1766. I have picked almost at random a few of the schools he mentions.

23 De Saussure, *A Foreign View of England in the Reign of George I and George II*, translated by Van Muyden, London, 1902. De Saussure was in London in 1725–36.

24 For much of the information about Fleet marriages I have drawn on Mark Herber, *Clandestine Marriages in the Chapel and Rules of the Fleet Prison 1680–1754*, London, 1998.

25 Francis Place, *Autobiography*, British Library Add MS 35142.

26 *The Post Boy*, 1741, quoted by George, op. cit.

27 J. R. Hutchinson, *The Press-Gang Afloat and Ashore*, London, 1915.

28 Thomas Pennant, *Account of London*, London, 1790, quoted in George, op. cit.

29 Hugh Phillips, *Mid-Georgian London*, London, 1964. Mr Phillips places Keith's house, where his curates practised, on the corner of East Chapel Street and Curzon Street, separated from his May Fair Chapel by East Chapel Street. Mr Herber places the May Fair Chapel 'near to the parish church of St George, Hanover Square'. I have in this instance preferred Curzon Street. Either location would be preferable, one would think, to the Fleet or its Liberties.

30 *The Gentleman's Magazine*, March 1754.

31 Herber, op. cit.

32 Ibid.

33 Grose, op. cit.

34 *The Gentleman's Magazine*, November 1767.

35 *The Gentleman's Magazine*, September 1763.

36 *The Gentleman's Magazine*, December 1772.

37 Grose, op. cit.

38 Harry Margary, *Cries of London first published c. 1754*, Lympne, 1978.

39 F. M. Eden, *The State of the Poor: A History of the Labouring Classes in England*, London, 1797.

40 His shop card is included in Ambrose Heal, *London Tradesmen's Cards of the Eighteenth Century*, London, 1925.

41 Grose, op. cit. Anyone who wore woollen stockings before the advent of nylons will recognise this. As schoolgirls we used to blacken our heels with ink, to disguise the huge holes that seemed to happen overnight.

42 Ibid.

43 George, op. cit.

44 T. Firmin, *Proposals for the Employment of the Poor*, London, 1682, quoted by George op. cit. In Grose, op. cit., a tallyman is a 'broker that lets out clothes to women of the town' – that is, prostitutes. I suppose he could combine both trades.

45 Grose, op. cit. The ubiquity of the pawnshop lasted until the easy credit given by 'plastic' nowadays. I once pawned a watch my father had given me. The

pawnbroker, a genial man, said, 'We haven't seen this watch for many years.' My father had also been a student in London. I did redeem it in due course.

46 Place, op. cit.

47 Grose, op. cit.

48 See Tobias Smollett, *Roderick Random*, London, 1748, in which an agile lady is arrested for debt ' "... will you be pleased to be carried to my house or to jail?" "If I must be confined, said she, I would rather be in your house than in a common jail". "Well well, answered he, if you have money enough in your pocket, you shall be entertained like a princess." But when she acquainted him with her poverty, he swore he never gave credit and ordered one of his myrmidons to call a coach to carry her to the Marshalsea at once.' She got away, and had a free drink as well.

49 *The Gentleman's Magazine*, June 1759.

50 Place, op. cit. Place's father kept a sponging-house at one stage.

51 *The Gentleman's Magazine*, January 1759. Can this majestic language have come from the pen of Dr Johnson, who was writing for *The Gentleman's Magazine* at the time?

52 *The Gentleman's Magazine*, June 1761.

53 *The Gentleman's Magazine*, October 1761.

54 *The Gentleman's Magazine*, October 1761.

55 Julian Litton, 'The English Funeral' in Margaret Cox (ed.), *Grave Concerns: Death and Burial in England 1700–1850*, York, 1998.

56 George, op. cit.

57 There is a tiny scrap of paper preserved in the Public Record Office, dated 1750: PRO IR 10.15. It reads: 'William Mathew's Bill on John Mathews, for victuals drink washing lodging and money lent – £1 8s 3d. Expenses carrying him to London 8s. Expenses for his funeral £1 1s.'

58 *Low-Life*, op. cit.

Chapter 10: Philanthropy (pp. 77–87)

1 Anon., *An Account of the General Dispensary for the Relief of the Poor*, London, 1770, 1776 edition.

2 Anon., *An Estimate of the Manners and Principles of the Times*, London, 1757.

3 Henry Fielding, *The History of Tom Jones, a Foundling*, London, 1749.

4 *London Chronicle*, 25 February 1764.

5 I was able to read the Foundation's records in the London Metropolitan Archives. Passages in quotation marks are from those records. I have also drawn on Ruth McClure, *Coram's Children*, Yale, 1981.

6 The site of the Foundling Hospital was sold in the 1920s, but some of it is still an open space called Coram's Fields, where no adult is admitted unless accompanied by a child. The open arcades where the children played and worked are the only parts of the original Hospital left. The Hospital's work is still carried on by the Thomas Coram Foundation.

7 Some of these tokens are in the Hospital's archives: scraps of pink and white checked cloth; an ivory fish; even a bottle top marked 'ale'.

8 The children learnt to read their catechism, and also the Instructions to Apprentices that they would be given when they left. I set them out in full because they seem to exemplify the kindly practical benevolence that pervaded the Hospital:

You are placed out Apprentice by the Governors of this Hospital. You were taken into it very young, quite helpless, forsaken & deserted by Parents and Friends. Out of charity have you been fed, clothed, and instructed; which many have wanted [lacked].

You have been taught to fear God, to love Him, to be honest, careful, laborious [hardworking] and diligent. As you hope for Success in this World and Happiness in the next, you are to be mindful of what has been taught you. You are to behave honestly, justly, soberly, and carefully in everything, to everybody, and especially towards your Master/Mistress and family; and to execute all lawful commands with Industry, Cheerfulness and good Manners.

You may find temptations to do wickedly, when you are in the world; but by all means fly from them. Tho' you may have done a wrong thing, you will, by sincere confession, more easily obtain forgiveness than if by an obstinate Lye you make the fault the greater, and thereby deserve a far greater punishment. Lying is looked upon to be the beginning of everything that is bad, and a person used to it is never believed, esteemed or trusted.

Be not ashamed that you were bred in this Hospital. Own it; and say that it was thro' the good Providence of God that you were taken care of. Bless Him for it; and be thankful to those worthy Benefactors who have contributed to your maintenance and support. And if it ever be in your Power, make a grateful Acknowledgement to the Hospital for the Benefits you have received.

Be constant in your prayers, and going to Church; and avoid Gaming, Swearing and all evil discourses: by this means the Blessing of God will follow your honest Labours, and you will also gain the goodwill of all good persons.

If you follow the Instructions which have all along been taught you, and which we now give you, you may be happy; otherwise you will bring on yourself Misery Shame and Want.

Note, Your Master will provide you Meat, Drink, Washing, Lodging and Clothing: and [for boys only] he has agreed to pay you Five Pounds a Year for the Three last years of your Apprenticeship.

9 *The Gentleman's Magazine*, February 1747.

10 Captain Coram was as he requested buried under the altar of the Chapel. When the site was sold his bones were moved to St Andrew's, Holborn, near Hatton Garden.

11 *The Gentleman's Magazine*, June 1747.

12 A trade sprang up, of transporting babies from far and near. A tinker accepted a guinea from a man in Bristol, to take a baby to the Hospital. He pocketed the guinea and drowned the baby. A man had to lower his rate of eight guineas per trip from Yorkshire with eight babies in his panniers, because of competition. Of

eight babies consigned to London in one wagon, all died except one whose mother followed on foot and managed to feed it.

13 *The Gentleman's Magazine* of those dates.

14 All passages in quotation marks are taken from the Society's archives, which are in the National Maritime Museum. I have also drawn on James Stephen Taylor, *Jonas Hanway, Founder of the Marine Society*, London, 1985.

15 The stature of the applicants to the Marine Society provides an index of the health of the poor. The tallest fifteen-year-old was under 4'9". Thirteen-year-olds were on average 4'3½" tall, *10 inches less* than children of that age in the 1960s. John Landers, *Death and the Metropolis*, Cambridge, 1993.

16 William Shaw, *Bibliography of the Collection of Books and Tracts in Commerce, Currency and Poor Law 1557–1763 by Joseph Massie*, London, 1937.

17 James Pellar Malcolm, *Anecdotes of London*, London, 1810.

18 Betsy Rodgers, *Cloak of Charity*, London, 1949.

19 The clothes were two gowns, three day caps, two night caps, three neckbands, three pairs of stockings, three shifts, two under petticoats, one upper petticoat, two pairs of shoes, one 'pair of bodice', which I think meant stays, one pair of knitted garters and three checked aprons. Some of these would do for two years, such as the aprons, but not the shoes, out of which children grow practically overnight. But all in all, the provision was not miserly.

20 John Entick, *A New and Accurate History and Survey of London, Westminster and Southwark*, London, 1766.

21 Malcolm, op. cit.

22 William Thornton, *A New, Complete and Universal History, Description and Survey of the Cities of London and Westminster*, London, 1784.

23 Thea Molleson and Margaret Cox (eds), *The Spitalfields Project*, York, 1993.

24 Entick, op. cit.

25 M. Dorothy George, *English Life in the Eighteenth Century*, London, 1925.

26 J. R. Hutchinson, *The Press-Gang Afloat and Ashore*, London, 1915.

27 *The Gentleman's Magazine*, November 1751.

28 *The Gentleman's Magazine*, January 1767.

29 *The Gentleman's Magazine*, March 1746 and December 1749.

30 *The Gentleman's Magazine*, January 1768.

31 *The Gentleman's Magazine*, March 1767.

32 Francis Grose, *A Classical Dictionary of the Vulgar Tongue*, London, 1785.

33 Samuel Johnson, *The Idler* no. 22, 16 September 1758.

34 *The Gentleman's Magazine*, December 1763.

35 Malcolm, op. cit.

Chapter 11: The Sick Poor (pp. 88–100)

1 John Entick, *A New and Accurate History and Survey of London, Westminster and Southwark*, London, 1766.

2 *The Gentleman's Magazine*, April 1758.

3 John Howard, Appendix to *The State of the Prisons in England and Wales*, Warrington,

1780. Howard is remembered more for his description of prisons, but he also personally surveyed all London's hospitals. By the time his findings were published, ten years had passed since the end of our period, so I have not relied on his account of their current state unless it seems likely that his account could apply almost ten years earlier, but I have used his comments on the original structures.

4 Guy Williams, *The Age of Agony*, London, 1975.

5 Howard, op cit. The fees may have increased by 1789, but they were not new.

6 Entick, op. cit.

7 Ibid.

8 Ben Weinreb and Christopher Hibbert (eds), *The London Encyclopaedia*, London 1983, from which I have gratefully taken other facts on London's hospitals.

9 *London Chronicle*, 2 April 1763, from which the figures for St Bart's are also taken.

10 Pennant, *A Tour of London and Oxford*, London, 1806.

11 P. J. Grosley, *A Tour to London*, translated by Thomas Nugent, London, 1772. M. Grosley was in London in 1765.

12 Weinreb and Hibbert, op. cit.

13 Howard, op. cit.

14 This, at least, was the theory. But the practice of charging fees, however they were described, to these destitute and desperate patients continued, which is why Dr Marsden founded the Royal Free Hospital in 1828.

15 *The Gentleman's Magazine*, April 1748.

16 *The Gentleman's Magazine*, November 1754, reflecting on the death of Dr Mead.

17 David Owen, *English Philanthropy*, London, 1965.

18 Entick, op. cit.

19 *The Gentleman's Magazine*, November 1754.

20 William Thornton, *A New, Complete and Universal History, Description and Survey of the Cities of London and Westminster*, London, 1784.

21 *The Gentleman's Magazine*, April 1748.

22 Before the National Health Service took over hospitals, they usually had a banner across their front, saying 'All Contributions Gratefully Received', voluntary presents being their only source of income, apart from those which still retained ancient endowments. This may be difficult to imagine, for those who have grown up with state-funded hospitals.

23 Owen, op. cit.

24 *The Gentleman's Magazine*, June 1752.

25 *The Gentleman's Magazine*, November 1753.

26 *The Gentleman's Magazine*, January 1757.

27 'Lock' from the French word for the rags, *loques*, used to dress the sores of lepers, and venereal lesions; not anything to do with locking the patients in.

28 *The Gentleman's Magazine*, October 1767.

29 For those with morbid and curious minds, I will quote the description in Williams, op. cit., of a typical case. It begins with red spots on the forehead, spreading to the scalp and the whole of the body. On its way, it can cause blindness, or death by suffocation if the mouth membranes swell and obstruct breathing. In two or three days, the vesicles fill with pus. The sufferer is by now unrecognisable and delirious. In eleven or twelve days, if death has not cut this

awful story short, the pustules dry up and the scabs eventually drop away. Lord Macaulay described it as: 'turning the babe into a changeling at which the mother shuddered and making the eyes and cheeks of the betrothed maiden objects of horror to the lover'.

30 The following hospitals opened:

    1749: The Lying-in Hospital for married women

    1750: The City Lying-in Hospital

    1752: Queen Charlotte's Hospital for married *and unmarried* women

    1757: The Royal Maternity Hospital

    1765: The Westminster Lying-in Hospital

31 Roy Porter, *The Greatest Benefit to Mankind*, London, 1997.

32 M. Dorothy George, *London Life in the Eighteenth Century*, London, 1925.

33 Thomas Hunt (ed.), *The Medical Society of London 1773–1973*, London, 1972.

34 Anon., *A General Account of the Dispensary for the Relief of the Infant Poor*, London, 1772. There had been suggestions that a hospital for sick children should be opened, but 'if you take away a sick child from its Parent or Nurse you break its heart immediately' and the idea was dropped.

35 James Pellar Malcolm, *Anecdotes of London*, London, 1810.

36 *Daily Advertiser*, 8 December 1743.

37 Entick, op. cit.

38 Williams, op. cit.

39 Anon., *Low-Life*, London, 1764.

40 John Pringle, FRCP RS, *Observations on the Nature and Cure of Hospital and Jayl Fevers*, London, 1750.

41 Edward Barry, MD, *A Treatise on a Consumption of the Lungs*, London, 1728.

Chapter 12: Work (pp. 101–112)

1 Anon., *Low-Life*, London, 1754.

2 Jonas Hanway, *A Sentimental History of Chimney Sweepers in London and Westminster*, London, 1785.

3 In Scotland and on the continent chimneys were swept by dropping something like a weighted holly bush or a special brush *down* the chimney from above. This system does not seem to have been used in London. But the more you think of it the more improbable it becomes, that children were sent *up* the chimney to clean it. A properly built chimney would be smooth on the inside, having been 'parged' with fire-resistant clay. It would have bends in it, dictated by the architect's insistence that fireplaces in main rooms should be centrally placed in the wall. You can't stack one fireplace on top of another and make each open on to the same chimney, because this would let cold air into the flue. The fire on the lowest floor would not draw well, and the smoke might escape into higher rooms, through their fireplaces. Each fire has to have its own flue. So you have to bend each flue round the fireplace immediately above, and back, so that it joins the others in a tidy group at roof level. This could take a lot of space, so the flues were made as narrow as consistent with getting a good up-draught.

This might be as narrow as nine inches, or even less. What you see of a fireplace – the six feet of breadth in an inglenook, convenient for roasting a whole cow, or the modest basket grate of a Victorian bedroom fireplace – dictates the width of the flue only for a short distance, perhaps as far as ceiling height. After that the flue narrows. When it emerges onto the roof in a chimney it is much narrower than when it began at the chimneypiece below.

Kitchen fires were still made for roasting. Spits could be as much as six feet long, in grand kitchens. Possibly the flues of these fires, which would be the ones most in use, were wider, and may have been straighter since the fire did not have to be fashionably in the middle of the wall, like the ones on display upstairs. But efficient chimney design would still have required the kitchen flue to narrow as it went up. Possibly a child could get some way up one of these chimneys, despite its smooth inner surface. But the only part of any chimney that it would be practicable for a child to sweep would be the first stage of it, before it narrows. This would be consistent with the horror stories of putting a child up the chimney while the fire is still burning.

What happened to the rest of the chimney? Firing a gun up it, a method of chimney-sweeping in old houses when wood was burned on wide hearths with straight chimneys, would not work in eighteenth-century houses where the chimneys were unlikely to be straight. Anyway, imagine firing an eighteenth-century firearm up such a confined space. It would bring the parging down, and maybe the bricks, as well as the soot. The answer has to be, I don't know. Perhaps the soot was just left to accumulate until it fell down and made an appalling mess. Perhaps the rods carried by their masters, the chimney-sweeps themselves, sufficed for at least part of the chimney. But one thing is sure: no climbing boys went up the whole chimney, to the top.

This is a summary of a discussion with Tony Grice of Culworth Engineering Ltd, experts in chimney systems, to whom I am most grateful.

4 M. Dorothy George, *London Life in the Eighteenth Century*, London, 1925. Dr George quotes a case of 1788 in which a ten-year-old boy was sent up a chimney that had been on fire for 48 hours. His master came and found fault with him 'in so angry a manner as to occasion fright, by which means he fell down into the fire and was much burned and crippled for life'.

5 Francis Grose, *A Classical Dictionary of the Vulgar Tongue*, London, 1785.

6 John Stow, *Survey of London*, London, 1598, corrected by John Strype 1720, 1754 edition. There is a pitiful picture of these children in *Low-Life*: at midnight they are 'sleeping on the bulks of houses scratching themselves as they lie, being sadly pestered with lice, rags, empty stomachs and guilty consciences'.

7 Harry Margary, *Cries of London first published c. 1754*, Lympne, 1978.

8 Per Kalm, *Account of his Visit to England on his Way to America in 1748*, translated by Joseph Lucas, London, 1892. The flower-sellers were still sitting round the base of Eros in Piccadilly up to the beginning of the last war.

9 George, op. cit.

10 Kalm, op. cit., and George, op. cit. It looks as if the 'Distressed Poet' of Hogarth's print is about to default on his milk bill. A well-dressed milkmaid is angrily showing him her talley stick. Her yoke is over one arm. She presumably made her debt-collecting rounds after her delivery rounds.

11 Most of what follows is drawn from Walter M. Stern, *The Porters of London*, London, 1960.

12 In the eighteenth-century wave of philanthropy, this was noticed, and a Society for the Relief of the Ruptured Poor was duly set up, but after our period.

13 Malarchy Postlethwaite, *Universal Directory of Trade and Commerce*, London, 1766.

14 There has been as much academic debate about the origin of trade unions as about the beginning of the industrial revolution. This, for what it is worth, is the conclusion I have reached, from the contemporary records I have read. For more descriptions of trades, see George, op. cit. The picture she paints is roughly the same for all trades. I use 'scab' in its modern sense. Grose, op. cit., defines 'scab' as 'a worthless man or company'.

15 George, op. cit.

16 *London Chronicle*, 12 December 1761, quoted in George, op. cit.

17 *Public Advertiser*, 18 February 1769: advertisement by S. Cole and Co., weavers. 'A quantity of flowered and striped silks of last year's pattern will be sold extremely low', quoted in George, op. cit.

18 William Thornton, *A New, Complete and Universal History, Description and Survey of the Cities of London and Westminster*, London, 1784.

19 *The Gentleman's Magazine*, April 1764.

20 George Rudé, *Hanoverian London*, London, 1971.

21 *The Gentleman's Magazine*, October 1767.

22 Rudé, op. cit.

23 Bernardino Ramazzini, *De Morbis Artificium* [Industrial Diseases], published in English, 2nd edition, London, 1750.

24 Peter Linebaugh, *The London Hanged*, London, 1991.

25 *The Gentleman's Magazine*, July 1751.

26 *The Gentleman's Magazine*, September 1751.

27 Linebaugh, op. cit.

28 Joseph Reddington (ed.), *Home Office Papers 1768–69*, London, 1878.

29 Linebaugh, op. cit. The hangman took the right hand of one of the dead men, Murphy, and stroked it on the cheek of a child suffering from scrofula.

30 *The Gentleman's Magazine*, April 1768.

31 Ibid.

32 Reddington (ed.), *Home Office Papers*, 15 May 1768.

33 Ibid. 26 Aug 1768.

34 Quoted in *London Journal*, vol. 4, 1978.

35 Ibid.

36 Reddington (ed.), *Home Office Papers*, July 1768.

37 *The Gentleman's Magazine*, 19 May 1750, among many such reports.

38 At that time, warships were classified according to the number of guns they carried. There were 12 1st-rate ships with a total of 4,132 sailors; 21 2nd-rate ships, with a total of 4,470 sailors; 36 3rd-rate ships with a total of 6,142 sailors; and 46 4th- and 5th-rate ships with a joint total of 4,140 sailors, according to Malarchy Postlethwaite, op. cit. Some ships were paid off in Portsmouth, but some in London, producing, subject to the press-gangs, a surge of happy mariners.

39 *The Gentleman's Magazine*, May 1768.

40 Ramazzini, op. cit., from which the rest of this section is taken.

41 Ibid.

42 Postlethwaite, op. cit.

43 Grose, op. cit. Benjamin Franklin felt he was unusual in his 'constant attendance [at work], (I never making a Saint Monday)'. W. T. Franklin, *Memoirs of Benjamin Franklin*, London, 1833. The frontispiece of *Low Life* published in 1754 is a picture of a pub with various men and one woman, identified by the tools of their trades, enjoying a drink. It is called 'Saint Monday'.

44 *The Gentleman's Magazine*, September 1756.

45 Much of this section is taken from J. R. Hutchinson, *The Press-Gang Afloat and Ashore*, London, 1915. It is hard to see how the British Navy won so many battles in the eighteenth century with these crews. The system was not dismantled until 1833.

46 *London Evening Post*, 1 January 1747.

47 Francis Place, *Autobiography*, British Library Add MS 35142.

48 Hutchinson, op. cit.

49 *The Gentleman's Magazine*, April 1756.

50 *The Gentleman's Magazine*, December 1761.

51 *The Gentleman's Magazine*, July 1755.

52 *The Gentleman's Magazine*, October 1770.

53 *The Gentleman's Magazine*, November 1770.

54 *Public Advertiser*, 15 January 1771.

55 Ibid.

56 *The Gentleman's Magazine*, August 1738.

Chapter 13: Slaves, Servants and Domestic Work (pp. 113–122)

1 James Boswell, *The Life of Samuel Johnson*, London, 1791.

2 Reddington (ed.), *Parliamentary History of England*, vol. XIV, 1743–53, London, 1813.

3 Quoted in James Walvin, *The Black Presence*, London, 1971.

4 Ibid., quoting the *Daily Ledger*, 31 December 1761.

5 *The Gentleman's Magazine*, January 1763. Samuel Johnson had a negro servant who had been brought to England in 1750 as a slave, but had been 'given his liberty' in his master's will.

6 *The Gentleman's Magazine*, December 1768.

7 *The Gentleman's Magazine*, November 1771.

8 Quoted in Walvin, op. cit.

9 Ibid.

10 Boswell, op. cit.

11 Malarchy Postlethwaite, *Tract on the Negro-Trade*, London, 1746, quoted in Walvin, op. cit.

12 Walvin, op. cit.

13 *London Chronicle*, 16 February 1764.

14 Anon., *An Estimate of the Necessary Charges of a Family in the Middling Station of Life*,

quoted in Dorothy Davis, *A History of Shopping*, London, 1966.

15 Isaac Ware, *Complete Body of Architecture*, London, 1756.

16 J. Jean Hecht, *The Domestic Servant Class in Eighteenth Century England*, London, 1956.

17 Francis Place, *Autobiography*, British Library Add MS 35142.

18 Mary Collier, *The Woman's Labour* (the washerwoman) in Roger Lonsdale (ed.), *The New Oxford Book of Eighteenth-Century Verse*, Oxford, 1984.

19 *The Gentleman's Magazine*, March 1763, a graphic account of the murder of Lord Dacre's butler by a footman which describes the lay-out of the house. It had, among other advantages, a 'laundry-house'.

20 G. Eland (ed.), *Purefoy Letters 1735–53*, London, 1931.

21 Francis Grose, *A Classical Dictionary of the Vulgar Tongue*, London, 1785.

22 Anon., *Apology for Pawnbroking*, 1744, quoted in Davis, op. cit.

23 Joseph Massie, *Letter to Bourchier Cleeve re Massie's Calculation of Taxes*, London, 1757. This is an enormous amount, difficult to imagine in these days of washing powders. But if you can remember a pound packet of sugar – eight of them, each week.

24 *The Gentleman's Magazine*, May 1751.

25 Mark Laird and John Harvey, 'The garden plan for 13, Upper Gower Street, London', *Garden History*, vol. 25, no. 2, winter 1997.

26 Gladys Scott Thomson, *The Russells in Bloomsbury Square 1669–1771*, London, 1940.

27 I have used a facsimile published in 1971 by Huntingdon Laboratories Inc., Huntingdon, of the fourth edition, 1762.

28 Ambrose Heal, *London Tradesmen's Cards of the Eighteenth Century*, London, 1925.

29 Per Kalm, *Account of his Visit to England on his Way to America in 1748*, translated by Joseph Lucas, London, 1892.

30 Ibid.

31 Grose, op. cit.

32 Boswell, op. cit.

33 *The Gentleman's Magazine*, Supplement, 1766.

34 Grose, op. cit.

35 *The Gentleman's Magazine*, February 1761.

36 John Stow, *Survey of London*, London, 1598, corrected by John Strype 1720, 1754 edition.

37 De Saussure, *A Foreign View of England in the Reign of George I and George II*, translated by Van Muyden, London, 1902. De Saussure was in London in 1725–36. The custom got worse after then.

38 *London Chronicle*, vol. 7, January–June 1760.

39 *The Gentleman's Magazine*, May 1764.

40 Hecht, op. cit.

41 Gavin Hannah (ed.), *The Deserted Village: The Diary of an Oxfordshire Rector, James Newton*, Stroud, 1992.

42 Hecht, op. cit.

43 *London Chronicle*, vol. 3, 1758, quoted in Hecht, op. cit.

44 I once heard two nannies interpreting advertisements by employers. The only bits I remember now are 'fun-loving' = must be prepared to sleep with employer's

husband, and 'foreign holidays' = every evening baby-sitting, in a foreign place, while the employers are out on the tiles.

45 Hecht, op. cit.

46 Anon., *Low-Life*, London, 1764.

Chapter 14: Amusements (pp. 123–132)

1 I am indebted to the archivist of United Distillers, who kindly sent me a copy of the relevant chapter of John Doxat *The Gin Book*, London, 1989, with a most informative letter. I am similarly indebted to Seagram Distillers plc for a copy of an article by John E. Linnell in the autumn 1957 issue of the house magazine of the former Distillers Company, entitled *The House of Burnet*.

2 This useful word does not appear in Dr Johnson's *Dictionary*.

3 Joseph Massie, *Calculation of the Present Taxes*, 2nd edition, London, 1761.

4 Jenny Uglow's *Hogarth: A Life and a World*, London, 1997, taught me to 'read' Hogarth's pictures.

5 All these are from Peter Linebaugh, *The London Hanged*, London, 1991. The rest are from Francis Grose, *A Classical Dictionary of the Vulgar Tongue*, London, 1785.

6 Bradstreet, *The Life and Uncommon Adventures of Captain Bradstreet*, London, 1754.

7 Francis Place, *Autobiography*, BL Add MS 35142.

8 *London Chronicle*, 19 October 1762.

9 *The Gentleman's Magazine*, November 1769.

10 James Pellar Malcolm, *Anecdotes of London*, London, 1810.

11 De Saussure, *A Foreign View of England in the Reigns of George I and George II*, translated by Van Muyden, London, 1902.

12 *London Evening Post*, 23 October 1764.

13 George Rudé, *Hanoverian London*, London, 1971.

14 De Saussure, op. cit.

15 Place, op. cit.

16 *The Gentleman's Magazine*, July 1749.

17 Grose, op. cit. It was called 'docking'.

18 From a petition by 300 substantial citizens to the King, who refused to pardon the young man. His bones had to rest content with a memorial stone commemorating his 'zeal for his countrymen and an honest detestation for Public Stews [brothels]'. Jasper Goodwill, *The Ladies' Magazine*, November 1749.

19 *The Gentleman's Magazine*, November 1749.

20 *The Gentleman's Magazine*, April 1756.

21 *The Gentleman's Magazine*, July 1759, November 1761, April 1763. One of the sodomites was saved from being 'pelted' by a passing press-gang; the other was killed.

22 De Saussure, op. cit.

23 There used to be a small square stone in the middle of the tarmac on the western edge of the traffic vortex at Marble Arch, marking the site. I have not been able to see it, lately.

24 *The Gentleman's Magazine*, October 1767. This seems to have been unusual. The

normal transport was in carts, giving the crowds a better view.

25 In Spitalfields where some rioting weavers were hanged, in Shadwell where seven men involved in the fights between coal-heavers and sailors were hanged, in Bethnal Green where two rioters were hanged 'amid an innumerable concourse of spectators', and in Panton Street/Haymarket where a murderer was hanged and his body hung in chains, near the scene of his crime: pleasant for people visiting the Prince of Wales in nearby Leicester Fields. The murderer of a court official was hanged in Bow Street, but his body was removed to Finchley Common to be hung in chains there.

26 That sentence was imposed on William Prendergast for treasonable practices in 'New York, America', but he was given a free pardon instead. Reddington (ed.), *Home Office Papers*, 1766.

27 *The Gentleman's Magazine*, February 1753.

28 *The Gentleman's Magazine*, May 1770.

29 *The Gentleman's Magazine*, July 1761.

30 *The Gentleman's Magazine*, February 1751. Eight criminals were hanged at Tyburn, including three boys. The feet of one of them were chained together 'to prevent a rescue'.

31 *The Gentleman's Magazine*, January 1767.

32 *The Gentleman's Magazine*, August 1769.

33 L. Radzinowicz, *A History of English Criminal Law*, London, 1968.

34 William Thornton, *A New, Complete and Universal History, Description and Survey of the Cities of London and Westminster*, London, 1784.

35 P. J. Grosley, *A Tour to London*, translated by Thomas Nugent, London, 1772.

36 *The Gentleman's Magazine*, June 1771.

37 *The Gentleman's Magazine*, December 1758. What did they do with it? There is no clue in the report. The only other detail given is that the man was a Roman Catholic.

38 Grosley, op. cit.

39 Ibid.

40 Ibid.

41 Place, op. cit.

42 Malcolm, op. cit.

43 His engraving of *The Lottery* in 1724 is a comparatively pedestrian political satire.

44 *The Gentleman's Magazine*, November 1751.

45 M. Dorothy George, *London Life in the Eighteenth Century*, London, 1925. It is curious how little contemporary evidence there is, of the effect of the lottery on the poor, presumably because it impoverished them further but did not 'imbecillitate' them, which might have harmed the middle classes. The lottery was abolished in 1826 through the efforts of William Wilberforce, who turned his attention to it after he had achieved the abolition of slavery.

46 Thornton, op. cit.

47 *The Gentleman's Magazine*, June 1750.

48 John Entick, *A New and Accurate History and Survey of London, Westminster and Southwark*, London, 1766.

49 See Chapter 4.

50 *The Gentleman's Magazine*, October 1768.

Chapter 15: Crime and Punishment (pp. 133–149)

1 L. Radzinowicz, *A History of English Criminal Law*, London, 1968.
2 Francis Grose, *A Classical Dictionary of the Vulgar Tongue*, London, 1785.
3 *The Gentleman's Magazine*, March 1764.
4 *The Gentleman's Magazine*, March 1765.
5 Anon., *Low-Life*, London, 1764.
6 Ibid.
7 De Saussure, *A Foreign View of England in the Reigns of George I and George II*, translated by Van Muyden, London, 1902. De Saussure was in London in 1725–36.
8 F. A. Pottle (ed.), *Boswell's London Journal 1762–1763*, London, 1951.
9 Horace Walpole, *Letters*, Everyman edition, London, 1926: letter to the Countess of Ossory, 7 October 1781.
10 Lowell Blair (ed. and trans.), *Casanova's Memoirs*, London, 1958.
11 Peter Linebaugh, *The London Hanged*, London, 1991.
12 *The Gentleman's Magazine*, June 1771.
13 *The Ladies' Magazine*, 2 June 1750.
14 *The Gentleman's Magazine*, July 1755.
15 *The Gentleman's Magazine*, August 1757.
16 *The Gentleman's Magazine*, December 1747.
17 *The Gentleman's Magazine*, September 1747.
18 Grose, op. cit.
19 *London Chronicle*, 5 February 1763.
20 *London Chronicle*, 15 March 1763. It seems extraordinary that her husband didn't know how old she was.
21 *London Chronicle*, 15 and 26 December 1773.
22 *The Gentleman's Magazine*, April 1753.
23 The conditions before 1770 appear from the evidence of Sir John Fielding before a committee of the House of Commons on his *Plan for preventing Burglaries and Robberies* in 1751.
24 *Low-Life*, op. cit.
25 Walpole, op. cit., 21 July 1742.
26 James Pellar Malcolm, *Anecdotes of London*, London, 1810.
27 Francis Place, *Autobiography*, BL Add MS 35142.
28 M. Dorothy George, *London Life in the Eighteenth Century*, London, 1925. Dr George says of Fielding's appointment that it 'marked a turning-point in the social history of London'. In general, she found the period 1740–60 a hinge, as it were, between the bad old world and the brave new world.
29 *The Gentleman's Magazine*, January 1764.
30 In 1764 the body of an executed criminal was 'at his own request carried [away] and laid at the door of [the man who had prosecuted him], the mob threatening to pull down the man's house'. *The Gentleman's Magazine*, June 1764. In 1771 a mob of 2,000 people set on the principal witness in a trial that had resulted in the execution of two weavers and 'continued pelting him with brickbats ... they kept stoning him till he died in the greatest agony'. *The Gentleman's Magazine*, April 1771.

31 In 1769 Sir John Fielding 'recommended that the persons in custody on account of the outrages in Spitalfields should be prosecuted at public expense. His Majesty has approved.' Joseph Reddington (ed.), *Home Office Papers 1766–69*, London, 1878.

32 Grose, op. cit.

33 Lowell Blair, op. cit.

34 *The Gentleman's Magazine*, February 1769.

35 *The Gentleman's Magazine*, July 1770; Radzinowicz, op. cit.

36 D. Potter, *Historical Introduction to English Law*, London, 1958.

37 Grose, op. cit.

38 *The Gentleman's Magazine*, August 1762.

39 Radzinowicz, op. cit.

40 *The Gentleman's Magazine*, September 1767.

41 Place, op. cit.

42 *Low-Life*, op. cit.

43 *The Gentleman's Magazine*, 30 September 1770.

44 P. J. Grosley, *A Tour to London*, translated by Thomas Nugent, London, 1772. M. Grosley was in London in 1765.

45 *The Gentleman's Magazine*, May 1752.

46 James Boswell, *The Life of Samuel Johnson*, London, 1791.

47 *The Gentleman's Magazine*, February 1750.

48 Hans Zinsser, *Rats, Lice and History*, London 1935, a marvellous read long out of print in the UK.

49 *The Gentleman's Magazine*, January 1753.

50 *The Gentleman's Magazine*, January 1764.

51 Malcolm, op. cit.

52 *Abstract from Mr Howard's Account of the English Prisons and Hospitals*, London, 1789.

53 *The Gentleman's Magazine*, September 1764.

54 *The Gentleman's Magazine*, January 1765.

55 *London Evening Post*, 23 October 1764.

56 *The Gentleman's Magazine*, July 1763.

57 *The Gentleman's Magazine*, July 1771.

58 William Alexander, *The History of Women*, London, 1779.

59 Radzinowicz, op. cit.

60 A. Roger Ekirch, *Bound for America: The Transportation of British Convicts to the Colonies 1718–1775*, Oxford, 1987, on which the following section is based.

61 This word is not in Johnson's *Dictionary*. It means 'a line of animals, slaves, etc. fastened together' (*Concise Oxford Dictionary*). It is startling to find it used of English men in London.

62 *The Gentleman's Magazine*, June 1750.

63 *The Gentleman's Magazine*, December 1750.

Chapter 16: Dentistry, Health and Medical Care (pp. 153–173)

1 Thomas Beardmore, London, 1768, quoted in Roger King, 'John Hunter and

the natural history of the human teeth', *Journal of the History of Medicine*, vol. 49, no. 4 (October 1994).

2 Ambrose Heal, *London Tradesmen's Cards of the Eighteenth Century*, London, 1925.

3 S. Menzies Campbell, *Dentistry Then and Now*, Glasgow, 1963.

4 Ibid.

5 *The Gentleman's Magazine*, January 1764.

6 John Woodforde, *The Strange Story of False Teeth*, London, 1968.

7 Chesterfield, *Letters to his Son*, London, 1774.

8 Thea Molleson and Margaret Cox, *The Spitalfields Project*, vol. 2: The Anthropology, York, 1993. I hope I am making a reasonable deduction from this meticulous research.

9 Frederick Hoffman, *A Treatise on the Teeth, their Disorders and Cure*, London, 1753, quoted in Campbell, op. cit.

10 Elizabeth Bennion, *Antique Dental Instruments*, London, 1986.

11 Ibid.

12 G. Eland (ed.), *Purefoy Letters 1735–53*, London, 1931.

13 William Andrews, *Almanac*, 1750.

14 Bennion, op. cit.

15 Peter Laslett, *The World We Have Lost – Further Explored*, 3rd edition, London, 1983.

16 Professor E. A. Wrigley, personal letter.

17 The figures in the Bills were of christenings and burials in the Anglican Church. Babies born to parents who for religious or financial reasons did not have them christened, and whose deaths were followed by disposal of the body in non-Anglican rites, or no rites at all, were not included.

18 William Smellie, *A Treatise on the Theory and Practice of Midwifery*, London, 1752.

19 Joseph Hurlock, *A Practical Treatise on Dentition*, London, 1742.

20 Smellie, op. cit.

21 Hurlock, op. cit.

22 *Encyclopedia Britannica*, Edinburgh, 1773.

23 Anon., *The Ladies Dispensatory or Every Woman her own Physician*, London, 1739.

24 Francis Place, *Autobiography*, BL Add MS 35142.

25 Thomas Hunt (ed.), *The Medical Society of London 1773–1973*, London, 1972.

26 John Landers, *Death and the Metropolis*, Cambridge, 1993; also a private letter from Dr Landers.

27 *The Gentleman's Magazine*, November 1747.

28 *The Gentleman's Magazine*, March 1766.

29 *The Gentleman's Magazine*, February 1768.

30 Eliza Smith, *The Compleat Housewife*, 16th edition, London, 1758.

31 John Wesley, *Primitive Physic*, 5th edition, London, 1755.

32 A Society of Physicians in London, *Medical Observations and Inquiries*, vol. IV, London, 1771.

33 *The Gentleman's Magazine*, December 1752. There was much irate correspondence in *The Gentleman's Magazine*, but nothing was done.

34 Landers, op. cit.

35 John Fothergill, *An Account of the Sore Throat Attended with ulcers*, 4th edition, London, 1754. 'The parotid glands swell ... and grow hard.'

36 George Cheyne, *The English Malady*, London, 1733.

37 Quoted in Roy Porter and G. S. Rousseau, *Gout: The Patrician Malady*, London, 1998.

38 Review in *The Gentleman's Magazine*, June 1771, of Dr Cadogan's Dissertation on the Gout.

39 Wesley, op. cit.

40 Porter and Rousseau, op. cit.

41 *London Evening Post*, 19 February 1747.

42 Eland, op. cit.

43 Elizabeth Burton, *The Georgians at Home*, London, 1967.

44 F. A. Pottle (ed.), *Boswell's London Journal 1762–1763*, London, 1951.

45 *The Ladies Dispensatory*, op. cit.

46 The generally accepted view supposed a chain of causation beginning in the Caribbean islands, pausing at the siege of Naples in 1494 and thence spreading world-wide. Martin Lister in his *Dissertation on the Pox* of 1694 added a link at the initial stage – that it was transmitted to man in tropical America by an iguana. It is unclear to me who was doing what, to which, to cause this. Guy Williams, *The Age of Agony*, London, 1975.

47 Richard Mead, *A Mechanical Account of Poisons*, 4th edition, London, 1747.

48 'In love, a man may lose his heart with dignity; but if he loses his nose, he loses his character into the bargain.' Chesterfield, op. cit.

49 Boswell 'resolved to take London as one takes mercury: to intermit it whenever I should find it affects my brain as one intermits the use of mercury when it affects the mouth.' *Boswell in Extremes 1776–1778*, ed. C. McC. Weir and F. A. Pottle, London, 1970.

50 *Encyclopedia Britannica*, op. cit.

51 *Medical Observations and Queries by a Society of Physicians in London*, vol. I, London, 1757.

52 Ibid., vol. II, 1762.

53 Wesley, op. cit.

54 I am grateful to Dr M. P. Eames for his guidance on the use of mercury, and on other aspects of eighteenth-century prescriptions. He told me that mercury would have had no effect on nervous colic. I forgot to ask Dr Eames about the effect of a live puppy.

55 Wesley, op. cit.

56 A suicide attempt by this agonising method was reported in the *London Chronicle*, 3 September 1760.

57 Landers, op. cit.

58 Review of Dr Battie's *Treatise on Madness* in the *London Chronicle*, vol. II, 1757.

59 *London Chronicle*, 22 January 1763.

60 *The Gentleman's Magazine*, April 1763.

61 *The Gentleman's Magazine*, August 1769.

62 *The Gentleman's Magazine*, April 1772.

63 *The Gentleman's Magazine*, December 1763. There is no indication of how he used the cherries and toothpick. How did similar stories end if the victim were not so resourceful?

64 Smith, op. cit.

65 Eliza Smith's book included nearly a hundred pages of medical recipes. Perhaps my favourite is 'To cure spitting of blood if a vein is broken. Take mice-dung beaten to powder, as much as will lie on a sixpence...'

66 *The Ladies Dispensatory*, op. cit.

67 This lasted until quite recently. When I was a child, in Scotland, there was a book beside the bed where my sister and I slept, in my paternal grandfather's house, called 'What every young boy should know'. I read it, as I read everything, even the whole of Scott and Dickens, but it was as incomprehensible to me as a page of Scott's peasant dialogue. It appeared to concern some action that would cause your hand to drop off, but what it was remained unclear to me.

68 Such as those in the Wellcome Institute for the History of Medicine, W MS 3539.

69 *Owen's Weekly Chronicle*, 19 February 1763.

70 *The Gentleman's Magazine*, August 1748.

71 Ibid.

72 *London Evening Post*, 28 April 1752.

73 *London Chronicle*, vol. I, 1764.

74 *Public Advertiser*, 14 January 1771.

75 *Daily Advertiser*, 20 May 1741.

76 Patent no. 887 of 1767: the specification includes an elaborate drawing of all the bits.

77 James Boswell, *The Life of Samuel Johnson*, London, 1791.

78 Seasons, *Almanac*, 1760.

79 Quoted in Hugh Phillips, *Mid-Georgian London*, London, 1964.

80 I am indebted to M. Rowbottom and Charles Susskind, *Electricity and Medicine: A History of their Interaction*, London, 1984, for this, my own grasp of electricity being that of Thurber's aunt, who knew that it leaks out of sockets overnight. The gentlemen who wrote the *Encyclopedia Britannica* in 1773 were also 'entirely ignorant of the electric fluid', but looked forward to the day when 'an electric machine might be contrived to go by wind or water, and a convenient room might be annexed to it in which a floor might be raised on electrics, and a person might sit down, read, sleep or even walk about during the electrification'. Up to then a 'charged' person tended to get a luminous nose and produce a 'sharp crack' if he touched someone else, the usefulness of which was perhaps limited.

81 *The Gentleman's Magazine*, June and November 1748.

82 *The Gentleman's Magazine*, October 1749.

83 *The Gentleman's Magazine*, May 1753.

84 John Wesley, *Journal*, London, 1827.

85 *The Gentleman's Magazine*, March 1763.

86 Wesley, *Journal*, op. cit. By now Wesley had read 'Dr Priestley's ingenious book' on it.

87 Boswell, op. cit.

88 Heal, op. cit.

89 Anon., *Low-Life*, London, 1764.

90 *London Evening Post*, 21 April 1747.

91 *Low-Life*, op. cit.

92 Richard Mead, *A Mechanical Account of Poisons*, London, 1702, 4th edition 1747.

93 *The Gentleman's Magazine*, Supplement, 1769. I can only hope this is not a veiled reference to the myth I have referred to above, that intercourse with an uninfected partner would rid the sufferer of venereal disease.

94 Dr Hill, *The Old Man's Guide to Health and Longer Life*, 5th edition, London, 1764.

Chapter 17: Childhood, Schooling and Religion (pp. 174–184)

1 Iona and Peter Opie, *The Singing Game*, Oxford, 1985.

2 Information kindly provided by Hamleys plc.

3 S. Roscoe, *John Newberry and his Successors*, Wormley (Herts), 1973.

4 Peter Hunt (ed.), *Children's Literature*, Oxford, 1995.

5 F. R. B. Whitehouse, *Table Games of Georgian and Victorian Times*, Royston, 1971.

6 Anthony Burton, *Children's Pleasures*, London, 1996.

7 Francis Place, *Autobiography*, BL Add MS 35142.

8 P. J. Grosley, *A Tour to London*, translated by Thomas Nugent, London, 1772. M. Grosley was in London in 1765.

9 James Boswell, *The Life of Samuel Johnson*, London, 1791.

10 John Wesley, *Journal*, London, 1827.

11 Ambrose Heal, *London Tradesmen's Cards of the Eighteenth Century*, London, 1925.

12 Letter of 2 March 1737, quoted in Ruth McClure, *Coram's Children*, Yale, 1981.

13 Gladys Scott Thomson, *The Russells in Bloomsbury Square 1669–1771*, London, 1940.

14 Grosley, op. cit.

15 A Scottish village school that I attended during part of the last war went in for punishment by 'strapping' on the hand. The master used to hold the leather strap behind his back as he stood in front of the cast-iron stove comfortably warming himself, and keeping the heat away from us. The strap got so hard that it was like 'a stout cane' and certainly 'bruised the hands sorely'. I regarded its infliction as a useful lesson in not being found out.

16 Heal, op. cit.

17 I. Parker, *Dissenting Academies in England*, Cambridge, 1914.

18 William Thornton, *A New, Complete and Universal History, Description and Survey of the Cities of London and Westminster*, London, 1784.

19 Thomson, op. cit.

20 Chesterfield, *Letters to his Son*, London, 1774.

21 Professor Kahn Freund, teaching Roman law in the London School of Economics in 1947, dumbfounded his class by addressing us in Latin. Worse, he pronounced it like Austrian. It was a stimulating experience, and possibly one of the last occasions on which Latin was used as a conversational medium.

22 Grosley, op. cit.

23 Chesterfield, op. cit.

24 *London Chronicle*, 3 January 1764.

25 *Public Advertiser*, 15 January 1771.

26 W. A. Speck, *Stability and Strife: England 1714–60*, London, 1977.

27 Grosley, op. cit. He does not unfortunately specify the trade.

28 Susan Lawrence, *Charitable Knowledge*, Cambridge, 1996.

29 *The Gentleman's Magazine*, May 1772.

30 Anon., *Tradesman's Directory*, London, 1756.

31 Robert Poole, ' "Give us our eleven days" – Calendar reform in eighteenth-century England', *Past and Present*, no. 149, November 1995. Contrary to widely held belief, it transpires that, partial though people were to rioting, they never did riot about their eleven days, because their grievances were anticipated and provided for. Mr Poole disentangles the Julian calendar adopted by the Christian Church in 325 from the Gregorian calendar adopted by some continental countries in 1582. By then the two calendars were ten days adrift, which turned into eleven in 1700, a leap year. Lord Chesterfield's bill not only rerouted English calendars on to Gregorian rails, but restarted the year on 1 January instead of 25 March, for some purposes. Unfortunately, the tax system still used the old dates so that the last day of the financial year was 25 March: add eleven days and you get to 5 April, which is still with us.

32 John Entick, *A New and Accurate History and Survey of London, Westminster and Southwark*, London, 1766.

33 Ibid.

34 Grosley, op. cit.

35 *The Gentleman's Magazine*, September 1756.

36 Wesley, op. cit. Wesley could reach a crowd of several thousand. Benjamin Franklin found, by experiment, that a speaker could be heard by a crowd of 25,000: W. T. Franklin, *Memoirs of Benjamin Franklin*, London, 1833.

37 Anon., *Low-Life*, London, 1765.

38 Horace Walpole, *Letters*, Everyman edition, London, 1936.

39 Boswell, op. cit.

Chapter 18: A Woman's World (pp. 185–198)

1 Samuel Johnson, *Rasselas*, London, 1759.

2 *The Gentleman's Magazine*, May 1746. Nova Scotia had been British, in the British view, since 1713, but the French did not always agree. Cape Breton was later renamed Halifax. The assisted emigration in the year after the Jacobite rebellion raises the possibility that some of these emigrants may have been Scots, or at least of Jacobite sympathies.

3 *The Gentleman's Magazine*, July 1749.

4 *The Gentleman's Magazine*, August 1752.

5 *London Chronicle*, 20 October 1761.

6 *London Chronicle*, 19 July 1763.

7 Peter Laslett, *The World We Have Lost – Further Explored*, London, 1971.

8 *London Chronicle*, 31 July 1760.

9 *The Gentleman's Magazine*, August 1764.

10 Bartle Grant (ed.), *The Receipt Book of Elizabeth Raper*, London, 1924, which begins with entries from her Journal. 'I could have loved and valued him, but upon my soul the moment I think him to cool I am off without a Pang.' She married

someone else of whom her parents must have approved, since they found her an
extra £200 a year.

11 For an illuminating description of Hogarth's work, see Jenny Uglow, *Hogarth: A
Life and a World*, London, 1997.

12 *The Gentleman's Magazine*, 18 January 1751.

13 *The Gentleman's Magazine*. You would have thought that someone could have found
out his name.

14 William Alexander, *The History of Women*, London, 1779.

15 Joseph Reddington (ed.), *Parliamentary History of England*, vol. XV, 1753–65, London,
1813. This speech was part of the debate on Lord Hardwicke's Act, considered
below.

16 Anon., *The Complete Letter-Writer*, Edinburgh, 1768.

17 For a fuller discussion of the pre-1753 position see the author's *Restoration London*,
London, 1997.

18 *Davids* v. *Wilson*, reported in *The Gentleman's Magazine*, August 1747.

19 *The Gentleman's Magazine*, September 1762.

20 *The Gentleman's Magazine*, November 1761.

21 *The Gentleman's Magazine*, September 1764.

22 *The Gentleman's Magazine*, September 1768. It would have been a very slow journey
in a hearse, if they were intending to go all the way at a funereal pace. She must
have been glad to get out.

23 *The Gentleman's Magazine*, January 1769.

24 M. H. Port 'West End palaces: the aristocratic town house in London', *London
Journal*, no. 20, 1995.

25 Ibid.

26 Hannah Glasse, *The Art of Cookery made Plain and Easy*, London, 1747, published
in facsimile by Prospect Books, London, 1995.

27 *The Gentleman's Magazine*, February 1753.

28 *The Gentleman's Magazine*, October 1753. Turtles still sometimes arrive in home
waters. One was washed ashore in 1998 weighing 225 kg: *Daily Telegraph*, 9
February 1998.

29 John Stow, *Survey of London*, London, 1598, corrected by John Strype 1720, 1754
edition.

30 Hugh Phillips, *Mid-Georgian London*, London, 1965. I had always imagined
shepherds leading their sheep along the Mayfair streets, but the market owed its
name to a previous owner called Shepherd – such a disappointment. The fair
was suppressed by the end of the century.

31 I am most grateful to Miss Muller of Fortnum and Mason, who kindly sent me
a copy of *The Delectable History of Fortnum and Mason*, tracing the history of the
shop from 1707.

32 Information kindly provided by R. Twining and Company Ltd, which still trades
from the same premises.

33 *Public Advertiser*, 19 January 1771.

34 *Public Advertiser*, 19 January 1771.

35 Facsimile published by Harry Margary, Lympne, 1978.

36 Ambrose Heal, *London Tradesmen's Cards of the Eighteenth Century*, London, 1925.

37 Malarchy Postlethwaite, *Universal Dictionary of Trade and Commerce*, London, 1766.

38 Eliza Smith, *The Compleat Housewife*, London, 1758.

39 Elizabeth Raffald, *The Experienced English Housekeeper*, Manchester, 1769, republished Lewes, 1997.

40 Ibid.

41 John Farley, *The London Art of Cookery*, 3rd edition, London, 1785. He gave the cook a choice whether to kill the pig herself or not. At least it would be fresh.

42 Smith, op. cit.

43 Farley, op. cit.

44 Francis Grose, *A Classical Dictionary of the Vulgar Tongue*, London, 1785.

45 Ibid.

46 Farley, op. cit.

47 Ibid.

48 Raffald, op. cit. All the cookery writers whose books I read give numerous recipes of this kind.

49 The heart, liver and lungs.

50 Farley, op. cit.

51 Raffald, op. cit.

52 Ibid.

53 Ibid. Larks were generally regarded as edible then.

54 Horace Walpole was asked to dinner at Northumberland House then. *Letters*, Everyman edition, London, 1936: 7 April 1765.

55 P. J. Grosley, *A Tour to London*, translated by Thomas Nugent, London, 1765. M. Grosley was in London in 1765.

56 Samuel Johnson, *Dictionary*, London, 1755.

57 A model of the pleasure garden, even down to its twinkling lights. C. S. Sykes, *Private Palaces*, London, 1985.

58 Chesterfield, *Letters to his Son*, London, 1778.

59 Grosley, op. cit.

60 De Saussure, *A Foreign View of England in the Reign of George I and George II*, translated by Van Muyden, London, 1902. De Saussure was in London in 1725–36.

61 Grosley, op. cit.

62 *The Gentleman's Magazine*, March 1763. The footman who went for them had in this instance just murdered the butler. The case provides a fascinating sight of the routine of a large house in Bruton Street.

63 *The Gentleman's Magazine*, May 1760.

64 Per Kalm, *Account of his Visit to England on his Way to America in 1748*, translated by Joseph Lucas, London, 1892.

65 Dr Johnson, op. cit.

66 *The Gentleman's Magazine*, November 1755.

67 Grosley, op. cit.

68 *The Complete Letter-Writer*, op. cit.

69 Grosley, op. cit.

70 *London Evening Post*, 30 December 1747.

71 Joseph Massie, *Letter to Bourchier Cleeve re Massie's Calculation of Taxes*, London, 1757.

72 *Boswell's London Journal*, ed. F. A. Pottle, London, 1951.

73 Donald Burrows, *Handel*, Oxford, 1994, citing an article by William Frosch, 'The

"case" of George Frederic Handel', *New England Journal of Medicine*, vol. 321, September 1989.

74 Laslett, op. cit. The latest figure now, for families that have children at all, is 1.8.

75 Grose, op. cit.

76 This, and much else in this section, is derived from Angus McLaren, *Reproductive Rituals*, London, 1984.

77 Grose, op. cit.

Chapter 19: The Middling Rank of Men (pp. 199–214)

1 *Daily Advertiser*, 8 December 1743.

2 Hugh Phillips, *Mid-Georgian London*, London, 1965.

3 Samuel Johnson, *Dictionary*, London, 1755.

4 Michael Reed, *The Georgian Triumph*, London, 1983.

5 P. J. Grosley, *A Tour to London*, translated by Thomas Nugent, London, 1772. M. Grosley was in London in 1765.

6 James Boswell, *The Life of Samuel Johnson*, London, 1791. Years later, when Johnson was old and ill, he reassembled what remained of his original club 'to ensure himself society in the evening for three days in the week'. Boswell was in Scotland at the time, but Johnson proposed him *in absentia*. 'Boswell (said he) is a very clubable [*sic*] man.'

7 John Stow, *Survey of London*, London 1598, corrected by John Strype 1720, 1754 edition.

8 Grosley, op. cit.

9 Malarchy Postlethwaite, *Universal Directory of Trade and Commerce*, London, 1766. By 1740 Britain was taking over two-thirds of the total Russian export of hemp and more than half of its exports of flax; also tar, iron from the Urals and silk from Armenian merchants who controlled the supply of raw silk from Persia. The Russia Company, the oldest chartered company, secured trading rights and safeguarded British interests in Russia. In 1748 it moved its permanent office from Waldo and Batson's coffee-house to an office in the Royal Exchange. David Macmillan, 'The Russia Company of London in the eighteenth century', *The Guildhall Miscellany*, vol. IV, no. 4, April 1973. No doubt Russian merchants visited London from time to time on a 'visiting firemen' basis. The mention of Japan is surprising. The Dutch, alone among European nations, had a precarious foothold there. Basil Guy, 'Japan', in Jeremy Black and Roy Porter (eds), *The Penguin Dictionary of Eighteenth-Century History*, Harmondsworth, 1996.

10 John Entick, *A New and Accurate History and Survey of London, Westminster and Southwark*, London, 1766.

11 From Anon., *Apology for Pawnbroking*, quoted in Dorothy Davis, *A History of Shopping*, London, 1966.

12 Davis, op. cit.

13 *Gazetteer and London Daily Advertiser*, 2 March 1763.

14 Postlethwaite, op. cit.

15 *The Gentleman's Magazine*, October 1768.

16 Chesterfield, *Letters to his Son*, London, 1774.

17 Stow, op. cit.

18 A. S. Turberville (ed.), *Johnson's England*, Oxford, 1933.

19 Phillips, op. cit.

20 James Pellar Malcolm, *Anecdotes of London*, London, 1810. The nearest I ever came to that was at Assizes once, when Queen's Counsel got his gown caught in the seat mechanism and was unable to rise to address the judge. Fortunately, I had my embroidery scissors with me – not, of course, in use at that moment – and was able to cut him free.

21 As always when discussing Hogarth, I am indebted to Jenny Uglow, *Hogarth: A Life and a World*, London, 1997.

22 Francis Grose, *A Classical Dictionary of the Vulgar Tongue*, London, 1785.

23 *London Chronicle*. When I lived in Gray's Inn, dogs were prohibited but the notice did not extend to monkeys. The gardener played the trumpet, but as far as I know there were no Dulcineas there.

24 Postlethwaite, op. cit.

25 Ruth McClure, *Coram's Children*, Yale, 1971.

26 Anon., *Low-Life*, London, 1764.

27 *London Evening Post*, 6 January 1747.

28 2 May 1758.

29 The central figure has opened the abdomen of the cadaver with a large knife. His shirt sleeves are rolled up, but he has not taken off his wig. Two colleagues are demonstrating the ankles and the eyes. With less risk of blood they are wearing their usual coats. The front row of spectators, one of whom is reading a book, are all wearing hats and wigs, and look like medicos themselves, but the back of the theatre is filled with standing figures, exchanging conversation as they watch.

30 *Low-Life*, op. cit.

31 Oliver Goldsmith, *Critical Review*, 10 November 1759.

32 Figures from G. R. Cragg, *The Church and the Age of Reason*, Harmondsworth, 1960.

33 E. H. Pearce, *The Sons of the Clergy: Some Records of 275 Years*, London, 1928. I also consulted the Society's records in the London Metropolitan Archives.

34 Entick, op. cit.

35 Whiffler: a harbinger, probably one with a horn or trumpet. Samuel Johnson, *Dictionary*, 9th edition, London, 1805.

36 Alan Guy, *Œconomy and Discipline*, Manchester, 1985.

37 *The Gentleman's Magazine*, February 1759.

38 Simes, *The Military Medley*, London, 1768, quoted in Guy, op. cit.

39 *The Gentleman's Magazine*, July 1772.

40 *The Ladies Magazine*, 1750. An early instance of money laundering.

41 T. H. White, *The Age of Scandal*, London, 1950.

42 *The Gentleman's Magazine*, December 1755.

43 *The Gentleman's Magazine*, December 1750.

44 *The Gentleman's Magazine*, June 1752.

45 *The Gentleman's Magazine*, January 1751.

46 Phillips, op. cit.

47 *The Gentleman's Magazine*, May 1752.

48 *The Gentleman's Magazine*, August 1754.

49 Reed, op. cit.

50 Rowland Bowen, *Cricket: A History*, London, 1970, and Turberville, op. cit.

51 *London Chronicle*, August 1763.

52 Grose, op. cit.

53 Phillips, op. cit.

54 Ibid.

55 Walter Besant, *London in the Eighteenth Century*, London, 1902.

56 Entick, op. cit.

57 *The Gentleman's Magazine*, April 1755.

58 *The Gentleman's Magazine*, November 1757.

59 *Daily Advertiser*, 8 December 1743.

60 *The Gentleman's Magazine*, November 1767.

61 Gavin Hannah (ed.), *The Deserted Village: The Diary of an Oxfordshire Rector, James Newton*, Stroud, 1992.

62 William Thornton, *A New, Complete and Universal History, Description and Survey of the Cities of London and Westminster*, London, 1784.

63 Gavin Hannah, op. cit.

64 *Daily Advertiser*, 20 May 1741.

65 Boswell, op. cit.

66 Grosley, op. cit.

67 Lowell Blair (ed. and trans.), *Casanova's Memoirs*, London, 1958.

68 *Daily Advertiser*, 8 December 1743. It offered 'several appartments for the conveniency of sweating, bathing and cupping, both ladies and gentlemen ... likewise an exceeding good cook'. Perhaps, perhaps not.

69 *Public Advertiser*, 14 January 1771.

70 The *London Chronicle* reported two cases in 1762. A woman had to stand once in the pillory at the end of Fetter Lane – so near her premises in Fleet Street that her customers surely greeted her. She was fined a shilling and given a month in prison. A man who ran a brothel in Whitefriars got a spell in the same pillory, three months inside and a fine of 5s.

71 Ibid.

72 De Saussure, *A Foreign View of England in the Reign of George I and George II*, translated by Van Muyden, London, 1902. It is said, in Harry Margary's *The A–Z of Georgian London*, London, 1981, to be included in Rocque's 1747 map, downstream from Somerset House and even the Tower, but I cannot identify it as a 'two-storey building' there, or anywhere on the river. A print of Somerset House by Knyff in about 1720 shows the Folly as a large flat-roofed houseboat, moored immediately opposite Somerset House. According to vol. X, the Companion volume, of *The Diary of Samuel Pepys*, ed. Latham and Matthews, London, 1983, it was 'a wooden house of (expensive) entertainment built on barges anchored in river off Somerset House. Described 1661 as a floating playhouse ... Much used in summer. In the 1690s rebuilt and renamed The Royal Diversion.' I would not fancy its chances of negotiating the rapids under London Bridge so as to moor *below* the Tower. Wherever it was, it sounds enchanting.

73 *London Chronicle*, 24 January 1764.

74 Charles Ryscamp, and F. A. Pottle (eds), *Boswell: The Ominous Years 1774–1776*, London, 1963.

75 Tim Hitchcock, *English Sexualities 1700–1800*, Basingstoke, 1997.

76 *The Gentleman's Magazine*, July 1764.

77 *The Gentleman's Magazine*, June 1757.

78 F. A. Pottle (ed.), *Boswell's London Journal 1762–1763*, London, 1951.

79 Tobias Smollett, *Roderick Random*, London, 1748.

80 Hitchcock, op. cit.

81 *The Gentleman's Magazine*, January 1750.

82 Hitchcock, op. cit.

Chapter 20: Fashion and Beauty (pp. 215–229)

1 C. and P. Cunnington, *The History of Underclothes*, London, 1951.

2 Not exactly straw; it could be the kind of bent grass or marram that grows on the Norfolk coast. Its leaves roll up into cylinders like straw. P. and R. A. Mactaggart, 'Some aspects of the use of non-fashionable stays', *The Proceedings of the 7th Annual Conference of the Costume Society*, 1973.

3 Norah Waugh, *Corsets and Crinolines*, London, 1954. No matter how admirable the descriptions in this and the above book, nothing could equal being allowed to handle stays, with shoes and dresses, in the Costume and Textile Study Centre, Carrow House Norwich, part of Norfolk Museum Service – see note 5 below.

4 *Daily Advertiser*, 20 May 1741. How did she lose her stays? Will her husband notice their absence? She will have other pairs, but still . . .

5 In Carrow House, Norwich, the Textile and Costume Research Centre of the Norfolk Museum Service, which has an incomparable collection of costume and embroidery, and the kindest of staff.

6 Mactaggart, op. cit. The husband and his wife wrote the article; the wife wore the stays.

7 *The Gentleman's Magazine*, 2 June 1750.

8 A Society of Gentlemen, *A New and Complete Dictionary of Arts and Sciences*, London, 1754.

9 Mactaggart, op. cit. I am most grateful to Ian Chipperfield, staymaker, of Great Yarmouth, for making this, and much other information about stays, available to me.

10 *The Gentleman's Magazine*, December 1753.

11 Henry Fielding, *Shamela*, London, 1741.

12 P. J. Grosley, *A Tour to London*, translated by Thomas Nugent, London, 1772. M. Grosley was here in 1765. Possibly it was his translator who got himself so tied in knots about the acres of visible bosom.

13 Cunnington and Cunnington, op. cit. There is the material for an Austenesque novel here.

14 Mactaggart, op. cit.

15 Cunnington and Cunnington, op. cit.

16 A dress in the Norwich Centre (see note 5 above) was open down the front of

the skirt, worn with a separate matching underskirt. The hip fullness, which was pronounced but not exaggerated, was held out by circles of cane or marram grass about the size of a hand-held embroidery frame. It was difficult to see how this would work, without the frames drooping downwards, and the wearer had left no user's manual. I have seen no other reference to such a device.

17 G. Eland (ed.), *Purefoy Letters 1735–53*, London, 1931. The writer was 68. She had a 20-inch waist.

18 Cunnington and Cunnington, op. cit.

19 Anon., *The Enormous Abomination of the Hoop-Petticoat*, cited in Cunnington and Cunnington, op. cit.

20 This, which has not been noted by any of the writers I have quoted, is from personal experience of the crinoline petticoats that were briefly in fashion for evening wear, in my youth. One had to be careful, sitting down, to get the substructure to subside round you rather than sticking up in the front, which would have been disastrous in the knickerless days of the eighteenth century.

21 *The Gentleman's Magazine*, January 1750.

22 *The Gentleman's Magazine*, August 1747.

23 Norah Waugh, *The Cut of Women's Clothes 1660–1930*, London, 1968.

24 Gladys Scott Thomson, *The Russells in Bloomsbury Square 1669–1771*, London, 1940.

25 Clare Browne (ed.), *Silk Designs of the Eighteenth Century from the Victoria and Albert Museum*, London, 1990.

26 Eland, op. cit.

27 *The Gentleman's Magazine*, December 1753.

28 Cunnington and Cunnington, op. cit.

29 Anon., *Low-Life*, London, 1765.

30 Malarchy Postlethwaite, *Univeral Dictionary of Trade and Commerce*, London, 1766.

31 *The Gentleman's Magazine*, June 1769.

32 *The Gentleman's Magazine*, November 1769.

33 Stella Tillyard, *Aristocrats*, London, 1994, quoting a letter from Lady Sarah Lennox.

34 Diana Scarisbrick, *Jewellery*, London, 1984.

35 *The Gentleman's Magazine*, September 1761.

36 *The Gentleman's Magazine*, January 1755.

37 *London Evening Post*, 21 April 1747.

38 *Public Advertiser*, 15 January 1771.

39 Cunnington and Cunnington, op. cit.

40 Eliza Smith, *The Compleat Housewife*, London, 1758; republished Studio Editions, London, 1994.

41 Still known, such is male conservatism, as a codpiece, as the Tudor penis-sheaths had been. Francis Grose, *A Classical Dictionary of the Vulgar Tongue*, London, 1785.

42 Norah Waugh, *The Cut of Men's Clothes*, London, 1964.

43 Dorothy Davis, *A History of Shopping*, London, 1966.

44 Thomson, op. cit.

45 *Public Advertiser*, 14 January 1771.

46 Gavin Hannah (ed.), *The Deserted Village: The Diary of an Oxfordshire Rector, James Newton*, Stroud, 1992.

47 James Boswell, *The Life of Samuel Johnson*, London, 1791.

48 *Public Advertiser*, 15 January 1771. Mr Christie was selling 'beautiful shapes for gentlemen's waistcoats' by auction.

49 *London Evening Post*, 28 April 1752.

50 Cunnington, *Costume*, London, 1966, from which I have also taken the information on shirts.

51 Grosley, op. cit.

52 *Public Advertiser*, 18 January 1771.

53 Eland, op. cit. Mrs Purefoy sounds the kind of lady who would not put up with a less than perfect job on the blue damask gown she sent to London in 1764 'to be cleaned or dyed'. A silk dyer set up in business in 1788 to dye both for the trade and for private customers, in 1788, and some of his records survive. His system was exactly as now – name of customer, description of goods to be dyed, ticket number, price. He charged 1s 6d to dye a pair of silk breeches black, and 10s 6d to clean a silver muslin dress. He also dyed household things such as curtains and upholstery. Alan Mansfield, 'Dyeing and cleaning clothes in the late eighteenth and early nineteenth century', *Costume: The Journal of the Costume Society*, no. 2, 1968.

54 *London Evening Post*, 8 October 1751.

55 Hannah Glasse, *The Servants' Directory*, 4th edition, London, 1762.

56 These were not, of course, the modern shape, but what we would call mob-caps made from a circle of material gathered so that the edge made a face-framing frill, and sometimes with ribbons or lace lappets to tie under the chin.

57 Peter Gilchrist, *A Treatise on Hair*, quoted in Richard Corson, *Fashions in Hair*, London, 1965, from which I have taken much of the information on hair and wigs.

58 Quotation from *The London Magazine* in Waugh, *The Cut of Women's Clothes*, op. cit.

59 Grosley, op. cit.

60 Richard Corson, *Fashions in Hair*, London, 1965.

61 Grosley, op. cit.

62 Francis Place, *Autobiography*, BL Add MS 35142. He was born in 1771. The 'leads' he describes must have been like the rods used nowadays in perming hair. They must have weighed a ton, but one must suffer to be 'with it', or as Francis would have said in his youth, 'a Middy'.

63 *The Gentleman's Magazine*, February 1765.

64 Per Kalm, *Account of his Visit to England on his Way to America in 1748*, translated by Joseph Lucas, London, 1892.

65 Advertisement of January 1761 quoted in Corson, op. cit.

66 *Daily Advertiser*, 8 December 1743.

67 *The Connoisseur*, 24 April 1755, quoted in Corson, op. cit.

68 Grose, op. cit. Unfortunately, the word was also used for the private parts of a woman, but reading Grose's *Dictionary*, one cannot but conclude that most words were.

69 Corson, op. cit.

70 Grose, op. cit.

71 William Thornton, *A New, Complete and Universal History, Description and Survey of the Cities of London and Westminster*, London, 1784. When asked by the major of the

Tower how he did, 'Why Sir I am doing very well for I am fitting myself for a place where hardly any majors go and very few lieutenant generals.'

72 *Low-Life*, op. cit.

73 A sign of a London heat wave is when barristers are given leave to remove their wigs, in the High Court. Wearing a barrister's wig on top of long hair in a bun, in Dar es Salaam, before air conditioning, as I did, was tricky. The sweat from my scalp – and I never thought of shaving it, as an eighteenth-century person would have done – tended to drip off my ears on to the documents, already tattered by white ants.

74 Charles Ryskamp and F. A. Pottle (eds), *Boswell: The Ominous Years 1774–1776*, London, 1963.

75 *London Evening Post*, 30 December 1747.

76 *Daily Advertiser*, 8 December 1743.

77 Betsy Rodgers, *Cloak of Charity*, London, 1949.

78 Grose, op. cit.

79 Ambrose Heal, *London Tradesmen's Cards of the Eighteenth Century*, London, 1925.

80 Boswell, op. cit.

81 See the author's *Restoration London*, London, 1997.

82 *The Gentleman's Magazine*, March 1751.

83 *The Gentleman's Magazine*, November 1751.

84 *London Chronicle*, 25 October 1760. I have not seen a reference to this in other mourning periods, but it seems reasonable to assume that it always applied. The vestige of colour in the shoulder knots enabled the footmen's employer to be identified.

85 *The Gentleman's Magazine*, September 1767. The habit of wearing a black band to signify mourning was a kind one that stopped only recently. It warned the outside world that you had reason for being less than cheerful, just as in the days of smallpox vaccination in the upper arm – still done in this century – a white band warned people not to touch your painful arm for a few days.

Chapter 21: Interiors and Gardens (pp. 230–244)

1 M. Dorothy George, *London Life in the Eighteenth Century*, London, 1925.

2 F. A. Pottle (ed.), *Boswell's London Journal 1762–1763*, London, 1951.

3 Ibid.

4 F. Brady and F. A. Pottle (eds), *Boswell in Search of a Wife 1766–1769*, London, 1956.

5 Lowell Blair (ed. and trans.), *Casanova's Memoirs*, London, 1958.

6 *The Gentleman's Magazine* of August 1762 gives the window tax rates, per window, as 1s per week for up to twelve windows, 1s 6d for over twelve. By June 1766 it had increased slightly. Anyone with a house of more than 25 windows had to pay 2s a window. It being human nature to avoid taxes whenever possible, this led to blocking up windows.

7 P. J. Grosley, *A Tour to London*, translated by Thomas Nugent, London, 1772.

8 G. Eland (ed.), *The Purefoy Letters*, London, 1931. Mrs Purefoy, a redoubtable lady who lived in the country, had this house on a 40-year lease from 1710. I don't know her rent. She was telling her man of business in London to 'put up a bill on my house in Cursitors Alley that it is to be let ... The rent is £42 per annum if you should light of a chap [*sic*].'

9 From an anonymous pamphlet, *Apology for Pawnbroking*, quoted in Dorothy Davis, *A History of Shopping*, London, 1966.

10 Apologies. I have tried to find a short clear guide, but failed.

11 Eliza Smith, *The Compleat Housewife*, London, 1758, republished Studio Editions, London, 1994.

12 112 pounds; US 100 pounds.

13 William Salmon, *Palladio Londiniensis*, London, 1752.

14 Information from the third Annual Conference and Workshop of the Traditional Paint Forum, held at Sion House in November 1997.

15 Bernardino Ramazzini, *A Treatise on the Diseases of Tradesmen*, translated into English and published in London, 1705: for long, the only work on industrial diseases.

16 Charles Saumarez-Smith, *Eighteenth-Century Decoration*, London, 1983.

17 Salmon, op. cit.

18 As is well known (to the French), the British murdered Napoleon with arsenic. When his body was taken from St Helena to Paris it was found that his hair contained a high level of arsenic: proof positive. It is more probable that he died of natural causes, and the arsenic vaporised from the fashionable green wallpaper in his bedroom.

19 Ramazzini, op. cit. A friend who is a painter/interior decorator was advised by the old painters she knew always to drink milk before starting work to avoid the effect of the fumes, despite the absence of fumes from modern paint.

20 Ware says 'sculpture' here, but in the context he must have meant stucco.

21 Most of the information on wallpapers comes from Treve Rosoman, *London Wallpapers: Their Manufacture and Use 1690–1840*, London, 1992.

22 Saumarez-Smith, op. cit.

23 Peter Thornton, *Authentic Décor*, London, 1984.

24 *The Gentleman's Magazine*, April 1760.

25 Lord Chesterfield, quoted in C. S. Sykes, *Private Palaces*, London, 1985.

26 John Carwitham, *Various Kinds of Floor Decoration ... being useful designs for ornamenting the Floors ... in Pavements of Stone, or Marble, or with painted Floor cloths*, London, 1739, quoted in Saumarez-Smith, op. cit.

27 Saumarez-Smith, op. cit.

28 Ambrose Heal, *London Tradesmen's Cards of the Eighteenth Century*, London, 1925.

29 J. Munro Bell, *Chippendale, Sheraton and Hepplewhite, Furniture Designers*, London, 1900.

30 Thornton, op. cit.

31 Eland, op. cit. One's heart bleeds for her. At least the user's manual she eventually got was written in English.

32 Ibid.

33 The information in this section comes from the magnificent Silver Room in the Victoria and Albert Museum.

34 Per Kalm, *Account of his Visit to England on his Way to America in 1748*, translated by Joseph Lucas, London, 1892.

35 Isaac Ware, *The Complete Body of Architecture*, London, 1756.

36 *London Evening Post*, 10 October 1747.

37 Grosley, op. cit.

38 Hugh Phillips, *Mid-Georgian London*, London, 1964. Mr Phillips describes these gardens from an enlargement of a print of 1731.

39 Gladys Scott Thomson, *The Russells in Bloomsbury Square 1669–1771*, London, 1940.

40 *Encyclopedia Britannica*, London, 1773.

41 R. Todd Langstaffe-Gowan has kindly allowed me to use the Spence material from his unpublished PhD thesis. His book on small London Georgian gardens will be published in 2000.

42 John H. Harvey, *The Availability of Hardy Plants of the Late Eighteenth Century*, Glastonbury, 1988.

43 John Rutter and Daniel Carter, *Modern Eden or the Gardener's Universal Guide*, London, 1769. I am supposing that the average London garden could not accommodate a kitchen garden or a 20-feet-high greenhouse, let alone a 'cool walk under the shelter of some naturally spreading elms'.

44 Ibid.

45 Alison Kelly, 'Coade stone in Georgian gardens', *Garden History: The Journal of the Garden History Society*, vol. 16, no. 2, 1988.

46 Kalm, op. cit.

47 Richard Bradley, *New Improvements in Planting and Gardening*, London, 1724.

48 *Gazetteer and London Daily Advertiser*, March 1763.

49 *The Flower-Gardener's New and Compendious Director*, reviewed in *The Gentleman's Magazine*, January 1754.

50 *The Gentleman's Magazine*, March 1747. Electricity was the miracle of modern science, then. The writer suggested that it would also help 'foecundated eggs' to hatch, bees and silkworms to work harder...

51 *London Chronicle*, vol. 17, January–July 1765.

52 Her handbill, preserved in the John Johnson collection in the Bodleian Library.

53 *London Evening Post*, 23 October 1764.

54 David Solman, *Loddiges of Hackney: The Largest Hothouse in the World*, London, 1995. In 1771 Busch was headhunted by Catherine Empress of Russia to lay out her gardens 'in the English taste'. Meanwhile, his business was carried on by another German emigré, Joachim Loddiges. By the 1850s urban development engulfed the nursery at Hackney and it closed. Paxton bought the last of the Loddige stock, for the Crystal Palace, including a palm weighing 15 tons that was pulled from Hackney to Sydenham by 32 horses.

55 Todd Langstaffe-Gowan, 'Gardening and the middle classes', in Mireille Galinou (ed.) *London's Pride: The Glorious History of the Capital's Gardens*, London, 1990.

56 Anon., *Low-Life*, London, 1764.

57 5th edition, London, 1764.

Chapter 22: Parties of Pleasure (pp. 245–261)

1 Horace Walpole, *Letters*, Everyman edition, London, 1926.
2 Epitaph quoted in *The Gentleman's Magazine*, August 1767.
3 Hugh Phillips, *The Thames about 1750*, London, 1951.
4 *The Gentleman's Magazine*, August 1765.
5 *The Midwife or Old Woman's Magazine*.
6 Walpole, op. cit.
7 P. J. Grosley, *A Tour to London*, translated by Thomas Nugent, London, 1772. M. Grosley was in London in 1765.
8 Quoted from *England's Gazetteer* by E. Beresford Chancellor, *The Eighteenth Century in London*, London, 1933.
9 *The Gentleman's Magazine*, May 1764.
10 Lowell Blair (ed. and trans.), *Casanova's Memoirs*, London, 1958.
11 Per Kalm, *Account of his Visit to England on his Way to America in 1748*, translated by Joseph Lucas, London, 1892.
12 Walpole, op. cit.
13 *London Chronicle*, 6 July 1762.
14 James Boswell, *The Life of Samuel Johnson*, London, 1791.
15 Walpole, op. cit.
16 James Curl, 'Spas and pleasure gardens of London from the seventeenth to the nineteenth century', *Garden History: The Journal of the Garden History Society*, vol. 12, no. 1, 1984.
17 David Harley, 'A sword in a madman's hand', in Roy Porter (ed.), *The Medical History of Waters and Spas*, Medical History Supplement 10, 1990.
18 John Stow, *Survey of London*, London, 1598, corrected by John Strype 1720, 1754 edition.
19 William Alexander, *The History of Women*, London, 1779. He was a bit of a misogynist, but probably accurate enough here.
20 G. Eland (ed.), *Purefoy Letters 1735–53*, London, 1931.
21 Grosley, op. cit.
22 Dorothy Davis, *A History of Shopping*, London, 1966.
23 *The Gentleman's Magazine*, May 1764. This is taken from the report of a fire in Bishopsgate, giving a ground plan of the damage.
24 Samuel Johnson, *The Idler*, 20 January 1759.
25 Ambrose Heal, of the well-known bed company, made a collection of them from which I have already often quoted: *Tradesmen's Cards in the Eighteenth Century*, London, 1925.
26 *London Chronicle*, vol. 15 January–June 1764.
27 John Entick, *A New and Accurate History and Survey of London, Westminster and Southwark*, London, 1766.
28 Grosley, op. cit.
29 Kalm, op. cit.
30 William Thornton, *A New, Complete and Universal History, Description and Survey of the Cities of London and Westminster*, London, 1784. The Tower had housed the royal menagerie since the Middle Ages. Lions and leopards belonged there as part of the royal heraldry, and miscellaneous gifts to the monarch by other monarchs

usually ended up there. The Zoological Gardens in Regent's Park opened in 1834.

31 Anon, *A Historical Description of the Tower of London and its Curiosities*, London, 1757: price 6d.

32 The animals in Johannesburg Zoo have names, for fund-raising purposes. I remember a female orang-utang with long orange hair, called Fergie.

33 Thornton, op. cit.

34 Ibid.

35 A young man called John Henry Mauclerc collected such throw-aways and even scribbled his impressions on some of them. His collection was recently sold by Marlborough Rare Books of Bond Street. I have drawn on their catalogue for the following section. Some of the flyers can be dated, all are attributable to the 1750s–1760s.

36 One wonders whether Mr Mauclerc was a medico. The unfortunate exhibit sounds very like the 'Elephant Man' of Victorian London, who suffered from an extreme form of skin lesions. Whatever they both had, it was certainly not elephantiasis.

37 *London Chronicle*, 9 May 1765.

38 Richard D. Altick, *The Shows of London*, London, 1978.

39 *London Chronicle*, 13 March 1761.

40 Grosley, op. cit.

41 *The Gentleman's Magazine*, June 1762.

42 *London Chronicle*, June 1762.

43 Altick, op. cit.

44 *The Gentleman's Magazine*, August 1762.

45 Joseph Reddington (ed.), *Home Office Papers 1760–65*, London, 1878.

46 *London Chronicle*, 14 February 1765.

47 *The Gentleman's Magazine*, August 1766.

48 *The Gentleman's Magazine*, March 1765.

49 Grosley, op. cit.

50 Thornton, op. cit.

51 James Pellar Malcolm, *Anecdotes of London*, London, 1810.

52 Grosley, op. cit.

53 Thornton, op. cit. That riot was on 24 February 1762.

54 Lowell Blair, op. cit.

55 *The Gentleman's Magazine*, July 1761, an article on theatrical history.

56 *London Chronicle*, 22 November 1760.

57 F. A. Pottle (ed.), *Boswell's London Journal 1762–1763*, London, 1951.

58 *The Gentleman's Magazine*, September 1770.

59 Francis Grose, *A Classical Dictionary of the Vulgar Tongue*, London, 1785.

60 This is not listed in the List of Works in Donald Burrows, *Handel*, Oxford, 1994. Perhaps it was not by Handel. Or could it be that Wesley had dozed off, in a performance of *Judas Maccabeus*? Or *Joshua*? Or even *Jephtha*?

61 John Wesley, *Journal*, London, 1827.

62 Burrows, op. cit.

63 Ruth McClure, *Coram's Children*, Yale, 1981.

64 Ibid., as to the fashionables.

65 *The Gentleman's Magazine*, September 1761.

66 Boswell, *Life of Johnson*, op. cit.

67 Roger Parker (ed.), *The Oxford Illustrated History of Opera*, Oxford, 1994. The last castrato opera singer was heard in London in 1826.

68 *The Gentleman's Magazine*, April 1751.

69 It is in the National Portrait Gallery.

70 Charles Saumarez-Smith, *Eighteenth-Century Decoration*, London, 1993.

71 Painted in 1736 and 1737: still there.

72 Rhian Harris and Robin Simon (eds), *Enlightened Self-Interest: The Foundling Hospital and Hogarth*, London, 1997.

73 John Gwynn, *London and Westminster Improved*, London, 1766. Gwynn always took a gloomy view.

74 *The Gentleman's Magazine*, October 1768.

75 Hugh Phillips, *Mid-Georgian London*, London, 1964.

76 Casanova, op. cit.

77 A. S. Turberville (ed.), *Johnson's England*, Oxford, 1933.

78 *The Gentleman's Magazine*, March 1770.

79 Ibid.

80 *The Gentleman's Magazine*, May 1770. Her heyday was coming to an end. Competition ruined her, she tried her hand at marketing ass's milk but ended her days in a debtors' prison.

81 *The Gentleman's Magazine*, May 1770.

82 Gladys Scott Thomson, *The Russells in Bloomsbury Square 1669–1771*, London, 1940.

83 On the lines of – and I choose a less awful one –

> Haste every nymph and each swain to the grove
> For Venus is here, 'tis the season for love.

Not much worse than any pop song, I suppose.

84 *Gazetteer and Daily Advertiser*, 2 March 1763.

85 *Daily Advertiser*, 8 December 1743.

Chapter 23: Manners, Speech, Conversation and Customs (pp. 262–273)

1 For much of this section I am indebted to Joan Wildeblood, *The Polite World*, Oxford, 1965, as well as to Lord Chesterfield, of course.

2 Anon., *The Polite Academy*, London, 1762, quoted in Wildeblood, op. cit.

3 I cannot help remembering the customary salutation at Scottish dances, in my youth – perhaps it's different now. Switching his sporran to the side with a swashbuckling but necessary gesture, your prospective partner for the quickstep would say, 'Will ye hae this ane wi' me?'

4 Wildeblood notes, and you will be glad to know, that since 1955 an ambassador presenting his credentials to the Queen is allowed to cut out this walking backwards bit, and just turn at the door and – bow.

5 Astonishing how often modern men in costume dramas, and even in court, get this wrong, which I have known to irritate a judge so profoundly that he said,

'I cannot hear you, Mr So-and-so.' The proper response is not to shout louder, but to take your hands out of your pockets.

6 The desiccated spinster making her way to church in Hogarth's *Morning*, in a chilly winter dawn, carries her fan like that, which looks slightly awkward. Hogarth never painted a detail without significance. Can she be saying that she plans to go on after church to a tryst? Jenny Uglow in *Hogarth*, London, 1997, speculates that the 'prudish spinster' may 'secretly be on the look-out for a lover', but does not refer to the fan.

7 P. J. Grosley, *A Tour to London*, translated by Thomas Nugent, London, 1772. M. Grosley was in London in 1765.

8 Lowell Blair (ed. and trans.), *Casanova's Memoirs*, London, 1958.

9 James Pellar Malcolm, *Anecdotes of London*, London, 1810.

10 Grosley, op. cit.

11 Thomas Sheridan, *Elements of English*, London, 1786. Sheridan was Irish.

12 James Boswell, *The Life of Samuel Johnson*, London, 1791.

13 Preface to his *Dictionary*.

14 William Matthews, *Cockney Past and Present*, London, 1938.

15 William Thornton, *A New, Complete and Universal History, Description and Survey of the Cities of London and Westminster*, London, 1784.

16 Ibid.

17 *The Gentleman's Magazine*, August 1748.

18 Thornton, op. cit.

19 John Wesley, *Journal*, London, 1827.

20 *The Gentleman's Magazine*, September 1763.

21 H. H. Lamb, *Climate History and the Modern World*, London, 1995.

22 *The Gentleman's Magazine*, February 1746.

23 Lamb, op. cit.

24 Thornton, op. cit.

25 *The Gentleman's Magazine*, February 1760.

26 *The Gentleman's Magazine*, January 1763.

27 *Public Advertiser*, 15 January 1771.

28 *London Chronicle*, 21 May 1763.

29 Wesley, op. cit.

30 *The Ladies' Complete Pocket-Book*, 1760.

31 Samuel Richardson, *Pamela*, London, 1740.

32 Quoted in A. S. Turberville (ed.), *Johnson's England*, Oxford, 1933.

33 Francis Grose, *A Classical Dictionary of the Vulgar Tongue*, London, 1785.

34 Ambrose Heal, *London Tradesmen's Cards of the Eighteenth Century*, London, 1925.

35 Bartle Grant (ed.), *The Receipt Book of Elizabeth Raper 1756–70*, London, 1924.

36 Margaret Cox (ed.), *Grave Concerns: Death and Burial in England 1700–1850*, York, 1998.

37 Campbell, *London Tradesmen*, London, 1747.

38 V. Moger (ed.) *The Pleasure of your Company*, London, 1980.

39 Heal, op. cit.

40 *The Gentleman's Magazine*, October 1757.

Chapter 24: High Society (pp. 275–285)

1 Chesterfield, *Letters to his Son*, London, 1774.
2 C. S. Sykes, *Private Palaces*, London, 1985.
3 *London Evening Post*, 1 January 1747.
4 The Spencer family's history is summarised in Joseph Friedman, *Spencer House*, London, 1993.
5 Ibid. Even in this house there were only two water closets, on the ground floor.
6 Illustrated in Sykes, op. cit.
7 Chesterfield, op. cit. Authors would not necessarily be gratified by being chosen for this. Several friends have told me that they keep a copy of my first book, *Restoration London*, in the loo, for a quick read. As far as I know, however, the copies are intact.
8 Sykes, op. cit.
9 *London Chronicle*, 6 June 1764, quoted in Sykes, op. cit. The chandeliers must have been a nightmare to clean. In those pre-electric days the level of illumination often gives an indication of the sumptuousness of the party.
10 Hugh Phillips, *Mid-Georgian London*, London, 1965.
11 Sykes, op. cit.
12 *The Gentleman's Magazine*, November 1769.
13 *The Gentleman's Magazine*, June 1765.
14 Diana Scarisbrick, *Jewellery*, London, 1984.
15 James Pellar Malcolm, *Anecdotes of London*, London, 1810.
16 *The Gentleman's Magazine*, October 1768.
17 C. and P. Cunnington, *Handbook of English Costume in the Eighteenth Century*, London, 1951. In fact the patterns of Spitalfields silk tended to be more attractive than the more ponderous French patterns. A clever salesman could raise his price by branding his goods as smuggled, and sell them with ostentatious caution, when they were perfectly normal English goods.
18 P. J. Grosley, *A Tour to London*, translated by Joseph Nugent, London, 1772.
19 *The Gentleman's Magazine*, May 1749.
20 Grosley, op. cit.
21 Ibid.
22 The evidence was reported in detail, there being then no prohibition of publication of salacious details in divorce cases: *The Gentleman's Magazine*, July 1770. There is a convenient summary in C. N. Galtey, *'Farmer' George's Black Sheep*, Bourne End, Bucks, 1985.
23 In case this joke falls flat, need I explain that horns were the sign of a cuckold, a deceived husband?
24 *The Gentleman's Magazine*, February 1754. Neither party was named in the report.
25 Ruth McClure, *Coram's Children*, Yale, 1981.
26 The excerpts in quotation marks are taken from the account of his trial in the *Newgate Calendar* (Folio Society edition), London, 1951.
27 William Thornton, *A New, Complete and Universal History, Description and Survey of the Cities of London and Westminster*, London, 1784.
28 *The Gentleman's Magazine*, April 1760.

29 *The Gentleman's Magazine*, May 1760.
30 *London Chronicle*, 6–8 May 1760.
31 Phillips, op. cit.
32 The passages in quotation marks are taken from Grosley, op. cit.

Chapter 25: The King (pp. 286–292)

1 The various alliances, treaties and campaigns are admirably explained by Charles
Chenevix Trench, *George II*, London, 1973. For those who find it impossible to
follow even his lucid account, I recommend W. C. Sellar and R. J. Yeatman,
1066 and All That, London, 1930:

> Rules of War in the Eighteenth Century
>
> Although the Succession of Wars went on nearly the whole time in the eighteenth
> century, the countries kept on making a treaty called the Treaty of Paris (or Utrecht).
> This Treaty was a Good Thing and laid down the Rules for fighting the wars; these
> were:
>
> (1) that there should be a mutual restitution of conquests except that England should
> keep Gibraltar, Malta, Minorca, Canada, India, etc.;
> (2) that France should hand over to England the West Indian islands of San
> Flamingo, Tapioca, Sago, Dago, Besique and Contango, while the Dutch were
> always to have Lumbago and the Laxative Islands;
> (3) that everyone, however Infantile or even insane, should renounce all claim to
> the Spanish throne;
> (4) that the King (or Queen) of France should admit that the King (or Queen) of
> England was King (or Queen) of England and should not harbour the Young
> Pretender, but that the fortifications of Dunkirk should be disgruntled and raised
> to the ground.
>
> Thus, as soon as the fortifications of Dunkirk had been gruntled again, or the Young
> Pretender was found in a harbour in France, or it was discovered that the Dutch
> had not got Lumbago etc., the countries knew it was time for the treaty to be signed
> again, so that the War could continue in an orderly manner.

2 Chenevix Trench, op. cit.
3 Ibid.
4 Now that the British Library is separate from the British Museum, the King's
Library, by a brilliant piece of planning, forms the literal as well as metaphorical
core of the library in its new building. One of the first alterations King George
III made to Buckingham House was to build on three libraries. He must have
regretted his grandfather's uncharacteristic generosity in giving away his books.
5 *The Gentleman's Magazine*, May 1752.
6 Hugh Phillips, *Mid-Georgian London*, 1964.
7 Reproduced in Diana Donald, *The Age of Caricature: Satirical Prints in the Reign of
George III*, Yale, 1966.
8 Quoted in John Brooke, *King George III*, London, 1972. It was written about 1766.

9 Ibid., foreword.

10 James Pellar Malcolm, *Anecdotes of London*, London, 1810.

11 The picture is by Zoffany, in the royal collection, reproduced in Charles Saumarez-Smith, *Eighteenth-Century Decoration*, London, 1993.

12 *The Gentleman's Magazine*, June 1763.

13 P. J. Grosley, *A Tour to London*, translated by Thomas Nugent, London, 1772.

14 *The Gentleman's Magazine*, February 1762.

15 *The Gentleman's Magazine*, July 1765.

16 *The Gentleman's Magazine*. I wonder what became of her.

17 *The Gentleman's Magazine*, December 1748.

18 John Entick, *A New and Accurate History and Survey of London, Westminster and Southwark*, London, 1766.

19 *The Gentleman's Magazine*, May 1766.

20 *The Gentleman's Magazine*, April 1768.

21 James Boswell, *The Life of Samuel Johnson*, London, 1791.

22 Brooke, op. cit.

23 Boswell, op. cit.

Appendix: Cost of Living, Currency and Prices (pp. 293–298)

1 Anon., *Tradesman's Directory*, London, 1756.

2 *The Gentleman's Magazine*, November 1754.

3 *The Gentleman's Magazine*, March 1759.

4 For an account of these see the author's *Restoration London*, London, 1997. The currency situation does not seem to have improved much in the intervening hundred years.

5 *The Gentleman's Magazine*, January 1753.

6 Eland (ed.), *Purefoy Letters 1735–1753*, London, 1931.

7 *Tradesman's Directory*, op. cit.

8 *The Gentleman's Magazine*, November 1754.

9 *The Gentleman's Magazine*, December 1759.

10 Glyn Williams, *The Prize of All the Oceans*, London, 1999.

11 *The Gentleman's Magazine*, September 1762.

12 *The Gentleman's Magazine*, July 1763.

13 *The Gentleman's Magazine*, August 1763.

Index

A New and Correct PLAN OF THE CITIES AND SUBURBS OF LONDON & WESTMINSTER & BOROUGH OF SOUTHWARK

London Printed for and Sold by Rob.t Sayer Map & Printseller near Sr.